COLLECTED POEMS

by Samuel Beckett

plays

WAITING FOR GODOT
ALL THAT FALL & OTHER PLAYS FOR RADIO AND SCREEN
ENDGAME
KRAPP'S LAST TAPE & OTHER SHORTER PLAYS
HAPPY DAYS

prose

MORE PRICKS THAN KICKS
MURPHY
WATT
MOLLOY
MALONE DIES
THE UNNAMABLE
THE EXPELLED / THE CALMATIVE / THE END / FIRST LOVE
HOW IT IS
TEXTS FOR NOTHING AND OTHER SHORTER PROSE 1950–1976
MERCIER AND CAMIER
COMPANY / ILL SEEN ILL SAID / WORSTWARD HO / STIRRINGS STILL

poetry

SELECTED POEMS 1930–1989

THE COLLECTED POEMS OF
Samuel Beckett

A critical edition

edited by Seán Lawlor *and* John Pilling

faber and faber

This edition first published in 2012
by Faber and Faber Ltd
Bloomsbury House
74–77 Great Russell Street
London WC1B 3DA

Designed by Ron Costley
Typeset by CB editions, London
Printed in England by T. J. International Ltd, Padstow, Cornwall

A CIP record for this book
is available from the British Library

ISBN 978-0-571-24985-5

10 9 8 7 6 5 4 3 2 1

in memoriam Seán Lawlor (died 10 August 2011)

Seán and I finished this edition of Beckett's *Collected Poems* four months before he died. It saddens me that he was not able to see the book through to publication. But this edition – his inspiration from the outset, his invitation to me to become co-editor having been generously offered and very gratefully received – is a lasting reminder of what a great loss to Beckett scholarship Seán's passing represents.

Salve aeternum mihi . . .
aeternumque vale.

JP
Reading, MMXI

Contents

Preface

The intention is to provide for the first time a comprehensive (if not complete) edition of Samuel Beckett's poems and verse translations. Interpretative materials (including variant readings) are given in the editorial commentary, and significant variant versions are given in the Appendix.

No previous edition has attempted to publish the poems in the order in which we present them here, which:
– broadly reflects the order of composition (where known)
– preserves the integrity of previous collections where these represent SB's known wishes
– clarifies the confusion created by previous so-called collected works.

Thus, we begin with *Echo's Bones and Other Precipitates*, the only volume of poems in English which Beckett ever published as a distinct collection. In the case of uncollected poems, where these have appeared in little magazines, we privilege SB's post-publication revisions which have never appeared in print. We have, generally, followed the order of previous collections of the French poems, which are less problematic and generally better edited.

   Previous editions incorporating selections from Beckett's translations (e.g. Calder 2002, Wheatley 2009) have included the texts of the original poems *en face*, which in most cases was not how they first appeared, and have not even been consistent in this connection. To have followed this practice here would have run counter to our wish to present Beckett's translations as poems able to stand on their own merits, and could not have been carried out in any consistent manner without greatly, and in our view needlessly, expanding the size of the volume. The commentary supplies all the details of how the translations first appeared. In the case of 'Long after Chamfort' we have included Chamfort's original prose as a way of demonstrating at least a part of what SB meant in giving his texts this title, irrespective of whether this is absolutely consistent with our own practice in other instances.

This new and more comprehensive edition of Beckett's poems and translations has been undertaken in order to put this whole dimension of his writing career in a somewhat clearer perspective than has thus far proved possible, not least because the materials towards it have in recent years become much more easily accessible than they previously were.

This edition privileges the only two genuine collections Beckett saw through the press (*Echo's Bones* . . . and *Poèmes 37–39*) by keeping them together at the beginning and end of our first ('Pre-War') section. Subsections in both parts of the edition seek to situate related, or in other ways ancillary, items as close to poems which are comparable in character as is feasible, and Beckett's translations are also grouped together, separated across the 'Pre-War' and 'Post-War' divide.

A number of poems are published here for the first time, and many translations are reprinted here from long defunct periodicals and little magazines for the first time in several decades. The majority of the jettisoned poems of the 1930s were so heavily revised as to clearly represent SB's last, best thoughts. We have, therefore, chosen to publish them in the main corpus of this collection and to reprint the original versions in the Appendix, with only a few annotations supplementing the very full documentation of them (much of which was obviously derived directly from Beckett himself) in Lawrence Harvey's *Samuel Beckett: Poet and Critic* (1970), still the only full-length published treatment of Beckett as poet. Annotations elsewhere address the issues in what became, after the initial 'spontaneous combustion of the spirit' (letter to TM of 18.10.32; LSB1, 134), effectively work in progress, if not permanently so. The headnotes to each entry are not intended to offer a 'totalised' reading of a given poem, but simply to supply all the relevant information available on the circumstances of composition. The individual notes are primarily designed to trace the interactions operating across and between poems, and across and between them and Beckett's other writings.

A chronological principle is applied as far as this has proved possible, given that so many dates of composition, especially in the early years, are irrecoverable in the light of currently available evidence, and may never be precisely dated. This principle obviously cannot be slavishly adopted where particular items form a natural group. Some 'identifications' (*Disjecta*, 19) are naturally more speculative than others, and some omissions in the two sections which are given over to translations have seemed sensible and necessary, if these are not to overemphasise Beckett's role as a facilitator rather than as a creative figure speaking for himself, irrespective of how his work on his own behalf might be received.

The addition of a commentary seems proper in view of the exceptional difficulty of this most neglected part of Beckett's oeuvre, a difficulty which has no doubt affected the ability of interested parties to access the poems at all, or which has meant that only isolated aperçus have proved of much value. Beckett had a fondness for his poems (and at least some of his translations), but he perhaps presumed too much upon the ability of his readers to follow the twists and turns, and the exceptional allusiveness, of a quicksilver mind. As the horoscope in *Murphy* puts it: 'Few minds are better concocted than this native's' (23); but the concoction makes for a heady brew. Beckett may – and in fact the public reception suggests he must – have overvalued his poems, as anyone might. But it was in poetry that he confronted himself most intimately, even if this confrontation was in conflict with his instinct to protect himself by way of ventriloquism, disguise or deviousness.

Given that Beckett felt 'from self so estranged' (letter to TM of 18.10.56; *LSB2*, 663), it is not very surprising that the 'combustion' of composition, whether 'spontaneous' or otherwise (letter to TM of 18.10.32; *LSB1*, 134), tended to produce results which are themselves often very strange. This edition is designed to reduce, but at the same time to respect, some of this strangeness, and to put into the reader's hand a book which the editors hope will facilitate, while it cannot guarantee, a meeting of minds.

The first sentence of Beckett's 1929 Joyce essay reads: 'The danger is in the neatness of identifications' (*Disjecta*, 19). There can be no 'neatness' in the circumstances; but perhaps some of the 'danger' is removed. The poems themselves, however, always keep 'danger' alive, and the translations are, obviously enough, peculiarly vulnerable to the feeling of failure which, for Beckett, became something of an *idée fixe*. Here, in this connection, readers can at least make up their minds for themselves as to where Beckett succeeds and fails, whether in his own voice or in a more ventriloqual role, by accessing more materials than have ever previously been gathered together all in one place.

EDITORIAL CONVENTIONS ADOPTED

Line numbers for Beckett's poems are given in bold in the Commentary.

Where Beckett left his poems untitled the first line (or in some cases, a part thereof) has been used as the nominated title in the table of contents.

The notes in the commentary are organised by general headnote, followed by variants and line-by-line annotations. In some cases, minor variants are integrated into the line-by-line annotations.

The commentary includes details of first publication of Beckett's poems, and of anthologisings and reprintings that are contemporary with the work, or which occurred within SB's lifetime.

The Editors
London; Reading
April 2011

Acknowledgements

For permissions in respect of unpublished material the Editors would like to thank Edward Beckett and the Beckett Estate in association with Rosica Colin Ltd. For permission to reprint published material they would like to thank Paul Keegan of Faber and Faber and, in the case of the *Letters of Samuel Beckett 1929–1940* and *1941–1956*, the Syndics of Cambridge University Press. For other permissions thanks are expressed to the Trustees of the Beckett International Foundation, University of Reading (Director, Dr Mark Nixon; with special thanks to Verity Andrews and Guy Baxter); to the Keeper of Manuscripts at Trinity College Dublin (Dr Bernard Meehan); to the Harry Ransom Humanities Research Center, University of Texas at Austin; to Kelly Brown of Special Collections at Washington University Library, St Louis, Missouri; to Robert O'Neill at the Burns Library, Boston College, Massachusetts; to Megan Mulder of Special Collections, Z. Smith Reynolds Library, Wake Forest University; to Jarron Jewell at the Winthrop Palmer Collection, B. Davis-Schwartz Memorial Library, Long Island University; to Professor Breon Mitchell and David K. Frazier, Lilly Library, Bloomington, Indiana; and to Les Héritiers Matisse, Paris.

The Editors owe an immense debt of gratitude to Professor James Knowlson for painstakingly reading the manuscript and making numerous very helpful suggestions, querying some of our manuscript transcriptions, and correcting errors in French and Italian. Although some errors must no doubt remain, there would have been many more without Jim's close attention to detail. Of the numerous scholars whose input was invaluable in one way or another we would especially like to thank: the late Professor Ruby Cohn; the late Professor Lawrence E. Harvey; Professor C. J. Ackerley (University of Otago); Professor S. E. Gontarski (Florida State University); Professor Dirk Van Hulle (University of Antwerp); Dr Maria José Carrera (University of Valladolid); Dr Daniela Caselli (University of Manchester); Dr Peter Fifield (University of York); Dr Sara Poole (University of Reading); Dr David Wheatley (University of Hull). For information conveyed to us in letters, emails or other private communications we thank: Anne Atik; the late Avigdor Arikha; the late A. J. Leventhal; Dr John Bolin (University of Oxford); Dr David Tucker (University of Sussex); Professor Lois Overbeck (Emory University); Bruno Cuneo (Chile); Trish Hayes (BBC Written Archives, Caversham); and Peter Selley of Sotheby's Ltd.

Charles Boyle, faced with an unenviable task, was our excellent copy-editor, for which relief much thanks.

Jim Knowlson and, in a no less valued supportive capacity, Mark Nixon could not have been of more help to me in the proof-reading of this edition if they had tried. My warmest thanks to them both for heroic efforts well beyond the call of duty under-taken on behalf of a much missed mutual friend, and for saving the surviving editor of the book embarrassments galore. Errors or omissions ('e.o.o.e', as 'Home Olga' expresses it) remain solely attributable to me.

For their personal support over a number of years, and for keeping us almost sane, we thank Trilby Lawlor and Jenny Halstead, who could not have been more long-suffering, and to whom this book is dedicated.

JP, December 2011

Samuel Beckett: Collected Poems

PART 1   Pre-War

Echo's Bones and Other Precipitates

The Vulture

dragging his hunger through the sky
of my skull shell of sky and earth

stooping to the prone who must
soon take up their life and walk

mocked by a tissue that may not serve
till hunger earth and sky be offal

Enueg I

Exeo in a spasm
tired of my darling's red sputum
from the Portobello Private Nursing Home
its secret things
and toil to the crest of the surge of the steep perilous bridge
and lapse down blankly under the scream of the hoarding
round the bright stiff banner of the hoarding
into a black west
throttled with clouds.

10   Above the mansions the algum-trees
the mountains
my skull sullenly
clot of anger
skewered aloft strangled in the cang of the wind
bites like a dog against its chastisement.

I trundle along rapidly now on my ruined feet
flush with the livid canal;
at Parnell Bridge a dying barge
carrying a cargo of nails and timber
20   rocks itself softly in the foaming cloister of the lock;
on the far bank a gang of down and outs would seem to be
    mending a beam.

Then for miles only wind
and the weals creeping alongside on the water
and the world opening up to the south
across a travesty of champaign to the mountains
and the stillborn evening turning a filthy green
manuring the night fungus
and the mind annulled
wrecked in wind.

I splashed past a little wearish old man,
Democritus,
scuttling along between a crutch and a stick,
his stump caught up horribly, like a claw, under his breech,
    smoking.
Then because a field on the left went up in a sudden blaze
of shouting and urgent whistling and scarlet and blue ganzies
I stopped and climbed the bank to see the game.
A child fidgeting at the gate called up:
'Would we be let in Mister?'
'Certainly' I said 'you would.'
But, afraid, he set off down the road.
'Well' I called after him 'why wouldn't you go on in?'
'Oh' he said, knowingly,
'I was in that field before and I got put out.'
So on,
derelict,
as from a bush of gorse on fire in the mountain after dark,
or, in Sumatra, the jungle hymen,
the still flagrant rafflesia.

Next:
a lamentable family of grey verminous hens,
perishing out in the sunk field,
trembling, half asleep, against the closed door of a shed,
with no means of roosting.
The great mushy toadstool,
green-black,
oozing up after me,
soaking up the tattered sky like an ink of pestilence,
in my skull the wind going fetid,
the water . . .

Next:
on the hill down from the Fox and Geese into Chapelizod
a small malevolent goat, exiled on the road,
remotely pucking the gate of his field;
the Isolde Stores a great perturbation of sweaty heroes,
in their Sunday best,

come hastening down for a pint of nepenthe or moly or half and
     half
from watching the hurlers above in Kilmainham.

Blotches of doomed yellow in the pit of the Liffey;
the fingers of the ladders hooked over the parapet,
soliciting;
a slush of vigilant gulls in the grey spew of the sewer.

Ah the banner
the banner of meat bleeding
on the silk of the seas and the arctic flowers
that do not exist.

Enueg II

world world world world
and the face grave
cloud against the evening

de morituris nihil nisi

and the face crumbling shyly
too late to darken the sky
blushing away into the evening
shuddering away like a gaffe

veronica mundi
10   veronica munda
give us a wipe for the love of Jesus

sweating like Judas
tired of dying
tired of policemen
feet in marmalade
perspiring profusely
heart in marmalade
smoke more fruit
the old heart the old heart
20   breaking outside congress
doch I assure thee

lying on O'Connell Bridge
goggling at the tulips of the evening
the green tulips
shining round the corner like an anthrax
shining on Guinness's barges

the overtone the face
too late to brighten the sky
doch doch I assure thee

Alba

before morning you shall be here
and Dante and the Logos and all strata and mysteries
and the branded moon
beyond the white plane of music
that you shall establish here before morning

    grave suave singing silk
    stoop to the black firmament of areca
    rain on the bamboos flower of smoke alley of willows

who though you stoop with fingers of compassion
10   to endorse the dust
shall not add to your bounty
whose beauty shall be a sheet before me
a statement of itself drawn across the tempest of emblems
so that there is no sun and no unveiling
and no host
only I and then the sheet
and bulk dead

Dortmunder

In the magic the Homer dusk
past the red spire of sanctuary
I null she royal hulk
hasten to the violet lamp to the thin K'in music of the bawd.
She stands before me in the bright stall
sustaining the jade splinters
the scarred signaculum of purity quiet
the eyes the eyes black till the plagal east
shall resolve the long night phrase.
10   Then, as a scroll, folded,
and the glory of her dissolution enlarged
in me, Habbakuk, mard of all sinners.
Schopenhauer is dead, the bawd
puts her lute away.

Sanies I

all the livelong way this day of sweet showers from Portrane on
    the seashore
Donabate sad swans of Turvey Swords
pounding along in three ratios like a sonata
like a Ritter with pommelled scrotum atra cura on the step
Botticelli from the fork down pestling the transmission
tires bleeding voiding zeep the highway
all heaven in the sphincter
the sphincter

müüüüüüüüde now
10   potwalloping now through the promenaders
this trusty all-steel this super-real
bound for home like a good boy
where I was born with a pop with the green of the larches
ah to be back in the caul now with no trusts
no fingers no spoilt love
belting along in the meantime clutching the bike
the billows of the nubile the cere wrack
pot-valiant caulless waisted in rags hatless
for mamma papa chicken and ham
20   warm Grave too say the word
happy days snap the stem shed a tear
this day Spy Wedsday seven pentades past
oh the larches the pain drawn like a cork
the glans he took the day off up hill and down dale
with a ponderous fawn from the Liverpool London and Globe
back the shadows lengthen the sycomores are sobbing
to roly-poly oh to me a spanking boy
buckets of fizz childbed is thirsty work
for the midwife he is gory
30   for the proud parent he washes down a gob of gladness
for footsore Achates also he pants his pleasure
sparkling beestings for me
tired now hair ebbing gums ebbing ebbing home

good as gold now in the prime after a brief prodigality
yea and suave
suave urbane beyond good and evil
biding my time without rancour you may take your oath
distraught half-crooked courting the sneers of these fauns these
    smart nymphs
clipped like a pederast as to one trouser-end
40   sucking in my bloated lantern behind a Wild Woodbine
cinched to death in a filthy slicker
flinging the proud Swift forward breasting the swell of Stürmers
I see main verb at last
her whom alone in the accusative
I have dismounted to love
gliding towards me dauntless nautch-girl on the face of the waters
dauntless daughter of desires in the old black and flamingo
get along with you now take the six the seven the eight or the
    little single-decker
take a bus for all I care walk cadge a lift
50   home to the cob of your web in Holles Street
and let the tiger go on smiling
in our hearts that funds ways home

Sanies II

there was a happy land
the American Bar
in Rue Mouffetard
there were red eggs there
I have a dirty I say henorrhoids
coming from the bath
the steam the delight the sherbet
the chagrin of the old skinnymalinks
slouching happy body
10   loose in my stinking old suit
sailing slouching up to Puvis the gauntlet of tulips
lash lash me with yaller tulips I will let down
my stinking old trousers
my love she sewed up the pockets alive the live-oh she did she
     said that was better
spotless then within the brown rags gliding
frescoward free up the fjord of dyed eggs and thongbells
I disappear don't you know into the local
the mackerel are at billiards there they are crying the scores
the Barfrau makes a big impression with her mighty bottom
20   Dante and blissful Beatrice are there
prior to Vita Nuova
the balls splash no luck comrade
Gracieuse is there Belle-Belle down the drain
booted Percinet with his cobalt jowl
they are necking gobble-gobble
suck is not suck that alters
lo Alighieri has got off au revoir to all that
I break down quite in a titter of despite
hark
30   upon the saloon a terrible hush
a shiver convulses Madame de la Motte
it courses it peals down her collops
the great bottom foams into stillness
quick quick the cavaletto supplejacks for mumbo-jumbo

vivas puellas mortui incurrrrrsant boves
oh subito subito ere she recover the cang bamboo for bastinado
a bitter moon fessade à la mode
oh Becky spare me I have done thee no wrong spare me damn
    thee
spare me good Becky
40   call off thine adders Becky I will compensate thee in full
Lord have mercy upon
Christ have mercy upon us

Lord have mercy upon us

Serena I

without the grand old British Museum
Thales and the Aretino
on the bosom of the Regent's Park the phlox
crackles under the thunder
scarlet beauty in our world dead fish adrift
all things full of gods
pressed down and bleeding
a weaver-bird is tangerine the harpy is past caring
the condor likewise in his mangy boa
they stare out across monkey-hill the elephants
Ireland
the light creeps down their old home canyon
sucks me aloof to that old reliable
the burning btm of George the drill
ah across the way a adder
broaches her rat
white as snow
in her dazzling oven strom of peristalsis
limae labor

ah father father that art in heaven

I find me taking the Crystal Palace
for the Blessed Isles from Primrose Hill
alas I must be that kind of person
hence in Ken Wood who shall find me
my breath held in the midst of thickets
none but the most quarried lovers

I surprise me moved by the many a funnel hinged
for the obeisance to Tower Bridge
the viper's curtsy to and from the City
till in the dusk a lighter
blind with pride
tosses aside the scarf of the bascules

then in the grey hold of the ambulance
throbbing on the brink ebb of sighs
then I hug me below among the canaille
until a guttersnipe blast his cernèd eyes
demanding 'ave I done with the Mirror
I stump off in a fearful rage under Married Men's Quarters
Bloody Tower
40   and afar off at all speed screw me up Wren's giant bully
and curse the day caged panting on the platform
under the flaring urn
I was not born Defoe

but in Ken Wood
who shall find me

my brother the fly
the common housefly
sidling out of darkness into light
fastens on his place in the sun
50   whets his six legs
revels in his planes his poisers
it is the autumn of his life
he could not serve typhoid and mammon

Serena II

this clonic earth

see-saw she is blurred in sleep
she is fat half dead the rest is free-wheeling
part the black shag the pelt
is ashen woad
snarl and howl in the wood wake all the birds
hound the harlots out of the ferns
this damfool twilight threshing in the brake
bleating to be bloodied
10   this crapulent hush
tear its heart out

in her dreams she trembles again
way back in the dark old days panting
in the claws of the Pins in the stress of her hour
the bag writhes she thinks she is dying
the light fails it is time to lie down
Clew Bay vat of xanthic flowers
Croagh Patrick waned Hindu to spite a pilgrim
she is ready she has lain down above all the islands of glory
20   straining now this Sabbath evening of garlands
with a yo-heave-ho of able-bodied swans
out from the doomed land their reefs of tresses
in a hag she drops her young
the whales in Blacksod Bay are dancing
the asphodels come running the flags after
she thinks she is dying she is ashamed

she took me up on to a watershed
whence like the rubrics of a childhood
behold Meath shining through a chink in the hills
30   posses of larches there is no going back on
a rout of tracks and streams fleeing to the sea
kindergartens of steeples and then the harbour

like a woman making to cover her breasts
and left me

with whatever trust of panic we went out
with so much shall we return
there shall be no loss of panic between a man and his dog
bitch though he be

sodden packet of Churchman
40 muzzling the cairn
it is worse than dream
the light randy slut can't be easy
this clonic earth
all these phantoms shuddering out of focus
it is useless to close the eyes
all the chords of the earth broken like a woman pianist's
the toads abroad again on their rounds
sidling up to their snares
the fairy-tales of Meath ended
50 so say your prayers now and go to bed
your prayers before the lamps start to sing behind the larches
here at these knees of stone
then to bye-bye on the bones

Serena III

fix this pothook of beauty on this palette
you never know it might be final

or leave her she is paradise and then
plush hymens on your eyeballs

or on Butt Bridge blush for shame
the mixed declension of those mammae
cock up thy moon thine and thine only
up up up to the star of evening
swoon upon the arch-gasometer
10   on Misery Hill brand-new carnation
swoon upon the little purple
house of prayer
something heart of Mary
the Bull and Pool Beg that will never meet
not in this world

whereas dart away through the cavorting scapes
bucket o'er Victoria Bridge that's the idea
slow down slink down the Ringsend Road
Irishtown Sandymount puzzle find the Hell Fire
20   the Merrion Flats scored with a thrillion sigmas
Jesus Christ Son of God Saviour His Finger
girls taken strippin that's the idea
on the Bootersgrad breakwind and water
the tide making the dun gulls in a panic
the sands quicken in your hot heart
hide yourself not in the Rock keep on the move
keep on the move

Malacoda

thrice he came
the undertaker's man
impassible behind his scutal bowler

to measure
is he not paid to measure
this incorruptible in the vestibule
this malebranca knee-deep in the lilies
Malacoda knee-deep in the lilies
Malacoda for all the expert awe
10 that felts his perineum mutes his signal
sighing up through the heavy air
must it be it must be it must be
find the weeds engage them in the garden
hear she may see she need not

to coffin
with assistant ungulata
find the weeds engage their attention
hear she must see she need not

to cover
20 to be sure cover cover all over
your targe allow me hold your sulphur
divine dogday glass set fair
stay Scarmilion stay stay
lay this Huysum on the box
mind the imago it is he
hear she must see she must
all aboard all souls
half-mast aye aye

nay

Da Tagte Es

redeem the surrogate goodbyes
the sheet astream in your hand
who have no more for the land
and the glass unmisted above your eyes

Echo's Bones

asylum under my tread all this day
their muffled revels as the flesh falls
breaking without fear or favour wind
the gantelope of sense and nonsense run
taken by the maggots for what they are

Uncollected Early Poems from the Leventhal Papers

Moly

The lips of her desire are grey
and parted like a silk loop
threatening
a slight wanton wound.
She preys wearily
on sensitive wild things
proud to be torn
by the grave crouch of her beauty.
But she will die and her snare
10   tendered so patiently
to my vigilant sorrow
will break and hang
in a pitiful crescent.

For Future Reference

My cherished chemist friend
Borodine
lured me aloofly
down from the cornice
into the basement
and there
drew tubes of acid and alkali out of his breast
to a rainbow sol-fa
                    mad dumb-bells spare me!
10   fiddling deft and expert
with the double-jointed nut-crackers of the hen's ovaries.
But I stilled my cringing
I did
and I smote him
                    ah my strength!
smashed
mashed
                    peace my incisors!
brayed him and flayed him
20   with a ready are-you-steady
cuff-discharge.

But did I?

And then the bright waters
beneath the broad board
the trembling blade of the streamlined divers
and down to our waiting
to our enforced buoyancy
come floating the words of
the Mutilator
30   and the work of his finger-joints
observe gen'l'men one of
the consequences of the displacement of
click!

the jaws.
The hair shall be grey
above the left temple
the hair shall be grey there
                    abracadabra!
                    sweet wedge of birds faithless!
40   God blast you yes it is we see
God bless you professor
we can't clap or we'd sink
three cheers for the perhaps pitiful professor.
Next per shaving, next . .
Well of all the . .
that little bullet-headed bristle-cropped
cyanosed rat of a pure politician
that I thought was experimenting with barbed wire in the Punjab
up he comes foaming to the slip
50   and tells me I'm putting no guts in my kick.
Well I just swam away nimbly
blushing and hopeless
with the little swift strokes that I like and . .
Oops!
over the stream and the tall green bank
in a strong shallow bow
and his face all twisted calm and patient
and the board-ledge doing its best to illustrate
Bruno's identification of contraries
60   Into the water or on to the stones?
no matter at all he cannot come back
from far bay or quarry
yes here he is
he must have come under
for the second edition
coming
house innings set half or anything.

If he cannot come twice
or forget his lesson
70   or break his leg
he might forget me

they all might.

So the snowy floor of the parrot's cell
burning at dawn
the palate of my strange mouth.

To Be Sung Loud

Rahab of the holy battlements
blade of brightness dripping
in the moth of pearl trembling
in the ashes of the firmament.
Puttanina mia!
you hid them happy in the high flax
pale before the fords
of Jordan and the dry red waters
and you lowered a pledge of scarlet hemp.
10   Ah radiant and angry,
Beatrice,
she is foul with the victory
of the bloodless fingers,
and she is proud,
and thou,
thou art my mother and my beloved,
thou art spears of pale fire,
pyre of my doubting,
and God's sorrow,
20   and my sorrows.

Casket of Pralinen for a Daughter of
a Dissipated Mandarin

Is he long enough in the leg?
Certainly, but his face . . .!
But Rosinette, my little doe,
is it not Bartholo, synthetic grey cat, prince of candles regent?
Reserve Thyrsis, my pet,
reserve him for your daylight ones.

And hold your head well over the paper, my precious,
or you risk to weep to no end on the blotting.
That soup thus arrosée, will you ever forget it,
10   on the first of the first
spoon-feeding the gladiator,
oiling the feather for rusty wedlock,
and dawn cracking all along the line?
Assumption of the innocents in slaver,
two fake Celts in one fake God.

The egg there at the head of the table with the bright lemon
    whiskers,
that is the Homo;
and there in the midst of them
occupying, you will observe, the pivotal position,
20   you can tell by the apposite gesture of the hand clutching the
    money-scrotum,
the doomed betrayer;
and that I fancy is cyanosed Tom
disbelieving
in the Sherry Cobbler that is my;
and here of course at the other extreme,
facing the Master on His right hand,
far, far from the bosom,
we have John,
John the bright boy of the class,
30   the lamb moistening with a cud of pure mucus

his mouth for a toad.
The brightest and best –
until we come to the in memoriam drunk
on the eleventh's eleventh eleven years after –
of all balls, banquets or parties.

Now Mr Beckett,
I want you to make a real effort,
I want you to cinch up your song:

What is this that is more
40   than the anguish of beauty,
this gale of pain that was not prepared
in the caves of her eyes?

Is it enough,
a stitch in the hem of the garment?
To-night her gaze would be less
than sun coming into a cage.

I am ashamed in the end
of this dud artistry,
I am ashamed of presuming
50   to align words,
of everything but the ingenuous fibres
that suffer honestly.

I don't blush,
but I am ashamed.

Fool, do you hope to undo
the knot of God's pain?

Goodness gracious, but that was a soft one!
Yes, I do think that was perhaps inclined to be just a shade too
    self-conscious.
Abfahrt!
60 Platznehmen for a hiccup on chocolate wheels
to our old friend.

Settle your hats and sit easy:

>Beauty, thou turd of prey,
>wing from my sorrow
>when memory willy-nilly
>comes in pills of purge
>in the bowels of my sorrow,
>have no pity,
>spatter her, soil her, till I love her.

70 Albion Albion mourn for him mourn,
    mourn I mean for William Wordsworth,
    for who is there now to discern in Mantegna's
    foreshortened butchers of salvation
    recognition of transcendent right and might?
    Sheep he wrote, the very much doubting
    son of the soil, sheep not sleep,
    Gloucester's no bimbo
    and he's in Limbo
    so all is well with the Petit Suisse of human kindness.

80 Night, my night, is freighted
    with a scurry of black pigs bleeding
    beneath the surf,
    but that seems to have no bearing,
    for they are gone, my Brussels Braut,
    they are all gone.

To My Daughter

Aholiba charm of my blear eyes
there is a cave above Zoar
and a comely donkey is there

do not bother bringing wine
he is no connexion of ours

child of my sorrow Belacqua will never
swim before your rut in vermilion on the wall
never will you see that glabrous cod
flaunting a Babylonian belt
and even supposing you did
he would not be worth sending to fetch

and I tell you there is a fed ass
lepping with impurée of cantharides
in the hill above Zoar

what more do you want

Text 1

oh and I dreamed he would come and come come come and cull
me bonny bony double-bed cony swiftly my springal and my
thin Wicklow twingle-twangler comfort my days of roses days of
beauty week of redness with mad shame to my lips of shame to
my shamehill for the newest of news the shemost of shenews is
I'm lust-be-lepered and unwell oh I'd liefer be a sparrow for my
puckfisted coxcomb bird to bird and branch or a cave of coal with
veins of gold for my wicked doty's potystick trimly to besom gone
the hartshorn and the cowslip wine gone and the lettuce nibbled
up nibbled up and gone nor the last day of beauty of the red time
opened its rose struck with its thorn oh I'm all of a gallimaufry and
a salady salmagundi singly and single to bed she said I'll have no
toadspit about this house and whose quab was I I'd like to know
that from my cheerfully cornuted Dublin landloper and whose foal
hackney mare toeing the line like a Viennese Täubchen take my tip
and clap a lock on your Greek galligaskins ere I'm quick and living
in hopes and glad to go snacks with my twingle-twangler and grow
grow into the earth mother of whom clapdish and foreshop

Text 2

Ce n'est au pélican
pas si pitoyable
ni à l'égyptienne
pas si pure
mais à ma douce Lucie
opticienne oui et peaussière aussi
qui ne m'a pas guéri
mais qui aurait pu
et à mon doux Jude
10   dont j'ai adororé un peu de la dépouille
que j'adresse la cause désespérée
qui a l'air d être la mienne

Text 3

Miserere oh colon
oh passionate ilium
just for to give the la.

Proust's cook is in the study,
she is grieving in a general way for the abstract intestine,
she is so engrossed that she does not hear the screams of her
    assistant,
a sloven she,
and the dying spit of a Paduan Virtue,
for alas she has stripped her last asparagus,
10   now she is smashed on delivery.
She rises,
her heart is full of murder and tears,
she hunts down the pullet with oaths,
fiercely she tears his little head off.

Shew those teeth here to your first-born,
spent baby,
and take a good pull on my buxom calabash.
Is it not a mercy that there is no duty to pay
on milch mammae?
20   Niño, you need a shave,
but vaseline omnia vincit.

Open thou my lips
and
(if one dare make a suggestion)
thine eye of skyflesh.
Am I a token of Godcraft,
the masterpiece of a scourged apprentice?
Having neither tail nor brass bones
shall I cease to lament?
30   Shall I dry my eyes and think no more about it
being not Behemoth?

Not so but perhaps
at the sight and sound of
a Florentine peacock's grave fandango.

I am Asdente, I threw away my packthread.
No blade has smoothed the furrowed cheeks
that my tears corrode,
and my varicose veins take my kneeling thoughts
from the piteous pelican.
40   I am Asdente I tell you
and my advice to every Narcissy is:
quick tip losers and be made happy for ever,
bode as that man who with his crosier
twice spoiled the sport of serpents
and in Arcadia of all places.
Madam, he said respectfully, casting down his eyes,
take it from me,
swan, flame or shower of gold,
it is one to ten at the time,
50   that is the ratio at peroration.

We are proud in our pain,
our life was not blind.
Worms breed in the red tears
as they slouch unnamed
scorned by the black ferry
despairing of death
who shall not scour in swift joy
the bright hill's girdle
nor tremble with the dark pride of torture
60   and the bitter dignity of an ingenious damnation.

Lo-Ruhama Lo-Ruhama
pity is quick with death.
Presumptuous passionate fool come now
and stand cold
on the cold moon.

Whoroscope

What's that?
An egg?
By the brothers Boot it stinks fresh.
Give it to Gillot.

Galileo how are you
and his consecutive thirds!
That penny Copernican lead-swinging son of a sutler!
We're moving, he said, we're off – Porca Madonna!
the way a ferryman would be, or a clockwork hare.
10   That's not moving, that's <u>moving</u>.

What's that?
A little green fry or a mushroomy one?
Two lashed ova with prostichiutto?
How long did she womb it, the feathery one?
Three days and four nights?
Give it to Gillot.

Faulhaber, Beeckman and Peter the Red,
come now in the cloudy avalanche
or Gassendi's sun-red crystalline cloud
20   and I'll pebble you all your hen-and-a-half ones
or I'll pebble a lens under the quilt in the midst of day.
To think he was my own brother, Battling Pete,
and not a premise out of him
no more than if Pa were still in it.
Hey! pass over those coppers,
sweet millèd sweat of my burning liver!
Them were the days I sat in the hot-cupboard
throwing Jesuits out of the skylight.

Who's that?
30   Hals?
Let him wait.

My wall-eyed dotey!
I hid and you sook.
And Francine my precious fruit
of a house-and-parlour foetus!
What an exfoliation!
The little grey flayed epidermis and scarlet tonsils!
My one child
scourged by a fever to stagnant blood,
40   murky blood,
blood!
Oh Harvey sir,
how shall the red and white, tell me that sir,
the many in the few, answer me that sir,
eddy through your cracked ticker?
The heart of my king is safe in a box
in a vault of my God.

What's that?
How long?
50   Sit on it.

A gale of evil flung my despair of ease
against the keen spires
of the one
lady,
not once or twice but . . .
(hatch it curse you!)
in one sun's drowning.
Now I am particularly anxious that the devout in authority
should pay attention to what I am saying.
60   So on with the silk hose over the worsted
and the morbid leather,
and away to Ancona on the bright Adriatic,
and au plaisir to the yellow key of the Rosicrucians.
(I see I said leather when of course I mean canvas,
the douce canvas.)
They don't know what the master of them that do did,
that the nares throb to the kiss of all foul and sweet air,
and the drums and the strange palate,

and the sorrowful cornea,
70 and thus it is that if,
as it is asserted,
and to put the case with rapid reverence,
we eat Him bread
and drink Him wine,
it is simply that he has the knack,
he has mastered the art,
of jigging as close to his jigging Doppelganger,
or as far from same,
and as sad or as gay,
80 as required by atomic tempo of species.
How's that, Antonio?

For the love of Bacon will you chicken me up that egg?
Shall I gorge cave-phantoms?

Anna Maria!
She reads Torah and says her love is crucified.
Leider! Leider! she bloomed and withered,
a pale abusive parakeet in a mainstreet window.
Nay, I believe, I assure you,
upon my word of honour I do,
90 every syllable.
Fallor, ergo sum!
The coy lecher!
He tolle'd and legge'd
and he buttoned across a redemptorist cardigan.
Very well, then:
I'm a bold boy I know,
so I'm not my son
(even supposing I were a concierge)
nor Joachim my father's
100 but the chip of a perfect block that is neither old nor new,
the lonely petal of a high bright rose.

Art thou then ripe at last,
my wan, my svelte, my double-breasted turd?
My! but she do smell prime!

She has aborted to a tee!
I shall eat her with a fish-fork,
white and yoke and down.
Then I shall rise and move moving
to the whore of the snows,
the homicidal harridan,
the pope the puke he bleached her soul,
her hands are dripping red with sunrise,
Christina the Ripper.
Oh Weulles spare the blood of a Frank
who has climbed the bitter stairs
(René du Perron . . .!)
and grant me my second
starless inscrutable hour.

Tristesse Janale

C'est toi, o beauté blême des subtiles concierges,
La Chose kantienne, l'icone bilitique;
C'est toi, muette énigme des aphasiques vierges,
Qui centres mes désirs d'un trait antithétique.

O mystique carquois! O flèches de Télèphe!
Correlatif de toi! Abîme et dure sonde!
Sois éternellement le greffé et la greffe,
Ma superfétatoire et frêle furibonde!

Ultime coquillage et palais de la bouche
10   Mallarméenne et emblème de Michel-Ange,
Consume-toi, o neutre, en extases farouches,
Barbouille-toi, bigène, de crispations de fange,

Et co-ordonne enfin, lacustre conifère,
Tes tensions ambigues de crête et de cratère.

Spring Song

STYX! STYX!
I shall shriek that in German with
yes I shall
I shall link hands and simply scream that
into her face
pumping foam from her bitter mouth
and then die ganze Nacht gehasst
Nacht gehasst
Nacht gehasst
10 die ganze bloody Nacht gehasst
till bright daylight in the subjunctive minor
what I call the subjunctive minor
on the stirabout of my lovely neighbour shine

I tell you my ruined toes do nip the livelong night
to nip the tip of the prow of the live plank
the trembling
and my dogsbody do jut forward crucified Victory o'er the
    foaming quarry
a hard gush cocks me forth rigor algor of wings
my taut bust tis my smoker's heart
20 it flickers and thuds
Ann! Ann!
the beacon my sister's bathing-cap pierces the storm
bright pang presto silver medusa in the eye of the slush
gracefully on the boiling concrete tosses my family
show dept! I screech that down into the tempest
show dept! show dept!
ub to d'navel mister ub to d'navel

ub to d'navel . . . . . !

I hear the pelt of a royal puma crackle with filth
30 and in the grey cadence of her hour
their hour

the angels sizzle from her scabs
behold her against the wall
behold her spilt in the shadow
the shadow the stuprum of biding
and aïe! under the cresset under the moon
the jaws the corded throat
the gums the fang of the tongue
doch Grock I assure thee
40 and the grey sordes for is it not their hour
they have rend-toi
within
oh open no doors here open no doors
scarlet torches for the fat queen
open no doors the walls are dying
she has made the covenant with her eyes
but the woman her husband the bed-warrior
he lifts her purple skirt he do
her lids stick she knuckles them with the keen jewels
50 hee! hee! scarlet without and within
the long puce jupe rattles up – brava!

Cain don't care he toils up his firmament
it's all in the night's work
he shakes his brand sullenly he scatters light from his brand
that's what he's paid for that's what he's spared for
light on the just and the
the cresset the grey jaws the rictus
that's what he's there for

now behold the bloated angels they are in the high gorges
60 from afar they discern him
babbo inviolate carrion babbo reeking for a bloodslide
babbo very 'andsome in the diadem of his wound
and still moist from his extreme bath
they settle on him rookery of widows
proudly they caw the tidings
oh! oh! the dead king leads the crags
ovariotomee!
geld him by stealth by dead of night

keep the clepsydra on the boil
70 and tell he added harshly that putid pute of a daughter of mine
tell her from me will you to
quit acting the little Princess Grisild of Denmark

hark a loud clot in the valley
a high red cacklebelch
it is the peacostrich most wunnerful animal
he comes threshing he comes flaming down the couloir
it is Thanatos
tread softly it is the tiger the rigor of post-partum
it is the placenta of the departed
80 softly haply tis their sweet night of love they have throttled a fat
    boy for a bolster

no she sleeps her flecked mouth is smiling
open the door brother carry her chastely to the throneroom
quiet your eyes brother blind them on her grey throat
exult in her bodice how it smells
it is green it has stiffened on her
it was their hour I tell you they had rend-toi
now the music is over the loud music
he has come down from his white gorges Thanatos has shrouded
    him
the angels are on foot let them slink home

it is high time lover

it is high time lover
hochzeit lover
to lay thy belted livery all adown
bring the whole scrotum of tricks up on to an high mountain
even as that priapean bard that did
in arles of his being merely
dirt in the dirt floor
of his chapel now a stable
on the bank of Loire
10   where now the magi and a hayrake
wake him without ceasing
except at harvest home when the latter is removed

it may be a plant
but
tears covering all risks
you take a time exposure and you
weep into your hat

then shall brimstone lend its fire
juniper crackle on the pyre
20   spinning-jenny drown
vermuth and vervain plaster the old pox
oil of vitriol cover the earth
big with her bric-à-brac
the scurf of beauty go mad in the gale
the dicky-bird egged out of captivity
the dove sperming at the beak plucked quick
and anteros
cloud of latter rain
lay the moon

Uncollected Poems

At last I find

At last I find in my confusèd soul,
Dark with the dark flame of the cypresses,
The certitude that I cannot be whole,
Consummate, finally achieved, unless

I be consumed and fused in the white heat
Of her sad finite essence, so that none
Shall sever us who are at last complete
Eternally, irrevocably one,

One with the birdless, cloudless, colourless skies,
One with the bright purity of the fire
Of which we are and for which we must die
A rapturous strange death and be entire,

Like syzygetic stars, supernly bright,
Conjoined in One and in the Infinite!

Calvary by Night

the water
the waste of water

in the womb of water
an pansy leaps

rocket of bloom flare flower of night wilt for me
on the breasts of the water it has closed it has made
an act of floral presence on the water
the tranquil act of its cycle on the waste
from the spouting forth
to the re-enwombing
untroubled bow of petalline sweet-smellingness
kingfisher abated
drowned for me
lamb of insustenance mine

till the clamour of a blue bloom
beat on the walls of the womb of
the waste of
the water

Home Olga

J might be made sit up for a jade of hope (and exile, don't you
    know)
And Jesus and Jesuits juggernauted in the haemorrhoidal isle,
Modo et forma anal maiden, giggling to death in stomacho.
E for the erythrite of love and silence and the sweet noo style,
Swoops and loops of love and silence in the eye of the sun and
    view of the mew,
Juvante Jah and a Jain or two and the tip of a friendly yiddophile.
O for an opal of faith and cunning winking adieu, adieu, adieu;
Yesterday shall be to-morrow, riddle me that my rapparee;
Che sarà sarà che fu, there's more than Homer knows how to
    spew,
10   Exempli gratia: ecce himself and the pickthank agnus – e.o.o.e.

Seats of Honour

Mammon's bottoms,
La Goulue's, mine, a cob's,
Whipt, caressed,
My mother's breast.

But God's,
A goat's, an ass's,
Alien beauty,
The Divine Comedy.

Gnome

Spend the years of learning squandering
Courage for the years of wandering
Through the world politely turning
From the loutishness of learning.

Up he went

Up he went and in he passed
And down he came with such endeavour
As he shall rue until at last
He rematriculate for ever.

Cascando

1

why not merely the despaired of
occasion of
wordshed

is it not better abort than be barren

the hours after you are gone are so leaden
they will always start dragging too soon
the grapples clawing blindly the bed of want
bringing up the bones the old loves
sockets filled once with eyes like yours
all always is it better too soon than never
the black want splashing their faces
saying again nine days never floated the loved
nor nine months
nor nine lives

2

saying again
if you do not teach me I shall not learn
saying again there is a last
even of last times
last times of begging
last times of loving
of knowing not knowing pretending
a last even of last times of saying
if you do not love me I shall not be loved
if I do not love you I shall not love

the churn of stale words in the heart again
love love love thud of the old plunger
pestling the unalterable
whey of words

terrified again
30 of not loving
of loving and not you
of being loved and not by you
of knowing not knowing pretending
pretending

I and all the others that will love you
if they love you

  3

unless they love you

Ooftish

offer it up plank it down
Golgotha was only the potegg
cancer angina it is all one to us
cough up your T.B. don't be stingy
no trifle is too trifing not even a thrombus
anything venereal is especially welcome
that old toga in the mothballs
don't be sentimental you won't be wanting it again
send it along we'll put it in the pot with the rest
10   with your love requited and unrequited
the things taken too late the things taken too soon
the spirit aching bullock's scrotum
you won't cure it you won't endure it
it is you it equals you any fool has to pity you
so parcel up the whole issue and send it along
the whole misery diagnosed undiagnosed misdiagnosed
get your friends to do the same we'll make use of it
we'll make sense of it we'll put it in the pot with the rest
it all boils down to blood of lamb

Translations

Delta

To thee
I have willed the life drained
in secret transfusions, the life chained
in a coil of restlessness, unaware, self-angry.

When time leans on his dykes
then thine
be his allconsciousness
and memory flower forth in a flame
from the dark sanctuary, and shine
10   more brightly, as now, the rain over, the dragon's-blood
on the walls and the green against the branches.

Of thee
I know nothing, only
the tidings sustaining my going,
and shall I find
thee shape or the fumes of a dream
drawing life
from the river's fever boiling darkly
against the tide.

20   Of thee nothing in the grey hours and the hours
torn by a flame of sulphur,
only
the whistle of the tug
whose prow has ridden forth into the bright gulf.

Drunken Boat

Downstream on impassive rivers suddenly
I felt the towline of the boatmen slacken.
Redskins had taken them in a scream and stripped them and
Skewered them to the glaring stakes for targets.

Then, delivered from my straining boatmen,
From the trivial racket of trivial crews and from
The freights of Flemish grain and English cotton,
I made my own course down the passive rivers.

Blanker than the brain of a child I fled
10   Through winter, I scoured the furious jolts of the tides,
In an uproar and a chaos of Peninsulas,
Exultant, from their moorings in triumph torn.

I started awake to tempestuous hallowings.
Nine nights I danced like a cork on the billows, I danced
On the breakers, sacrificial, for ever and ever,
And the crass eye of the lanterns was expunged.

More firmly bland than to children apples' firm pulp,
Soaked the green water through my hull of pine,
Scattering helm and grappling and washing me
20   Of the stains, the vomitings and blue wine.

Thenceforward, fused in the poem, milk of stars,
Of the sea, I coiled through deeps of cloudless green,
Where, dimly, they come swaying down,
Rapt and sad, singly, the drowned;

Where, under the sky's haemorrhage, slowly tossing
In thuds of fever, arch-alcohol of song,
Pumping over the blues in sudden stains,
The bitter rednesses of love ferment.

I know the heavens split with lightnings and the currents
Of the sea and its surgings and its spoutings; I know evening,
And dawn exalted like a cloud of doves.
And my eyes have fixed phantasmagoria.

I have seen, as shed by ancient tragic footlights,
Out from the horror of the low sun's mystic stains,
Long weals of violet creep across the sea
And peals of ague rattle down its slats.

I have dreamt the green night's drifts of dazzled snow,
The slow climb of kisses to the eyes of the seas,
The circulation of unheard of saps,
And the yellow-blue alarum of phosphors singing.

I have followed months long the maddened herds of the surf
Storming the reefs, mindless of the feet,
The radiant feet of the Marys that constrain
The stampedes of the broken-winded Oceans.

I have fouled, be it known, unspeakable Floridas, tangle of
The flowers of the eyes of panthers in the skins of
Men and the taut rainbows curbing,
Beyond the brows of the seas, the glaucous herds.

I have seen Leviathan sprawl rotting in the reeds
Of the great seething swamp-nets;
The calm sea disembowelled in waterslides
And the cataracting of the doomed horizons.

Iridescent waters, glaciers, suns of silver, flagrant skies,
And dark creeks' secret ledges, horror-strewn,
Where giant reptiles, pullulant with lice,
Lapse with dark perfumes from the writhing trees.

I would have shown to children those dorados
Of the blue wave, those golden fish, those singing fish;
In spumes of flowers I have risen from my anchors
And canticles of wind have blessed my wings.

Then toward me, rocking softly on its sobbing,
Weary of the torment of the poles and zones,
The sea would lift its yellow polyps on flowers
Of gloom and hold me – like a woman kneeling –

A stranded sanctuary for screeching birds,
Flaxen-eyed, shiteing on my trembling decks,
Till down they swayed to sleep, the drowned, spreadeagled,
And, sundering the fine tendrils, floated me.

Now I who was wrecked in the inlets' tangled hair
70 And flung beyond birds aloft by the hurricane,
Whose carcass drunk with water Monitors
And Hanseatic sloops could not have salved;

Who, reeking and free in a fume of purple spray,
Have pierced the skies that flame as a wall would flame
For a chosen poet's rapture, and stream and flame
With solar lichen and with azure snot;

Who scudded, with my escort of black sea-horses,
Fury of timber, scarred with electric moons,
When Sirius flogged into a drift of ashes
80 The furnace-cratered cobalt of the skies;

I who heard in trembling across a waste of leagues
The turgent Stroms and Behemoths moan their rut,
I weaving for ever voids of spellbound blue,
Now remember Europe and her ancient ramparts.

I saw archipelagoes of stars and islands launched me
Aloft on the deep delirium of their skies:
Are these the fathomless nights of your sleep and exile,
Million of golden birds, oh Vigour to be?

But no more tears. Dawns have broken my heart,
90 And every moon is torment, every sun bitterness;
I am bloated with the stagnant fumes of acrid loving –
May I split from stem to stern and founder, ah founder!

I want none of Europe's waters unless it be
The cold black puddle where a child, full of sadness,
Squatting, looses a boat as frail
As a moth into the fragrant evening.

Steeped in the languors of the swell, I may
Absorb no more the wake of the cotton-freighters,
Nor breast the arrogant oriflammes and banners,
100   Nor swim beneath the leer of the pontoons.

ANDRÉ BRETON

The Free Union

My woman whose tresses are wood-fire
Whose thoughts are heat-lightning
Whose body is hour-glass
My woman whose body is otter in tiger jaws
My woman whose mouth is cockade and bouquet of stars of the
    last magnitude
Whose teeth are spoor of a white mouse on the white earth
Whose tongue is grated glass and amber
My woman whose tongue is stabbed Host
Whose tongue is doll that opens and shuts its eyes
10   Whose tongue is stone past belief
My woman whose lashes are pothooks' down-strokes
Whose brows are rim of nest of swallow
My woman whose temples are slate of roof of greenhouse
And fug on windows
My woman whose shoulders are champagne
And fountain frozen o'er its dolphins
My woman whose wrists are matches
My woman whose fingers are hazard and ace of hearts
Whose fingers are hay
20   My woman whose armpits are beechmast and marten
And Midsummer Night
And privet and nest of
Whose arms are foam of sea and lock
And corn and mill mixed
My woman whose legs are spindles moving
In gestures of clockwork and despair
My woman whose calves are pith of elder
Whose feet are bunch of keys whose feet are caulkers drinking
My woman whose neck is impearled barley
30   My woman whose throat is golden Vale
And tryst in the bed yea the bed of the torrent
Whose breasts are night
My woman whose breasts are salt sea molehill
My woman whose breasts are crucible of ruby

Whose breasts are spectrum of rose through dew
My woman whose belly is fan of the days unfurling
Whose belly is giant claw
My woman whose back is bird soaring plumb
Whose back is quick-silver
40 Whose back is brightness
Whose nape is rolled stone and moist chalk
And fall of the glass that held the wine
My woman whose hips are skiff
Whose hips are candelabrum whose hips are arrow-feather
And stem of feather of white peacock
And numb balance
My woman whose rumps are sandstone and amianth
My woman whose rumps are shoulders of swan
My woman whose rumps are spring-time
50 Whose sex is iris
My woman whose sex is placer and ornithorynchus
My woman whose sex is mirror
My woman whose eyes full of tears
Whose eyes are compass needle are violet panoply
My woman whose eyes are savanna
My woman whose eyes are water to drink in prison
My woman whose eyes are wood under the axe for ever
Whose eyes are level of water level of air earth and fire

Lethal Relief

The statue of Lautréamont
Its plinth of quinine tabloids
In the open country
The author of the Poetical Works lies flat on his face
And near at hand the hiloderm a shady customer keeps vigil
His left ear is glued to the ground it is a glass case it contains
A prong of lightning the artist has not failed to figure aloft
In the form of a Turk's head the blue balloon
The Swan of Montevideo with wings unfurled ready to flap at a
    moment's notice
10   Should the problem of luring the other swans from the horizon
    arise
Opens upon the false universe two eyes of different hues
The one of sulphate of iron on vines of the lashes the other of
    sparkling mire
He beholds the vast funnelled hexagon where now in no time the
    machines
By man in dressings rabidly swaddled
Shall lie a-writhing
With his radium bougie he quickens the dregs of the human
    crucible
With his sex of feathers and his brain of bull-paper
He presides at the twice nocturnal ceremonies whose object due
    allowance for fire having been made is the interversion of the
    hearts of the bird and the man
Convulsionary in ordinary I have access to his side
20   The ravishing women who introduce me into the rose-padded
    compartment
Where a hammock that they have been at pains to contrive with
    their tresses for
Me is reserved for
Me for all eternity
Exhort me before taking their departure not to catch a chill in the
    perusal of the daily

It transpires that the statue in whose latitude the squitch of my
    nerve terminals
Weighs anchor is tuned each night like a piano

Lady Love

She is standing on my lids
And her hair is in my hair
She has the colour of my eye
She has the body of my hand
In my shade she is engulfed
As a stone against the sky

She will never close her eyes
And she does not let me sleep
And her dreams in the bright day
10   Make the suns evaporate
And me laugh cry and laugh
Speak when I have nothing to say

Out of Sight in the Direction of My Body

All the trees all their boughs all their leaves
The grass at the base the rocks the massed houses
Afar the sea that thine eye washes
Those images of one day and the next
The vices the virtues that are so imperfect
The transparence of men that pass in the streets of hazard
And women that pass in a fume from thy dour questing
The fixed ideas virgin-lipped leaden-hearted
The vices the virtues that are so imperfect
10   The eyes consenting resembling the eyes thou didst vanquish
The confusion of the bodies the lassitudes the ardours
The imitation of the words the attitudes the ideas
The vices the virtues that are so imperfect

Love, is man unfinished.

PAUL ELUARD

Scarcely Disfigured

Farewell sadness
Greeting sadness
Thou art inscribed in the lines of the ceiling
Thou art inscribed in the eyes that I love
Thou art not altogether want
For the poorest lips denounce thee
Smiling
Greeting sadness
Love of the bodies that are lovable
10   Mightiness of love that lovable
Starts up as a bodiless beast
Head of hope defeated
Sadness countenance of beauty

The Invention

The right hand winnows the sand
Every transformation is possible
Afar on the stones the sun whets his fever to have done
The description of the landscape is not very important
The pleasant space· of harvesting and no longer.

> Clear with my two eyes
> As water and fire.

*

What is the role of the root?
Despair has broken all his bonds
10   He carries his hands to his head
One seven one four one two one one
A hundred women in the street
Whom I shall never see again.

*

The art of living, liberal art, the art of dying well, the art of thinking, incoherent art, the art of smoking, the art of enjoying, the art
of the Middle Ages, decorative art, the art of reasoning, the art of
reasoning well, poetic art, mechanic art, erotic art, the art of being a grandfather, the art of the dance, the art of seeing, the art of
being accomplished, the art of caressing, Japanese art, the art of
20   playing, the art of eating, the art of torturing.

*

Yet I have never found what I write in what I love.

Second Nature

In honour of the dumb the blind the deaf
Shouldering the great black stone
The things of time passing simply away

But then for the others knowing things by their names
The sear of every metamorphosis
The unbroken chain of dawns in the brain
The implacable cries shattering words

Furrowing the mouth furrowing the eyes
Where furious colours dispel the mists of vigil
10   Set up love against life that the dead dream of
The low-living share the others are slaves
Of love as some are slaves of freedom

Scene

At the hour when the first symptoms of mental viduity make
    themselves felt
A negro is to be seen always the same negro
In a most thoroughfare ostensibly swanking a red tie
He always sports the same beige hat
He has the features of spite he looks at no one
And no one looks at him

I love neither roads nor mountains nor forests
Bridges leave me cold
I do not see their arches as eyes I am not in the habit of walking
    on brows
10   I am in the habit of walking in quarters where there are the most
    women
And then I am interested only in women
The negro also for at the hour when boredom and fatigue
Daunt and detach me from desires
From myself
Then I meet him always
I am detached he is spiteful
His tie is certainly wrought iron with a coat of red-lead
False forge fire
But whether or not he is there out of spite
20   It is certain that I only notice him for want of something better
    to do

The shadows are yoked to an obvious determination to see
    nothing
But forth from its nest the evening staggers
What is that signal those signals those alarums
It is the last astonishment of the evening
The women departing slip off their chemises of light
All of a single sudden not a soul remains
When we are gone the light is alone

    *

The carmine loft has nooks of jade
And jasper if the eye shuns nacre
30   The mouth is the mouth of the blood the elder
Cranes its neck for the milk of the blade
A flint has cowed the tempestuous night
Risk infant trips up daring
Stones on the stubble birds on the tiles
Fire in the harvests in the breasts
Playing with the pollen of the breath of the night
Hewn at the hands of the winds the water
Catches up her skirts and the scrolls of wave
Set the spark of dawn aflame
40   And in her black bodice a corpse seduces
The scarabs of the grass and of the dead boughs

     *

In a so thoroughfare

Universe-Solitude

1
A woman every night
Journeys secretly.

2
Villages of weariness
Where the arms of girls are bare
As jets of water
Where their youth increasing in them
Laughs and laughs and laughs on tiptoe

Villages of weariness
Where everybody is the same.

3
10   To see the eyes that cloister you
And the laughter that receives you.

4
I want to kiss thee I do kiss thee
I want to leave thee thou art tired
But when our strengths are at the ebb
Thou puttest on an armour more perilous than an arm.

5
The body and the profane honours
Incredible conspiracy
Of the angles soft as wings.
But the hand caressing me
20   It is my laughter that unclasps it
It is my throat that clings to it
That ends it

Incredible conspiracy
Of the discoveries and surprises.

6

Phantom of thy nudity
Phantom child of thy simplicity
Child victor carnal sleep
Of unreal liberties.

7

It is the breath the yestersun
Joining thy lips
And it is the caress the fresh caress
To scour the frail seas of thy shame
To fashion them in gloom
It is the mirrors of jasmine
The problem of calm.

8

Disarmed
She knows of no enemy.

9

She stretches herself
That she may feel less alone.

10

I admired descending upon thee
Time in the chariot of space
Our memories transported me

Much room is denied thee
For ever with me.

11

Rending her kisses and her fears
She wakes in the night
To wonder at all that has replaced her.

PAUL ELUARD

Confections

1
Simplicity yea even to write
To-day at least the hand is there

2
It is meet to scrutinize
The inquisitive
When one is weary

3
The violence of sea-winds
Ships old faces
A permanent abode
Weapons to defend one
A shot one only
Stupefaction of the father
Dead this long time

4
All these people eat
They are gluttonous they are happy
The more they laugh the more they eat

5
Above the hat-wear
A regiment of ospreys gallops past
It is a regiment of foot-wear
All the disillusioned fetishists and their complete collections
Off to the devil

6
Cataclysms of gold well-gotten
And of silver ill-gotten

7
The birds perfume the woods
The rocks their great nocturnal lakes

8
Play at profile and win
Let a bird abide in its wings

9
Rapt
I dwell in this thorn and my claw alights
On the sweet breasts of poverty and crime

10
30 Why are they made to run
They are not made to run
Arriving underdue
Departing overdue

What a road back
When slowness takes a hand

Proofs of the contrary
And futility

11
Gold-filings a treasure a platinum
Puddle deep in a horrible valley
40 Whose denizens have lost their hands
It takes the players out of themselves

12
The drawing-room with its black tongue licks its master
Embalms him performs the office of eternity

13
The Beresina forded by a sandy jug-dugged woman

14
He takes her in his arms
Bright gleams for a second playing
On the shoulder-blades the shoulders and the breasts
Then hidden by a cloud

She carries her hand to her heart
50 She pales she quakes
Whose then was the cry

But he if he still lives
He shall be rediscovered
In a strange town

15
The blood flowing on the flags
Furnishes me with sandals
I sit on a chair in the middle of the street
I observe the little Creole girls
Coming out of school smoking pipes

16
60 Do not see reality as I am

17
All life even as an agate has poured itself
Into the seams of my countenance and cast
A death-mask of unrivalled beauty

18
The black trees the white trees
Are younger than nature
In order to recover this freak of birth one must
Age

19
Fatal sun of the quick
One cannot keep thy heart

TRISTAN TZARA

from The Approximative Man

– it was a day softer than a woman
under the beds I saw
heavy masses of shadow
ready to fall on the sleeping felons
in the soft palms of their beds
I saw hanging from the haloes' ears
watching masses heavy and black-fisted
and stalking in the middle writing without respite
rain breaking grey wings and prisms
10   and brief phosphorescent wills lost amid laughter's hatchings
their trotting awakening the fields the eyes had closed
noiselessly screwing themselves to the screw on the well's curb
the wild grass's few pants
and then the birds' catacombs the birds
flying away through the submissive tentacles
the tamed brothers in the mirror
the dolls' eyes fixed on the fatherlands' paddocks
where earth is flung into puddles of corpses and urine
farther on I have seen eyelashes pressing round birds – a polar
    crown
20   and the powerful falls of the birds of light
upon the inflamed world of days without escape
and then I saw no more
somebody noisily shut the door
– woman friend weeping at the bottom of the hold –
night grew withered within me

Reminder

I have opened my eyes on loves without limit
and the new shadow on the new land
a silence trod on our bodies it was only the flash of a day
and the eye closed fright

sweet absence of words tangling the shadow
the calls became plaintive so far away still was the spring
and you soft spring-like flesh
lost bitter

will you no longer bear my leisure my woes
10   shadows of frail ash in that grass which avoids you
I have rattled the dream and drummed without respite under
    alien vaults
thy steps have come after me until late in the soul

a confusion of croakings happened to be on my way
I have rejected the depressing friendship of distant calls
I no longer cloud my eyes with the sight of loves without limit
lost without limit and turned to dumb friendships

ERNST MOERMAN

Louis Armstrong

suddenly in the midst of a game of lotto with his sisters
Armstrong let a roar out of him that he had the raw meat
red wet flesh for Louis
and he up and he sliced him two rumplips
since when his trumpet bubbles
their fust buss

poppies burn on the black earth
he weds the flood he lulls her

some of these days muffled in ooze
10   down down down down
pang of white in my hair

after you're gone
Narcissus lean and slippered

you're driving me crazy and the trumpet
is Ole Bull it chassés aghast
out of the throes of morning
down the giddy catgut
and *confessing* and my woe slavers
the black music it can't be easy
20   it threshes the old heart into a spin
into a blaze

Louis lil' ole fader Mississippi
his voice gushes into the lake
the rain spouts back into heaven
his arrows from afar they fizz through the wild horses
they fang you and me
then they fly home

flurry of lightning in the earth
sockets for his rootbound song
30   nights of Harlem scored with his nails
snow black slush when his heart rises

his she-notes they have more tentacles than the sea
they woo me they close my eyes
they suck me out of the world

Poèmes 37–39

they come
different and the same
with each it is different and the same
with each the absence of love is different
with each the absence of love is the same

—

elles viennent
autres et pareilles
avec chacune c'est autre et c'est pareil
avec chacune l'absence d'amour est autre
avec chacune l'absence d'amour est pareille

à elle l'acte calme
les pores savants le sexe bon enfant
l'attente pas trop lente les regrets pas trop longs l'absence
au service de la présence
les quelques haillons d'azur dans la tête les points enfin morts
    du cœur
toute la tardive grâce d'une pluie cessant
au tomber d'une nuit
d'août

à elle vide
10   lui pur
d'amour

être là sans mâchoires sans dents
où s'en va le plaisir de perdre
avec celui à peine inférieur
de gagner
et Roscelin et on attend
adverbe oh petit cadeau
vide vide sinon des loques de chanson
mon père m'a donné un mari
ou en faisant la fleur
10 qu'elle mouille
tant qu'elle voudra jusqu'à l'élégie
des sabots ferrés encore loin des Halles
ou l'eau de la canaille pestant dans les tuyaux
ou plus rien
qu'elle mouille puisque c'est ainsi
parfasse tout le superflu
et vienne
à la bouche idiote à la main formicante
au bloc cave à l'œil qui écoute
20 de lointains coups de ciseaux argentins

Ascension

à travers la mince cloison
ce jour où un enfant
prodigue à sa façon
rentra dans sa famille
j'entends la voix
elle est émue elle commente
la coupe du monde de football

toujours trop jeune

en même temps par la fenêtre ouverte
par les airs tout court
sourdement
la houle des fidèles

son sang gicla avec abondance
sur les draps sur les pois de senteur sur son mec
de ses doigts dégoûtants il ferma les paupières
sur les grands yeux verts étonnés

elle rôde légère
sur ma tombe d'air

10

La Mouche

entre la scène et moi
la vitre
vide sauf elle

ventre à terre
sanglée dans ses boyaux noirs
antennes affolées ailes liées
pattes crochues bouche suçant à vide
sabrant l'azur s'écrasant contre l'invisible
sous mon pouce impuissant elle fait chavirer
10   la mer et le ciel serein

musique de l'indifférence
cœur temps air feu sable
du silence éboulement d'amours
couvre leurs voix et que
je ne m'entende plus
me taire

bois seul
bouffe brûle fornique crève seul comme devant
les absents sont morts les présents puent
sors tes yeux détourne-les sur les roseaux
se taquinent-ils ou les aïs
pas la peine il y a le vent
et l'état de veille

ainsi a-t-on beau
par le beau temps et par le mauvais
enfermé chez soi enfermé chez eux
comme si c'était d'hier se rappeler le mammouth
le dinothérium les premiers baisers
les périodes glaciaires n'apportant rien de neuf
la grande chaleur du treizième de leur ère
sur Lisbonne fumante Kant froidement penché
rêver en générations de chênes et oublier son père
10   ses yeux s'il portait la moustache
s'il était bon de quoi il est mort
on n'en est pas moins mangé sans appétit
par le mauvais temps et par le pire
enfermé chez soi enfermé chez eux

Dieppe

encore le dernier reflux
le galet mort
le demi-tour puis les pas
vers les vieilles lumières

Dieppe

again the last ebb
the dead shingle
the turning then the steps
towards the lights of old

Rue de Vaugirard

à mi-hauteur
je débraye et béant de candeur
expose la plaque aux lumières et aux ombres
puis repars fortifié
d'un négatif irrécusable

Arènes de Lutèce

De là où nous sommes assis plus haut que les gradins
je nous vois entrer du côté de la Rue des Arènes,
hésiter, regarder en l'air, puis pesamment
venir vers nous à travers le sable sombre,
de plus en plus laids, aussi laids que les autres,
mais muets. Un petit chien vert
entre en courant du côté de la Rue Monge,
elle s'arrête, elle le suit des yeux,
il traverse l'arène, il disparaît
10   derrière le socle du savant Gabriel de Mortillet.
Elle se retourne, je suis parti, je gravis seul
les marches rustiques, je touche de ma main gauche
la rampe rustique, elle est en béton. Elle hésite,
fait un pas vers la sortie de la Rue Monge, puis me suit.
J'ai un frisson, c'est moi qui me rejoins,
c'est avec d'autres yeux que maintenant je regarde
le sable, les flaques d'eau sous la bruine,
une petite fille traînant derrière elle un cerceau,
un couple, qui sait des amoureux, la main dans la main,
20   les gradins vides, les hautes maisons, le ciel
qui nous éclaire trop tard.
Je me retourne, je suis étonné
de trouver là son triste visage.

jusque dans la caverne ciel et sol
et une à une les vieilles voix
d'outre-tombe
et lentement la même lumière
qui sur les plaines d'Enna en longs viols
macérait naguère les capillaires
et les mêmes lois
que naguère
et lentement au loin qui éteint
10   Proserpine et Atropos
adorable de vide douteux
encore la bouche d'ombre

Samuel Beckett: Collected Poems

PART 2   Post-War

.

Saint-Lô

Vire will wind in other shadows
unborn through the bright ways tremble
and the old mind ghost-forsaken
sink into its havoc

Antipepsis

And the number was uneven
In the green of holy Stephen
Where before the ass the cart
Was harnessed for a foreign part.
In this should not be seen the sign
Of hasard, no, but of design,
For of the two, by common consent,
The cart was the more intelligent.
Whose exceptionally pia
10   Mater hatched this grand idea
Is not known. He or she,
Smiling, unmolested, free,
By this one act the mind become
A providential vacuum,
Continues still to stroll amok,
To eat, drink, piss, shit, fart and fuck,
Assuming that the fucking season
Did not expire with that of reason.
Now through the city spreads apace
20   The cry: A thought has taken place!
A human thought! Ochone! Ochone!
Purissima Virgo! We're undone!
Bitched, buggered and bewilderèd!
Bring forth your dead! Bring forth your dead!

Poems from Novels and Plays

who may tell the tale
of the old man?
weigh absence in a scale?
mete want with a span?
the sum assess
of the world's woes?
nothingness
in words enclose?

Watt will not
abate one jot
but of what

of the coming to
of the being at
of the going from
Knott's habitat

of the long way
of the short stay
10   of the going back home
the way he had come

of the empty heart
of the empty hands
of the dim mind wayfaring
through barren lands

of a flame with dark winds
hedged about
going out
gone out

20   of the empty heart
of the empty hands
of the dark mind stumbling
through barren lands

that is of what
Watt will not
abate one tot

Age is when to a man
Huddled o'er the ingle
Shivering for the hag
To put the pan in the bed
And bring the toddy
She comes in the ashes
Who loved could not be won
Or won not loved
Or some other trouble
Comes in the ashes
Like in that old light
The face in the ashes
That old starlight
On the earth again.

Six Poèmes

bon bon il est un pays
où l'oubli où pèse l'oubli
doucement sur les mondes innommés
là la tête on la tait la tête est muette
et on sait non on ne sait rien
le chant des bouches mortes meurt
sur la grève il a fait le voyage
il n'y a rien à pleurer

ma solitude je la connais allez je la connais mal
10   j'ai le temps c'est ce que je me dis j'ai le temps
mais quel temps os affamé le temps du chien
du ciel pâlissant sans cesse mon grain de ciel
du rayon qui grimpe ocellé tremblant
des microns des années ténèbres

vous voulez que j'aille d'A à B je ne peux pas
je ne peux pas sortir je suis dans un pays sans traces
oui oui c'est une belle chose que vous avez là une bien belle
    chose
qu'est-ce que c'est ne me posez plus de questions
spirale poussière d'instants qu'est-ce que c'est le même
20   le calme l'amour la haine le calme le calme

Mort de A.D.

et là être là encore là
pressé contre ma vieille planche vérolée du noir
des jours et nuits broyés aveuglément
à être là à ne pas fuir et fuir et être là
courbé vers l'aveu du temps mourant
d'avoir été ce qu'il fut fait ce qu'il fit
de moi de mon ami mort hier l'œil luisant
les dents longues haletant dans sa barbe dévorant
la vie des saints une vie par jour de vie
10   revivant dans la nuit ses noirs péchés
mort hier pendant que je vivais
et être là buvant plus haut que l'orage
la coulpe du temps irrémissible
agrippé au vieux bois témoin des départs
témoin des retours

vive morte ma seule saison
lis blancs chrysanthèmes
nids vifs abandonnés
boue des feuilles d'avril
beaux jours gris de givre

je suis ce cours de sable qui glisse
entre le galet et la dune
la pluie d'été pleut sur ma vie
sur moi ma vie qui me fuit me poursuit
et finira le jour de son commencement

cher instant je te vois
dans ce rideau de brume qui recule
où je n'aurai plus à fouler ces longs seuils mouvants
et vivrai le temps d'une porte
10   qui s'ouvre et se referme

    —

my way is in the sand flowing
between the shingle and the dune
the summer rain rains on my life
on me my life harrying fleeing
to its beginning to its end

my peace is there in the receding mist
when I may cease from treading these long shifting thresholds
and live the space of a door
that opens and shuts

que ferais-je sans ce monde sans visage sans questions
où être ne dure qu'un instant où chaque instant
verse dans le vide dans l'oubli d'avoir été
sans cette onde où à la fin
corps et ombre ensemble s'engloutissent
que ferais-je sans ce silence gouffre des murmures
haletant furieux vers le secours vers l'amour
sans ce ciel qui s'élève
sur la poussière de ses lests

10   que ferais-je je ferais comme hier comme aujourd'hui
regardant par mon hublot si je ne suis pas seul
à errer et à virer loin de toute vie
dans un espace pantin
sans voix parmi les voix
enfermées avec moi

—

what would I do without this world faceless incurious
where to be lasts but an instant where every instant
spills in the void the ignorance of having been
without this wave where in the end
body and shadow together are engulfed
what would I do without this silence where the murmurs die
the pantings the frenzies towards succour towards love
without this sky that soars
above its ballast dust

10   what would I do what I did yesterday and the day before
peering out of my deadlight looking for another
wandering like me eddying far from all the living
in a convulsive space
among the voices voiceless
that throng my hiddenness

je voudrais que mon amour meure
qu'il pleuve sur le cimetière
et les ruelles où je vais
pleurant celle qui crut m'aimer

—

I would like my love to die
and the rain to be raining on the graveyard
and on me walking the streets
mourning her who thought she loved me

Translations

Apoem 4

I belong to the Earth. I am a rendez-vous: tents pitched on my tongue, lodgers in my right fist (whenceforward fist *manœuvring* pen and Revels of Wrath). Don't blame me for this state of affairs, forgive me while you can. As soon as I could stride I barged in, on Humanity: dud governments, conquistadores sweating the big drum, dungbeetles of mind, gross whites, magistrates and whores in furs, informing lice, darling lieutenants, exclusive mother-monsters, clergymen, quarter-wits, totists and receivers – in a word soon learned one is ever far from home. Can't have that. I terrorised my pals, ad libid., my esteemed pals. No, no, no lifestory to-day. Multiplication of *all the senses* desirable. Matter of Pure Medecine, to put it mildly. In short, I was in the Army, hence felon like my million spits – in self-defence I understand. And so on.

You at war, you who press your lips on Her's, at every leaving. Well! Arrest me! Hard on fall, ha, flop into mirror, superstitious plump for seven years luck, Hard. 'Twas more. *They* defiled, under the finest trees. I chewed my heartcud, then damned the expense. I dissolved brooding. *Thou shalt not sleep Thine eye is old junk* Seasons fondled spoons I taunted my ogres, their steels, their clarions Similarly was butterfly in their net Servingman ranker *Small boy in search of bellyful: cold meats al fresco, dreams later* The world was their dungeon! humane killer! I have strayed on Grammar's strands: skivvies, sluts, bawds, bombardears; but more particularly how much more noxious by far, clear-starchers ironing Death's frills. (Embellish her, loose her witching on the track the field of honour, meet for calf-love). The truth being on the contrary that Death is *most alarming*, from this point of view. The blood was black, indiscreet. The most flourishing young men, the most athletic, did not escape, in spite of the lesson learnt. O vanities. Their frail victories are ever in my thoughts, over nature's wallets and the druggery of willing women. Once pressed into death, they *consented* to the hour of joy. Me they postponed to the morrow. I too was long gone, curdled. But to-day I will aline them here, to tremble again between the lines. (Indispensable to read between the lines,

impossible to overstate the importance of this.) In the war then the finest scenery was nothing to me but wounds, great gummed jaws. Between the panoramas no communion, no osmose. With quasi-majestic common consent the Officers turned their backs on freedom; can't recall a single exception! unless they were tour-
ists and in what are tourists poets *I ask you?* those travellers un-concerned with seeing the *sights*. (In art no plan, but all settlement bull by horns pains conquest inroad *forced moves*). To pass the war on to sing it nourish it seemed my lot, involving its recurring to me leitmotiv, which is absolutely practically out of the question. So again the philharmonic tutti or mounted police. I scarified inno-cent roses *whose only sin was redness*, beheaded the condors of the daily Andes *cousins-german of my fouled eyelids*, slightly disguised Poetry as a diver, as a gasmasked combattant, as an airman meteor between the Universal shirt and skin. Equipped with phonolithic
heart I gave tongue with the yellers yappers hoothers fluthers with man tuskhandled deviltusked – like most of the maneaters, agreed *No difficulty there*. Better! better befell me in equal atonement in-flexible despot cowering slave; I therefore confess I succumbed to the defence of the fatherland, the luxury of a colonial empire, the besotted bravos of a clatter of cornerboys *countrymen of mine*. Me I loathed in time, put to death. My familiars slunk maybe, fearful for OUR skin. I trembled on the brink. Shocking offhand, all of a sudden, my private-skeleton – cold sweats streaming streaming. Poet of Poetry patient aggressor and of all members of kingdoms
animal mineral vegetable bearing thereto resemblance from front back side, I could have set up for myself and jogged along in the shade of a whim; had first-fruits, viands, spleen; resided clandes-tinely; corrupted *others'* offspring; and so on. But freely I gave audi-ence to playwrights, to fashionable dress-designers, too freely. By many a narrow gorge I went and flagrant isthmus, for glory's sake. Schlitters or mariners in stellar pose *but on the verge of telling a lie rather than wrong the fishers of past pearls I choose with a thump on the jut of the chin to knock the phrase flat. (Dull mystery, don't be polite; alas, unbearable, all speech constrained to silence par-
taking of the fascist act. In which I was frequently my own victim, as it happened.)* The war then, with its incivilities, rent my body, mortified my mind, like an excrement. Having reached the age of reason *or the age-limit as the case may be*, I cried: 'Milkmen and

mad soilsmen excepted Who will wake me?' Merely the first words
of a crucified adult. (Useful! I took thought for my wife, for my still
foetal child, but both beyond already this ultimate Regime.) The
archives of the World are no longer in safety: The nags tore their
chests of firedamp of beryl of soot of *no importance* The marbles
went bad black blue fox diamond *for life* The cork crumbled to the
rivers' great despair The fruit the vegetables withered on wattles
my body peoples galleys continents skyhigh The smoke wallowed
openly in breasts rumps fats clusters of women like chandeliers
dangling from the hooks of a town in ruins The anthracite lost
its taste of traveller And I personally opened an asylum so vast
that the nation of the mad found room therein for the future of
several branch establishments. The truth is I'm still at the elim-
inatory stages. In any other circumstances I should have been so
pleased to begin God with a wave, a shoulder, a helicopter, *something visible*. Whereas I was sucked into the dawn. What rapidity!
and translucency! what a caesarean! All at once. A single meal! The
20th century has belched a man. I was full of pride, suspicious of
my angel. Pride! crevasse that it is the duty of every self-respecting
Nature-lover (i.e., for your guidance, the art-critic with his universal belly) to explore with a lantern, so as, not to do anything
about it *what matters is to mean well* in ignorance of the common-
est kind *that of the gentleman passing judgment* and so as not to
make matters even worse, I refer to the style of the firm and the
individual bearing. I skirted then, all fair in war! the fluvial legs
of reality, the spine of monsoon-pallid beasts, the drape *between
the rising and the setting sun* of mannequins their hips awrithe in
me admiring eye. No. No no, not that. On the contrary a revolt-
ing firmament, nothing more. Ergo sum total I halfdowned tools,
whereas on the other threshold of the tunnel the ganger signed
on planets, phosphor pills. O lens! O round eye on plate! I resent-
ed successively the platform *because clown*, the hall *where gloves
kid the iron hand*, the *excessively antifamily* box, the hygienic avenues. Of all the manors loved of yore not one came forward! O
the hair of the dog! Nothing naturally prevented me from eschew-
ing stereoscopic films, tracer bullets, nervous rockets, gritty hair
or nail grenades, borborygmous bombs emitting great sculpture
don't waste scrap! brands of I know not what spontaneous generation. Dresser! dishes damned . . . At times I played a part; yet never

felt proof as I would have wished *notwithstanding precautions, body armour, western magic in the past from proximate purloined* or demented, whatever my pretensions, to the throne of Life or to make a long story short the poet's armchair. O the panes the panes the feet severed! Was I a drunkard or the jobless throwing myself out of the window like a piano stuffed to the bung? O down with the music to come that coughs and digs its grave. Up to the penis in I went to the seablood of a shattered maid. Thus than War the ghost can raise no viler pleasure, amidst the sheaves of flowers the harangues the moved awed mob the machines fresh from the factory the purveyors wondrous swollen. But apart from these touching frivolities need I say what onslaught of polity erratic, occasional, morbid, *true to tradition?* I had worn the dunce's cap, a fact that had to be brought to the notice of the bishops and more docile parishioners. I reeked, my pals joined the pack, the fur flew, etc. Antiquated therefore I return from war, fair game for remorse jeers codology and *compulsory* disarmament. Except that now *I've quit* I'm a conscientious objector.

At this life latitude love appears. Ivory tower or sundew for the arachnid. Not a word on the subject of the necessities, wretched lying novice longings or gourmet's stomachbelch. I verify the state of man, past, present and to come. A trifle compared with true love so sensitive to geographical niceties, but with what flank adhesions to the comedy of good manners. Is there then definitely no alternative to conspicuousness by absence? I blow mysself up like a fanatic, right in the middle of the nuptial rites. Here come the women in love haunting pocket pharos pier pole phallus. I would deem this something quite new in the spectral line, but incontinent their hindlegs go limp and my head is broken, I am naught but the rag of yesternight's radiant star. I say to myself, Unfortunate ocean! Poltroon! Suddenly: *The town is underground! the town is underground! the town is underground!* Then I escape with my life? Through the roots the bulbs the yams I glimpse the balls' the jazzbands' plastic queen. I hasten, clogs darken my sky. And invite a panther to waltz. O *my* darling. On the wharf of her muscles soon I envisage *beyond compare* the proofs sublime of poetic swindle. I whizbang awhistwhack his highness and do my stuff. She undoes herself up. I adore her, lying *not clear who* on the hard ground, in her lidojungle lair, in the shade of a kaki-laden heart. It's Sunday on Thursday, her love is the week of Sundays. At every sigh she sighs goodby, for every tie comes asunder. *O my panther that goes her own pirogue* Goodbye . . . The town sleeps its drunken sleep. Shame brands the brows of the women in flight. Now I daub me for the wantons, as the sacrament requires. Tallyhist! Tallyhist! dog *I sniff out the Venus mount.* Or horse in realm of fancy amble. Ah, numberless I have borne them lewd bold childish wavering: enough to unhinge your loins! and take their number! to make sure never again, etc. There was a time when I had truck with schoolgirls plump *but* smelling of chalk or butter. *O their blarney.* They grew up without latin and their lips went tart. They grew gallows ripe, our subjunctive tripe made flesh and love, whose gullets to slit the dominie itched, with a squint in his eye and a taste for romance. With my testicled friends on a toss of the dice I staked their charms. I had thirteen to my bow, unheard of luck, indecent. *Really?* – What matters is not so much to vulgarise as to caulk the brainseams. For long bellydancing thighs start from mine eyes. *If only they were mere ideas!* It is quite impossible for me to escape from the *gas*-chamber or the *town*-sewer without breaking to smithereens the finest pleasure in the world. Foreigners console me not at all, is it possible I am in the most fraternal country known? Whose treasures I mistrust, where beauty cries for hunger. Her sheepfold, interspace! shaggy vale! too tender motor that graduates my loving! tis every morning she has to have her toe and finger nails painted and repainted, as though she were not fancy enough *the way she is*. I suffered the ooze of a thousand beeswaxed female Whites and the vomit green of *art* Negresses sapped by absinthe. Then paved the palate and the *rumps* of Optionals of quite another race, etc. And now from the last word in frigidaires I extort a bunch of keys a polynesia of locks: real young *adjective* women. O what systems then. What a poor thing written poetry is beside this montage. Would I could celebrate the equations achieved thanks to Them. I see them again, on the job: fresh figs open to the very globule, sugarjuice changing with eclipse and climate, expensive soaps that *finally* literally harrowed my ducts *including the urethra*. I call them to mind, triplex perhaps or acoustics *I couldn't say:* The one goddess ligid and sofomous arched over the iris with bengal cock, and her pussies that spoiled me The other like a train

160

170

180

of thought, less violent than honey, bomb agog *boom boom* to pose
for the photographer and bring forth The next with straight sword
her hilt her tongue her gems afox on fairs and rounds, who mine
from log in languor stretched rose pith at dawn her bearings gone
What others? The ardent The teaser The festive The undinist The
gloved The itinerant The numidian The eleventh The hussie The
median The tightfit The pitibal The kleptomaenad The clitorid-
ian The phosphorimel? O women incarcerate, I kept you free from
the deliverer, we being ourselves or nothing. *You were repudiated.*
What romanticism had ensued, but for the fear of scandal. *For-*
get and forgive. The fact is fond memory brings how luscious we
clipped. The moon at the full I drank my fill. The moon, gentleman, was a mousehole, an owlhole, a tolerance womb. I inserted
my middle finger, palmed. I coiled the nimbus. And it rained foam
at the foot of the monsignor tree, cream on the crown of my sex-
cylinder equipped *pro* the arabesques of dayspring and *con* the too
too gallant gonococci. All things considered I should have said that
I drank *to perfection.* For Woman, fowl escaped from a diamond
lorry, may, duly sabred, in a moment of weakness turn into a cascade. I drank then philtres as it were, weak as water; nevertheless
at times an hour assumed the importance of a week and so on ...
The Casino's corset flew off or the Follies': clover, oats, nugget,
prospectus, cataract *I still have enough bad taste: to write that im-*
ages burn! and ought to be made blaze tram crammed with cur-
rants pudding on an Irish virgin's siding *The writer who don't let*
words come in is a eunuch, etc. The incident is closed, I embark. It
seems only yesterday that I was accused of trying to murder a ewe,
phantom at the outside of my one-and-twentieth birthday : my
wedding-day. In memory of this *last love* I plead not guilty; for the
World with its Morals and Hardys lawful unions Tates and Bradys
and P.C. Sades, the lighttight World and the law-abiding immaculate Hog that I was all but, we died in concert. Calmed, nightly I
set out to coast about a woman still the same, whom I love, in the
name of the oppressed peoples.

Remains poetry, that is the account of man and his various vital
situations *and poetry to-day being purely and simply the pastime*
of licensed apes or laggards purple in the face, the fine flower of
bilge, the hoist to politics, the scramble for applause, etc. I will be an

apoet the Apoet too no doubt, consigning with care to poetry's gal-
vanic zone no man's land and subterraneans, even as it oxygenated
230 ever. I cast my whip to the stars and take a shower, being sensual.
Whereupon the Future sprawling on its back: but no dictatorship
of sound or colour or phrase or letter or smell of silence, no red
tape, no committees, no medical board, no votes for all. It won't
be long now perhaps before I have poetry in pigeon-holes. Twould
have been an insult to free man in all his splendour, to science,
the arts, the generations but for whom tralala . . . Grabbed by the
tousles and whipped off the ground, tripped up and dumped in
the vaults of Our Lord – I come asunder in three parts *Natural
History illustration;* and my trunk drifts up to tide. *That's* life! all
240 our harangues recorded, all our lusts for women, all our bread-
and-milk disquisitions, nothing but bawdy civil dealings with X,
Y, Z. But there is no obligation to vanish for two pins, I am not of
the putrid spawn of senators. *One fine evening* I mustered a few
friends, more or less banished from their Native Lands. We bashed
and penissed once and for all the pinups of the antique disposi-
tion. Since when the banks spend thrift in a creel full of crabs on
wheels. It was more than we could bear. We ravished the secrets
of a sphere, security in other words. Politicians after all never had
the vaguest idea what the Bible was about or Marx and Rimbaud
250 or Nietzsche and Lautréamont, never did anything but wash their
hands at the mere mention of Jesus. Had to be enfrenzied bells,
willows, crystal, the sounding planets loudened, *in the interests
of an eventual communication with the without.* I want Miracles.
The miracle is a man without a chain round his neck. Poetry is
thus in position. I hear the trumpet, the cavalry. The feudal universe is ablaze. At last I have captured the voice's prism. I am on a
rail. The stations, the depots sink under the rain. The level-cross-
ing men go weak in the legs. I smash the crockery of the towns, etc
. . . Now the air cracks, the prisoners are downcast, etc. Wretched
260 men-at-arms, wretched pretenders to the executive Power! You
made of Paris a boudoir, of New York a brothel, of London a cross,
of Nagasaki a stroke of fire . . . Excellent inflation of the west! Poor
imbecile copyists *dead to the thing* have you seen the test of the
sun, Orient! igny petry! and its shafts? Did you ever hear of the
deep African Strings, or the Heel of the red Americas? As for me I
know after *a quarter century of hard there* your foundries, strategic

points, spitals, reinforced concrete, migraine avenues, your simi-
an chimneys and their havana tophats. – In the window, *just fancy!*
I eye from top to toe Death that bedizened tenant of your copro-
270 phagous civilisation . . . And what about your *Great Men* with the
keeners doing the homeguard step behind them . . . Well, I leave
them to the march of Time. My night at least is single-minded. *Our*
government proceeds directly from the stalags or the field-units or
the beltbusting virgins, and the eye of the ages. As for the urinals,
they served to relieve us of our elegancies our mentality *à la mode.*
Poetry cancelled its lease. To such extents *an hysterical cock crows*
itself hoarse on the dunghill of the historical: the Gallic Cock that
I sport with pleasure in my mouth a fatherland Flower live long
Plumage Cherry, etc. But without the preparations cease . . . This
280 epoch *Conspew the hideous Conspew the majordomos Conspew*
This epoch, I repeat, will be superseded. I will harry its holy Sisters
its Bureau O the fuse of an act of love And the poet cancels the in-
terdicts No customs barrier The coiling flames devour the twined
barrage of reason. It is said *My hearings whistle The alarm unsticks*
the plugs of wax Hauling of linen bulbs springs I insurrect in a bath
of steam The properties were volcanic To be sure to be sure Can't
do anything about anything Any more than you I come a cropper
The carillons bite their tails I bring to light a begged question It is
foresaid that you shall see the triumph at last of the weak over the
290 strong, the confined over the gaoler, the child over his unlawful
parents, the ploughman over the reveller, the poet over the apoth-
ecary, the citizen over the racialist. Humanity lets go the brakes . . .
In his kayak, flouting the rapids, the romany *friend.* The regular
. . . Woman is a starter. At the third rebuke the swimmers sprint
Neither angels Nor gnomes Nor radars . . . Nor am I idle, polishing
a scarab due to sail: my near and dear, our young ladies, mammy
scolded as usual We touch the other shore I olebulldoze through
the dead towns Sweetheart is in black tights My hair is as white as
snow Yoicks Why Where are you I crash into the mirrors Spatter
300 with dragon's-blood the female fauna All you want is another dash
of paint. Nothing doing nothing doing O my jaguars The hues of
nature change I tread soft on eggs on bowls Ah ah ah Childishness
is all Ah ah ah I seek a gracious louse the poisoned bullet of gold I
find a hole in an Indian's chest Yet another tragedy The lodges sub-
side on foxgloves of bronze I compose the grass But the *fact pri-*

mordial is I am more particularly at daggers drawn with American
Europe It will mean the end is near I enchased a last tank Whence
visored to sever the sore throat of self Shed its brine at last I clarion
Trepan Sharksilver Cyclone like a stuka In a last attempt I start life
310   from its lair: a roe, at times a lion. – Beyond all poetry written ci-
phered episodic architectural O the mushes of a brain O the crude
oils O the perils of the nightfalls of a brain I can no more A bundle
I am nothing but a bundle of nerves That's why I'm at the mercy
of a needle *You understand* A needle What's wanted is a rush from
east to west I was ahead of time The future is behind me It's no
longer I who speak It's my understudy I am led Game Fish Bird
Psyche Mirador Hold them in flight Don't ring up I abide a figure
Between heaven and earth No reality then without the organpoint
Its rush Watch out Between the enchaptered peoples see the trop-
320   ics striving the orgy of the aerolites like menstruous women in the
sky the hithering thithering thunderbolts the lavas' foaming froth
the cathedrals asimmer the steamed stars the shampoo till the
coiffing fingers are worn to the bone or perhaps a thinker's scalp:
customer writhing without a word among the contemporary alka-
lis Immeasurable indispensable geological metamorphosis Loud
cheers When I wake the races will have interbred.

Should I have fed the medecine-men red ants of my health? – In
the normal course of events I would have followed the usual pre-
scriptions. But there is no getting past the fact that I've ceased to
330   be a sunguard. The old order is changed: utterly. But not a word on
that subject, for the good reason that a really quite astounding or-
ganism has superseded the man I was. *Already the promised end:
for the here and now, with its armed words loosed in the corridor of
a so-called confidential revolution, minute by minute takes a different name. I bury the soft sluggish words, faithful to their page
– their concentration camp. A poet was only an alias.* I am cured.
Now, left over, I go back to where I belong . . . So no need of olif-
ants or stern alarums, we'll be among friends: transparent unions,
ruby soldiers of the northern lights, impuberal chorus girls, nurs-
340   es of Atlantis, masterringers of the Woods and Forests, overskilled
workers, peasants of light, philadelphians of the cardinal points,
founders of public stars and ALL CITIZENS ADULT OR NOT.

131

HENRI MICHAUX

To Right nor Left

According to my already long experience, the Universe is a great
big superficial complicated brute of a business, appearing always
or nearly always at the same stage of the day, and then so fast and
firm apparently that we call it 'reality'.

It appears in fact coherent, but not for long, and soon it collaps-
es into the deep indifferent gulf.

Thenceforward no great further effort is required for us to sleep
sound.

*

Many a weighty word is spoken that a littler may be still. But this
10   mighty one comes not unaided. And as it is of nothing worth,
unwarmed by pressure all about, piles and piles of them are
needed, that a life may rise and behind that life the person be
obscured.

In the shadow of walls of paper the wretched file past.

But fresh layers are always forthcoming, to consolidate the ex-
isting barrage, for it requires to be sustained.

Every morning (every evening also) the agent of mass performs
its obturation. All make haste, their small change at the ready, ea-
ger with firm hold to grasp at last truth's sticky organ. But there
20   is nothing there but paper, a barrage of paper, ever thicker, ever
stronger, that never a little word may slip past the bulwarks of
the weighty. In the turmoil fresh gangs appear, the tumult never
ceases, and life goes by, drummed out by the years.

*

Because the old are well aware that the young cannot bear the
sight of them, will not have them about them, will fly from them
to the furthest possible remove, they have taken the precaution,
among other precautions, to engender children, young of their
own, present and available, unable to escape, constrained to attend, to be petted (squirming), ordered about and finally (which

³⁰ is even more delicious) hamstrung by the blackmail of affection and sacrifice.

It would thus appear that the old have got hold of the right end of the stick. Alas, such is not the case. For it usually happens that the young they long to have about them are not their own young, their sons, their grandsons (nor even their daughters, not their type, unfortunately). No, these they would rather see festering and rotting in the manure. Those they covet are other, glimpsed in the street, the Underground, and they open then their breasts with the dagger of impossible adoption, deserted by the young yearned
⁴⁰ after with such yearning, while the hardening mask of age widens, deepens on their faces, a bark never to be stripped.

And the royal gift of a tender girl-face, bright-eyed, with skin so pure and finely woven that it is better not thought of, goes to another family that probably does not value it, but talks bitterly of failed examinations and damaged family pride.

So all the old in fact miss their mark, or almost all.

*

The volume of a week, still better of a month, and the less said about a year the sooner mended, is a thing so difficult to consider that some, driven by this fleeting spectacle to despair or nearly,
⁵⁰ are darkly enflamed to perform unheard of deeds, deeds deemed by them the most flagrant of the heroic category, in the hope of being able one day to recall some tatter of this galloping, unpinnable existence — to call one day their own, one only, doomed otherwise to join the others in the dust and refuse. One out of the thousands they think thus to retrieve. And though they are mistaken, for one and all with the possible exception of a few seconds slip finally from their mind, yet is their failure not entire. For other gentlemen, of the 'informed' variety, have not forgotten that it was a memorable day, an eventful day, have noted it down and bear it
⁶⁰ in mind. That is to say that they bear in mind the note they have made. For of the day itself they do not know the millionth part, nor feel of that millionth part the shadow of the odour of its truth. Whereas the living one who lived it at his risk and peril turns back towards it with groaning, back towards that day for all his efforts fading, and though he strain in a tiny space to keep it aloft, clear

of the other days. But with their dishevelment it soon is one and mingled, in utter and inextricable confusion.

He has lived.

*

Merde!

70   It would appear, says Solpiquet, that this word has no meaning, nor but seldom any relevance. It is that nevertheless which in fact annihilates the noble and ruins the possessor.

The rich fear the poor for their facile use of filthy language evocative of miserable (admitted) conditions of living, From this poor human bestiality they turn their thought aside with all their strength. And suddenly an unfortunate word forces it violently upon them and an instant brings to naught years of luxury.

Thus it is indispensable, if one is to remain rich and undisturbed by such stenching offal, to be surrounded by persons of polish, 80 no less apprehensive of being themselves defiled than attentive to this peculiarity in their friends.

Now when we consider, briefly as beseems us, in all its viscosity our bodily machine, and furthermore the fact that the very best opinion, the most indulgent tribunals, have never countenanced its free and ultimate operations otherwise than in the company of another, and even then within a soundproof compartment, we may easily understand the exceptional success, in a society of courtiers and in its subsequent imitations, of Monsieur Racine, unreadable incidentally for foreigners, of all men the most detached, in the al-90 lusiveness and polish of his language, from the mention of human nature's physiological misfortunes, and the best fitted to please all those who relish their nobility.

Since then many things have happened, apart from our advances in plumbing, that make it easier to keep certain immediacies at a distance. And it may be safely asserted that the great mingling of classes and societies, of the means of information and recreation now within the reach of almost all, have done more to devaluate nobility than slump and bankruptcy.

Nevertheless the word '*merde*' retains an unquestionable po-100 tency of demoralization and deflation.

With regard to the thing itself, no change has taken place. We all must do it, if we insist on remaining alive, and the Pope himself is no exception.

All he can do, all we can do, is this: Not speak of it.

*

Among the most disagreeable operations is that of reviewing one's past. It is for this reason that a man, when he is called a fool, is so painfully impressed. For this obliges him to turn back, to re-interpret an infinite series of events in which he had supposed himself to figure with intelligence, in order to discover that he had in fact done so with stupidity. This is an immense and disintegrating labour, a trudging as it were on repudiated feet towards far horizons.

Faced by these vistas of vertigo the fool, in his extreme wisdom, sensibly decides that he is not a fool.

Alone some sorry fools persist, in the teeth of common sense.

I cannot urge too strongly against this dismal attempt at elucidation.

*

The great difficulty for a generation of children desirous of opening fire on a generation of adults consists in finding a point of vantage. But there is worse to come. For the firing once begun, the children grow into adults, without exception.

It is thanks to this notable swindle, too late discovered, that millions have been enabled to advance in years, unscathed and almost without pain. When at last their eyes were opened, the time for suicide itself was past. Thus human life has persisted down the centuries.

Édouard Manet

That a tragic destiny, omitting pilfering Death, accomplice of all, glory of man, should brand, hard, hostile, one all liveliness and grace, troubles me — not the outcry against him who has, from this time forth, renewed the great pictural tradition according to his instinct, nor posthumous gratitude: but, in the depth of chagrin, the virile ingenuousness of a satyr in putty-coloured great-coat, beard and scant fair hair greying with an air. In short, mocker at Tortini's, elegant; in the studio, the fury that flung him at an empty canvas, as though he had never painted before – the preco-
10 cious gift of old disquiet here embodied in discovery and sudden acquittance: a lesson to the daily mindful witness, me, that every time, anew, one stakes oneself wholly, being none other than all others, indistinct, at will. Memory: he said, then, so well: 'The eye, a hand', that I muse again. This eye – Manet – this child eye of old urban stock, new, set on things, on persons, virgin and abstract, preserved, only yesterday, the immediate freshness of meeting, in the claws of glancing smile, in mockery then, before the pose, of the fatigues of a twentieth sitting. His hand – the pressure felt clear and prompt affirming in what mystery the limpid vision coursed
20 within it, to establish, vivid, pale, profound, keen, haunted with dark, the new and French masterpiece.

The Work of the Painter

To Picasso

I

Surround this yellow with shapeless white of egg
Wrap this white of egg in fine pliant blue
In vain the straight black line comes from you
Dawn is behind your picture

And walls innumerable fall
Behind your picture and you with staring eye
Like a blind man like a madman
Raise a high sword towards the void

One hand why not a second hand
And why not the feather-naked mouth
Why not a smile and why not tears
At the edge of the canvas where the little nails play

Here is the others' day give shadows their chance
And with a flicker of the lids renounce

II

You raised a high sword
Like a flag against the wind
You raised your gaze against the shadow and the wind
Of the dumbfounding gloom

You would not share
Nothing is to be expected of nothing
On you the stone will not fall
Nor the obliging praise

Hard scorner advance renouncing
Deep in your refusal pleasure springs
Art could be a grimace
You subdue it to a simple door

Open on life

    III
And the trite image of the grapes
On the cloth the trite
30   Image of the sword
Raised towards the void note of exclamation
Note of consternation and amaze
Who shall hold it against me

Who shall hold against you the immemorial
Pose of every man a prey to shadow
The others are shadow but the others bear
A burden as heavy as yours
You are a ray of the star of shadow
That determines light

40   We are not amused by those who speak of shadow
In the catacombs of death
Those who believe in disaster and beguile their death
With a thousand and one thornless vanities
We carry our sack of coal
To the fire that confounds us

    IV
The madmen brothers of nothing said
All begins with images
I join by images
All dawns to the high day

50   My mind is at ease
About our longings they are pleasant
Gentle and violent like scythes
In the tender reddening grass

To-day we want to eat
Together or else play and laugh
To-day I should like to go
To Soviet Russia or else rest

With my heart the bride's
With the power of well-doing
60 And hope strong as a sheaf
Of hands tied upon a kiss

V

Picasso my mad friend
My wise friend beyond bourns
There is nothing on our earth
That is not purer than your name

I like to say so I like to say
That all your gestures are signed
For it is thence that men
Bring the warrant of their stature

70 And their stature is different
And their stature is still the same
It rests on the cobble-stone
It rests on their desires

VI

It is a question of seaweed ever
Of tresses of pieces of ground
A question of true friends
With fevers of ripe fruit

Of old death and young flowers
In bundles that do not decay
80 Life gives its whole heart
And death gives its secret

A question of true friends
Kindred down the ages
Creation every day
In the careless good-day

    VII
Curtain there is no curtain
But some steps to climb
Some steps to build
Without toil without care
90   Work will become delight
We never doubted it we know well
That suffering is a surcharge and we want
New texts virgin canvases after love

Eyes like anvils
Vision like the horizon
Hands on the threshold of knowing
Like biscuits in wine

And the one end to be first everywhere
Shared day caress without degree
100   Dear comrade yours to be the first
Last in the world in a first world

RENÉ CHAR

Courbet: The Stone Breakers

Sand straw live softly softly take the wine
Gather the down-drifting dovecot feathers
Parch with the avid water-channel
Stay girls barefoot going
Pierce their chrysalids
Drink lightly carelessly the well suffered blood

We devour the grey fire's pest among the stones
While in the village they plot and plan
The best place still for men is the ruined roads
10   The tomatoes in the gardens are borne to us on the twilight air
And of our women's next spite forgetfulness
And the smart of thirst aching in our knees

Sons this night our labour of dust
Will be visible in the sky
Already the oil rises from the lead again.

Picasso Goes for a Walk

on a perfectly round real china plate
an apple poses
face to face
with a painter of reality
trying in vain to paint
the apple as it is
but it is
having none
the apple
10   has its own views
knows a trick or two
the apple
and before you can say knife is turning
on its real plate
slyly round and round
softly without stirring
and like a Duke of Guise disguised as a gas lamp
so as not to have his portrait taken against his wishes
the apple assumes the guise of a fair fruit in disguise
20   and it is then
that the painter of reality
begins to realize
that all the appearances of the apple are against him
and it is then
like the unfortunate pauper
like the necessitous wretch of a sudden at the mercy of no matter
    what merciful charitable organisation redoubtable with mercy
    charity and redoubtability
that the unfortunate painter of reality
of a sudden falls a helpless prey
to a thronging multitude of associations of ideas
30   and the apple as it turns evokes the apple-tree
the earthly paradise Adam and then Eve
the espalier the eye Cox the pie

Canada the Hesperides Normandy the Pippin and the Bloody
    Butcher
the serpent's tooth the innocent flower
and original sin
and the origins of art
and Switzerland with William Tell
and Isaac Newton himself
winner at the Universal Gravitation Exhibition of more than one
    gold medal
40   and the dazed painter loses sight of his model
and falls asleep
it is then that Picasso
happening to pass as he happens to pass
everywhere every day
invincibly at home
sees the apple the plate and the sleeping painter
what an idea to paint an apple
says Picasso
and Picasso eats the apple
50   and the apple says thanks
and Picasso breaks the plate
and smiling goes on his way
and the painter torn from his dreams
like a tooth
finds himself all alone before his unfinished canvas
and in the midst of his broken crockery
the terrifying pips of reality

ALFRED JARRY

from The Painting Machine

The River and the Meadow

The river has a big soft face, for the slaps of the oars, a neck with many folds, blue skin with green lanugo. In its arms, on its heart, it holds the little chrysalis-shaped isle. The green-robed meadow falls asleep, pillowed in the hollow of its neck and shoulder.

Love

In Love like gauze changing like the skies the soul is entangled, assumes the masked face of a chrysalis. It walks on upturned skulls. Behind the wall where it shelters talons brandish arms. Poison is its baptism. Ancient monsters, of which the wall is made, laugh in their green beards. The heart remains red and blue, violet in the artificial distance of the gauze it weaves, changing like the skies.

The Jester

His fine round hump hides the world, his red cheek likewise gnaws the tapestry lions. He has clubs and diamonds on his garments' crimson silk and towards the sun and green he casts the holy water of his sprinkler hung with bells.

A Mere Witch

Her hump well back, her belly out, her hair whistling in the rush of the broom that skewers her, she passes under the claws, heaven's vegetation red, the way's forefingers pointing towards the Devil.

Zone

In the end you are weary of this ancient world

This morning the bridges are bleating Eiffel Tower oh herd

Weary of living in Roman antiquity and Greek

Here even the motor-cars look antique
Religion alone has stayed young religion
Has stayed simple like the hangars at Port Aviation

You alone in Europe Christianity are not ancient
The most modern European is you Pope Pius X
And you whom the windows watch shame restrains
10   From entering a church this morning and confessing your sins
You read the handbills the catalogues the singing posters
So much for poetry this morning and the prose is in the papers
Special editions full of crimes
Celebrities and other attractions for 25 centimes

This morning I saw a pretty street whose name is gone
Clean and shining clarion of the sun
Where from Monday morning to Saturday evening four times a
    day
Directors workers and beautiful shorthand typists go their way
And thrice in the morning the siren makes its moan
20   And a bell bays savagely coming up to noon
The inscriptions on walls and signs
The notices and plates squawk parrot-wise
I love the grace of this industrial street
In Paris between the Avenue des Ternes and the Rue Aumont-
    Thiéville

There it is the young street and you still but a small child
Your mother always dresses you in blue and white
You are very pious and with René Dalize your oldest crony

Nothing delights you more than church ceremony
It is nine at night the lowered gas burns blue you steal away
30   From the dormitory and all night in the college chapel pray
Whilst everlastingly the flaming glory of Christ
Wheels in adorable depths of amethyst
It is the fair lily that we all revere
It is the torch burning in the wind its auburn hair
It is the rosepale son of the mother of grief
It is the tree with the world's prayers ever in leaf
It is of honour and eternity the double beam
It is the six-branched star it is God
Who Friday dies and Sunday rises from the dead
40   It is Christ who better than airmen wings his flight
Holding the record of the world for height

Pupil Christ of the eye
Twentieth pupil of the centuries it is no novice
And changed into a bird this century soars like Jesus
The devils in the deeps look up and say they see a
Nimitation of Simon Magus in Judea
Craft by name by nature craft they cry
About the pretty flyer the angels fly
Enoch Elijah Apollonius of Tyana hover
50   With Icarus round the first airworthy ever
For those whom the Eucharist transports they now and then
    make way
Host-elevating priests ascending endlessly
The aeroplane alights at last with outstretched pinions
Then the sky is filled with swallows in their millions
The rooks come flocking the owls the hawks
Flamingoes from Africa and ibises and storks
The roc bird famed in song and story soars
With Adam's skull the first head in its claws
The eagle stoops screaming from heaven's verge
60   From America comes the little humming-bird
From China the long and supple
One-winged peehees that fly in couples
Behold the dove spirit without alloy
That ocellate peacock and lyre-bird convoy

The phoenix flame-devoured flame-revived
All with its ardent ash an instant hides
Leaving the perilous straits the sirens three
Divinely singing join the company
And eagle phoenix peehees fraternize
70   One and all with the machine that flies

Now you walk in Paris alone among the crowd
Herds of bellowing buses hemming you about
Anguish of love parching you within
As though you were never to be loved again
If you lived in olden times you would get you to a cloister
You are ashamed when you catch yourself at a paternoster
You are your own mocker and like hellfire your laughter crackles
Golden on your life's hearth fall the sparks of your laughter
It is a picture in a dark museum hung
80   And you sometimes go and contemplate it long

To-day you walk in Paris the women are blood-red
It was and would I could forget it was at beauty's ebb

From the midst of fervent flames Our Lady beheld me at Chartres
The blood of your Sacred Heart flooded me in Montmartre
I am sick with hearing the words of bliss
The love I endure is like a syphilis
And the image that possesses you and never leaves your side
In anguish and insomnia keeps you alive

Now you are on the Riviera among
90   The lemon-trees that flower all year long
With your friends you go for a sail on the sea
One is from Nice one from Menton and two from La Turbie
The polypuses in the depths fill us with horror
And in the seaweed fishes swim emblems of the Saviour

You are in an inn-garden near Prague
You feel perfectly happy a rose is on the table
And you observe instead of writing your story in prose
The chafer asleep in the heart of the rose

Appalled you see your image in the agates of Saint Vitus
100 That day you were fit to die with sadness
You look like Lazarus frantic in the daylight
The hands of the clock in the Jewish quarter go to left from right
And you too live slowly backwards
Climbing up to the Hradchin or listening as night falls
To Czech songs being sung in taverns

Here you are in Marseilles among the water-melons

Here you are in Coblentz at the Giant's Hostelry

Here you are in Rome under a Japanese medlar-tree

Here you are in Amsterdam with an ill-favoured maiden
110 You find her beautiful she is engaged to a student in Leyden
There they let their rooms in Latin cubicula locanda
I remember I spent three days there and as many in Gouda

You are in Paris with the examining magistrate
They clap you in gaol like a common reprobate

Grievous and joyous voyages you made
Before you knew what falsehood was and age
At twenty you suffered from love and at thirty again
My life was folly and my days in vain
You dare not look at your hands tears haunt my eyes
120 For you for her I love and all the old miseries

Weeping you watch the wretched emigrants
They believe in God they pray the women suckle their infants
They fill with their smell the station of Saint-Lazare
Like the wise men from the east they have faith in their star
They hope to prosper in the Argentine
And to come home having made their fortune
A family transports a red eiderdown as you your heart
An eiderdown as unreal as our dreams
Some go no further doss in the stews
130 Of the Rue des Rosiers or the Rue des Ecouffes

Often in the streets I have seen them in the gloaming
Taking the air and like chessmen seldom moving
They are mostly Jews the wives wear wigs and in
The depths of shadowy dens bloodless sit on and on

You stand at the bar of a crapulous café
Drinking coffee at two sous a time in the midst of the unhappy

It is night you are in a restaurant it is superior

These women are decent enough they have their troubles
    however
All even the ugliest one have made their lovers suffer

140   She is a Jersey police-constable's daughter

Her hands I had not seen are chapped and hard

The seams of her belly go to my heart

To a poor harlot horribly laughing I humble my mouth

You are alone morning is at hand
In the streets the milkmen rattle their cans

Like a dark beauty night withdraws
Watchful Leah or Ferdine the false

And you drink this alcohol burning like your life
Your life that you drink like spirit of wine

150   You walk towards Auteuil you want to walk home and sleep
Among your fetishes from Guinea and the South Seas
Christs of another creed another guise
The lowly Christs of dim expectancies

Adieu Adieu

Sun corseless head

Message from Earth

Father Goethe who are above the heavens
among the Dominations and the Thrones
and sleep and watch with eyes astare
sluices of your downpouring light:
if you may leave the fond arm of the Father,
break the Law and the Archangel's ring,
and, though the finger of opprobrium points,
leave the choirs of your joy and come,
descending like a glacier in the warm season
10   or the wild albatross winging to its shore.

It seems that in your timelessness is spread
the immemorial net of all our ways
and that you are beset with names long gone
wrapping you round as in a mail of fire:
Earth, Demeter, Gea and Prakriti.
Of us you are mindful perhaps as of a fable
and, with the sorrow of the unremembered,
will mourn when you find again the tender child
who drank of the breast and relished the wild honey
20   and broke the shells and pored upon the ores.

You saw us, when the sun was languishing
and Orion with Andromeda dissolved,
crouch in the shadow of your cedar-tree,
like reindeer caught in traps or bisons
stricken with fear.
We are, as in your visionary jest,
The people with twisted mouth and cloven tongue,
the race inebriate with yes and no,
with oneness and divorce,
30   and muttering with the Falsifier still
darkly a broken smatter of your words.

We are still living in the cave

of green light shot with guile,
where the larva bloodless breeds
and polyps merge in Madrepore.
And bat-grease and owls' sullen down
shed still a night that fain would be eternal
and feed for ever on its black bitumen.

Try and discern your livid progeny
40 half mad Cordelia, half Eumenide:
you will find only sameness in this cave
never scoured by the biting brine.
And you will discover, Demiurge, as you go,
the casket underneath a block of stone,
whither in a peering midnight dead men come
to taste the mustard of the pit of hell.

Yet it will even be by this day's grace
that in the cambric of the skies the wind
is lulled, and hushed the wave.
50 What time you seek to permeate the earth,
stricken like a beast, with your river of life,
and slake the fevered's thirst
and signal to the chosen.
And in the air a stir of answer trembles,
a quiver of good news, a thistle-down,
and never a hint in what assails our flesh
of roughness or of hurt,
nought but a whispering of loving lips,
less than a hiss: scarce a breath.

Selections from *Anthology of Mexican Poetry*

FRANCISCO DE TERRAZAS

Sonnet

I dreamed that I was thrown from a crag
by one who held my will in servitude,
and all but fallen to the griping jaws
of a wild beast in wait for me below.

In terror, gropingly, I cast around
for wherewith to uphold me with my hands,
and the one closed about a trenchant sword,
and the other twined about a little herb.

Little and little the herb came swift away,
and the sword ever sorer vexed my hand
as I more fiercely clutched its cruel edges . . .

Oh wretched me, and how from self estranged,
that I rejoice to see me mangled thus
for dread of ending, dying, my distress!

10

I am not moved

I am not moved to love thee, Lord God,
by the heaven thou hast promised me;
I am not moved by the sore dreaded hell
to forbear me from offending thee.

I am moved by thee, Lord; I am moved
seeing thee nailed upon a cross and mocked;
I am moved seeing thy body all over wounds;
I am moved by thy contumely and death.

I am moved, last, by thy love, in such a wise
10   that though there were no heaven I still should love thee
and still should dread thee though there were no hell.

I need no gift of thee to make me love thee;
for though as now I hope I nothing hoped
as now I love thee I should love thee still.

Time demands

Time demands I give of me account;
the account demands, if I would give it, time:
for he, without account, who lost such time,
how shall he, without time, give such account?

Time cares not to take time into account,
for that the account was not made up in time;
for time would only take account of time
if in the account of time time found account.

What account shall ever reach unto such time?
What time reach ever unto such account?
What life without account but without time?

I live, I have no time, give no account,
knowing that I must give account of time
and that the time must come to give account.

from Song on Beholding an Enlightenment

[. . .]

Thus richly clad the Mead,
when sorrowful
– stricken with fears,
his heart immersed in care –
upon the belvedere a Monk appeared
who could no longer
suffer his own self,
as by increasing pangs he is assailed;
with brimming eyes
10   and fitful pulse
and halting breath
and with a profane tumult in his thoughts.
To hill and dale,
seeing them thus adorned, he bends his gaze,
so haply they might still
the inner turmoil of his discourses.
Suspended all his sense
in a profound amaze,
on what he sees he lives;
20   for there he nought discerns
save only hill and field
that gently lull his grief
– as tumult slackens
and the close rig of pain
when falls the wind
that lashed the heart to storm
– till by a tuneful Goldfinch,
augur of calm to come,
he is aroused
30   from this dead life.

[. . .]

Thus he spoke,
and already made resolve
– blind and in despair –
to renounce his holy state,
when he beheld,
soaring, beating the air,
a Hawk appear
– Pirate whose sustenance
is plunder, feathered bolt,
10   wandering meteor, vertiginous comet.
Well armed with talons,
his beak a furbished sword,
he speeds his course,
spreading his body's sails.
Plumy craft, he towers
even to the clouds, to feign himself a cloud,
and thence – eyeing
the Goldfinch singing,
happy and careless,
20   heedless of peril,
the Hawk, poising,
stoops boltlike from the clouds
with such muffled thunder
that it is heard by none
but by the Bird who, terrorstruck,
beheld himself between the talons mangled
so unawares
that he together ended
his life and song,
30   breathing his latest accent from the wound,
leaving by his baneful death the flowers
beset with fears
and weeping piteously
such innocence so injured and aggrieved.

To a Dead Actress

Here lies the purple sleeping and here lie
elegance and grace and loveliness,
and here that clarion of dulcitude
whose voice was lent to life's harmonious numbers.

Trumpet of love, no more thy clamant strain
with sonorous softness summons to the fray;
now in the tenebrous obscurity
with thine lies stricken many a tuneful soul.

Poesy thanks to thee was manifest
10 and with a fairer, surer life endued;
and – loving, cold, disdainful – thou didst feign

so well that even Death was unresolved
if thou didst simulate him as one dead
or didst submit to him as one alive.

Diuturnal infirmity

Diuturnal infirmity of hope,
thou that sustainest thus my fainting years,
and on the equal edge of weal and woe
holdest in equilibrium the scales

forever in suspense, forever loath
to tilt, thy wiles obeying that forbid
the coming ever to excess of measure
either of confidence or of despair.

Who rid thee of the name of homicide?
10   For thou art crueler still, if well we mark
that thou suspendest the deluded soul

between a wretched and a happy lot,
not to the end that life may be preserved,
but to inflict a more protracted death.

JUANA DE ASBAJE

from First Dream

But Venus first
with her fair gentle morning-star
shone through the dayspring,
and old Tithonus' beauteous spouse
– Amazon in radiance clad –
armed against the night,
fair though martial
and though plaintive brave,
showed her lovely brow
10   crowned with morning glimmers,
tender yet intrepid harbinger
of the fierce luminary
that came, mustering his van
of tiro gleams
and his rearward
of stouter veteran lights
against her, usurping tyrant
of day's empire, who,
girt with gloom's black bays
20   sways with dread nocturnal sceptre
the shades,
herself by them appalled.
But the fair forerunner,
herald of the bright sun,
scarce flew her banner in the orient sky,
calling all the sweet if warlike
clarions of the birds to arms,
their featly artless
sonorous bugles,
30   when the doomed tyrant, trembling,
distraught with dread misgiving,
striving the while
to launch her vaunted might, opposing
the shield of her funereal cloak
in vain to the unerring

shafts of light
with the rash unavailing
valiance of despair,
sensible of her faintness to withstand,
40   prone already to commit to flight,
more than to might, the means of her salvation,
wound her raucous horn,
summoning her black battalions
to orderly retreat.
Forthwith she was assailed
with nearer plenitude of rays
that streaked the highest pitch
of the world's lofty towers.
The sun in truth, its circuit closed, drew near,
50   limning with gold on sapphire blue a thousand
times a thousand points and gleaming scarves,
and from its luminous circumference
innumerable rays of pure light streamed,
scoring the sky's cerulean plain,
and serried fell on her who was but now
the baneful tyrant of their empire.
She, flying in headlong rout,
mid her own horrors stumbling
trampling on her shade,
60   strove, with her now blindly fleeing host
of shadows harried by the overtaking light,
to gain the western verge which loomed at last
before her impetuous course.
Then, by her very downfall vivified,
plunging in ever more precipitant ruin,
with renewed rebellion she resolves,
in that part of the globe
forsaken by the day,
to wear the crown,
70   what time upon our hemisphere the sun
the radiance of his fair golden tresses shed,
with equable diffusion of just light
apportioning to visible things their colours
and still restoring

to outward sense its full efficacy,
committing to surer light
the world illuminated and myself awake.

IGNACIO RODRÍGUEZ GALVÁN

from The Prophecy of Cuauhtémoc

Space is azure and the mountains bathe
in vivid azure and in azure shade.
The breath of blithesome youth is everywhere,
and the singing birds toss to and fro
upon the gentle breezes' restlessness.
All things incite to joy; and yet my soul
is muffled in a cloak of death; and drop
by drop my wounded heart bleeds slow away.
My mind is a black bottomless abyss,
10   and in it thought goes blindly wandering
like a lost dove in an unfathomed cave.

Was it reality or dream? . . . Vain question . . .
A dream assuredly, for a deep dream
is the voracious passion that consumes me;
it was a dream, no more, the joy that touched
my cheek with faint caress; a dream the accents
of that voice that lulled my grief to sleep;
a dream that smile, a dream that blandishment
and that soft gaze . . . I suddenly awoke;
20   and the fair Eden vanished from my sight
as the wave that rides in from the sea
and scatters; there is nothing left to me
except the cruel memory that wrings
my soul and without ceasing gnaws my heart.

        .   .   .   .   .

Make· haste, dreams, make haste! And deck my brow
with deadly nightshade: I desire to dream.
From their graves resuscitate the dead,
that I may see them, touch them, shuddering . . .

I have fed my life with what I felt,
30 with the horror I felt and with the sorrow.
Dream, in thy safe keeping let me come
to this world's end . . .

To the Wind

When I was a child I lay in dread,
listening to you moaning at my door,
and fancying I heard the sorrowful
and grievous dirge of some unearthly being.

When I was a youth your tumult spoke
phrases with meaning that my mind divined;
and, blowing through the camp, in after years
your harsh voice kept on crying 'Fatherland.'

Now, in the dark nights, I hear you beating
10   against my incoercible prison-bars;
but my misfortunes have already told me

that you are wind, no more, when you complain,
wind when raging, wind when murmuring,
wind when you come and wind when you depart.

Before a Corpse

Well! there you lie already . . . on the board
where the far horizon of our knowledge
dilates and darkens to a vaster verge.

Where implacable experience
unanswerably states the higher laws
to which existence is subservient.

Where that glorious luminary shines
whose light extinguishes the difference
that separates the master from the slave.

10   Where the voice of fable is heard no more
and reality speaks out aloud
and superstition vanishes away.

Where crisis presses on to where it may
decipher the solution of the problem
whose mere enouncement fills us with dismay,

that which arises from a premised reason
and hangs upon your lips to be unsealed
in the tremendous voice of final truth.

There you lie . . . beyond the ignoble strife
20   in which it was vouchsafed to you at last
to break the bonds that held you fast to pain.

There is no more light within your eyes,
lifeless and inert your tenement rests,
its end forsaken and its means destroyed.

Vanitas! they seeing you will say
whose creed is that the empire of life
ends at the point where that of death begins.

And deeming that your mission is fulfilled,
they will come to you and with their eyes
30 wish you for eternity farewell.

But it is false! . . . your mission is not fulfilled,
for out of nothingness we are not born,
and into nothingness we do not die.

Existence is a circle, and we err
when we assign to it for measurement
the limits of the cradle and the grave.

The mother is the mould, and nothing more,
that gives us form, the transitory form
with which we make our thankless way through life.

40 Yet neither was that form the first assumed
by our existence, neither will it be,
to-morrow, when it perishes, the last.

Yet a little and you, your last breath sped,
will be restored to earth and to its womb
which is the source of universal life.

And there your dust, in seeming so remote
from life, will quicken once again beneath
the fecundating might of rain and summer.

And with the springing up from root to grain,
50 a witness to the plant you will arise
to the high realm of sovereign alchemy;

or it may be, converted into corn,
returned to the sad hearth where the sad spouse,
wanting for bread, is with you in her dreams.

What time the larva from your cloven grave's
uncovered depths ascends, its being changed
into the being of a butterfly,

and faltering in its first uncertain flight,
comes to the desolate pillow of your love,
60   bearer of your kisses from the dead.

And in the midst of all this inner change
your skull, instinct with an impetuous life,
instead of thoughts will bring forth flowers, flowers

within whose chalice timidly the tear
perchance will glisten that your loved one shed
on your departure, bidding you farewell.

The journey's end is in the grave, for in
the grave the flame irrevocably dies
that in the cloister of our spirit burned.

70   And yet within that mansion at whose door
our breath is quenched, there breathes another breath
by which we are awaked to life anew.

There an end is made of strength and talent,
there an end is made of pain and pleasure,
there an end is made of faith and feeling,

there an end is made of earthly joys,
and the idiot and the sage together
sink to the abode where all are equal.

Yet in that same place where the soul is spent
80   and spent the body, in that selfsame place
the dying being is a nascent being.

The powerful and fecundating pit
annexes to itself the being that was
and from it draws and shapes the being to be.

To unforgiving history it abandons
a name, indifferent and unconcerned
whether it die or whether it endure.

It receives the clay and it alone,
and, altering its form and destiny,
90   ensures that it shall live eternally.

The grave holds nothing but a skeleton;
and life within this mortuary vault
continues secretly to find its substance.

For when this transient existence ends
to which with such solicitude we cling,
matter, immortal as glory, is endowed
with other semblances, but never dies.

Envoy

On your altars I have spent my incense,
shed my last remaining roses' petals.
Where the shrines of my goddesses arose
is nothing now but a vast waste of sand.

I sought to enter your soul, and what a fall,
what a wildering midst ruins and pits!
To such things I have given so much thought
that all my thought is pain and thought of pain.

Ended! . . . And what remains of such exceeding
10   rapture? In you neither moral grief
nor aftertaste of lust, nor taste of tears.

In me what deep and dreadful cataclysm!
What darkness in my conscience and what dread,
and what a nausea of self-disgust!

Golden

Beneath the evening gold,
above the golden corn,
the mill moves slow
its jagged sails.

Above the golden corn
hugely it shovels down
from sky to earth
the evening hoard.

LUIS G. URBINA

The Ancient Tear

As in the depths of an ancient cavern
lost in the recesses of the mountain,
silently, these centuries, a drop
of water falls;
so in my dark and solitary heart,
in the most hidden secret of my vitals,
I have heard, this long time past, a tear
slowly falling.
What dark cranny filters it to me?
10 From what mysterious springs does it distil?
To what fertile torrent is it faithless?
From what far source is it to me consigned?
Who knows? . . . When I was a child my tears
were the celestial dew that morning sheds;
when I was a youth they were a storm-cloud,
a tempest of passion and a rain of anguish.
Later, in a wintry eventide,
my tears were snowfall . . .
Now I weep no more . . . my life is arid
20 and my soul serene.
And yet . . . why do I feel the dropping thus,
tear after tear,
of some exhaustless spring of tenderness,
some indefatigable vein of grief?
Who knows! . . . It is not I, but those who were
my sad progenitors; it is my race;
the afflicted spirits,
the flagellated flesh;
age-long panting after the impossible,
30 mystic hopes,
sudden and unbridled melancholy,
ineffectual and savage anger.
In me at my begetting human suffering
left its marks,
its cries, its blasphemies, its supplications.

My heritage it is that weeps, my heritage,
in the depths of my soul.
The grief of my ancestors in my heart
collects, as in a chalice, tear by tear.
40 So I shall pass it on, when the day comes,
when from the seemly womb of the beloved,
kisses made incarnate, other beings,
transformations of my life, proceed.
I am at my desk. The afternoon
is kindly. My room is bright with sun.
Outside, in the garden, I hear the voices
of the children, their laughter and their singing.
And I think: unhappy creatures, perhaps
already, at this hour of merriment,
50 in your blithe hearts there seeps, unknown to you,
silent and tenacious, the ancient tear! . . .

An Old Burden

Who is yonder siren so distressed
of voice, so white of flesh, so dark of tress?
– A ray of moon bathing in the fountain,
a ray of moon . . .

Who roams the house, crying out my name?
Who calls me in the nights so tremulously?
– A flurry of wind moaning in the tower,
a flurry of wind.

Who art thou, say, archangel, thou whose wings
10   flame in the evening's divine fire, thou
who soarest through air's glory?
– The passing clouds:
see, mere clouds.

Who dipped in water, God, her necklaces?
Rain of diamonds on azure velvet.
– The image of the sky trembling in the stream,
the image of the sky.

Lord! beauty then is nought but mirage, nought.
Thou art sure: be thou my ultimate Lord.
20   Where find thee, in the air, on earth, in me?
– A glimmer of dream will guide thee in every abyss,
a glimmer of dream.

JOSÉ JUAN TABLADA

Haiku of the Flowerpot

I
The multicoloured mushroom seems
a Japanese toad's
parasol.

II
The dragon-fly strives patiently
to fasten its transparent cross
to the bare and trembling bough.

III
Ants on inert cricket crawling.
Memory
of Gulliver in Lilliput.

IV
Mingled, in the quiet evening,
chimes of angelus and bats
and swallows fly.

V
The little fly-tormented ass,
while he is being burdened, dreams
of emerald Elysian Fields . . .

VI
The tiny monkey looks at me . . .
He would like to tell me something
that escapes his mind!

VII
Beneath my window the moon on the roofs,
and the cats' silhouettes,
and their Chinese music.

VIII
Amidst the blue and white waves
the rolling swim of dolphins,
arabesques of wings and anchors.

IX
Smitten by the solar sun
the glass sea breaks to shivers.

X
The clock seems gnawing at the midnight feast,
echoed by the rat's
minute-hand.

XI
30   Red cold
guffaw of summer,
slice
of watermelon!

Romance of the Living Corpse

There are hours I imagine
that I am dead;
that I perceive only forms
wound in the shrouds of time;
that I am scarce a phantasm
seen by some in dreams;
that I am a sleepless bird
in its blindness blindly singing;
that I fled thither – I know not when –
10   whither 'she' and 'he' departed;
that I seek them, seek
them and see them not,
and that I am a shadow among shadows,
in endless night.

But of a sudden life
dawns on fire
and I hear a voice that calls me,
as before, crying loud;
and thronging desire
20   at the sight runs riot
and the senses ramp
like ravening lions . . .
And here, here dwells a soul
so close, so deep within,
that to tear it from my breast
were to tear forth my own . . .
And I am the same again,
dreaming I am awake
and astride on life
30   as on an unbridled colt . . .

You alone, you who came
like a secret gift to me,
you for whom the night sings
and the silence lightens;
you alone, you who came
from your glorious circle's centre
with loving flight
down to my hell;
you alone, while your hands
40   stray in my hair
and your eyes rest on mine
before the kiss,
you alone can tell me
if I am alive or dead.

RAMÓN LÓPEZ VELARDE

My Cousin Agueda

My godmother invited my cousin
Agueda to spend the day
with us, and my cousin
came with a conflicting
prestige of starch and fearful
ceremonious weeds.

Agueda appeared, sonorous
with starch, and her green eyes
and ruddy cheeks protected
10   me against the fearsome
weeds.

    I was a small boy,
knew O was the round one,
and Agueda knitting,
mild and persevering,
in the echoing gallery,
gave me unknown shivers.
(I think I even owe her the heroically
morbid habit of soliloquy.)

20   At dinner-time in the quiet
shadowy dining-room,
I was spellbound by the brittle
intermittent noise of dishes
and the caressing timbre
of my cousin's voice.

    Agueda was
(weeds, green pupils, ruddy cheeks)
a polychromatic basket of
apples and grapes
30   in the ebony of an ancient cupboard.

RAMÓN LÓPEZ VELARDE

Ants

To warm life passing singing with the grace
of a woman without wile or veil,
to unconquered beauty, enamouring, saving,
responds, amid the magic hour's elation,
a rancour of ants in my voracious veins.

The pit of silence and the swarm of sound,
the flour cloven like a double trophy
on fertile busts, the Hell of my belief,
the rattle of death and prelude to the nest,
10   chastise the ceaseless truant formication.

But soon my ants will deny me their embrace
and from my poor and diligent fingers fly
as a cold bagasse is forgotten on the sand;
and your mouth, cypher of erotic prowess,
your mouth that is my rubric, food, adornment,
your mouth that in its flaunting tongue vibrates
like a reprobate flame escaping from a kiln
into a throng of bitter howling gales
where the moon prowls intent to ravish you,
20   your mouth will smell of shroud and crushed grass
of opiate and respond, wick and wax.

Before my ants abandon me, Amada,
let them journey the journey of your mouth
to gorge viatica of the sanguinary fruit
provoking me from Saracen oases.

Before your lips die for my sorrow give
them to me on the graveyard's critical threshold,
their bread and perfume, venom and cautery.

To-and-Fro of Saint Theresa

She weaves away at the bower,
sword shuttling in the loom,
branchy, hitherandthithering
Saint Theresa's moon.

The eyes in sparkling flight
caught among the lashes
free and captive give
battle and sue for peace.

A wizened darky trembles
10   entangled in his guitar,
a runaway bridegroom in
a slip of a wench's arms.

Wench in an hour won,
free though consenting, and alien.
How all flows, how all
departs whence all abides!

From the flowers' cups
drops of essence shed:
all in the instant that ends
20   in another is begun.

Below the sea escapes
in the same light it hales
and escaping never
escapes from the hands of earth.

On his lively mare the rider
of the air passes and passes
not: he bides in the shadow,
rowelling jingling spurs.

It is life journeyed through
as to a far remove!
A coming and going, a being
in flight and ever near!

A being beside me, and she
dead these years!
A deluding of all as by
Zeno with his arrow!

Time twines into the voice;
languor takes the song.
With agile feet the angels
suffer to come on earth.

Flying quiet moon,
heron self-ensnared,
in scrolls of leaves she moves
and moves not, wheels and wheels not.

The Word Is Graven

The painter
Only barely
The lordly wandering playboy
With his fresh wondering eyes
Fresh wondering colour
Ironic
Eirenic
Heroic smile
Midst eggs, the young of goats, great flowers
10 Tender
Opens his eyes
His paintbox and his heart
To the creation
Which the other
Painter opening his eyes
His paintbox and his heart
Created
Heaping beauty smiling
On beauty smiling
20 Into being the world
I see him upside down
Set all things right side up
For a paradise of paradox and pardon

The creation of man is unique
Yet all the beasts are there, in the beginning on the waters. And
    man is herd when man is Joseph. Tamer of the wild when
    David. And all the beasts are there in Messianic times. The
    waters are there, the beginning waters with the beasts upon.
    Then the Red Sea, Jordan, Nile, with man upon.
Stone is there, even in the Tables of the Law. But also as witness in
    the Stone of Shechem. And as hindrance for Samson.
And the tree is over Joshua. And the tree is the Ark brought to
    Jerusalem.
The angels are there, with Abraham twice, with Jacob twice, with

Joshua twice, and two before Solomon, and with Samuel, and
in the dream of Solomon, and in the vision of Isaiah.
The palms are there, the women, Rebecca, the Well of Jacob, and
the prophetesses Mary and Deborah.
30   The struggles are there, the struggle of David.
And the encounters.
And the sacrifices, Noah's, Manoah's, and the Circumcision, and
the sacrifice of Abraham.
The blessings are there, of Jacob on Isaac, of Ephraim and of
Manasseh, of Moses on Joshua, and the anointing of Saul, and
the anointing of Solomon.
The drunkenness of Noah, the drunkenness of Lot, and Samson
and Dalilah, and David and Bathsheba, and the refusal of
Joseph.
The prisons are there, the prison of Jeremiah, and Jeremiah in
tears.
The deaths are there, of Sarah, and Moses, and Saul, and
Absalom, and the Mount of Olives.
The visions are there, the burning bush, and Elijah on Mount
Carmel, and Anna invoking the Eternal and King David, and
the Song of the Ark, and the Song of David, and man led by the
Eternal, and the dream and praying of Isaiah, and Jeremiah,
and the vision of Ezekiel, and the vision of Elijah and Elijah
caught up to heaven.
The deliverance of Jerusalem, and the fall of Jerusalem, and the
prophecy concerning Jerusalem.
The miracles are there, the serpent and the candlestick, Jericho,
the offering of Elijah, and the child raised by Elijah from the
dead.
40   Sweeps of light and dark, whirling banners of fume. Wailing. Not
wings, name them not wings, nor rocks, these forms as firm as
rock, as soaring as wing. Ah faint soul. Is not this the god I saw
in Russian fable?
Art thou not much amazed, God, before Thy creature?
But his, to think upon it, the eternity and beyond of time. How
faint a creature, here, is man.

None but only Rembrandt before Chagall, Rembrandt walking in
the streets of Amsterdam, to have so fiercely lived the book.

None but only Rembrandt and Blake
And sometimes Tintoretto
To have sung so the Book of Books.
And all grief in an eye-shielding hand.
Here is man and the angel.
More man than man is angel.
50 The hills are little heaps under the sky
Like eastern monasteries.
And fairy roads under the dim sky.
By Raphael this shepherd from
An undiscovered Arcadia.
Colourless spray of colour.
And after Abraham Jacob,
Job's harbinger.
And Joseph's fall.
And the wild gay setting forth.
60 The Creator like a thief

On absent mountains.
Does he speak?
He is the silent Logos
Wheeling of an inchoate sun.

On the deep now, eyes, throbbing in the warmth of the nest. The
anxious forehead sights the dove.

The beast is there
Lambent
And Apollo
Is it not Apollo
70 Far from manifold
Isra

The waters.
Bubbles on the sea
And the oriflamme of the wings.

Jordan.
Stones on the waters

Sacred on the sacred waters.

Nile.
The tiny creature, so tiny, alone
80   In its tininess glides
On the waters
By the reeds
Thinking.

The stones.
The tables are hewn rocks under a black cloud.
His horn has become a pillar of fire
Under the strong hand of the cloud of smoke.
Then above the crumbled stones
The man Samson stronger than stone.
90   Triumph of a man beast
Hardly thinking, faintly thinking.

The trees.
Down of the tree over Joshua
And of his beard
And the ark brought to Jerusalm, like a lyre.

The angels.
First Abraham unimposing
Little more
Than a little old man
100   Between the angels and the huge clustered flowers.
And gladly we would know
The names of these three angels
And how they sat at rest
Among their wings
And gladly these
With sweetest prayers smooth.

The angels have furled their wings.
The little old man is there
In sore affliction.

110 The angels are at rest, then descended.
   Are they ascending? Are they descending?
   Their wings are before them.

   The wrestling with the angel.
   The angel is more man
   Than the man more beast
   Than man
   But questioning.
   Like sails the angels are filled
   With the wind of the Spirit.

120 Great wings of butterflies
   Streams of shining mist
   Wing shields
   Over the uttermost woe.

   The women the palms, Rebecca the first idyll.
   Three realms, three signs.
   Between the palms and the king.
   Fair circles of Bathsheba.

   The prophetesses.
   Still torrent of Deborah's gown
130 Windblown table of stone.

   The encounters.
   Joseph, piety fallen, pity fallen.
   Moses and Aaron rejoicing almost
   almost amazed.
   Great stark figures whispering
   Before the Eternal
   Bodies ending in everlasting pillars.

   Jacob towards Egypt, oh thronging wilderness.
   Man is weary before the setting forth
140 All future past.

   The third is but the king.

They meet, work miracle.
Majesty of Moses ruining at his peak
Seeing the unseeable wonder
Uttering oracle.

The drunkenness. He is quiet.
Dionysus climbs the stage
In nakedness to officiate.
Not so Noah.

150   Unconsciousness of Noah begetting
Unconsciousness of Lot.

The sacrifices.
Man prostrate on the earth.
The beasts hemmed in as in a burning bush.
Candlestick flames of fire.

Now on his son flesh of his flesh
In the nest of his beard
And oh the great hands of the priest father
Streaming like a Rembrandt with ancientness.
160   And the woman fulfilled beyond her dreams.

The prisons. The beard of Jeremiah
In a wall and shrill
His lamentation
And his hair still
Thick and black.

The deaths. Of Sarah, nigh the first of dolours.
Colourless, radiant.
Then the five-branched star.
Darkness deepens on every hand, the light
170   Shines in the midst because on every hand
Darkness deepens

Second mighty death.
The feet are weary, the hand still speaks.

The Spirit of God is on the rocks.
Cataracts of shadowy light.
God himself is questioning.
Third mighty death.
His soul was music.

David brought low.
180   Absalom in glory dark already.
Thinking veils.

Drawn by the tree
Absalom almost angel.
The ass departs.

Forever is everlasting
Setting sun
Under the towers
David weeps for Absalom.
All suffering is in an eye-shielding hand.

190   The blessings. The hands, here the great hands
Are filled with blessing
The eye transpiercing
The man Jacob.

The flame licks the sun.
In the gloom the grove the posy breathes
And softly burns.

The voice is dark, I hear the voice.
The ringlets tremble.
Jehovah is all but absent in His light.
200   Rain of light.
Cathode anode the eyes.
Torrent of fire. The voice is strong. The voice is a high door.

Man is a heap
Of watchful worship.

David lofty still and exceeding strange
King whose eye is an arc
And the royal mantle
And the crowned forehead.

Higher even
210 Than the head
Singer of unending song.
Scarce loftier
The Eternal.
Both sure
Each strong by the other's strength
The man perhaps more assured
But how vast and shining are the wings of God.

Isaiah boulder of prayer
Ablaze with light
220 Torrent still with peace
The eyes see high and far,

Jeremiah sun in God's heart.
The man is dark, he is touched
By the light, and high
His stature,

The story of Jerusalem.
Anger abroad in the sky
Striding.
As a marvellous rabbi veils his eyes
230 With its great hands the Spirit passes.

Elijah, the chariot
That flamed aloft
With its flame horses.
And its wheels roll higher than the clouds.

Prophecy concerning Jerusalem.
By whom uttered? By Elijah.
Bitter sorrow and dark.

Elijah is nothing
But a mighty cry.
240   The pentacle
Blazes forth.

In Chagall that old vehemence again
That voice and throat and odour of man
And stateliness of prayer.
And slowly that strain of suffering
Upborne by the angels
By the beast trod down
In pain by pain illumined
Questioning in anguish and in thirst
250   Of anguish
Mustered by pain
Indifferent in the end
Through fortitude
Murmuring secrets
Self-amazed
More at itself than in itself overthrown
Crying out
Overbearing
Assuaged
260   Astonished radiance
Submissive beast
In sweet unction
Overbearing
Even for the sun
Home on high
Among the trumpets
Assuaged.

Chagall too unlocks the springs, quenches the fire, tames the
    rock, till the air thrills.
Over the earthly flings the triumphant splendours.
270   Restores old Israel to his vigour
And swathes him in veils of prayer.

Six Poems

In me, civil war.
My orange tree my knees displease;
my cascade rails against my bones;
mine between my heart to choose
and a stabbed island stertorous
in my valise, between my history book
and head crammed with throttled memories.
Mucous membrane Word!
Thing that wouldst be human!
10   In me, civil war.

                *

Fresh sighs for sale!
Prime doubts a penny!
Scowls going at a loss!
When I'm sold out I'll go
far from me and these among
be born again;
a mango warm from the bough,
a more than feline kiss,
a few objects without name.
10   Fresh hopes for sale!
Prime sooth a penny!
Smiles going at a loss!
Bargains, bargains, in and out of reason!

                *

Knife,
unaided were you knife,
then without purpose! and soon
to perish for no need of naming you.
Knife,
you were no knife

without my eyes to scour you,
my sweat to rust you over.
And I,
10   without your metal,
the moon it claws,
were but leaf,
foam that is weary,
a fin under a door,
a remnant of chewed medlar . . .
You through us know you as you,
I me as me through me before your face.
Knife of flesh, man of steel,
incarnate in each other each lives on.
20   Me you constrained to understand myself:
I bleed!
You to be understood yourself constrained,
and break!
Oh culpable encounter!
Knife, pure knife,
must be invented anew,
and man, sole man:
two to each other never to be known.

    *

He can only live in shivers
he gathers up and pieces together
in fond disarray.
This bit was the bent for happiness,
that a love might once have been,
this scrap of hide
the remains of childhood.
He fears identity that foal
borne in offering by the stream
10   to the fishes of prey.

    *

Why must the day
undo its eve,
autumn summer,
grown years the years agrowing?
Gardens under these
have rotted.
Suns like cast-off
raiment perish
beyond this noontide.
10 He has no more questions.
There is a music he loves.

     *

Now that he has drained
the cask of fancy dry
reality has him plagued
like a bubo-stricken rat.
No oak but turns
to coffin at his touch,
no waters scanned
but summon to their bed.
All he has left is the absolute
10 or the odd fly at evening
to tear from its wings.

Later Poems

Long after Chamfort

Wit in fools has something shocking
Like cabhorses galloping.

> Le sot qui a un moment d'esprit étonne et scandalise comme des
> chevaux de fiacre qui galopent.

The trouble with tragedy is the fuss it makes
About life and death and other tuppenny aches.

> Le théâtre tragique a le grand inconvénient moral de mettre trop
> d'importance à la vie et à la mort.

Better on your arse than on your feet,
Flat on your back than either, dead than the lot.

> Quand on soutient que les gens les moins sensibles sont, à tout
> prendre, les plus heureux, je me rappelle le proverbe indien: 'Il
> vaut mieux être assis que debout, couché qu'assis, mort que tout
> cela.'

Live and clean forget from day to day,
Mop life up as fast as it dribbles away.

> Quand on a été bien tourmenté, bien fatigué par sa propre sensi-
> bilité, on s'aperçoit qu'il faut vivre au jour le jour, oublier beau-
> coup, enfin éponger la vie à mesure qu'elle s'écoule.

Ask of all-healing, all-consoling thought
Salve and solace for the woe it wrought.

La pensée console de tout et remédie à tout. Si quelquefois elle
vous fait du mal, demandez-lui le remède du mal qu'elle vous a
fait, elle vous le donnera.

Hope is a knave befools us evermore,
Which till I lost no happiness was mine.
I strike from hell's to grave on heaven's door:
All hope abandon ye who enter in.

L'espérance n'est qu'un charlatan qui nous trompe sans cesse; et,
pour moi, le bonheur n'a commencé que lorsque je l'ai eu perdu.
Je mettrais volontiers sur la porte du paradis le vers que le Dante
a mis sur celle de l'enfer: *Lasciate ogni speranza etc.*

sleep till death
healeth
come ease
this life disease

Vivre est une maladie dont le sommeil nous soulage toutes les
seize heures. C'est un palliatif; la mort est le remède.

how hollow heart and full
of filth thou art

Que le cœur de l'homme est creux et plein d'ordure.

hors crâne seul dedans
quelque part quelquefois
comme quelque chose

crâne abri dernier
pris dans le dehors
tel Bocca dans la glace

l'œil à l'alarme infime
s'ouvre bée se rescelle
n'y ayant plus rien

10   ainsi quelquefois
comme quelque chose
de la vie pas forcément

something there

something there
where
out there
out where
outside
what
the head what else
something there somewhere outside
the head

10   at the faint sound so brief
it is gone and the whole globe
not yet bare
the eye
opens wide
wide
till in the end
nothing more
shutters it again

so the odd time
20   out there
somewhere out there
like as if
as if
something
not life
necessarily

dread nay

head fast
in out as dead
till rending
long still
faint stir
unseal the eye
till still again
seal again

head sphere
10   ashen smooth
one eye
no hint when to
then glare
cyclop no
one side
eerily

on face
of out spread
vast in
20   the highmost
snow white
sheeting all
asylum head
sole blot

faster than where
in hellice eyes
stream till
frozen to
jaws rail
30   gnaw gnash
teeth with stork
clack chatter

come through
no sense and gone
while eye
shocked wide
with white
still to bare
stir dread
40   nay to nought

sudden in
ashen smooth
aghast
glittering rent
till sudden
smooth again
stir so past
never been

at ray
50   in latibule
long dark
stir of dread
till breach
long sealed
dark again
still again

so ere
long still
long nought
60   rent so
so stir
long past
head fast
in out as dead

Roundelay

on all that strand
at end of day
steps sole sound
long sole sound
until unbidden stay
then no sound
on all that strand
long no sound
until unbidden go
steps sole sound
long sole sound
on all that strand
at end of day

10

thither

thither
a far cry
for one
so little
fair daffodils
march then

then there
then there

then thence
daffodils
again
march then
again
a far cry
again
for one
so little

The Downs

the downs
summer days on the downs
hand in hand
one loving
one loved
back at night
the hut

no thought
thoughtless on
under the sun
hand in hand
one loving
the other loved
thoughtless back
night

on till the cliff
the edge
hand in hand
gazing down
the foam
no further
the edge
the foam

no speech
speechless on
under the sun
hand in hand
till the edge
speechless back
the hut
night

the bridge
winter night
wind
snow
gazing down
the flood
foaming on
black flood foaming on

40   no thought
gazing down
meaningless flood
foaming on
winter night
wind
snow
no meaning

light
from the banks
50   lamplight
to light the foam
the snow
faintly lit
the foam
the snow

one dead of night
in the dead still
he looked up
from his book

from that dark
to pore on other dark

till afar
taper faint
the eyes

10   in the dead still

till afar
his book as by
a hand not his
a hand on his
faintly closed

for good or ill

for good and ill

mirlitonnades

en face
le pire
jusqu'à ce
qu'il fasse rire

    *

rentrer
à la nuit
au logis
allumer

éteindre voir
la nuit voir
collé à la vitre
le visage

    *

somme toute
tout compte fait
un quart de milliasse
de quarts d'heure
sans compter
les temps morts

    *

fin fond du néant
au bout de quelle guette
l' œil crut entrevoir
remuer faiblement
la tête le calma disant
ce ne fut que dans ta tête

    *

silence tel que ce qui fut
avant jamais ne sera plus
par le murmure déchiré
d'une parole sans passé
d'avoir trop dit n'en pouvant plus
jurant de ne se taire plus

      *

écoute-les
s'ajouter
les mots
aux mots
sans mot
les pas
aux pas
un à
un

      *

lueurs lisières
de la navette
plus qu'un pas s'éteignent
demi-tour remiroitent

halte plutôt
loin des deux
chez soi sans soi
ni eux

      *

imagine si ceci
un jour ceci
un beau jour
imagine
si un jour
un beau jour ceci
si ceci
cessait
imagine

    *

d'abord
à plat sur du dur
la droite
ou la gauche
n'importe

ensuite
à plat sur la droite
ou la gauche
la gauche
ou la droite

enfin
à plat sur la gauche
ou la droite
n'importe
sur le tout
la tête

    *

flux cause
que toute chose
tout en étant
toute chose
donc celle-là
même celle-là
tout en étant
n'est pas
parlons-en

*

samedi répit
plus rire
depuis minuit
jusqu'à minuit
pas pleurer

*

chaque jour envie
d'être un jour en vie
non certes sans regret
un jour d'être né

*

nuit qui fais tant
implorer l'aube
nuit de grâce
tombe

*

rien nul
n'aura été
pour rien
tant été
rien
nul

*

à peine à bien mené
le dernier pas le pied
repose en attendant
comme le veut l'usage
que l'autre en fasse autant
comme le veut l'usage
et porte ainsi le faix
encore de l'avant
comme le veut l'usage
enfin jusqu'à présent

*

ce qu'ont les yeux
mal vu de bien
les doigts laissé
de bien filer
serre-les bien
les doigts les yeux
le bien revient
en mieux

*

ce qu'a de pis
le cœur connu
la tête pu
de pis se dire
fais-les
ressusciter
le pis revient
en pire

*

ne manquez pas à Tanger
le cimetière Saint-André
morts sous un fouillis
de fleurs surensevelis
banc à la mémoire
d'Arthur Keyser
de cœur avec lui
restes dessus assis

*

plus loin un autre commémore
Caroline Hay Taylor
fidèle à sa philosophie
qu'espoir il y a tant qu'il y a vie
d'Irlande elle s'enfuit aux cieux
en août mil neuf cent trente-deux

*

ne manquez pas à Stuttgart
la longue Rue Neckar
du néant là l'attrait
n'est plus ce qu'il était
tant le soupçon est fort
d'y être déjà et d'ores

*

vieil aller
vieux arrêts

aller
absent
absent
arrêter

    *

fous qui disiez
plus jamais
vite
redites

    *

pas à pas
nulle part
nul seul
ne sait comment
petits pas
nulle part
obstinément

    *

rêve
sans fin
ni trêve
à rien

    *

morte parmi
ses mouches mortes
un souffle coulis
berce l'araignée

    *

d'où
la voix qui dit
vis

d'une autre vie

    *

mots survivants
de la vie
encore un moment
tenez-lui compagnie

    *

fleuves et océans
l'ont laissé pour vivant
au ru de Courtablon
près la Mare-Chaudron

    *

de pied ferme
tout en n'attendant plus
il se passe devant
allant sans but

    *

sitôt sorti de l'ermitage
ce fut le calme après l'orage

    *

à l'instant de s'entendre dire
ne plus en avoir pour longtemps
la vie à lui enfin sourire
se mit de toutes ses dents

    *

la nuit venue où l'âme allait
enfin lui être réclamée
voilà-t-il pas qu'incontinent
il la rendit une heure avant

*

pas davantage
de souvenirs qu'à l'âge
d'avril un jour
d'un jour

*

son ombre une nuit
lui reparut
s'allongea pâlit
se dissolut

*

noire sœur
qui es aux enfers
à tort tranchant
et à travers
qu'est-ce que tu attends

*

le nain nonagénaire
dans un dernier murmure
de grâce au moins la bière
grandeur nature

*

à bout de songes un bouquin
au gîte à dire adieu astreint
de chasse lasse fit exprès
d'oublier le chandelier

     *

c'est l'heure
durcir
le cœur
partir

     *

comme au
berceau
toute parole bue
comme au
berceau
folie à nouveau mue

     *

lui
à son âge
lui faire ça à lui
sacré canal
lacrymal

     *

par une faille dans l'inexistence
s'infiltrent des miasmes d'oxygène
dans le silence du pseudo-silence
de la pénombre par bonheur à peine

     *

minuit mille ans d'ici
d'ici cinq cent midi
donc que minuit
cette nuit
ici

*

silence vide nue
ne vous aura jamais
tant été

vide silence

*

qu'à lever la tête
c'est la beauté
qu'à la
lever

'mirlitonnades' in English

there
the life late led
down there
all done unsaid

    *

ceiling

lid eye bid
bye bye

    *

bail bail till better
founder

    *

away dream all
away

    *

head on hands
hold me
unclasp
hold me

    *

again gone
with what to tell
on again
retell

    *

let ill alone
let ill
alone

    *

nothing blest
oh sweet
blest all

    *

ashes burning more than all
the burning all
to ashes

    *

on whence
no sense
but on
to whence
but on
no sense
so on
no whence
no sense

    *

poetic miscalculation

content from
Y to Z
95.1%
to the dearest decimal dead
incalescent
incipient

    *

look in thine arse and write

    *

tittle-tattle
marl through rattle

    *

Là

aller là où jamais avant
à peine là que là toujours
où que là où jamais avant
à peine là que là toujours

go where never before
no sooner there than there always
no matter where never before
no sooner there than there always

    *

Brief Dream

Go end there
One fine day
Where never till then
Till as much as to say
No matter where
No matter when

Epitaphs

il ne sait plus ce qu'on lui disait
il ne sait plus ce qu'il se disait

on ne lui dit plus rien
il ne se dit plus rien

en se disant qu'il y a rien à dire
plus rien à dire

　　*

ochone ochone
dead and not gone

　　*

Le médecin nage
le malade coule

　　*

Ci-gît qui y échappa tant
Qu'il n'en échappe que maintenant

Hereunder lies the above who up below
So hourly died that he lived on till now.

Comment dire

folie –
folie que de –
que de –
comment dire –
folie que de ce –
depuis –
folie depuis ce –
donné –
folie donné ce que de –
10   vu –
folie vu ce –
ce –
comment dire –
ceci –
ce ceci –
ceci-ci –
tout ce ceci-ci –
folie donné tout ce –
vu –
20   folie vu tout ce ceci-ci que de –
que de –
comment dire –
voir –
entrevoir –
croire entrevoir –
vouloir croire entrevoir –
folie que de vouloir croire entrevoir quoi –
quoi –
comment dire –
30   et où –
que de vouloir croire entrevoir quoi où –
où –
comment dire –
là –
là-bas –

loin –
loin là là-bas –
à peine –
loin là là-bas à peine quoi –
40 quoi –
comment dire –
vu tout ceci –
tout ce ceci-ci –
folie que de voir quoi –
entrevoir –
croire entrevoir –
vouloir croire entrevoir –
loin là là-bas à peine quoi –
folie que d'y vouloir croire entrevoir quoi –
50 quoi –
comment dire –

comment dire

what is the word

folly –
folly for to –
for to –
what is the word –
folly from this –
all this –
folly from all this –
given –
folly given all this –
10   seeing –
folly seeing all this –
this –
what is the word –
this this –
this this here –
all this this here –
folly given all this –
seeing –
folly seeing all this this here –
20   for to –
what is the word –
see –
glimpse –
seem to glimpse –
need to seem to glimpse –
folly for to need to seem to glimpse –
what –
what is the word –
and where –
30   folly for to need to seem to glimpse what where –
where –
what is the word –
there –
over there –
away over there –

afar –
afar away over there –
afaint –
afaint afar away over there what –
40   what –
what is the word –
seeing all this –
all this this –
all this this here –
folly for to see what –
glimpse –
seem to glimpse –
need to seem to glimpse –
afaint afar away over there what –
50   folly for to need to seem to glimpse afaint afar away over there
      what –
what –
what is the word –

what is the word

Samuel Beckett: Collected Poems

APPENDIX

For Future Reference

My cherished chemist friend
lured me aloofly
down from the cornice
into the basement
drew bottles of acid and alkali out of his breast
to a colourscale accompaniment
    (mad dumbells spare me!)
fiddling deft and expert
with the double jointed nutcrackers of the hen's ovaries
10   But I stilled my cringing
and smote him
yes oh my strength!
smashed
mashed
    (peace my incisors!)
flayed and crushed him
with a ready are you steady
cuff-discharge.
But did I?

20   And then the bright waters
beneath the broad board
the trembling blade of the streamlined divers
and down to our waiting
to my enforced buoyancy
came floating the words of
the Mutilator
and the work of his fingerjoints:
observe gentlemen one of
the consequences of the displacement of
30   (click!)
the muncher.
The hair shall be grey
above the left temple
the hair shall be grey there

        abracadabra!
        Sweet wedge of birds faithless!
    God blast you yes it is we see
    God bless you professor
    we can't clap or we'd sink
40 three cheers for the perhaps pitiful professor
    next per shaving? next per sh . . . . ?
    Well of all the . . . . !
    that little bullet-headed bristle-cropped
    red-faced rat of a pure mathematician
    that I thought was experimenting with barbed wire in the Punjab
    up he comes surging to the landing steps
    and tells me I'm putting no guts in my kick.
    Like this he says like this.
    Well I just swam out nimbly
50 blushing and hopeless
    with the little swift strokes that I like and . . . . . .
    Whoops!
    over the stream and the tall green bank
    in a strong shallow arch
    and his face all twisted calm and patient
    and the board ledge doing its best to illustrate
    Bruno's identification of contraries
    into the water or on to the stones?
    No matter at all he can't come back
60 from far bay or stony ground
    yes here he is
    (he must have come under)
    for the second edition
        coming
    house innings set half or anything . . .

    if he can't come twice
    or forgets his lesson
    or breaks his leg
    he might forget me
70 they all might . . . . !
    so the snowy floor of the parrot's cell
    burning at dawn
    the palaiate of my strange mouth.

From the only Poet to a shining Whore

For Henry Crowder to Sing

Rahab of the holy battlements,
bright dripping shaft
in the bright bright patient
pearl-brow dawn-dusk lover of the sun.

Puttanina mia!
You hid them happy in the high flax,
pale before the fords
of Jordan, and the dry red waters,
and you lowered a pledge
10   of scarlet hemp.

Oh radiant, oh angry, oh Beatrice,
she foul with the victory
of the bloodless fingers
and proud, and you, Beatrice, mother, sister, daughter, belovèd,
fierce pale flame
of doubt, and God's sorrow,
and my sorrow.

Casket of Pralinen for a Daughter of a Dissipated Mandarin

Is he long enough in the leg?
Già but his faice . . . .
Oh me little timid Rosinette
isn't it Bartholo, synthetic grey cat, regal candle?
Keep Thyrsis for your morning ones.

Hold your head well over the letter darling
or they'll fall on the blotting.
Will you ever forget that soupe arrosée
on the first of the first,
10   spoonfeeding the weeping gladiator

renewing our baptismal vows
and dawn cracking all along the line.
Slobbery assumption of the innocents
two Irish in one God.

Radiant lemon-whiskered Christ
and you obliging porte-phallic-portfolio
and blood-faced Tom
disbelieving
in the Closerie cocktail that is my
20   and of course John the bright boy of the class
swallowing an apostolic spit
THE BULLIEST FEED IN 'ISTORY
if the boy scouts hadn't booked a trough
for the eleventh's eleventh eleven years after.

Now me boy
take a hitch in your lyrical loinstring.
What is this that is more
than the anguish of Beauty,
this gale of pain that was not prepared
30   in the caves of her eyes?

Is it enough
a stitch in the hem of the garment of God?

To-night her gaze would be less
than a lark's barred sunlight.

Oh I am ashamed
of all clumsy artistry
I am ashamed of presuming
to arrange words
of everything but the ingenuous fibres
40   that suffer honestly.
Fool! do you hope to untangle
the knot of God's pain?

Melancholy Christ that was a soft one!

Oh yes I think that was perhaps just a very little inclined to be
    rather too self-conscious.

Schluss!
Now ladies and gents
a chocolate-coated hiccough to our old friend.
Put on your hats and sit easy.

Oh beauty !
50   oh thou predatory evacuation,
from the bowels of my regret –
readily affected
by the assimilation of a purging gobbet
from my memory's involuntary vomit –
violently projected,
oh beauty!
oh innocent and spluttering beautiful!

What price the Balbec express?
Albion Albion mourn for him mourn
60   thy cockerup Willy the idiot boy
the portly scullion's codpiece.
Now who'll discover in Mantegna's
butchery stout foreshortened Saviour
recognitions of transcendent
horse-power?
Sheep he wrote the very much doubting
genial illegible landscape gardener.
Gloucester's no bimbo
and he's in Limbo
70   so all's well with the gorgonzola cheese of human kindness.

Though the swine were slaughtered
beneath the waves
not far from the firm sand
they're gone they're gone
my Brussels Braut!

Hell Crane to Starling

Oholiba charm of my eyes
there is a cave above Tsoar
and a Spanish donkey there.

You needn't bring wine to that non-relation.

And he won't know
who changed his name
when Jehovah sprained the seam of his haunch
in Peniel in Peniel
after he's sent on the thirty camels
10   suckling for dear death
and so many fillies
that I don't want log tablets.
Mister Jacobson mister Hippolitus-in-hell Jacobson
we all know
how you tried to rejoin your da.
Bilha always blabs.

Because Benoni skirted aftercrop
of my aching loins
you'll never see him
20   reddening the wall in two dimensions
and if you did
you might spare the postage to Chaldea.

But there's a bloody fine ass
lepping with stout and impurée de pommes
in the hill above Tsoar.

Text

Miserere oh colon
oh passionate ilium
and Frances the cook in the study mourning
an abstract belly

instead of the writhing asparagus-plumer
smashed on delivery
by the most indifferential calculus
that never came out
or ever disdressed
10   a redknuckled slut of a Paduan Virtue.

Show that plate here to your bedfruit
spent baby
and take a good swig
at our buxom calabash.
There's more than bandit Glaxo
underneath me maternity toga.
So she sags and here's the other.
That's the real export or I'm a Jungfrau.
Now wipe your moustache and hand us the vaseline.

20   Open Thou my lips
and
(if one dare make a suggestion)
Thine eye of skyflesh.
Am I a token of Godcraft?
The masterpiece of a scourged apprentice?
Where is my hippopot's cedar tail
and belly muscles?
Shall I cease to lament
being not as the flashsneezing
30   non-suppliant airtight alligator?

Not so but perhaps
at the sight and the sound of
a screechy flatfooted Tuscany peacock's
Strauss fandango and recitative
not forgetting
he stinks eternal.

Alas my scorned packthread!
No blade has smoothed the furrowed cheeks
that my tears corrode.

40 My varicose veins take my kneeling thoughts
from the piteous pelican.

Quick tip losers narcissistic inverts.
Twice I parted two crawlers
dribbling their not connubial strangles
in Arcadia of all places.
Believe me Miss Ops
swan flame or shower of gold
its one to ten at the time
(no offence to your noble deathjerks)
50 I know I was at it seven . . .
the bitch she's blinded me!
Manto me dear
an iced sherbet and me blood's a solid.

We are proud in our pain
our life was not blind.
Worms breed in their red tears
as they slouch by unnamed
scorned by the black ferry
despairing of death
60 who shall not scour in swift joy
the bright hill's girdle
nor tremble with the dark pride of torture
and the bitter dignity of an ingenious damnation.

Lo-Ruhama Lo-Ruhama
pity is quick with death.
Presumptuous passionate fool come now
to the sad maimed shades
and stand cold
on the cold moon.

Whoroscope

What's that?
An egg?
By the brothers Boot it stinks fresh.
Give it to Gillot.

Galileo how are you
and his consecutive thirds!
The vile old Copernican lead-swinging son of a sutler!
We're moving he said we're off – Porca Madonna!
the way a boatswain would be, or a sack-of-potatoey charging
Pretender.
10   That's not moving, that's *moving*.

What's that?
A little green fry or a mushroomy one?
Two lashed ovaries with prostisciutto?
How long did she womb it, the feathery one?
Three days and four nights?
Give it to Gillot.

Faulhaber, Beeckman and Peter the Red,
come now in the cloudy avalanche or Gassendi's sun-red crystally
cloud
and I'll pebble you all your hen-and-a-half ones
20   or I'll pebble a lens under the quilt in the midst of day.

To think he was my own brother, Peter the Bruiser,
and not a syllogism out of him
no more than if Pa were still in it.
Hey! pass over those coppers,
sweet millèd sweat of my burning liver!
Them were the days I sat in the hot-cupboard throwing Jesuits
out of the skylight.

Who's that? Hals?
Let him wait.

My squinty doaty!
30 I hid and you sook.
And Francine my precious fruit of a house-and-parlour foetus!
What an exfoliation!
Her little grey flayed epidermis and scarlet tonsils!
My one child
scourged by a fever to stagnant murky blood –
blood!
Oh Harvey belovèd
how shall the red and white, the many in the few,
(dear bloodswirling Harvey)
40 eddy through that cracked beater?
And the fourth Henry came to the crypt of the arrow.

What's that?
How long?
Sit on it.

A wind of evil flung my despair of ease
against the sharp spires of the one
lady:
not once or twice but . . . .
(Kip of Christ hatch it!)
50 in one sun's drowning
(Jesuitasters please copy).
So on with the silk hose over the knitted, and the morbid leather –
what am I saying! the gentle canvas –
and away to Ancona on the bright Adriatic,
and farewell for a space to the yellow key of the Rosicrucians.
They don't know what the master of them that do did,
that the nose is touched by the kiss of all foul and sweet air,
and the drums, and the throne of the fæcal inlet,
and the eyes by its zig-zags.
60 So we drink Him and eat Him
and the watery Beaune and the stale cubes of Hovis
because He can jig
as near or as far from His Jigging Self
and as sad or lively as the chalice or the tray asks.
How's that, Antonio?

In the name of Bacon will you chicken me up that egg.
Shall I swallow cave-phantoms?

Anna Maria!
She reads Moses and says her love is crucified.
70   Leider! Leider! she bloomed and withered,
a pale abusive parakeet in a mainstreet window.

No I believe every word of it I assure you.
Fallor, ergo sum!
The coy old frôleur!
He tolle'd and legge'd
and he buttoned on his redemptorist waistcoat.
No matter, let it pass.
I'm a bold boy I know
so I'm not my son
80   (even if I were a concierge)
nor Joachim my father's
but the chip of a perfect block that's neither old nor new,
the lonely petal of a great high bright rose.

Are you ripe at last,
my slim pale double-breasted turd?
How rich she smells,
this abortion of a fledgling!
I will eat it with a fish fork.
White and yolk and feathers.
100   Then I will rise and move moving
toward Rahab of the snows,
the murdering matinal pope-confessed amazon,
Christina the ripper.
Oh Weulles spare the blood of a Frank
who has climbed the bitter steps,
(René du Perron . . . . !)
and grant me my second
starless inscrutable hour.

Notes

René Descartes, Seigneur du Perron, liked his omelette made of eggs hatched from eight to ten days; shorter or longer under the hen and the result, he says, is disgusting.

He kept his own birthday to himself so that no astrologer could cast his nativity.

The shuttle of a ripening egg combs the warp of his days.

line 3 In 1640 the brothers Boot refuted Aristotle in Dublin.

4 Descartes passed on the easier problems in analytical geometry to his valet Gillot.

5–10 Refer to his contempt for Galileo Jr., (whom he confused with the more musical Galileo Sr.), and to his expedient sophistry concerning the movement of the earth.

17 He solved problems submitted by these mathematicians.

21–6 The attempt at swindling on the part of his elder brother Pierre de la Bretaillière – The money he received as a soldier.

27 Franz Hals.

29–30 As a child he played with a little cross-eyed girl.

31–5 His daughter died of scarlet fever at the age of six.

37–40 Honoured Harvey for his discovery of the circulation of the blood, but would not admit that he had explained the motion of the heart.

41 The heart of Henri iv was received at the Jesuit college of La Flèche while Descartes was still a student there.

45–53 His visions and pilgrimage to Loretto.

56–65 His Eucharistic sophistry, in reply to the Jansenist Antoine Arnauld, who challenged him to reconcile his doctrine of matter with the doctrine of transubstantiation.

68 Schurmann, the Dutch blue-stocking, a pious pupil of Voët, the adversary of Descartes.

73–6 Saint Augustine has a revelation in the shrubbery and reads Saint Paul.

77–83 He proves God by exhaustion.

91–3 Christina, queen of Sweden. At Stockholm, in November, she required Descartes, who had remained in bed till midday all his life, to be with her at five o'clock in the morning.

94 Weulles, a Peripatetic Dutch physician at the Swedish court, and an enemy of Descartes.

Return to the Vestry

Lover
off with your braces
Slouch in unbuttoned ease
fill a sack take a porter climb a mountain
as he did
the deaf conceited lecherous laypriest
the vindictive old sausage-sprinkler
    dirt in a dirt floor
    in a chapel barn
10   by a stifled stream.
    Zoroaster
    politely factorized
    and a hay-rake
    guarantee his siesta
    except during the harvest season when the latter is removed.
    I may be mistaken
    but –
    tears covering all risks –
    I took a time exposure
20   and wept into my hat
So
swell the cairn and spill the doings.
Burn sulphur!
Juniper flame to a swirl of ashes!
Drown the Singer
I'm done with stitch anguish.
Now a compress of wormwood and verbena
on my fiery buttocks
Smother the place in Cerebos it stinks of breeding.
30   Here's the mange of beauty in a corporation bucket!
Shovel it into the winds!

Loose the sparrows.
Pluck that pigeon she dribbles fertility.
Mumps and a orchid to Fräulein Miranda.
Gentle Anteros
dark and dispassionate
come a grave snake with peace to my quarry
and choke my regret
noble Anteros
40   and coil at the door of my quarry tomb
and span its rim with a luminous awning
shallow and dim
as a grey tilt of silk
filtering sadly
the weary triumph of morning.

Or mock a duller impurity.

Serena II (untitled MacGreevy version)

this seps of a world

see-saw she is blurred in sleep
she is fat she is half dead the rest is freewheeling
part the black shag the pelt
is ashen woad
snarl and howl in the wood wake all the birds
hound the whores out of the ferns
this damfool twilight threshing in the brake
bleating to be bloodied
10   this crapulent hush
tear its heart out

in her dreams she leaps again
way back in the good old dark old days
in the womb of her dam panting
in the claws of the Pins in the stress of her hour
the womb writhes bagful of ferrets
first come first served no queuing in the womb

the light fails it is time to lie down
Clew Bay vat of xanthic flowers
20   Croagh Patrick waned Hindu to spite the pilgrims
she is ready to lie down above all the islands of glory
straining now this Sabbath evening of garlands
with a yo-heave-ho of able-bodied swans
out from the doomed land their reefs of stresses
whales in Blacksod Bay dancing
as to the sound of a trumpet
in a hag she drops her young
the asphodels come running the flags after
cloppety-clop all night she drops them
30   till dawn the trollop fillips the clots of love
from her infamous finger
she wakes whining

she was deep in heat when Pavlov came
with a cauter and a metronome he came
toiling on bottom gear through the celtic mizzle
to where stiff with nits
blotch and pearly ticks she lay
her hot snout pointing south
vermifuge quotha from this time forth
40   and donnerwetter she'll wet on my tomb

she took me up on to a high watershed
whence like the rubrics of a childhood
lo Meath shining through a chink in the mountains
posses of larches there is no going back on
a rout of tracks and streams fleeing to the sea
kindergartens of steeples and then the harbour
like a woman making to cover her breasts
and left me

with whatever trust of panic we went out
50   with so much shall we return
there shall be no loss of panic between a man and his dog
bitch though he be

sodden packet of Players
it is only a dream
muzzling the cairn
the light randy slut can't be easy
this clonic world
all these phantoms shuddering out of focus
it is better to close the eyes
60   all the chords of the earth broken like a bad pianist's
the toads abroad again on their rounds
sidling up to their snares
the fairy-tale of Meath ended
say your prayers now and go to bed
your prayers before the lamps start to sing behind the larches
here at these knees of stone
then to bye-bye on the bones

Mancando

1

Konntest du nicht
jene blosse Gelegenheit zum Wortvergiessen,
jene goldene
einfach sein?

Lieber Missgeburt als keine?

Kaum bist du fort, so wird
die Zeit zu Blei.
Dann immer zu früh
beginnen sie zu baggern,
blindlings mit den Haken
am Boden ihrer Not umher,
und Knochen, alte Lieben,
schale Lieben, Schädel
von Augen wie den deinen
einst erleuchtet,
heraufzubringen.
So werden sie alle
immer beginnen
müssen.

Besser zu früh als niemals?

Die schwarze Not
spritzt ihnen ins Gesicht.
Sie wiederholen
die alten Worte:
> Es bargen die Geliebte
> neun Tage nie,
> noch neun Monate
> noch neun Leben.

Die Geliebte!

2

30 Die grauen Worte:
   Lehrst du mich nicht
   lerne ich nie.
 Die schalen Worte:
   Es gibt ja ein letztes
   auch von letzten Malen,
   eine letzter Bitten,
   eine letzte letzter Lieben.
   Es kommen doch zu Ende
   Wissen, Zweifel, Trug,
40   zum Schweigen auch die Worte:
    Liebst du mich nicht,
    werd' ich nie geliebt,
    lieb' ich dich nicht,
    lieb' ich nie.

3

 Es dreschen des Herzens Flegel die faulen Worte,
 die schalen Worte,
 die unablässige
 Spreu von Worten.
 Es steigt das alte Grauen
50 ich könnte nicht mehr lieben,
 eine andere als dich lieben,
 von einer andern als dir
 geliebt werden,
 nicht geliebt werden.
 Das alte Grauen
 vor Wissen, Zweifel, Trug.
 Trug.

4

 So begann ich, so werden sie alle
 immer beginnen
60 müssen,
 wenn sie dich lieben.

 Ausser wenn sie dich lieben.

*

Poupée Pompette et vieux bébé
C'est l'amour qui nous unit
Au terme d'une longue vie
Qui ne fut pas toujours gaie
C'est vrai
Pas toujours gaie.

Hairy Mac and Sucky Molly
In the ending days and nights
Of unending melancholy
10   Love it is at last unites.

*

C'est l'amour qui nous conduit
La main dans la main vers Glasnévin
C'est le meilleur du chemin
A mon avis au tien aussi
Mais oui
A notre avis.

To the lifelong promised land
Of the nearest cemetery
With his Sucky hand in hand
10   Love it is at last leads Hairy.

Samuel Beckett: Collected Poems

COMMENTARY

Abbreviations

SB   Samuel Beckett

LSB1   *The Letters of Samuel Beckett 1929–1940*, (eds.) Martha Dow
Fehsenfeld and Lois More Overbeck, Cambridge: Cambridge
University Press, 2009

LSB2   *The Letters of Samuel Beckett 1941–1956*, (eds.) George
Craig, Martha Dow Fehsenfeld, Dan Gunn and Lois More
Overbeck, Cambridge: Cambridge University Press, 2011

EDITIONS REFERRED TO

EBOP   *Echo's Bones and Other Precipitates*, Paris: Europa Press,
1935

Dream   *Dream of Fair to Middling Women*, Dublin: Black Cat
Press (edited by Eoin O'Brien and Edith Fournier), 1992

Disjecta   *Disjecta: miscellaneous writings and a dramatic
fragment*, London: John Calder, 1983 (edited by Ruby Cohn)

MPTK   *More Pricks Than Kicks*, London: Faber and Faber, 2010
(edited by Cassandra Nelson)

PTD   *Proust* and *Three Dialogues with Georges Duthuit*, London:
John Calder, 1965

MANUSCRIPTS

BIF/UoR   Beckett International Foundation, University of
Reading

HRHRC   Harry Ransom Humanities Research Center, University
of Texas at Austin

TCD   Trinity College Dublin

AJL   A. J. Leventhal papers, HRHRC

CI   Calvin Israel-Samuel Beckett collection, Burns Library,
Boston College

GB   Georges Belmont papers (private hands)

GR   George Reavey papers, HRHRC

MDZ   Morton Dauwen Zabel papers, *Poetry* (Chicago),
University of Chicago, Illinois

RA   Richard Aldington papers, Southern Illinois University,
     Carbondale, Illinois
SOS   Seumas O'Sullivan papers, TCD
TM   Thomas MacGreevy correspondence with Samuel Beckett,
     TCD

OTHER MANUSCRIPTS CONSULTED

Georges Duthuit's correspondence with Samuel Beckett, Les
     Héritiers Matisse (Issy-les-Moulineaux/Paris)
Winthrop Palmer Collection of French and Irish Rare Books
     (Long Island University)
*'Whoroscope' Notebook, 'College' Notebook, 'Sam Francis'
     Notebook, 'Sottisier' Notebook* (UoR)

OTHER ABBREVIATIONS

Atik   Anne Atik, *How It Was: A Memoir of Samuel Beckett*,
     London: Faber and Faber, 2001
CPOB   Objet Beckett (Centre Pompidou/IMEC catalogue for
     Samuel Beckett Centenary Exhibition, 14 March–25 June 2007)
CPEF   Collected Poems in English and French (see under
     PREVIOUS COLLECTIONS OF BECKETT'S POEMS below)
DM   *The Dublin Magazine*
DN*   *Beckett's 'Dream' Notebook*, edited and with an
     introduction by John Pilling, Reading: Beckett International
     Foundation, 1999 [cited by asterisked item number, not page
     number]
F&F*   Raymond Federman and John Fletcher (eds.), *Samuel
     Beckett: his works and his critics*, Berkeley and Los Angeles, CA:
     University of California Press, 1970 [cited by asterisked item
     number and page number]
Harvey   Lawrence Harvey, *Samuel Beckett: Poet and Critic*,
     Princeton, NJ: Princeton University Press, 1970
Knowlson   James Knowlson, *Damned to Fame: the Life of
     Samuel Beckett*, London: Bloomsbury, 1996
Lake*   Carlton Lake (ed.), *No Symbols Where None Intended:
     Samuel Beckett at the Humanities Research Center*, Austin, TX:
     University of Texas at Austin, 1984 [cited by asterisked item
     number and page number]

Inf.   Dante's *Inferno*
Purg.   Dante's *Purgatorio*
Par.   Dante's *Paradiso*
  [All quotations from *The Divine Comedy* of Dante Alighieri
  (Italian text with translation and commentary by John D.
  Sinclair), London, Oxford, New York: Oxford University Press,
  1971]

All abbreviations not accounted for here are explained in the relevant entries. For all other source references see the Bibliography.

PREVIOUS COLLECTIONS OF BECKETT'S POEMS

Echo's Bones and Other Precipitates, Paris: Europa Press, 1935
Gedichte, Wiesbaden: Limes Verlag, 1959; 1976
Poems in English, London: John Calder, 1961; New York, Grove
  Press, 1963
Poems in English, New York: Grove Press, 1971 (Collected Works)
Poèmes, Paris: Editions de Minuit, 1968
Collected Poems in English and French, London: John Calder,
  1977; New York: Grove Atlantic, 1977
Collected Poems 1930–1978, London: John Calder, 1984
Poèmes suivi de mirlitonnades, Paris: Editions de Minuit, 1978,
  augmented impressions 1979, 1984 and 1992
Selected Poems, London: John Calder, 1999 ('Beckett Short no. 12')
Poems 1930–1989, London: John Calder, 2002
Poems, Short Fiction, Criticism (volume IV of *The Grove Samuel
  Beckett Centenary Edition*), New York: Grove Press, 2006
Selected Poems 1930–1989, London: Faber and Faber, 2009 (ed.
  David Wheatley)

OTHER WORKS OF BECKETT'S CONSULTED

Anthology of Mexican Poetry, London: Calder and Boyars, 1970
As The Story Was Told: uncollected and late prose [includes 'The
  Capital of the Ruins'], London: John Calder, 1990
*Beckett in Black and Red: The Translations for Nancy Cunard's
  Negro* (1934), ed. Alan Warren Friedman. Lexington: University
  Press of Kentucky, 2000
Company, etc. [includes *Ill Seen Ill Said, Worstward Ho, Stirrings*

Still], London: Faber and Faber, 2009 (ed. Dirk Van Hulle)

Comment c'est, Paris: Les Editions de Minuit, 2005

The Complete Dramatic Works, London: Faber and Faber, 1990

The Complete Short Prose 1929–1989, New York: Grove Press, 1995 (ed. S. E. Gontarski)

Drunken Boat, Reading: Whiteknights Press, 1976 (ed. James Knowlson and Felix Leakey)

Eleutheria, translated by Barbara Wright, London: Faber and Faber, 1996

The Expelled / The Calmative / The End with *First Love*, London: Faber and Faber, 2009 (ed. Christopher Ricks)

How It Is, London: Faber and Faber, 2009 (ed. Edouard Magessa O'Reilly)

Malone Dies, London: Faber and Faber, 2010 (ed. Peter Boxall)

Malone meurt, Paris: Les Editions de Minuit, 2001

Mercier and Camier, London: Faber and Faber, 2010 (ed. Seán Kennedy)

Molloy, London: Faber and Faber, 2009 (ed. Shane Weller)

Murphy, London: Faber and Faber, 2009 (ed. J. C. C. Mays)

Nouvelles et Textes pour rien, Paris: Les Editions de Minuit, 1991

Premier amour, Paris: Les Editions de Minuit, 1970

Texts for Nothing and other shorter prose, 1950–1976 [includes *Imagination Dead Imagine, The Lost Ones*], London: Faber and Faber, 2010 (ed. Mark Nixon)

The Unnamable, London: Faber and Faber, 2010 (ed. Steven Connor)

Watt, London: Faber and Faber, 2009 (ed. C. J. Ackerley)

Watt, Paris: Les Editions de Minuit, 2005

PART 1   Pre-War

ECHO'S BONES AND OTHER PRECIPITATES

EBOP was published (unpaginated) by George Reavey's Europa Press, Paris, in December 1935, the third of six titles launching his 'Europa Poets' series, and the only one not to feature art work. It was advertised as for sale at 3s 6d in its 'ordinary edition', with signed copies at 6s. Some nine months earlier SB had sent Reavey this revised title for the collection, which he had previously thought of as *Poems* ([15.3.35]; *LSB1*, 264), claiming it was 'more modeste' ('plus modeste'). *Echo's Bones* names the last of the thirteen poems in the collection, while *Precipitates* refers indirectly to 'The Vulture' by way of J. G. Robertson's *A History of German Literature* (revised 1931 edition, 352), which notes that Goethe's 1777 visit to the Harz Mountains 'left its poetic precipitate in the poem "Harzreise im Winter"'.

The reduction of 27 *POEMS* to 13 for *EBOP* must have been carried out with an eye to quality (see the headnote to the section 'Uncollected Early Poems from the Leventhal Papers' for further discussion of this), but was presumably primarily intended to give a 'through-composed' aspect to a collection of poems written intermittently over about four years. The numbered poems (with generic implications in the case of the *Enueg*s and the *Serena*s) suggest a coherence in the planning which in fact only emerged gradually, and in some cases apparently quite late on in the proceedings. The first and last poems, of six lines and five lines respectively, act as a kind of frame for the whole. 'Alba' and 'Dortmunder', although they differ in content, make a 'natural' pair. The 'Beatrice in the brothel' aspect of the latter is echoed in 'Sanies II'. Ethna MacCarthy, although she is not named, is the figure whom SB has most in mind in 'Alba', 'Serena I' and 'Serena III'. 'Malacoda' and 'Da Tagte Es' were both written relatively late (in the case of the former a final version was only achieved a few weeks before publication), and in both the missing figure of SB's father seems to lie behind the poetic impulse. The first word of 'Enueg I' ('Exeo . . .') establishes the feeling of an unfinished, perhaps unfinishable, journey that marks many of the poems. The collection as a whole, perhaps surprisingly in the circumstances, is 'very strong on architectonics' (*Dream*, 178), and – like the *Temps modernes* poems (q.v.) – these poems fit well alongside one another, in spite of the inevitable differences between them.

Sales of the 327 copies of *EBOP* were so poor that SB could tell A. J. Leventhal that he still had 'a fat pile' of them in his possession more than twenty years later (letter of 24.4.56; HRHRC; not in *LSB2*), although he said he had none left of the equally limited edition of the Hours Press 'Whoroscope': 'Pity I've given all mine away.' A couple of weeks earlier, however, in a letter to Nancy Cunard of 5.4.56 (*LSB2*, 611) SB speaks of 'even a few Whoroscopes' being still on his shelves. For a plan as to who should receive copies, especially review copies, of *EBOP* see Carlton Lake (*43[c], 30–1), with fewer than 28 copies envisaged as *hors commerce*. SB told TM: 'It will be a relief to have [the poems] out and abused' (*LSB1*, 283), but he was disappointed by such few reactions to them as he received, whether in public or in private (cf. *LSB1*, 295, and a letter to TM of 30.12.35, not in *LSB1*). Hence, no doubt, SB's emphasis on 'No professional reactions to the poems in any quarter that I know of', and the further comment: 'I am only interested in those I like having copies' (letter of 9.1.35 [i.e. 1936]; not in *LSB1*). According to SB, the *Dublin Magazine* (April–June 1936, 77–8) could only work up '5 lines of faint damn' (2.5.[36]; *LSB1*, 331–2). The anonymous reviewer had in fact confessed himself '[be]wildered but impressed' (cf. the response to 'Saint-Lô' [q.v.]), and even went on to quote 'The Vulture' in full, noting that 'The last line has a gigantic wing'. He also singled out 'Enueg I' and 'Enueg II' for praise, noting that 'the flight from emotion in "Enueg I" is a very real thing. Mr Beckett finds himself, I think, in those poems. And perhaps in "Alba". Others, because of his idiom – I am not sure of. There is a confusion of accidental phenomena that leaves me adrift. Adrift; but, in spite of myself, impressed.' The *Irish Times* did not review *EBOP*, but did notice the three poems from the collection, 'Malacoda', 'Enueg II' and 'Dortmunder' as reprinted in *transition* 24 (June 1936, 8–10); 'CM' wrote: 'They are "difficult", but not more so than the poems of many modern authors, and in no way to be com-

pared with the extravagances of some of the other contributors'
(25.7.36, 7). Noel Riley Fitch reprinted these three poems, following the same eccentric order, in *in transition: A Paris Anthology*,
London: Secker and Warburg (43–5). 'Malacoda' was (with 'Alba'
and 'Dortmunder') one of only three of the *EBOP* poems omitted
from the first issue of *Evergreen Review* (1957), which was effectively the first printing of the collection in the USA, in due course
to be superseded by the whole collection appearing in the Grove
Press *Poems in English* (1963), four years later than *Gedichte* (1959;
which presents the 'Enueg's, the two 'Sanies' and the three 'Serena's as numbered poems, together under the three generic titles)
and two years after the Calder *Poems in English* (1961).

The manner in which SB's first collection of poems was received, or how he expected them to be received, is in part reflected
in the dedication on the copy of *EBOP* which he signed for George
Reavey: '"mets ce que tu veux dans le vide . . ."' (Lake *41; 28–9),
a quotation from a poem beginning 'Que m'importe . . .', from
Reavey's collection *Signes d'Adieu*, Paris: Europa Press, 1935, 19.

The Vulture

'The Vulture' was the last of the *EBOP* poems to be written. SB
annotated the poem in his copy of *EBOP* at the HRHRC 'not without reference to Goethe's Dem Geier gleich . . .' (the opening line
of Goethe's 'Harzreise im Winter'). Goethe's poem clearly meant
a lot to SB, who writes of its 'Five lines, for ever in my head' in a
letter to Maria Jolas of 16.4.58 (HRHRC). These opening five lines
translate as 'Like a hawk poised, with scarce-quivering wings, on
lowering morning clouds, watching for prey, let my song hover'
(Penguin, 1964, 54). Goethe's invocation of the spirit of inspiration
as a hawk hovering on its prey is transformed by SB into what
P. J. Murphy has termed the '"Vulture" aesthetic' (*Reconstructing
Beckett: Language for Being in Samuel Beckett's Fiction*, Toronto:
University of Toronto Press, 1999, especially 15–18).

There are no known variants of 'The Vulture'.

SB was reading Ben Jonson's *Volpone* (in which there is a character named Voltore) early in 1935 (*LSB1*, 243). 'The Vulture' was

reprinted in the *Dublin Magazine* (April–June 1936, 77–8) as part of a review of *EBOP* (see above).

'The Vulture' was the first poem in the running order for the BBC broadcast of 'More Poems by Samuel Beckett' on 24.11.66, followed by 'Echo's Bones', 'Da Tagte Es', 'Serena I', 'Serena III', 'Sanies I', 'who may tell the tale' and 'Watt will not' [from *Watt*]; '[Spend] the years of learning' [i.e. 'Gnome']; and 'Age is when to a man' [from *Words and Music*] (cf. letters and memoranda at the BBC Written Archives, Caversham [15.2.66, 25.2.66, 25.5.66, 22.11.66], and F&F *506, 104). It was the eighth of the ten *EBOP* poems selected for the first issue of the *Evergreen Review* in 1957, placed between 'Serena III' and 'Da Tagte Es'. 'The Vulture' was not included in the broadcast of 14.4.76 which formed part of the BBC's 70th birthday tribute, compiled from the two previous programmes of readings of SB's poems by Jack MacGowran (8.3.66 and 24.11.66).

Notes

2   in a letter to the editor of *The Listener* of 5.5.57, SB discussed the use of the 'skull image' which 'he said recurs frequently in his work, namely *Malone*, the first poem in *Echo's Bones* and *Murphy* ("There is a chapter . . . on the topography of his skull: Amor intellectualis quo Murphy se ipsum amat")' (quoted in Sotheby's catalogue for literature sale, 8.7.2004, 71).
3   'stooping': the term used in falconry to describe a bird diving or swooping on its prey. Cf. 'stoop' in lines **7** and **9** of 'Alba'.
4   cf. Matthew 9:5–6. Malone writes: 'what it ['this ballsaching poppycock about life and death'] is all about exactly I could no more say, at the present moment, th[a]n take up my bed and walk' (*Malone Dies*, 52).
6   cf. 'the offal of experience' (*PTD*, 78), and 'Eye ravening patient in the haggard vulture face, perhaps it's carrion time' ('Text I', *Texts for Nothing*, 5).

Enueg I

The poem is an account of a long walk starting at the Portobello

Bridge on Dublin's Grand Canal and continuing along its banks as far as the area known as the Fox and Geese, where the poet turns away from the canal into the village of Chapelizod on the river Liffey. Its title comes from a medieval Provençal genre, the 'enueg' or 'complaint', which SB recorded in *DN* *505 from Jean Beck's *La Musique des troubadours*. There are prose reworkings of many phrases from the poem in *Dream*, 28, 55, 157. SB sent the poem to Seumas O'Sullivan, asking him 'Darf ich?' ['May I?'; cf. *Dream*, 96] (*LSB1*, 96), but the *Dublin Magazine* rejected it. Enclosing it in a letter to TM of 20.12.31 SB wrote: 'Herewith a pome [*sic*] that S O'S wouldn't have on account of the <u>red sputum</u>! I haven't tried to place it elsewhere, & thought I'd send it to you à tout hasard' (*LSB1*, 100). A letter to TM of 7.9.33 (not in *LSB1*) shows SB thinking of it as 'the canal Enueg', primarily to distinguish it from the 'little policeman Enueg', although the generic confusions in SB's mind prior to finally deciding on the contents for *EBOP* (cf. the notes to 'Alba' below) leaves the intended reference in the second instance uncertain.

Variants

Five are known, as sent to Seumas O'Sullivan (SOS; *LSB1*, 96–8), Thomas MacGreevy (TM), A. J. Leventhal (AJL), Richard Aldington (RA) and Morton Dauwen Zabel (MDZ; *LSB1*, 232–4); SOS, TM and MDZ bear the title 'Enueg'.

All variant versions earlier than *EBOP* offer evidence of SB 'fiddling' (letter of 27.8.[32] to TM; not in *LSB1*) over details rather than making any substantial and/or structural alterations. For all practical purposes SOS and TM are almost identical; AJL, RA and MDZ closely resemble the *EBOP* version in all but a few very minor details.

Line numbers here refer to the *EBOP* lineation.

All variant versions: **12** 'head'. **25** 'lamentable parody of champaign land'. **35** 'suddenly went up in a blaze'. **36** 'a bank to see' [MDZ: 'a bank to look at']. **44** 'Then on' [MDZ 'So on']. **50** 'pitiful'. **51** 'perished'. **53** 'no visible means'. **65** 'endimanchés'. **68** 'drowned'. **72** 'Ah!'. **74** 'flowers!'. **75** '(they do not exist) . . .' [no suspension points in MDZ, which is probably the closest in time to *EBOP*].

Minor variants common to SOS and TM: **14** 'cangue'.

43 'ground' ['field' in AJL, RA and MDZ]. **47** 'in my dream of
Sumatra' with commas around the phrase. **66** 'hurrying' ['hastening' in AJL, RA and MDZ]; 'or moly' not present [also absent
from AJL, but present in both RA and MDZ, so presumably a late
addition].

Notes

1 'in a spasm': cf. *Dream*, 64. SB had found the phrase in a poem
('Crón Tráth Na nDéithe' [Twilight of the Gods]) by his friend
Thomas MacGreevy, and praised him for it in a letter of late Au-
gust/early September 1931 (*LSB1*, 84).

2–3 SB is almost certainly thinking of his cousin Peggy Sinclair
with whom he was romantically involved at the time and who
later died of tuberculosis (3 May 1933 in Bad Wildungen Hospital
in Germany). There is, however, no record of Peggy's being admitted to the Portobello Private Nursing Home.

4 'secret things': Virgil leads Dante into Hell to the 'segrete cose'
(*Inf.*, III, 21). 'Secret things' refers to the objects of Belacqua's
voyeurism in 'Walking Out' (*MPTK*, 102). In a letter to Pamela
Mitchell SB uses the phrase in relation to his brother Frank's last
illness: '. . . and so soon it will have been another day and all the
secret things inside a little worse than they were and nothing
much been noticed' (18.6.54; not in *LSB2*). The phrase recurs in a
letter to Aidan Higgins of 22.4.58 (HRHRC).

5 the Portobello footbridge (for a photograph, see O'Brien,
201) across the Grand Canal, its two steep sides well described in
Harvey (127, fn 78).

6 cf. *Dream*, 55.

10 'algum trees', cf. 2 *Chronicles* 2:8 and *DN* *1007; however,
'Devlin didn't know what an algum tree was and I couldn't en-
lighten him' (SB to TM, 9.10.33, *LSB1*, 166).

12 'sullenly': 'sullen' is a word associated with the Alba in *Dream*
(207). It is the word used in the famous Carlyle-Wicksteed [prose]
translation of Dante for the 'Tristi fummo . . .' section of *Inferno*,
VII, a favourite SB reference point (see, e.g., the *'Whoroscope'
Notebook*). The word 'sullen' also figures in SB's favourite quotation from the play *The Beaux' Stratagem* by George Farquhar; cf.
'Whoroscope' Notebook and *Watt*, 207: 'a sullen, silent sot', misremembered as from a play ('the somebody's Revenge [. . .] is it')

by John Marston in a TM letter of 18.10.56 (*LSB2*, 663). In 'Spring Song' (q.v.) Cain 'shakes his brand sullenly' (line **54**).

13–15 a 'cang' is a Chinese portable pillory (cf. *Dream*, 55, 187; *DN* *405; 'Sanies II', **36**); *The Unnamable*, 45, 57, 68).

16 for the 'ruined feet' cf. *Dream*, 237, and the Belacqua of 'Dante and the Lobster' whose 'feet were in ruins' (*MPTK*, 8).

17 cf. 'that livid Dublin evening light on the shallows' (*LSB1*, 62), the 'livid strands' and 'livid tulips' of *Dream*, 31 and 157, and the 'livid Zurbar[á]n' of *Dream*, 72, and 'tulips' and 'pale-livid' in the TM version of 'Serena III' (*LSB1*, 167).

18 for a photograph, see O'Brien, 203.

19 'nails and timber': emblematic of Christ's passion, cf. *Molloy*, 24: 'It was a cargo of nails and timber, on its way to some carpenter I suppose.'

30–1 cf. 'little wearish old man (Democritus)' (*DN* *720; from Burton's *Anatomy of Melancholy*, 1.16). Democritus, who laughed at human folly while Heraclitus wept for it, is Belacqua's preferred philosopher in 'Yellow' (*MPTK*, 155), where in the event it is Democritus, in spite of his 'limits', who wins a kind of victory over Heraclitus. The word 'wearish' has the sense of 'sickly, feeble, delicate; lean, wizened, shrivelled' (*OED*); cf. Lord Gall's 'wearish voice' in the short story 'Echo's Bones' (7). SB described Krapp's 'cracked' voice as 'wearish' in the first draft of *Krapp's Last Tape* (Knowlson and Pilling, 1979, 81).

33 'smoking.' has a line to itself in variant versions, in *EBOP* and in *Poems in English*, a privilege not extended to the word since *CPEF*. We have with some reluctance accepted the *CPEF* lineation, now apparently the norm.

35 'ganzy', common Irish synonym for a sweater.

39 the unconventional punctuation is also found throughout *More Kicks than Pricks* (cf. Pilling, 2011, 16).

47–8 cf. 'bloodied rafflesia in sombre Sumatra' (*DN* *656; Nordau, *Degeneration*, 192). Transcribing Nordau's 'blood-red' as 'bloodied' may have suggested the image of this enormous, foul-smelling flower as 'the jungle hymen'. For 'hymen' cf. 'Serena III', line **4**, and *DN* *434; and for 'rafflesia' cf. *The Unnamable*: 'somewhere off the coast of Java and its jungles red with rafflesia' (*The Unnamable*, 29).

49 'Next': cf. *Dream*, e.g. 19, 114, 139.

57 and 64–7   cf. *Dream*, 28.

61   for the Fox and Geese, cf. *Dream*, 183; and (as here, preceded by Island Bridge, but also with a whore in a garret) *Dream*, 28. 'Chapelizod' and 'Isolde Stores' (lines **61**, **64**), while real Dublin locations, also have a Wagnerian and a Joycean resonance with the 'great perturbation of sweaty heroes' offering an ironic reading of the ancient myth.

62   'goat, exiled': alluding to the distribution of sheep and goats on the Day of Judgement.

64   cf. 'a great perturbation of tenses' (*DN* *733; Burton, 1, 33). The word 'perturbation' is used three times in *Dream* (11, 28, 133).

66   'nepenthe', the draught of forgetfulness given by Helen to Telemachus when he visits Nestor's palace (*DN* *886; Burton, III, 202); 'moly' [cf. 'Yoke of Liberty', and Molloy believing himself poisoned at Lousse's house], the potion given to Odysseus by Hermes to protect him from the enchantments of Circe (*DN* *712; Bérard, *Odyssée*, 169; *Odyssey*, X, 302 ff.).

68   'doomed': a late change, probably influenced by the stories 'Love and Lethe' ('the doomed Belacqua', *MPTK*, 79), and 'Yellow' of 1933. But of course SB's poem had seemed 'doomed', having failed to find favour with editors.

68   not for the first time in the poem (cf. **55–6**) the colours suggest a painting, and SB may have had Edvard Munch's 'The Scream' partly in mind. For 'yellow' cf. *DN* *519, 'xanthic' in 'Serena II', the story 'Yellow' (*MPTK*, 164; with 'yaller' on 159), '[Murphy's] yellow all revived' (*Murphy*, 24), etc.

71   cf. *Dream*, 157, for the gulls, a detail SB told TM he liked in Nancy Cunard's poem *Parallax* in two letters to him of July 1930 (*LSB1*, 25, 28). The 'slush' of gulls in 'a spew of yellow foam' in 'the mouth of the sewer' recurs in 'The End' (*The Expelled*, etc., 54).

72–5   translate the concluding lines of Rimbaud's 'Barbare' (*Les Illuminations*). For 'banner' cf. *Dream*, 98, and the little-known letter of 14.3.34 (not in *LSB1*) to Arland Ussher (HRHRC); for 'the arctic flowers' cf. *Mercier and Camier*: 'Like arctic flowers. In half an hour they'll be gone' (97); and for 'that do not exist' cf. *Dream*, 147: '(they do not exist)', closer to Rimbaud's final line. 'Barbare' is a prose-poem which also contains the repeated exclamation 'Douceurs!' (cf. *LSB1*, 72), a favourite exclamation in *Dream* (e.g. 31, 46, 85, 182; used in a letter to TM of 11.3.31; *LSB1*, 72). Beckett seems to have thought of this as an 'untranslatable word', presumably because it can shift its meaning from 'sweetnesses' to 'sweeteners' in the sense of bungs or bribes. Belmont (*Souvenirs*, 284) highlights SB's difficulties with the word, and a text by him in the Knowlson Collection (UoR) records SB having invited him to collaborate on translating Rimbaud's *Les Illuminations*, an idea which failed to materialise.

Enueg II

'Enueg II', like 'Alba', was written in early August 1931. They are the two earliest poems in the collection. 'Enueg II' was one of three poems (with 'Dortmunder' and 'Malacoda') republished from *EBOP* in *transition* in 1936 (*LSB1*, 334). The three poems were noticed in passing in the *Irish Times* of 25.7.36, 7. The TM version, the only known variant, is entitled 'Alba' (hence SB's reference to 'the other' as distinct from 'the "sheet" Alba' in the TM letter of 22.9.31; *LSB1*, 91). Lines **22–6** are reworked in *Dream*, 28.

Variants in version sent to MacGreevy [*31 lines*]

1   the first word is capitalised.
5   'discreetly' for 'shyly'.
9 and 10   upper case V: 'Veronica mundi / Veronica munda'.
12   'like a pig' for 'like Judas'.
20   'broken' for 'breaking'; there is an additional line before 'doch I assure thee': 'unsweetened up to date'.
22   'he stands' for 'lying', with a section break.
23   'goggling like a fool at the green tulips of the evening'.
29   'oh world / putain' in place of the final line. Cf. 'putid pute' in 'Spring Song' (line **70**), 'Puttanina mia!' in 'To be Sung Loud / From the only Poet to a shining Whore', and 'Be off, puttanina' (*Dream*, 51).

Notes

4   a variation on the Latin tag 'de moriturus nihil nisi bonum' ('of the dead nothing but good' – don't speak ill of the dead) that replaces the dead with those about to die and omits the final adjective.

9–11 St Veronica is said to have wiped the face of Jesus as he was carrying his cross and to have been rewarded with an imprint of his face on her towel. SB described 'give us a wipe' as the 'class of guttersnippet' that continued to please him, adding 'One has to buckle the wheel of one's poem somehow [. . .] or run the risk of Nordau's tolerance' (12.9.31, *LSB1*, 87). This was one of the phrases that, SB claimed to TM (letter of 9.10.31; not in *LSB1*), had led to Seumas O'Sullivan turning this poem down for the *Dublin Magazine*. The 'mundi'/'munda' alternation echoes the epitaph carved on the tomb of Rosamund, mistress of Henry II of England: 'Hic jacet in tomba Rosa mundi, non Rosa munda'. (Since 'mundi' means 'worldly' and 'munda' means 'clean', the epitaph implies Rosamund was a whore: 'Here lies the world's Rose, not Rose the chaste'; cf. the same distinction (applied to 'veronica') in *Dream*, 105–6; and, in a letter to AJL of 7.8.[34] (not in *LSB1*) in connection with Eluard's *La Rose Publique*. SB had found the tag in the Italian original of Mario Praz's *The Romantic Agony* (*DN* *327).

12 cf. 'I sweat like Judas' in a letter of 14.3.34 to Arland Ussher (HRHRC), and a German Diary entry of 9.10.36: 'sweating like Judas'. All these instances are a deliberately heterodox rewriting of biblical accounts of Jesus sweating on the Cross.

13 possibly an adaptation of the lines 'tired of living and scared of dying' in the song 'Ol' Man River', which premiered in Jerome Kern's *Show Boat* of 1926, the 1928 film version of which featured Paul Robeson singing the song that made him famous. Note also that seven of the ten lines in this section are of three words and that three sections of this poem are of three lines only. However, as SB says of Jack B. Yeats, these triads 'are related, not by rule of three, as two values to a third, but directly, as stages of an image' (*Disjecta*, 90).

15 SB's friend Georges Pelorson (later Georges Belmont) varied the French idiom 'j'ai les pieds en compote' by substituting 'marmalade' for 'compote' ('jam'); Knowlson, 1996, 135. SB uses the same phrase in *Dream*, 125, and in a letter to Nuala Costello (27.2.34; *LSB1*, 189).

18 cf. '<u>Smoke less</u>' (*LSB1*, 69, and *Dream*, 190).

19 'mon vieux cœur' was another phrase much favoured by Georges Pelorson (Knowlson, 1996, 135–6). Cf. *Dream*, 17, and 'the latest cardiac feather' (*LSB1*, 73), alluding to the heart palpitations suffered by SB from 1926 onwards.

21   for 'thee', repeated in the last line, cf. the deliberately slightly archaic elements in SB's 1930 version of Montale's 'Delta', and the notes to lines **15–17** of 'To Be Sung Loud'. The line is later adapted for use in 'Spring Song', line **39**, with 'Grock' added. The phrase 'I assure you' occurs at line **72** of the Hours Press 'Whoroscope' (see Appendix), here line **89**.

21–2   the space between these lines, which had been omitted in the version first published in *EBOP* (as SB pointed out to his publisher, George Reavey; undated '[after 13 October 1935]' letter, *LSB1*, 289), is here restored. There is a space in the TM version. The version published in *transition* 24 in September 1936 inserts the space between lines **20** and **21**, i.e. before rather than after 'doch I assure thee'.

24   cf. the note to line **17** of 'Enueg I', 'the green tulips' of a letter to TM of [?12].9.31 (*LSB1*, 88), and the 'livid tulips' in *Dream*, 157.

25   'anthrax': cf. *Dream*, 29.

26   cf. the same phrase in *Dream*, 28.

27–9   cf. the closing lines of 'Arènes de Lutèce', 'a face in the embers' (*The Unnamable*, 18), the 'face in the ashes' in 'Age is when to a man' (*Words and Music*), and the late television play . . . *but the clouds* . . ., which contains a graphic dramatisation of a face in the clouds.

Alba

'Alba' was written in early August 1931 making it, with 'Enueg II' (probably the earlier of the two poems), one of the earliest poems in *EBOP*. In the TM materials at TCD is a copy of the latter titled 'Alba', which suggests that 'Enueg II' as published in *EBOP* was, for a time at least, 'Alba 2', as per Charles Prentice's letter to SB of 27.7.32 (UoR); 'Alba 1' in the Leventhal typescripts equates to 'Alba' as published in *EBOP*. 'Alba 1' and 'Alba 2' are the thirteenth and fourteenth poems in the Leventhal Contents List, with 'Enueg 1' and 'Enueg 2' the tenth and eleventh. Prentice praises 'Alba 2' (a title otherwise unknown) as 'superb', although he thought it 'not so important or significant as ['Spring Song' and what became 'Sanies II']'. These confusions of titling, presumably the product of SB's occasionally hazy grasp of the genres of Provençal poetry, seem to be effectively settled by him referring to 'the "sheet" Alba' in a letter to TM of [*c*.22.9.31; *LSB1*, 91], and going on to quote two phrases from 'the other' [i.e. 'Enueg II' as published in *EBOP*, which, in the TCD MacGreevy material, exists in a version titled 'Alba'].

SB's copy in the HRHRC is annotated: '39 Trinity College Dublin' (Lake *42, 30). This recollection of SB's address while he was a lecturer at TCD is a poignant reminder of the time when his unrequited love for Ethna MacCarthy, the Alba of *Dream of Fair to Middling Women*, was at its most intense. 'Alba' was first published in the *Dublin Magazine* VI (n.s.) Oct.–Dec. 1931; in a letter to TM reporting on this SB told his friend that 'S O'S [. . .] & his bloody committee examined it longitudinally latitudinally & diagonally for fear of an obscene anagram!' (9.10.31; not in *LSB1*). A French translation by SB's friend Alfred Péron appeared in the last pre-war issue of Luc Descaunes's magazine *Soutes*, 9 (1938), 41 (F&F *144, 38; SB apparently thought his friend's effort 'not very good').

An 'alba' is a Provençal aubade or dawn song (cf. *DN* *505; from Beck). 'Alba' has frequently been reprinted, notably in *The Faber Book of Irish Verse*, edited by John Montague, 1974, 295.

In a letter to Donald McWhinnie of 7.5.57 SB wrote: 'I liked the way he read <u>Alba</u>', referring to A. J. Leventhal's Third Programme broadcast 'Samuel Beckett: Poet and Pessimist' (30.4.57), the text of which was subsequently published in *The Listener*, LVII (9.5.57), 746–7 (F&F *3006, *1299; [307], 180). The text of 'Alba' is published in full without variants on page 747. Leventhal also quoted the final section of 'Whoroscope', as published by the Hours Press, in full [746]. The late 1967 plan to broadcast 'Alba' and 'Dieppe III' [i.e. 'what would I do'] as verbal interludes on the 'Music Programme' of the BBC had to be postponed (memo of 2.10.67) until 24.5.68 when they were read by Jack McGowran under the title *Recital: Words and Music* at 10.40 p.m. on the Third Programme (BBC Written Archives, Caversham; cf. the notes to 'Cascando').

Variants

As well as the version that appeared in the *Dublin Magazine*
(DM), there are three typescript variants in the MacGreevy (TM),
Leventhal (AJL) and Israel (CI) collections. The Israel typescript
has handwritten notes indicating section breaks corresponding
to those in the poem as published.

1   'Before morning' in TM, DM and AJL. This is also how it is
represented at the point in *Dream* (148), where the opening line
is quoted alongside snatches of Dante, Baudelaire, Goethe and
Mallarmé as Belacqua, responding 'to the obscure need to verbal-
ise a wombtombing' (148), murmurs 'a syllable or two of incanta-
tion'.

5   'here' is missing from the fifth line in CI and Montague, which
reads 'that you shall establish before morning'.

8   'rain on the bamboos, flower of smoke, alley of willows' (with
commas) in TM.

9   TM and DM have 'like' for 'with'.

10   'to sign the dust' in TM, DM and AJL.

11   TM has 'can add nothing'; DM 'cannot add'.

13   TM has 'symbols' for 'emblems'.

TM and DM have commas at the end of lines 6, 7, 11, 12, 13 and 15.

Notes

1–4   the first four lines were quoted by Thomas MacGreevy
in his review of *Intercessions* by Denis Devlin (*Ireland To-day*,
Dublin, October 1937, 81–2) with the observation that 'Mr Beckett
gathers all his forces into single, precise statements'.

2–4   the vision of the Logos is anticipated in the *Paradiso*, II,
41–2: '. . . il disio / di veder quella essenza in che si vede / come
nostra natura e Dio s'unio' ('the desire to see His being in whom
is seen how our nature was joined to God'). See *Par.*, II, 59–60 ff.
and 'Dante and the Lobster' *(MPTK, 3)* for Beatrice's explanation
of the spots on the moon. Music was for SB at this time often a
soubriquet for the act of love (e.g. *Murphy*, see, for example, 89
and 147). The 'white plane of music' also refers to the music of
the spheres heard by Dante in *Par.*, I, 78 and to the white light of
dawn in *Par.*, I, 44. See also *Dream*, 181 and 193, for other instances
of 'white music'.

6–8 the central section is based on material that SB found in Louis Laloy, *La Musique chinoise* (75, 101; *DN* *498 and *499). Line 7 draws on Laloy's description of the Chinese lute (*qin* in the modern Pinyin romanisation or 'K'in' as in line **4** of 'Dortmunder'). Cf. the 'suave words' of the Alba in *Dream* (171), and 'yea and suave' in line **35** of 'Sanies I'.

9 cf. the woman taken in adultery. The scribes and Pharisees put it to Jesus that Moses, in the laws, set stoning as the penalty for adultery: 'But Jesus stooped down, and with *his* finger wrote on the ground, *as though he heard them not*' (John, 8:6). This imagery is reused in 'Serena III', line **21**. The 'stooping' of Jesus is viewed by the Polar Bear (*Dream*, 209; *MPTK*, 51) as an act of 'megalomaniacal impertinence', but it sufficiently intrigued SB for him to return to it in the sixth of the *Texts for Nothing* (26). SB often said he wondered what it was that Jesus was writing in the dust (Atik, 73), and 'stooping' is also found in 'The Vulture' (line **3**).

11–12 'bounty' and 'beauty' recall the description of Piccarda (*Purg.*, XXIV, 13: '. . . tra bella e bona / non so qual fosse più', 'I know not if she was more fair or good') and the play on pity and piety (*Inf.*, XX, 28) which exercises Belacqua in 'Dante and the Lobster' (*MPTK*, 11). For other occurences of the word 'beauty' in SB's poems see the note to line **63** of 'Casket . . .'.

13 for 'statement' (a key word in SB's early aesthetic, found in SB's lecture notes as taken by Rachel Burrows (TCD) (e.g. 17, 33, 35, 103, 105); in *Dream*, 26, and in a letter to TM of 18.10.32 (*LSB1*, 134): ' a statement and not a description'. In responding to a Poussin painting of Apollo and Daphne in his German Diaries for 18.3.37 SB drew a distinction between the withering laurels on Apollo's brow and the fresh laurel that Daphne turns into 'meaning more than the Gidean achievement that vanishes into an emblem and a refutation'. For 'emblems', cf. *Dream*, 187.

14 a negation of the sunshine and the unveiling in *Par.* III, 1 and 117: 'Quel sole che pria d'amor mi scaldò 'l petto' ('that sun that first warmed my breast with love') and 'non fu dal vel del cor già mai disciolta' ('she was never loosed from the veil of the heart'). SB also probably has Schopenhauer's 'veil of Maya' in mind.

15 'host', cf. the 'milizia' of *Par.*, XXX, 43 and XXXI, 2.

17 cf. 'the mysteries of bulk banished' (*Dream*, 182). SB may have been thinking of the 'many' crossing London Bridge in T. S. Eliot's *The Waste Land* (lines 62–3), an image derived from Dante, *Inf.*, III, 55–7.

Dortmunder

'Dortmunder' is another sort of *alba* and a pendant to 'Alba' in *EBOP*, where the two poems appear on facing pages. While 'Alba' meditates on idealised love, 'Dortmunder' recalls an earthier transaction with a prostitute. SB marked this poem in the 'autograph' HRHRC copy of *EBOP* 'Cassel [i.e. Kassel] revisited' (Lake, *42, 30) and Harvey commented that it was written there in January 1932 under the influence of Dortmunder beer (77). It was one of the '2 poems' sent to Samuel Putnam 'from Germany about middle January [. . .] One long ['Enueg I'], one short' (letter to Putnam of 3.4.[32] (*LSB1*, 107). There are copies of the poem with minor variants in the RA and MDZ papers. The CI version is the same as the published poem. 'Dortmunder' was republished from *EBOP*, with 'Enueg II' and 'Malacoda', in *transition* in 1936 (cf. *LSB1*, 334).

Variants

3 MDZ: 'I null and she royal hulk'.
7 not in RA.
10 no comma after 'Then' in MDZ.
13 no comma in RA and MDZ ; 'and' added: 'Schopenhauer is dead and the bawd'. RA spells 'Scopenhauer'.

Notes

Murphy telescopes the first and last lines of the poem into 'a dusk of lute music' (75). Neary is feeling very sorry for himself in a Chinese restaurant 'and a sorer lack than any wife or even mistress, were she Yang Kuei-fei herself, was a mind to pillow his beside'. Yang Kuei-fei was a 'famous concubine', as Beckett records in his '*Dream' Notebook* (*522; *Dream*, 52); her spectral presence in 'Dortmunder' elevates a brothel encounter.
1 'magic': Ronsard's 'Magie ou délivrance de l'amour', which inspired 'Return to the Vestry' / 'it is high time lover', is described

as 'the liquorish laypriest's Magic Ode' in *Dream*, 68, and is a
touchstone for Belacqua's flirtation with the Alba (*Dream*, 28,
174 and 175, where the Alba remarks '. . . If you are familiar with
it we could give earth to this conversation there'). 'Homer dusk'
refers to 'The hour when darkness fills the streets' (*DN* *715,
from Bérard, 177; cf. *Dream*, 28, *MPTK*, 45 and 174, and SB to TM,
18.10.32, *LSB*, 136, and 21.11.32, not included in *LSB1*). In the latter,
as here, the Homer dusk is coupled with red steeples.

3   'null', cf. *Dream*, 40, 121; 'royal': recalling the Chinese imperial
concubine Yang Kuei-fei. Cf. *DN* *522; *Dream*, 177.

4   'The Chinese lute | k'*în* |' (*DN* *498; *Dream*, 113); in modern
Pinyin 'qin'.

6   'jade splinters': a synaesthetic evocation of Chinese music,
perhaps drawn from SB's recollection of 'Confucius juggling with
the liu-liù on cubes of jade' (*DN* *496). SB told Harvey that jade
had a cold feel for him (Harvey notes, 28.3.62). It is the colour for
hope in 'Home Olga'.

7   cf. the Thomistic 'signaculum virginis, hymen' ('the hymen as
a token of virginity', *DN* *434); and the correlation of 'signaculum
sinus' or 'sign of the curve', with 'the Hogarthian sigma of beauty'
in a letter to Ruby Cohn of 17.7.75 (UoR).

8   cf. the 'plagal' or 'Amen cadence', thus the 'plagal east' as
dawn putting an end, in true *alba* fashion, to this night of love;
see also 'plagal finale (off the tonic)' (*DN* *503). For 'the eyes the
eyes black' cf. *Dream*, 49 and 111, and 'most pleasing, piercing
black eyes', *DN* *842 (Burton on the Virgin Mary).

9   cf. the 'longa nuech' of a Provençal poem by Folquet de Marseille, given the title 'Dans la nuit longue' in Beck's Troubadour
book (99).

10   from St Augustine, *Confessions* (*DN* *202; cf. *Dream*, 26), perhaps also by way of *A Portrait of the Artist as a Young Man*: 'The
Firmament was as a scroll rolled away' (121).

12   the Douai-Rheims version of Habbakuk suggests that the
Old Testament prophet may be incontinent in the face of God's
wrath: 'When I heard, my belly trembled . . .' (Habbakuk 3: 1); cf.
also the 'gush of mard' from Findlater's horse at the beginning of
Dream (1) and the 'mard of gold sculpppt' (*Dream*, 78).

13   cf. 'Schopenhauer says <u>defunctus</u> is a very beautiful word
– as long as one does not suicide. He might be right.' (SB to TM,

before 5.8.30, *LSB1*, 36). Cf. the last word of SB's *Proust* (1931; *PTD*, 93).

Sanies I

An early draft entitled 'WEG DU EINZIGE!', which was sent to MacGreevy on 13 May 1933, is reproduced in *LSB1*, 160–1. The poem is listed in the Leventhal contents as 'Weg Du Einzige', but there is no matching text. 'Sanies I' is an imaginative account of a long bicycle ride SB took on Easter Saturday (15 April) 1933 north of Dublin 'through Malahide and round the estuary to Portrane and back by Swords' as he told TM (24.3.33, *LSB1*, 154). In the course of the ride he muses on his 'authentic reminiscences of the two primal traumata (birth and weaning)', which, as he says in his Psychology Notes, 'are at the bottom of all myths and neuroses' (TCD MS 10971/8/35). SB had just turned 27, but feels himself to be, like Dante, 'nel mezzo del cammin di nostra vita' or halfway through the biblical span of three score years and ten (cf. line **22**). He had resigned from Trinity in January of the previous year, moved to Paris and completed his first novel, *Dream of Fair to Middling Women*, but it had failed to find a publisher and, unable to support himself from his writing, he had been forced to return to his family home at 'Cooldrinagh' where relations with his parents were strained. His relationship with Peggy Sinclair was long over, and Ethna MacCarthy, to whom he was strongly attracted, had recently taken up with A. J. Leventhal, whom she would live with and eventually marry. The shock of meeting Ethna with Leventhal brings the poem to its close (cf. *LSB1*, 154) and explains the original title which may be translated as 'Get Away You Only One!' The title under which it was published is taken from a medical term for a 'discharge from a sore' (*DN* *1035), and is found in *Dream* (108, 228) and later in 'Yellow' (*MPTK*, 159; the story was written in 1933, almost certainly well before SB's relatively late adoption of 'Sanies' as a genre indicator in *EBOP* alongside 'Enueg', 'Alba' and 'Serena', which are more or less genuine Provençal genres). In a letter to TM of 5.1.33 (*LSB1*, 149) SB speaks of an 'eschewal of verbal sanies', i.e. logorrhoea.

In the HRHRC 'autograph' copy of *EBOP* this poem is marked

'Exitus Redditus / this evening/ Montparnasse / 1957' by SB (Lake, *42, 30; cf. *Dream*, 129), applying his favourite tag from Thomas à Kempis, implying that nothing much has changed in 25 years.

Variant last lines (47–53) of 'Sanies I' as 'Weg Du Einzige!'
(MacGreevy version)

> get along with you now take the six the seven the eight or the
>   little single-decker
> home to your prison your parlour in Sandymount
> or take the Blue Line for all I care home to the cob of your web
>   in Sandymount
> your ma expects you anny minute
> I know her she is still then she gets up
> then too the tiger in our hearts is smiling
> that funds ways home

Other very minor variants occur on the TM equivalents for lines **4, 7, 8** [missing], **9, 13, 22, 23, 24, 33, 34, 35, 38, 39** and **46**.

Notes

1   cf. 'Whan that Aprille with his shoures soote' (Chaucer, *General Prologue to the Canterbury Tales*).
2   Harvey, 140, discovered that there were swans carved on top of the pillars outside Turvey House, which is not on a river although Eoin O'Brien, 240, refers to 'the swans that populate the waters of the area'; cf. the swans in line **21** of 'Serena II'.
3   'three ratios': the gears of the bicycle; 'sonata', cf. *Molloy*, 29.
4   'pommelled', a variation of 'pummelled' which recalls Heredia's poem 'Sur le Pont-Vieux', the source for 'he chisels no Cellinesque pommels' in SB's *Proust* (*PTD*, 8); cf. 'post equitem sedet atra cura' ('behind the rider sits dark care', Horace, *Odes*, III, 1, 40). Beckett had just had a guilt-ridden bicycling dream in which Rudmose-Brown, his old tutor at Trinity, appeared behind him on the bike, 'in a panic on the step' (SB to TM, 13.5.33, *LSB1*, 158). When Belacqua sets off for his honeymoon, his deceased wife is '*atra cura* in the dicky' ('What a Misfortune'; *MPTK*, 140).
5   the sturdy thighs of Botticelli's Venus; for Botticelli, cf. *Dream*, 15, and *MPTK*, 167.
6   for 'zeep', cf. *Dream*, 115, and 'Yellow', *MPTK*, 151.

7–8 cf. 'mania for proving capacity for self-control (sphincters)' (Philosophy Notes, TCD MS 10971/8/19).

9 'müde': 'weary' (German).

10 while 'potwalloping' suggests the bumpiness of the road contributing to the cyclist's discomfort, it is also a constitutional term for an Irish borough, often squalidly corrupt, in which any householder who could boil or 'wallop' a pot was entitled to vote. Swords (line **2**) was such a borough; Mr Taylor's public house in 'Fingal' (*MPTK*, 27; for a photograph, see O'Brien, 239) is in Swords. Cf. 'pot-valiant' in line **18**.

11 refers to an advertisement for Raleigh bikes, although line **42** reveals that the cyclist is mounted on a Swift.

13 'pop': cf. letter to George Reavey of 9.1.36: '"I am sure you were not born with a pop." But am I not sparkling?' (*LSB1*, 295); the larches (cf. line **23**) are an obsessional childhood image in much of SB's work; cf., for example, line **30**, 'Serena II', *Watt* (38), where one larch turns green each year a week before the others, *Molloy* (34), *A Piece of Monologue* (*Krapp's Last Tape and other shorter plays*, 117), 'Love and Lethe', 'Walking Out' and 'Draff' (*MPTK*, 87, 96 and 173).

14 cf. 'Fingal': 'I want very much to be back in the caul, on my back in the dark for ever' (*MPTK*, 22).

17 a brief image of the bicycle ride as a sea journey ('billows') ending in shipwreck ('wrack') taking in the sexual attraction of the nubile and the certainty of the winding sheet or cerecloth. 'cere wrack' may also play on Stephen Dedalus's account of *Hamlet* in *Ulysses* where Burbage as Hamlet stands before Shakespeare as the ghost 'beyond the rack of cerecloth' (241).

18 'pot-valiant': valiant or courageous through the influence of drink, perhaps from Smollett (*Humphry Clinker*, where SB found 'sirreverence' as entered in the 'For Interpolation' section of the *'Whoroscope' Notebook*), or by way of the *OED* where 'potwalloping' is the previous entry. Cf. 'Ruby, pot-valiant, let a loud scoff' (*MPTK*, 89). There is an error in the first edition of *MPTK* (1934, 134), with 'Lucy' replacing 'Ruby' (F&F*16, 14).

21 alluding to a popular Irish saying (Harvey, 143).

22 SB impressed upon Harvey that the reference was to his own 35th birthday (letter to Harvey, 20.2.67; Dartmouth College), and not to the wedding of his parents (Saturday, 31 August, 1901).

But neither of these 'explanations' seems in any way precisely applicable to a poem written in 1933, when SB was twenty-seven.

24   for 'he took the day off', cf. *Company*, etc., 7. For 'up hill and down dale', cf. *Dream*, 72 and the story 'Echo's Bones' (7); SB associates the phrase with a Brothers Grimm tale ('The Cat and the Mouse set up house', the source for the tag 'So it goes in the world' which he used on numerous occasions), as is revealed in letters of early 1955 and 16.12.55 to Pamela Mitchell (*LSB2*, 583).

25   Beckett's father, William, took a walk on the day of SB's birth with an obsequious acquaintance who worked for the Liverpool, London and Globe Insurance Company (James Knowlson, private communication).

31   a hidden pun likening William Beckett's companion to a family dog (cf. 'Serena II') by way of Aeneas' faithful companion, 'fidus Achates', in Virgil's *Aeneid*.

32   'beestings': the first milk taken by a newly born infant or other mammal. Cf. 'colostrum' (*DN* *982; *Dream*, 81, 195).

33   SB had a particular fondness for the word 'ebb' as witnessed by the poem 'Dieppe'. He also considered *Ebb* as a possible title for *Embers* (SB to Barbara Bray, 17.2.59 and 25.2.59; in a letter of 2.3.59 he has 'changed the title to *Embers*', the title thereafter). A notable extension of the word to hair, gums and going home. Cf. the 'ebb of sighs' in 'Serena I', line **34**.

35   'suave': cf. 'Alba', line **6**.

36   'beyond good and evil' invokes Nietzsche.

37   cf. 'biding' in *Dream* (26, 74), and in 'Spring Song', line **35**.

38   cf. the 'nymphs' in Mallarmé's 'L'Après-midi d'un faune', and *DN* *1118 (from Ovid).

39   cf. 'A peeping Tom in bicycle-clips' (*Dream*, 72).

40   SB is smoking as he rides; 'Wild Woodbine' – a brand of cigarette. In the 8.3.66 BBC broadcast Jack MacGowran leaves out 'in' and has 'the' for 'a', which are presumably not authorial revisions (cf. 'I would like . . .'), even though SB was present at the recording sessions. 'Sanies I' was also chosen for the 14.4.76 70th birthday broadcast.

41   a 'slicker' is a raincoat; for 'cinched', cf. 'Casket . . .', line **38**.

42   'Stürmers', 'lady-killers' (German). Cf. *DN* *580, where the German word is used to describe the eponymous hero of Diderot's *Le Neveu de Rameau*.

46   'nautch-girl', Indian dancing girl; cf. 'the hard breastless Greek slave or huntress the hard nautch-girl' and the 'sinuous nautch-gal' (*Dream*, 83 and 162).

47   cf. 'St Teresa: undaunted daughter of desires' (*DN* *695). The Alba is thus described (*Dream*, 54, 222, and *MPTK*, 48). Ethna MacCarthy favoured bright red at this time (Knowlson, 1996, 61). Cf. also line **13** of Beckett's translation of Paul Eluard's 'Scene': 'Daunt and detach me from desires'. For the 'flamingo', cf. the Alba in the story 'Echo's Bones' (19; Dartmouth College typescript).

50   Ethna MacCarthy lived in Holles Street, site of the National Maternity Hospital, the location of the 'Oxen of the Sun' episode in *Ulysses*. Sandymount, in the TM variant, alludes to Ethna McCarthy's parental home at 1c Sandymount Avenue.

51   cf. the well-known limerick 'There was a young lady of Riga', or, alternatively 'Niger' (Harvey, 149).

52   Leventhal apparently 'thought <u>funds ways home</u> had something to do with paying her tram fare!' (SB to TM, 13.5.[33], *LSB1*, 159). In the story 'Walking Out' the phrase suggests that it simply means to go home together (*MPTK*, 101). Cf. 'The penny pleasure of homing in the gloaming' (*LSB1*, 154).

Sanies II

'Sanies II' was begun during SB's second lengthy stay in Paris (February 1932 to 12 July 1932) and recalls his first experience of the city as lecturer at the École Normale Supérieure in 1929 (cf. Lake, *42, 30). There are no known variants. In the *POEMS* contents list it is listed as 'Happy Land'. Charles Prentice, in a phrase that recalls the Protestant hymn, refers to 'There is a Happy Land' (letter to SB of 27.7.32; UoR), and speaks of its 'horror'. It is certainly a wild poem, developing the brothel theme, first explored in 'Dortmunder', which is here given the phantasmagorical inflection of a fairy tale with a perverse twist derived from *Flagellation and the Flagellants* by William Cooper, the pseudonym of James Glass Bertram. SB recorded numerous entries from Cooper in his *Dream Notebook* and incorporated many terms from Cooper in the last third of the poem. Although the topographical details are from the Parisian Left Bank (rue Mouffetard, line **3**, the

hammam of the Grand Mosque, lines **6–7** and the Panthéon, line
11), the psycho-geography includes reminiscences of brothels in
Dublin and Germany. 'Sanies II' was apparently, with 'Serena I',
one of two poems that SB sent to George Reavey, which Reavey
was slow to acknowledge (letter to TM of 21.11.32, not in *LSB1*).
The RA typescript of the poem has the title 'Enueg II'.

Notes

2 'the American Bar in the rue Mouffetard' is entered in *DN*
*1073, but cannot be identified with any certainty. The so-called
'American Bar', specialising in cocktails, was a burgeoning feature
of Paris in the late 1920s and early 1930s; they were to be found
either as establishments in their own right, or so designated in
larger hotels and restaurants.
5 the red eggs (Easter eggs or perhaps eggs pickled in vinegar)
of the previous line give rise to a poor pun on haemorrhoids
(which may be associated with constipation, as eggs may be) that
is characteristic of the stream of consciousness elisions of the
poem. Cf. the 'long poem [. . .] waiting to be written about hens
and eggs' (*Dream*, 192), i.e. 'Whoroscope', written and published
before *Dream* was finished.
6–7 recall the Turkish Bath and its tea-room in the Grand
Mosque (1921) in the Place du Puits de l'Ermite below the Jardin
des Plantes. Cf. the 'Turkish bath' in Dublin (*LSB1*, 68) and the
Agamemnon notes to 'Spring Song'.
8 'skinnymalinks': according to Dolan's *Dictionary of Hiberno-
English*, 'a tall, bony person'.
9 cf. 'slouch[ing] towards Bethlehem to be born' (W. B. Yeats,
'The Second Coming'). The phrase 'sailing slouching' pre-echoes
the title of Jack B. Yeats's *Sailing Sailing Swiftly* (1933). For the
phrase 'happy body', a Beckettian way of 'decently' expressing the
expulsion of waste matter, cf. *Dream*, 199 (and 'A Wet Night').
11 Puvis de Chavannes, whose murals (cf. 'frescoward', line
16) decorate the nearby Panthéon. For 'gauntlet', cf. 'gantelope'
in the poem 'Echo's Bones', line **4**; for 'tulips', cf. a letter to TM of
[?12].9.31 (*LSB1*, 88).
13 cf. 'filthy old trousers' (*Dream*, 233).
14 cf. the refrain of 'Molly Malone', 'alive, alive-oh'. Molly is
sometimes represented as a prostitute.

18 'maquereau', French slang for pimps, bawds, procurers.

20 SB was greatly amused by the incongruous sight of a print of Dante and Beatrice on the wall of Becky Cooper's celebrated brothel (cf. O'Brien, 179, 366 fn 106) in Dublin in October 1931 (SB to TM, 9.10.31, not included in *LSB1* but quoted in Knowlson, 1996, 140). The print was of Henry Holliday's 'Dante and Beatrice' in the Walker Art Gallery, Liverpool, which depicts the moment when Dante, watching from the Ponte Santa Trinità in Florence, glimpses Beatrice and her companions coming along the Lung'arno. Falling in love with her, he changes his way of life and writes *La Vita Nuova* (*The New Life*).

23–4 characters from the *Contes* of the Comtesse d'Aulnoy. SB commented to Harvey that the names 'all have a brothel feeling about them' (Knowlson, 1996, 139). Belle-Belle is maid of honour at Belacqua's wedding in 'What a Misfortune' (*MPTK*, 138), and Belacqua himself is addressed as 'Bel Bel' by the Smeraldina (*MPTK*, 143, and *Dream*, 55).

26 cf. *Dream*, 108, and 'Let me not to the marriage of true minds / Admit impediments. Love is not love / Which alters when it alteration finds' (Shakespeare, Sonnet 116; also used in *Dream*, 108).

27 echoes Robert Graves's *Goodbye to All That*, published in 1929.

31 Madame de la Motte: Jeanne St. Rémi de la Valois, de la Motte, the last woman to be publicly whipped in France, was imprisoned in the nearby Hospice de la Salpétrière after being flogged and branded (*DN* *394 and *396). The Comtesse d'Aulnoy was married, aged 16, to Monsieur de la Motte, Baron d'Aulnoy, so that she too might be addressed as Madame de la Motte.

32 'collop': 'a thick fold of flesh on the body as evidence of a well-fed condition' (*OED*, Scots or dialect); cf. 'collop-wallop' applied to Findlater's horse in *Dream*, 1.

34 'cavaletto': a marble flogging block used in Roman prisons (*DN* *401); 'supplejack': rattans carried by officers and NCOs in the British army (*DN* *378); 'mumbo jumbo': 'in various foreign countries the Rod is still the badge of power . . . in Africa there is mumbo jumbo' (Cooper, 15, cf. *DN* *343).

35 adapts Plautus' *Assinaria*: 'vivos homines mortui incursant boves' ('dead bulls attack live men', substituting 'puellas', 'girls' for 'homines', 'men'; *DN* *357).

36 'subito subito': 'now now' (Italian); the cang is a Chinese portable pillory (cf. 'Enueg I', **14**, *Dream*, 55 and 187, *The Unnamable*, 42; from *DN* *353); 'bamboo for bastinado' (*DN* *399 and *404).

37 cf. 'bastinado à la mode' (*DN* *399), a Chinese beating on the soles of the feet, and 'fessade' (*DN* *353; *Dream*, 50 and 97), a beating on the buttocks; here combined in 'a fashionable beating'.

38–40 Becky Cooper, notorious Dublin brothel-keeper (cf. note to line **20**); 'thine adders' may refer to Becky Sharp, 'la Vipère' of Thackeray's *Vanity Fair* (cf. note to line **29** of 'Serena I') which Beckett had finished reading by 4 August 1932 (*LSB1*, 111).

41–3 the conclusion parodies T S Eliot's *Ash-Wednesday* (1930), several sections of which end in prayer (cf. *Disjecta*, 68; a letter to Nuala Costello of 27.2.34: *LSB1*, 188; and 'Musset's prayer' in a letter to Mary Manning Howe of 22.5.37, not in *LSB1*). The *kyrie* recurs in SB's German Diary (15.11.36) as a figure for art-as-prayer: 'The art (picture) that is a prayer sets up prayer in onlooker, i.e. <u>Priest</u>: Lord have mercy upon us. <u>People</u>: Christ have mercy upon us. What is name of this art?'

Serena I

SB's copy in the HRHRC is inscribed 'London/World's End' indicating the area in which he was living when he visited the landmarks encountered in 'Serena I': the British Museum, Regent's Park Zoo, Primrose Hill and Ken Wood, Tower Bridge, the Tower of London and the Monument. The poem itself, as is clear from SB's correspondence with MacGreevy, where it is described as 'a blank unsighted kind of thing' (13.9.32, *LSB1*, 121), was written at SB's parental home, 'Cooldrinagh', in Dublin, although it may have been begun in London. Enclosing it in a letter to TM of 8.10.32, SB described it as 'the only bit of writing that has happened to me since Paris [i.e. since late June/early July] and that does me no particular credit as far as I can judge' (*LSB1*, 129).] It appears under the title 'I put pen to this' amended to 'Cri de Cœur 1' in the *POEMS* contents list at the HRHRC.

A 'serena' is a Provençal evening song in which the lover expresses 'his unhappiness during the daytime and his longing for the night that will reunite him with his lover' (Harvey, 85). Harvey may be in direct debt to SB here, but the three 'Serena' poems hardly seem to accord closely with this definition, and the genre is not recorded by Beck. SB may have remembered that the word 'serena' ('siren') is used by Dante in a dream-sequence in *Purg.*, XIX, 19, with Dante the protagonist tempted by a siren-like figure. All three of the Serenas could be seen as, in a sense, 'siren-songs', although the charms our poet has to resist are less obviously beguiling than those Dante confronts. In 'Serena I' it is the limited appeal of Ireland (line 11) and, perhaps, 'the Blessed Isles' (line 22). In 'Serena II', 'the doomed land their reefs of tresses' (line 22) has a sirenic ring to it, while in the third section (lines 27–34) the poet seems to have succumbed to the charms of Siren Ireland. 'Serena III' acknowledges that 'she is paradise' (line 3) but ends in headlong flight. Whether indeed Beckett had something of the sort in mind, the enigmatic genre 'Serena' is certainly an improvement on the 'Cri de Cœur' that it replaced.

The earliest extant version of the poem (untitled) was sent to TM in a letter dated 8 October 1932 (*LSB1*, 126–33). On the same day Beckett described the poem to his publisher George Reavey in the following terms: 'I have an idea I enshrined Primrose Hill and Crystal Palace seen thence, as though I were Marcel Schwob peering through incipient cataract at a red moutier [see the references to Schwob below], in a long sad one that does me great credit. Très émouvant. There is also a drill's arse and Daniel Defoe [a 'factual' writer, SB told Harvey; Harvey notes, Dartmouth College]. They coexist very amiably' (*LSB1*, 124–5). In a letter to Nuala Costello (27.2.34, *LSB1*, 184–9) Beckett associates leading contemporary figures from psychoanalysis with the animals from London Zoo and he strengthens the allusion to 'Serena I' by concluding this little sortie with a direct quotation from the poem: 'Or go on to Hampstead and have a drink at the Spaniards and look at your brother the fly, oh the Spanish fly, moving out of darkness into light et sqq.' (cf. *LSB2*, 181). SB told TM (13.5.33; *LSB1*, 159) that their mutual friend A. J. Leventhal considered the poem 'One long spittle'. 'Serena I' seems to have been, with 'Sanies II', one of two poems that SB sent to George Reavey, which Reavey was slow to acknowledge (letter to TM of 21.11.32, not in *LSB1*).

In *EBOP* 'Serena I' and 'Serena II' have the same number of lines (53). In the TM versions the first has 66 lines, the second (see Appendix) has 67.

Variant opening lines (1-14) of 'Serena I'
(untitled MacGreevy version)

I put pen to this
vague carmen that
is so much pleasanter easier
more'n in my line nor prose
and my kakoethes or as they [RA 'some'] say evil propensity
ain't got Gott sei dank no butt
what I mean is I don't love her
nor scape of land sea or sky
nor our Saviour [RA 'the Lord God'] particularly
I haven't signed any contract either I couldn't quite bring it off
no my algos is puss in the corner I just feel fervent
ardent in a vague general way
and my lil erectile brain [misspelt in RA] God help her
thuds like a butcher's sex

Notes to the variant opening of 'Serena I':
2   'carmen', Latin: song. Cf. 'carmine quae legunt cacantes' (songs that are sung shitting), *DN* *727, *LSB1*, 94; cf. note to line **70** of 'Spring Song'.
5   'kakoethes', Greek: an incurable itch. Cf. SB to Harvey on 'the itch to make' (273), 'cacoethes (scribendi, loquendi)' (*DN* *1018; from Juvenal), *Dream*, 133 ('cacoethes scribendi, the doom of the best of penmen [Joyce]', and 'a cacoethes of hoisting' by Moll Gall in the story 'Echo's Bones' (19).
6   'Gott sei dank', Thank God (German).
11   'algos', Greek: pain.
12   cf. 'ardent' in *Dream*, 66, and 'ardour' in combination with 'fervour' in a letter to TM of 13.9.32 (*LSB1*, 121).

Lines **15–57** are indented in TM [**15–56** in RA], which has 'housefly' in line **60**.
RA variants: title: 'Enueg 2'; lines **21–2**: one line in TM; line **36** has 'the Isles of the Blest'; line **39** has 'my quiet breath' [cf. 'Dante and

the Lobster']; line **51** has 'have'; lines **50–1**: 'the urn beacon above [TM: 'aloft'] / that I were Daniel Defoe no less'; lines **58–9**: 'but there [TM: 'then'] again as I say / who is likely to come across me [TM: 'to run across me'] in Ken Wood'; line **62** has 'creeping'.

Notes

1   SB's first British Museum Reader's Card was issued on 28.7.32.
2   SB's Philosophy Notebook has the following entry for Thales: 'THALES (650) His primal substance <u>water</u>. Earth afloat (dead fish) on surface of primal substance. <u>All things are full of gods</u>' (TCD MS 10967/5). SB combined notes from a number of sources. The form of words is closest to John Burnet's *Early Greek Philosophy*, London: A&C Black, 1930, 47–8, but Peter Fifield has suggested (private communication) that SB's image of the world as a 'dead fish adrift' may have been prompted by Friedrich Ueberweg's suggestion that Thales' doctrine arises from the 'geognostic observations (as of sea shells in mountains)' (*History of Philosophy*, New York: Charles Scribner's Sons, 1889, 35). Thales also occurs in SB's Psychology Notes in the context of Otto Rank's *Trauma of Birth*: 'Thales his primal substance water (amnios)' (TCD MS 10971/8/36). Pietro Aretino (1492–1556): satirist, pornographer – hence SB's mention of the 'Florentine positions' in a letter of 4.8.32 to TM (*LSB1*, 113) – and writer of devotional works. SB's editor at *The New Review*, Samuel Putnam, had translated Aretino's letters, sonnets and dialogues for a two-volume limited edition (New York: Pascal Covici, 1926; 1,250 copies), which also includes a critical essay and Putnam's translation of a biographical study by Francesco De Sanctis. According to Harvey, SB 'admired the concrete language of both the Aretino and Defoe' (89); he was presumably obliged to read 'the Aretino' (cf. 'L'Aretin', in *Inf.*, XXX, 31) in the North Library of the British Museum, where restricted books were issued. In later life SB owned the two-volume selection from *L'Oeuvre du divin Arétin* (Paris: Bibliothèque des Curieux, 1909, reprinted 1933) with an introduction and notes by Guillaume Apollinaire (letter to George Reavey of 29.8.72; cf. the notes to 'Zone' below).
11   a trick of the light recalls Ireland as it does in *Murphy*: 'Celia also looked at the sky ... simply to have that unction of soft, sunless light on her eyes that was all she remembered of Ireland' (174).

14 'George the drill', a *Mandrillus sphinx* Old World monkey with a spectacular red and blue bottom, was a great favourite with keepers and public at London Zoo at the time.

18 'strom', 'river, stream' (German). In *Dream* and *MPTK* Beckett uses the word 'strom' to designate a general hubbub. Peristalsis is a series of coordinated, rhythmic muscle contractions that occur throughout the length of the gastrointestinal tract. It is an automatic and vital process that moves food through the digestive tract.

19 'the work of the file' (i.e. attention to detail), Horace, *Ars Poetica*, 291; cf. also Walter Draffin's '*Dream of Fair to Middling Women* held up in the *limae labor* stage for the past ten or fifteen years' (*MPTK*, 134). Cf. also Chas's description of his poetic progress, added to 'A Wet Night' but not present in *Dream*: '*Limae labor* [. . .] *et mora*' (*MPTK*, 45).

20 recollection of the Lord's Prayer (Matthew 6: 9–13). 'Ye cannot serve God and mammon' occurs at verse 24 of the same chapter.

21 a literal, if disorientating, translation of the French idiom 'je me trouve'; cf. 'I surprise me' for the common French idiom 'je m'étonne' (line **27**). The Crystal Palace, built for the Great Exhibition of 1851, was destroyed by fire 30 November–2 December 1936.

22 although the Blessed Isles have their place in Greek and Celtic mythology, SB probably had more exotic literary sources in mind. Yang Kuei-fei, the famous Chinese concubine who was strangled on the emperor's orders following a rebellion, is found on the Isles of the Blest (*DN* *522; cf. also *Murphy*, 74). The reference to Schwob in the letter to Reavey of 8.10.32 (*LSB1*, 125) leaves open the possibility that SB was here also remembering the 'îles enchantées' in Schwob's 'L'étoile de bois' (1897; *Oeuvres complètes*, I, Paris, 1928, 154).

23 cf. *Dream*, 124, where Belacqua '*has turned out simply to be not that kind of person*' (i.e. a liu).

24 SB quotes this line in English (with an initial capital), followed by line **26** (also with an initial capital), in a typewritten letter in French to Georges Duthuit dated 'lundi 27' (probably February 1950; *LSB2*, 179–83)).

25 the Aldington variant 'my quiet breath' (also in TM, *LSB1*, 131) here makes explicit the Keatsian allusion (to 'Ode to a Nightingale'; cf. the end of 'Dante and the Lobster', and a 1930 TM letter: *LSB1*, 21).

27–8 some larger vessels had hinged funnels which would enable them to pass below Tower Bridge without the need for it to open and so delay motor traffic.

28 for Tower Bridge, cf. a letter to TM (4.8.32, *LSB1*, 111).

29 'viper's curtsy': SB told MacGreevy (4.8.32, *LSB1*, 111) that he had been reading *Vanity Fair*. In the novel, a few pages after being described as a viper, Becky Sharp makes a 'respectful virgin-like curtsey to the gentleman' (20). Cf. the adder of line **15** and Becky's adders in 'Sanies II', line **40**.

30 'lighter': flat-bottomed boat, such as a Thames barge.

32 a bascule is a bridge that opens using counterbalance weights. Its two halves meet in a scarf joint.

33 there was a river ambulance station at South Wharf at Trinity Street.

35 'canaille', 'rabble, riff-raff' (French).

36 'cernèd', another gallicism: 'les yeux cernés' – rings under the eyes.

37 the *Daily Mirror*, then (as now) a popular newspaper.

38 Married Men's Quarters and the Bloody Tower are both within the Tower of London.

40–2 'Wren's giant bully', the Monument, built to commemorate the Great Fire of London. The original inscription maintained that Papists had started the fire. Cf. Pope's lines: 'Where London's column, pointing to the skies, / Like a tall bully, lifts the head and lyes;' ('Epistle to Bathurst', 339–40).

43 as a young child Daniel Defoe lived in one of only three houses that survived the Great Fire.

48 for 'sidling', cf. line **48** of 'Serena II'. 'Draff' reworks this imagery: the gardener 'slobbered out of darkness into light, he chose a place in the sun and settled, he was like a colossal fly trimming its load of typhus' (*MPTK*, 176; 'a place in the sun', from the *Pensées* of Pascal, is the last phrase in 'Walking Out'; *MPTK*, 105). Cf. also Schwob (op. cit., 161): 'Il se lassa de vivre dans l'ombre verte et obscure'.

49 cf. Pascal, *Pensées* no. 295, and the last words of 'Love and Lethe' (*MPTK*).

Serena II

Included untitled in a letter to MacGreevy of 4.11.32 (*LSB1*, 140–2; see Appendix), and described as 'the bitch and bones' in a TM letter of 5.1.33 (*LSB1*, 150). The first line of the 4.11.32 version, 'this seps of a world', serves as title in the *POEMS* contents list, where it is subsequently crossed out and replaced by 'Cri de coeur 2'. No text survives at the HRHRC. SB's note to the poem in his copy of *EBOP* at the HRHRC reads: 'Glencullen – Prince William's Seat Enniskerry'. Bair (187) comments that it was his favourite walk in all of Ireland (cf. *LSB1*, 136, 139). SB borrows details from a trip he made with his brother, Frank, to Galway and County Mayo in October 1932 for the dreams of his mother's Kerry Blue bitch (*LSB1*, 127–8).

Despite the grand sweep and close observations of 'Serena II', SB told Harvey (Harvey notes) that he considered this poem 'a complete failure'. For photographs of the places referred to, see O'Brien, 308–10.

Notes

1   'clonic', the term used in pathology to describe spasms in which violent muscular contractions occur. 'Seps' in TM, 'rotten'. Cf. 'On *this earth* that is Purgatory' [emphasis added], 'Dante... Bruno.Vico..Joyce', (*Disjecta*, 33).
2   the editors are extremely grateful to James Knowlson for drawing their attention to this variant of a familiar nursery rhyme: 'See-saw, Margery Daw, / Sold her bed and lay on the straw; / Was not she a dirty slut / To sell her bed and lie in the dirt.' This surely echoes in the poem, notably in the phrase 'the light randy slut' (line **42**).
2–5   describe the condition of the dog's coat.
6–10   the poet's exhortation to the sleeping bitch to get busy in the undergrowth.
8   the 'celtic mizzle' of the MacGreevy variant (see Appendix) suggests this is a Celtic Twilight (cf 'twilighters' in 'Recent Irish Poetry', *Disjecta*, 71).
14   the Twelve Pins of Connemara.
17–18   Clew Bay, Croagh Patrick and Blacksod Bay are in County

Mayo. Xanthic flowers in botany are those that have a tinge of yellow rather than cyan, but, in view of the bitch's 'think[ing] she is dying' (line **15**), SB may also have in mind Xanthos, the 'blond' horse of Achilles who predicted the death of the hero in Book 19 of *The Iliad*.

On the last Sunday in July (Garland Sunday) thousands of pilgrims, many of them barefoot, climb to the summit of Croagh Patrick (St Patrick's Mountain). SB referred to this area as the 'mountainous Joyce's country' and described 'Croagh Patrick standing up over everything, with an Arrarat [for Ararat] cloud always somewhere near the chapel on the summit' (SB to TM, 8.10.32, *LSB1*, 127). '[W]aned Hindu' suggests that, as the sun sets and the light on the mountain moves westward, Croagh Patrick is consumed with eastern darkness.

19 'laid' in the 1963 Grove Press *Poems in English* is presumably a printing error.

21 'able-bodied swans': cf. 'sad swans' (line **2** of 'Sanies I'). SB may have had Mallarmé's famous 'Swan' sonnet (cf. *Dream*, 148) somewhere in mind.

23 'hag': a firm spot in a bog.

24 cf. 'whales will come and shew themselves dancing at the sound of a trumpet' (*DN* *803; Burton, II, 116).

26 Harvey's notes register SB's sensitivity to the 'shame of animals who hide to die'; cf. SB's shame in lines **47** and **49** of 'Casket . . .', and in line **5** of 'Serena III'.

27 the sudden shift in location from the west of Ireland to the Dublin mountains may also entail a shift in the referential pronoun from the bitch to the poet's mother. (A similar shift from world to bitch occurs at the beginning of the poem.) SB told James Knowlson that his mother had taken him as a small boy to see this watershed at the Featherbed Pass on Glencullen where the river Liffey rises (UoR).

29 SB's nurse, Bridget ('Bibby') Bray, told the young Beckett old fairytales from her native County Meath [cf. line **49**] (Knowlson, 1996, 15–16).

30 'posses of larches', cf. line **13** of 'Sanies I', and 'Walking Out' (*MPTK*, 96).

32–3 'kindergartens of steeples', cf. Wicklow, 'a bloody little toy Kindergarten' and Dún Laoghaire full 'of steeples' (*MPTK*, 20). Cf.

'The long arms of the harbour [are] like an entreaty in the blue sea' (*MPTK*, 87), and 'Even the piers of the harbour can be distinguished, on very clear days, of the two harbours, tiny arms in the glassy sea outflung, known flat, seen raised' (*Mercier and Camier*, 81).

35–6   cf. line **6** of 'Alba'.

37–8   In SB's translation of René Crevel's 'Everyone thinks himself phoenix' in the September 1932 *This Quarter* is the sentence: 'The erotic element is always present between dog and master.' SB has moved here from Pan to 'panic'.

39   'Churchman': a brand of cigarettes. In a BBC broadcast of 8.3.66 Jack MacGowran reads 'packet of Churchman sodden'.

40   for the cairn, cf. O'Brien, 60.

45   'it is useless to close the eyes': apparently a rejection of the poetic upon which, by way of Rimbaud, SB had previously based his practice.

49   SB's 'Trueborn Jackeen' notes (TCD) pinpoint Meath as part of a historical 'heptarchy'. Cf. 'The stories of Mahood are ended' (*The Unnamable*, 59).

50–3   recall the photograph of SB praying at his mother's knee, which was taken as the source for Dorothy Elvery's painting 'Bedtime', reproduced in Beatrice Lady Glenavy's *Today We Will Only Gossip* and in the biographies by Bair and Cronin, and is alluded to early in *How It Is*.

Serena III

A copy of this poem is filed with a letter to MacGreevy dated 9 October 1933 (*LSB1*, 167–8). In the *POEMS* contents list it is entitled 'Gape at this pothook of beauty', amended to 'Cri de coeur 3'. Harvey's Dartmouth College notes tell us that 'Serena III' was inspired by SB's affection for Nuala Costello (but cf. note to line **17**). The poem, which begins in stasis and ends in headlong flight, contains a great deal of sexualised imagery and a tone of intense frustration that seems to apply indiscriminately to artistic creation and intimate personal relationships. It is the last of the journey poems in *EBOP*: starting from the Dublin quays it 'cavorts' (cf. line **16**) at breakneck speed south along the coast to Blackrock. MacGreevy's is the only known variant, although in late 1935 SB wrote to George Reavey, 'I have found MS of Serena III which you can have' (*LSB1*, 289). In a private communication Peter Selley of Sotheby's reports that a manuscript of 'Serena III', presumably the one which Reavey had owned, was sold at the Swann Galleries in New York on 4.6.81 for $1,000.

Variant opening, central section and conclusion to 'Serena III' (MacGreevy version)

1–2 'gape at this pothook of beauty on this palette / it is final if you like'.
3 'come down her' for 'or leave her'.
5–16 'on Butt Bridge take thought for yer buzzum / the mixed declension of those mammae / cock up thine arse there is no other word for it / cock her well up to the tulips that droop in the west / swoon upon the arch-gasometer / on Misery Hill brand-new pale-livid / oh a most ferocious west African baboon's / swoon on the lil puce / house of prayer / something Heart of Mary / the bull and Pool Beg that will never meet / not in this world'.
25 'your old heart' [cf. 'Enueg II'] for 'your hot heart'.

Notes

1 'fix': cf. 'A paragraph ought to fix her' (*Dream*, 49). For 'pot-hook of beauty' see William Hogarth's eulogy of the serpentine line in his *Analysis of Beauty* (1753; 'written with a view of fixing the fluctuating ideas of taste') and his self-portrait holding a palette inscribed with the 'line of beauty and grace'. 'Pothooks and hangers': ascending and descending letters, sometimes used to characterise a scrawl; 'Walking Out' has 'pot-hooks and hangers of civility' (*MPTK*, 98), while *Dream* has 'pothooks and hangers of peeping and creeping and instantaneity' (207). Compare Beckett's translation of Breton's 'bâtons d'écriture d'enfants' as 'pothooks' down-strokes' ('The Free Union', line **11**). A number of SB's early poems, especially the jettisoned ones, use 'beauty' as a motif (see the note to line **63** of 'Casket . . .'). The prepositional phrase in this line, 'on this palette', is the first of more than twenty such phrases in this relatively short poem.

This poem is mysteriously annotated 'James Barry' (the

eighteenth-century Irish painter) in the 'autograph' *EBOP* at the HRHRC, which may perhaps best be explained by reference to Barry's 'Adam and Eve' canvas (cf. 'paradise' in line **3**) in the National Gallery in Dublin. For photographs of the places referred to, see O'Brien, 62, 219, 222, 223.

4 cf. the 'jungle hymen' (line **48**) of 'Enueg I' and the 'scarred signaculum' of 'Dortmunder' (line **7**); a letter to Ruby Cohn of 17.7.75 connects the 'signaculum', or sign of the curve, to 'the Hogarthian sigma of beauty' (UoR). The velvety, voluptuous cataract of 'plush hymens' combines the idea of plug and push, to recall the 'eye suicide' of Rimbaud's 'Les Poètes de sept ans' in which the young poet sees stars from pressing his fists on his closed eyes (cf. SB to TM, 11.3.31, *LSB1*, 73), a recurrent motif in the 1933 story 'Echo's Bones'.

5 'Butt Bridge': over the Liffey; one of a number of Liffey bridges in *EBOP* (and also in *Dream* and *MPTK*). The original swivel steel bridge, erected in 1879 and named after Isaac Butt, leader of the Home Rule movement, was replaced by a concrete span bridge in 1932. Beckett may well have the earlier bridge in mind (cf. note to line **17**). Malone reminds himself that since he last went through his possessions, 'much water has passed beneath Butt Bridge, in both directions' (*Malone Dies*, 79).

6 the mixed declension in German combines masculine and feminine endings.

7 cf. *Dream*, 100, and 'cock up the other cheek' (from Matthew 5:39) of the parson in 'Draff' (*MPTK*, 178). For a similar exploitation of 'up' and 'down' (lines **8** and **18**), cf. 'Draff', almost certainly written very close in time to this poem.

9–10 'Misery Hill', by the basin of the Grand Canal, was so called because of the utter poverty in the area. In the 1930s, the gasometer was painted a deep red (O'Brien, 222). The revision removes the 'tulips [. . .] livid' connection which SB had favoured in 'Enueg I' and elsewhere.

11 'purple': an imperial or religious colour, but given a sexual context by SB in 'Dortmunder's' red spires and violet lamps and in the 'purple skirt', 'scarlet within and without' and 'long, puce jupe' of 'Spring Song', lines **48–51**. The word 'purple' here was 'puce' in the TM version.

13 ironically the missing word is 'Immaculate'; i.e. the Church of the Immaculate Heart of Mary on City Quay.

14 'Bull and Pool Beg': lighthouses on opposite sides of Dublin Bay where the Liffey meets the sea.

15 'in this world': by contrast with 'paradise' (line 3). Cf. 'this clonic earth', line 1 of 'Serena II', and 'this earth that is Purgatory' (*Disjecta*, 33).

17 SB crashed into the middle intersection of this 'terrible humped Victoria Bridge' *(MPTK*, 84) on Boxing Day, 1931, badly injuring Ethna MacCarthy. Thirty years later SB confessed to Lawrence Harvey that he would 'never forget the look in her father's eye afterwards' (Knowlson, 1996, 143). Harvey notes that the poem reflects SB's realisation that his relationship with Ethna would never prosper in the way he had long hoped; cf. the note to lines **21–2** below.

19 the ruins of the notorious Hell Fire Club, a site of historical, occult and prurient homosexual interest on the Killakee mountain, can be made out from Sandymount.

21–2 cf. note to 'Alba', line **9**. The woman taken in adultery is trivialised as 'girls taken strippin' (cf. SB's dreadful *jeu de mots* on the name of Nuala Costello – 'nu[e] à la côte à l'eau' – perhaps seen as a replacement for the unobtainable Ethna MacCarthy; Knowlson, 1996, 745 fn 85). Cf. also the 'finger of God' or 'digitus dei' *(MPTK*, 91).

23 the district of Booterstown, Russianised. For 'breakwind' cf. line **3** of 'Echo's Bones'.

24 cf. Nancy Cunard's gulls in her poem 'Parallax' (*LSB1*, 25; *LSB2*, 670), 'Enueg I' line **71** and the end of the novella 'The End'.

26 Blackrock, but also the Rock of Ages, as in a well-known hymn ('cleft for me').

27 cf. 'My sometime friend Belacqua' at the start of 'Ding-Dong' *(MPTK*, 31), moving 'constantly from place to place'.

Malacoda

This poem, begun shortly after the unexpected death of SB's father on 26 June 1933, did not assume its final form until October 1935, a month before publication. It is listed in the *POEMS* contents list as 'thrice he came', amended to 'The Undertaker's Man', which was still the title used by SB as late as 8.10.35, while he was expecting proofs, in a letter to TM saying it has been 'well changed, [with] the rest more or less as you know them' (*LSB1*, 283). There are no known variants. This poem and the two that follow it in *EBOP* may be regarded as successive attempts to come to terms with the death of the father Beckett loved deeply. Malacoda (literally 'Eviltail') is a demon in the fifth *bolgia* of the *Inferno* (Cantos XXI–XXII), 'a plausible rascally official, civil and submissive to superior authority, circumstantial and convincing in his lies' according to Sinclair (*Inf.*, 280). The undertaker in 'Draff' is called Mr Malacoda (*MPTK*, 174).

'Malacoda' was republished from *EBOP*, with 'Enueg II' and 'Dortmunder', in *transition* in 1936 (cf. *LSB1*, 334). Eugene Jolas reprinted it in his edited anthology *transition workshop* (New York: The Vanguard Press, Inc., 1949, 204).

Notes

3   'scutal', pertaining to a heraldic shield (cf. 'targe', line **21**), derives, via the Latin 'scutum' ('a shield'), from an Indo-Germanic root verb meaning 'to cover'.

3–4   We restore here the section break found in *EBOP*, which helps to foreground the three 'comings' (cf. Harvey, 108, 110). This break has not been respected in subsequent editions, in spite of the fact that it is present in *transition* (see headnote).

4   cf. 'Draff': 'Most respectfully desirous to measure [. . .] What could an inch or so possibly matter this way or that?' (*MPTK*, 174).

5   cf. Cain in 'Spring Song', line **52**, and *Dream*, 7, 130.

6   'incorruptible': in the *De Monarchia* (Book III, XV, 4) Dante distinguishes between the corruptible (body and soul considered together) and incorruptible (the soul). In *Inf.*, II.14, he describes Aeneas' father, Silvius, as going 'still subject to corruption' ('corrutibile ancora') to the underworld. The deceased Belacqua in the story 'Echo's Bones' (16; Dartmouth College typescript) is similarly 'incorruptible', and SB also uses the word in his 1934 review of 'Recent Irish Poetry' (*Disjecta*, 70). The Harvey notes at Dartmouth College show that SB and Harvey discussed the Dante associations on 30.4.62 (Knowlson, 1996, 498), which suggests there may be no need to suppose this an echo of the Funeral Service, e.g. 'so also is the resurrection of the dead. It is

sown in corruption; it is raised in incorruption' (1 Corinthians 16:42).

7 Malebranca (literally 'evil claw') is the name of the first demon addressed by Malacoda (*Inf.*, XXI, 37); cf. Scarmilion (line **23**; the driver of the hearse in 'Draff' is called 'Scarmiglione', *MPTK*, 176). '[K]nee-deep in the lilies' recalls Dean Inge's 'time of the lilies, Nature delivered from bondage' (*DN* *706).

10–11 Malacoda's 'signal' in the *Inferno* is a deafening fart (XXI, 139; cf. the 'uproarious endeavours' of his namesake in 'Draff'; *MPTK*, 169). This accounts for the heaviness of the air, which is also remarked upon by Dante (*Inf.*, IX, 82; XVI, 130; XXXI, 36). Cf. 'breaking [. . .] wind' in the third line of 'Echo's Bones'.

13 cf. 'Draff': 'she took herself off to prepare her weeds' (*MPTK*, 169).

12, 14 and **18** play on Beethoven's inscription over the fourth movement of the String Quartet in F major, op. 135: Der schwer gefaßte Entschluß. (Muß es sein?) – (Es muß sein!) (Sweet song of peace – must it be? It must be!). A favourite SB reference, found as late as in a 3.1.79 letter to Jocelyn Herbert (UoR).

16 'ungulata': cloven-hoofed animals; cf. 'Draff', *MPTK*, 174.

19 cf. 'Draff': 'The demon, quite unable to control his impatience to cover [. . .] so let the good man cover by all means' (*MPTK*, 175).

21 'targe': archaic word for shield.

22 'dog day[s]': traditionally a time of calamity associated with sultry weather, in *The Book of Common Prayer* extending from 6 July to August 17, close in time to William Beckett's death.

22 'glass': here the barometer ('Draff' leads one to suppose that the funeral of SB's father took place in good weather); in line **4** of 'Da Tagte Es' following, a mirror.

23 translates Dante's address to one of Malacoda's companions: 'Posa, posa, Scarmiglione!' (XXI, 105). In 'Draff', 'a strongly worded message [from the Smeraldina to the driver of the hearse, 'Scarmiglione'] exhorting him to temper full speed with due caution' is deliberately countermanded by Hairy Quin's instruction to 'Let her out [. . .] to the irreducible coefficient of safety' (*MPTK*, 176).

24 SB told Harvey (111, 149) that he had in mind a painting of a butterfly on a flower by Jan van Huysum. This painting has been identified as 'Flowers in a Terracotta Vase' in the National Gallery in London, which SB visited many times, although there is an equally splendid Van Huysum, with similar details, in the permanent collection of old masters at the Dulwich Picture Gallery, which SB also visited. The 'imago' is not only the mature butterfly, which the caterpillar turns into after metamorphosis, but also, as SB noted from Karin Stephen, *The Wish to Fall Ill*: 'Parent Imagos, fantastic creations reflecting the child's own intentions' (Psychology Notes, TCD MS 10971/7/4).

27–8 'all aboard [. . .] aye aye': cf. *Dream*, 204, 'Draff' (*MPTK*, 176), and the situation on the submarine at the end of the story 'Echo's Bones'.

Da Tagte Es

'Da Tagte Es' is annotated in SB's copy of *EBOP* at HRHRC: 'Walther von der Vogelweide?' SB quotes, in German, from a famous poem of Vogelweide's, without giving any source, in a letter of 14.3.34 to Arland Ussher (HRHRC); the quotation was probably taken from a footnote in J. G. Robertson's *History of German Literature*, which modernises Walther's Middle High German (123 fn 1); cf. F&F, 17. For 'Walther', see also 'The Calmative' (*The Expelled*, etc., 29) and *Stirrings Still* (*As the story was told*, 124). However, it seems more likely that the poem that SB was thinking of in writing 'Da Tagte Es' was Heinrich von Morungen's famous 'Tagelied', which he had also read in Robertson's *History*, and which ends each verse with the refrain 'dô tagte ez' (modernised as 'Da tagte es' [118 fn 3]). The Vogelweide quotation suggests that 'Da Tagte Es' must have been written in early 1934. The refrain from Morungen would more usually translate as 'it is daybreak' – the 'Tagelied' is an 'alba' – whereas here the sense is more 'it is the day', reflecting a shift from an erotic situation to the deathbed of a loved one. In this connection, see a letter that SB wrote to A. J. Leventhal, indicating that he had submitted the poem to the *Dublin Magazine*: '[Seumas O'Sullivan] has a quatrain of mine, due in the last awful issue, but perhaps he has smoked its indiscriminate application to death-bed and whoral foras' (7.8.35; not in *LSB1*). Cf. a letter to TM of 26.4.35 (not in *LSB1*): 'the *Dublin Magazine* is out, but my poem not in'.

It does not appear in the *POEMS* contents list, unless it is the

otherwise unknown poem 'Abundance of the Heart'. In a letter
of 7.8.35 to A. J. Leventhal (not in *LSB1*) SB refers to 'emotional
Vergreifen' (Ger: 'wrong notes'; very probably in relation to 'Da
Tagte Es'). The only known variant is a version in SB's own hand
for the *Great Book of Ireland* (reproduced in facsimile in *Irish
Studies Review*, no 1, Spring 1992, 11). This reverses the second and
third lines, leaving the rhyme scheme intact. Since SB's health
was in terminal decline and the manuscript contains a number
of false starts, this hardly constitutes an authoritative revision.
Nonetheless, it is very moving that he should have recalled the
poem in which he said farewell to his deceased father as his own
life was drawing to a close, and presumably this effectively settles
the issue of whether or not the 'death-bed' idea was dominant
over 'whoral foras' more than fifty years earlier (but see the notes
to lines 1 and 3 below).

Notes

1   among the 'surrogate goodbyes' which SB may have sought
to 'redeem' were the poem 'Malacoda' (at the time of writing 'Da
Tagte Es' still titled 'thrice he came' or 'The Undertaker's Man'),
which it echoes, and the two stories 'Draff' and 'Echo's Bones'
(the first shortly to appear in the 1934 Chatto and Windus *More
Pricks Than Kicks*, the second having been excluded from the
collection late in 1933). In both stories – but especially in 'Draff'
– Belacqua's fictional death is a kind of 'surrogate' for William
Beckett's in real life. Both stories make wild, 'Echo's Bones' very
wild, comedy out of heartbreak. The phrase 'surrogate adieu' in
a TM letter of 27.12.[34] (not in *LSB1*) is used by SB with reference
to the Sinclairs, whose daughter Peggy died a month earlier than
SB's father in 1933.
2   cf. Mallarmé's 'Brise marine': 'l'adieu suprême des mou-
choirs'; in *Dream* Mallarmé's poem also surfaces as 'the supreme
adieu' (3) and 'waved a Mallarmean farewell' (12), probably with
thoughts of another Mallarmé poem 'Adieu'. A different quotation
from 'Brise marine' is entered in the '*Sottisier*' *Notebook* (UoR MS
2901), and there is what seems to be a reference to Mallarmé's
poem in a letter to Barbara Bray of 16.2.78 (TCD).
3   cf. Thomas Moore's lyric (*Irish Melodies*) 'She is far from
the Land'. Moore's 'She' has been suppressed here, perhaps to

dislodge any potentially erotic implications. SB reuses the reference in 'The Expelled' (13). Compare 'sheets far from the lad' (*Finnegans Wake*, 395).

4   for 'the glass' cf. 'glass set fair' in 'Malacoda', line **22**; for 'unmisted' cf. final scene in Shakespeare's *King Lear*: 'Lend me a looking glass. / If that her breath will mist or stain the stone, / Why then she lives.' SB reuses the image in *Imagination Dead Imagine*: 'Hold a mirror to their lips, it mists' (*Texts for Nothing*, 89).

Echo's Bones

The title derives from Ovid (*DN* *1101). The poem was written after Charles Prentice of Chatto and Windus had rejected a story with the same title for inclusion in *MPTK* (letter of 13.11.33; UoR). In *Poems in English*, and subsequent Calder and Grove editions, the poem was followed by the date '1935', the year in which *EBOP* was published, as though this were the date of its composition, which makes it look like the most recent poem in the collection, whereas 'The Vulture', which appears at the head of the collection, was the last to be written. The handwritten version of the poem sent to TM (6.12.33, *LSB1*, 171) has the initial letter of each line capitalised. There is also a variant among the poems sent to *Poetry* (Chicago), now to be found among the MDZ papers. Peter Selley of Sotheby's has reported (private communication) the sale of an 8–line manuscript version of the poem on 14.9.78 in Hamilton, Ontario for 200 Canadian dollars. However this version, if accurately described (the autographed Chamfort addition to the collector Henry Wenning's copy of *Fin de Partie* has eight lines; see the headnote to 'Long after Chamfort'), is unknown to scholars. The HRHRC 'autograph' copy of *EBOP* is marked by SB: '"Echo's Bones were turned / to stone". / Ovid Metamorphoses?' (Lake *42, 30), although in this case it is a process of putrefaction that is so vividly imagined.

'Echo's Bones' was, very appropriately, the first poem in the running order of eleven poems (chosen from the two previous programmes of 8.3.66 and 24.11.66) in the BBC broadcast of 14.4.76 which formed part of a 70th-birthday tribute to SB, with readings by Jack MacGowran, who had died in 1973.

Variants

2   TM has 'rots' for 'falls'; MDZ has 'breaks'.
5   'worms' in MDZ.

Notes

1   cf. *Murphy* on the distinction between 'asylum' and 'exile' (48).
2   cf. Prospero: 'Our revels now are ended' (*The Tempest*, IV, i)
and the 'dying fall' of *Twelfth Night* (I, i).
3   the phrase 'without fear or favour' is used of the Alba in
MPTK (50; it replaces 'like a turdus' [from the notes to *The Waste
Land*] in *Dream*, 209), and again in the letter to Nuala Costello of
10.5.[34] (*LSB1*, 208).
4   cf. 'the gauntlet of tulips' in 'Sanies II', line 11. The image may
come from William Cooper's *Flagellation and the Flagellants*, but
cf. also 'gauntlope' in Fielding's *Tom Jones* (Book VII, chapter 11),
which SB was reading in November 1932 (*LSB1*, 139).

UNCOLLECTED EARLY POEMS FROM
THE LEVENTHAL PAPERS

At some point, probably in the middle of 1932, Beckett began the
process of collecting his poems together for a volume which was
originally to be entitled *POEMS*. The Leventhal collection at the
University of Texas at Austin includes a cover sheet, a contents
list (27 titles) and the text of 14 poems. Two of these ('Alba' and
'Enueg I') were included in *EBOP.* Most of the others are revised
versions of poems that had appeared in small magazines or, in
the case of 'Whoroscope', as a separate publication.

While it is impossible to determine the dates of Beckett's revisions of individual poems with any certainty, the order of titles in
the Leventhal contents list indicate these were carried out largely
between August 1932 and May 1933. But the difficulties which SB
experienced in deciding what to include and what to exclude
persisted. Eight months before George Reavey's plans for his new
'Europa Poets' series were finalised SB told A. J. Leventhal: 'My
poems are worthless' (28.7.34; not in *LSB1*). This may have been
the point at which he decided to jettison a number of poems,

although 'Moly' (later to be omitted from *EBOP*) was one of three poems sent to *Poetry* (Chicago) in November 1934 (*LSB1*, 230 ff.) and it remained one of the poems which SB thought of most highly. The final cull is perhaps most likely to have taken place closer to SB's collection acquiring a new title ([15.3.35]; *LSB1*, 264). Reavey's enterprising publishing spirit had sustained SB's hopes for a number of years, but how much he contributed to the decision-making process is not known, and SB's judgement must have been of paramount importance. It typifies SB's sense of how success might be achievable by way of Reavey that he should have mentioned to him 'my next book of poems' (23.2.37; *LSB1*, 455), and subsequently asked 'Will the E[uropean] L[iterary] B[ureau] publish <u>Poems in French & English</u>?' (22.4.[38]; *LSB1*, 618), as the first poems in French began to accumulate.

A number of the notes below demonstrate SB's earlier attempts to group disparately composed poems closer together, as if he were seeking in his work-in-progress to develop the 'through-composed' aspect so evident in *EBOP*.

The running order here is taken from the cover sheet, type-written with holograph corrections, in the Leventhal papers. The unrevised versions of seven of the poems appear in the same order in the Appendix.

Moly

Published as 'Yoke of Liberty' in *The European Caravan* (New York: Brewer, Warren and Putnam, 1931, 480; hereafter *EC*), but entitled 'Moly' in the Leventhal and Zabel versions (the latter being the copy text here). Harvey and Calder's *Poems 1930–1989* reproduce the text of the Leventhal version but under the original title (as it appears in *EC*, at least; *LSB1* index, 782, claims that 'Moly' was the 'initial title', albeit on no known grounds: SB to TM 18.10.32 [*LSB1*, 134] suggests otherwise, since it post-dates *EC* and refers to the poem as 'Moly'). 'Yoke of Liberty' alludes to Dante's *De Monarchia* (II.I). We publish the Zabel version, previously reprinted in *LSB1*, 231, since this appears to be later than Leventhal. Beckett had intended 'Moly', one of the few poems he commended in a letter to Thomas MacGreevy (18.10.1932, *LSB1*, 134), to open the *POEMS* collection. 'Moly' is, as Beckett noted, the 'antidote to Circe' (*DN* *712), the magical drug given to Odysseus by Hermes to protect him from the sorceress's charms. It occurs with another ancient magical potion, nepenthe, in 'Enueg I', and later Molloy imagines that Lousse's 'miserable molys' have poisoned him (53).

In a letter to TM of 9.10.31 SB told him: 'Seumas O'Sullivan wouldn't publish "the lips of her desire are grey". I sent it yesterday to *Everyman*. I can't remember whether I sent it to them before or not' (not in *LSB1*). It was probably also included in the 'stuff of mine – carmina quae legunt cacantes' [cf. 'carmen' in the TM variant text of 'Serena I'] sent to *transition* (*LSB1*, 94). At some point during conversations with Lawrence Harvey in 1962, SB underlined the importance of the poem by saying 'All the images are my own' (Harvey notes; cf. Harvey, 312–14). Given SB's continuing high estimation of the poem, it seems surprising that he should have omitted it from *EBOP*, unless of course he simply felt that, successful as it was as his own very personal expression, it did not fit with the other poems he had selected for that collection.

Variants

5   'she' (lower case) in *EC*; this is a typographical error.
11   'tamed and watchful sorrow' in *EC*; 'tamed watchful sorrow' in Leventhal, Harvey and Calder.

Notes

8   the subject of beauty is raised again in lines **40** and **63** of 'Casket . . .', in line **24** of 'it is high time lover', in line **1** of 'Tristesse Janale', in line **12** of 'Alba', in line **7** of 'Seats of Honour', in line **5** of 'Serena I', and in line **1** of 'Serena III'.
11   for 'sorrow': cf. lines **19** and **20** of 'To Be Sung Loud', lines **64** and **67** of 'Casket . . .', line **6** of 'To My Daughter', and 'Whoroscope's 'sorrowful cornea' (line **69**).

For Future Reference

First published in *transition*, 19–20, Spring–Summer, 1930, 342–3 (see Appendix). SB asked TM to send his own copy of *transition* so that the poem could be added to the ones that SB intended to show to Charles Prentice at Chatto (14.7.32; not in *LSB1*) – and subsequently revised for inclusion in *POEMS*. The *transition* version is republished in Harvey (299–301) and *Poems 1930–1989*. 'For Future Reference' records a dream of SB's about life at Portora (Harvey, 298). In *Dream* it is alluded to as 'the ducky diver' (68), recalling its boxing and diving imagery and the diver whose name (i.e. 'involuntary memory') it would serve no purpose to withhold (*PTD*, 32). Cf. SB to Barbara Bray in a letter of 16.8.63: 'I was champion boxer of Portora, only gave it up in TCD because I found I was getting more than I gave' (TCD).

'For Future Reference' was presumably one of the 'twice round pointed ones' ('Return to the Vestry' the other?) from SB's 'Central Lavatory' referred to by SB in a letter to TM of 25.8.[30] (*LSB1*, 43); for a little-known lavatorial squib written by SB in adolescence, see four lines from the poem in *LSB1*, 44; six lines from the 'poem' ('Come away, my love . . .') published in Knowlson 1996, 44, and the full 20-line version in Gerald Pakenham Stewart's *The Rough and the Smooth: an autobiography* (Waikanae, NZ: Heritage Press, 1994). (A privately recorded audiocassette of this, read by Patrick Magee, is in the Knowlson collection at UoR.)

Notes

1 Deirdre Bair identified Mr W. N. Tetley, the science and mathematics teacher at Portora, as the hated schoolmaster of the poem (32). She also said that he taught swimming, although Beckett told James Knowlson that nobody really took the boys for swimming (Interview 6, 22.4.89, Knowlson Archive, UoR).
2 the Russian composer Borodin(e) was a chemist by profession (cf. *Dream*, 210, and *MPTK*, 51). The spelling is either an attempt to make the composer sound more like a chemical element, or an attempt to approximate the correct Russian pronunciation.
4 cf. the cornices in Dante, *Purg.*, and the plans for *Murphy* in the early pages of the *'Whoroscope' Notebook*.
9 the punning 'dumb-bells' signal a transition from musical to boxing imagery. Cf. the boxing imagery in 'The Possessed' (*TCD: A College Miscellany* 37, 12 March 1931; *Disjecta*, 99–101), in the story 'Echo's Bones' ('So the battle raged . . .'; 13), and a letter to

Barbara Bray of 16.8.63 in which SB refers to his sometime boxing prowess.

11 'the hen's ovaries': cf. 'Whoroscope' and *Dream*, 192: the 'long poem'.

18 'incisors': cf. *Dream*, 86.

19 'brayed him': cf. *DN* *242, from Proverbs 27:22, and 'bray his heart', *Dream*, 4.

23–7 first occurrence of the diving board imagery, re-used in 'Spring Song' (line **15**), *Dream* (34), *Watt* (192), *Eleutheria* (118) and most famously in *Company* (10–11). SB told Anne Atik that it was a recurring dream for him (33).

35 cf. 'Moly' line **1**.

47 Harvey suggests that a Trinity friend of SB's who went into the Indian Civil Service was the model for this unflattering portrait (300). However, the photograph of Tetley in O'Brien also fits this description. Cf. note to 'cyanosed' for 'blood-faced' Tom in the revision of 'Casket . . .' (line **22**, indicating that both poems may have been revised at about the same time; cf. also *DN* *1020 and 'cyanosed' in *Dream* (62), 'Love and Lethe' (*MPTK*, 85), the story 'Echo's Bones' (22) and *Murphy* (102). '[B]lood-faced Tom' [Tommaso Masaccio] occurs in *Dream* (80).

49 cf. the 'foaming spit', in the other direction, of *Dream*, 136, and the 'foaming quarry' in line **17** of 'Spring Song'.

59 mention of Bruno may indicate that the poem was written as early as 1929 while Beckett was working on 'Dante...Bruno. Vico..Joyce'.

60 in *Dream*, suicides have already made their decision and it is into the water, from the bridge, of course, not the bank (27, 228).

68 probably with thoughts of W. B. Yeats's 'The Second Coming', combined with Heraclitus' dictum that no one can 'step down twice into the same stream' (Philosophy Notes, TCD MS 10967/24). The idea recurs in the short story 'Echo's Bones' (1), where a 'reborn' Belacqua in a way disproves it, in 'Le Monde et le Pantalon' (*Disjecta*, 128), and in 'The Expelled' (8).

75 reworks Verlaine's 'ma bouche est aride altérée' ('Chant d'amour brutal'). Cf. also the 'strange palate' of the revised version of 'Whoroscope' (line **68**), the 'bitter mouth' of line **6** of 'Spring Song', the 'palais de la bouche' of line **9** of 'Tristesse Janale' and *Dream*, 31.

To Be Sung Loud

'To Be Sung Loud' is a reworking of 'From the only Poet to a shining Whore (For Henry Crowder to Sing)' as published in *Henry-Music*, Hours Press, 1930, and republished in Harvey and *Poems 1930–1989*. The subtitle of the original composition in part explains the revised title. SB described 'From the only Poet . . .' as 'the Rahab tomfoolery', but Nancy Cunard's lover, Henry Crowder, for whom it was written, found it 'vey, vey bootiful and vey, vey fine in-deed' (SB to TM, ?17.7.30; *LSB1*, 25). The Hours Press published the poem set to Henry Crowder's music, so that the lineation adopted by Harvey and Calder is not evident. The phrases 'pearl brow' and 'dawn dusk' are not hyphenated in the Hours Press edition. There is a recent recording by Allan Harris of 'From the only Poet' included with Anthony Barnett's *Listening for Henry Crowder*. 'To Be Sung Loud' is published here, from the typescript in the Leventhal papers, for the first time.

'From the only Poet to a shining Whore' is given in the Appendix. The alterations are relatively minor but serve to tighten the beginning and ending of the poem.

Notes

1   Dante is the 'only Poet' of the original title and Rahab 'the shining Whore' who was spared when Jericho was destroyed (Joshua 2:1–21) because she had helped the Israelite spies to escape from the city. For Dante she is an example of justification by works rather than by faith and she appears appropriately in the Sphere of Venus (*Par.*, IX, 112–25). Rahab also made an appearance in 'Whoroscope' (holograph and Hours Press), although she was subsequently excised from the revised versions. The biblical and Dantesque imagery is given a distinctly erotic charge in the poem, the first half of which is addressed to the whore, the second to Dante's virginal inamorata Beatrice.

2–4   cf. the description of Rahab sparkling like a ray of sunlight in clear water (*Par.*, IX, 113–14) mixed with a recollection of Piccarda like a pearl on a white brow (*Par.*, III. 14). Beckett explained to Harvey that line 4 of 'From the only poet', 'pearl-brow dawn-dusk lover of the sky' was an image of 'the planet Venus as it appears against the background of the sun's light at dawn or dusk, light against light and visible only as a faint image of its real splendour' (306). In *DN* *1097 Beckett translates the nine lines from *Paradiso* III that describe Piccarda. This is the longest extant translation of Dante that Beckett made. Cf. the opening of 'Dante and the Lobster' where Belacqua, bored by Beatrice's explanation of the spots on the moon, is 'impatient to get on to Piccarda'. This imagery is here reworked to apply to Rahab rather than to the planet. The phrase 'moth of pearl' derives from 'mother of pearl' (cf. the 'pearl-brow' of *Dream*, 174). The Dante passage continued to intrigue, and also to perplex, SB much later in life, as is clear from a letter to Mary Manning Howe of 9.4.58 (HRHRC).

5   'My little whore!' Cf. *Dream*, 51, referring to the Syra-Cusa, and 'pute' in line **70** in 'Spring Song', also thinking of Lucia Joyce.

6–9   Rahab hid the Israelites in flax on her roof and the servants of the king of Jericho were sent on a wild goose chase to 'the fords of Jordan'; Rahab recalled the parting of the Red Sea and 'she bound a scarlet line in the window' as a sign that she was under the protection of Joshua (Joshua 2: 6–21).

11   cf. the 'Beatrice in the brothel' discussion of *Dream*, 102.

13   cf. 'bloodless nonchalance' (*Dream*, 80).

15–17   the three 'thou's, replacing a single 'you' in 'From the only Poet . . .', invite comparison with SB's practice in his version of Montale's 'Delta' and his translations from Eluard and Breton (q.v.), and with similar choices in 'Enueg II', in line **3** of 'it is high time lover', in line **25** of 'Text 3', and in line **39** of 'Spring Song'.

17   'pale fire': cf. Shakespeare, *Timon of Athens*, IV. iii. 438, and *Hamlet*, I. v. 90.

18   'pyre': cf. line **19** of 'it is high time lover'. For 'doubting', cf. line **75** of the revised 'Casket . . .'. Fire, flames and heat – usually with hellish associations, or in connection with desire rather than with the purifying fire of Dante – are frequently invoked in the early poems.

19   'sorrow': cf. line **11** of 'Moly', lines **64** and **67** of the revised 'Casket . . .', line **6** of 'To My Daughter', and 'Whoroscope', line **69**.

20   perhaps significantly, the final words of 'To Be Sung Loud' are 'my sorrows', in contrast to 'God's sorrow', whereas in 'From the only Poet . . .' the sorrow of God and the poet are both singular.

Casket of Pralinen for a Daughter of a Dissipated Mandarin

Originally published in *The European Caravan*, 1931 (476–8). Reprinted in Harvey and in *Poems 1930–1989*. Calder seems to have used Harvey as the copy text since he follows the section divisions in Harvey rather than in *EC*. The version given here, from the Leventhal papers, is published for the first time. The poem is addressed to the Smeraldina, whose father is known as the Mandarin in *Dream*, which may possibly suggest that this was the 'pome' sent to the real-life original of the Mandarin, 'Boss' Sinclair, although 'Whoroscope', published by the Hours Press, seems a more likely candidate (*LSB1*, 26; cf. the headnote to 'Whoroscope' below). It is an apology (of sorts) for the real events that are recorded as the 'disastrous Silvester' (New Year's Eve, 1929) in *Dream* (76–109), and which marked the effective end of SB's relationship with his cousin Peggy Sinclair, on whom the Smeraldina is modelled. The poem opens with the Smeraldina's mother addressing her distraught daughter on New Year's Day. It moves to a contemplation of Ewald Dülberg's painting of the Last Supper, which hung in the Sinclairs' drawing room in Kassel, before concluding in a lengthy appraisal of the poet's failure to find the right words to express 'the ingenuous fibres that suffer honestly' (**51–2**). 'Casket . . .' in its original form was presumably, with 'Hell Crane to Starling' and 'Text', one of the 'three turds from my Central Lavatory' which SB told TM that Jacob Bronowski had accepted for publication in the *European Caravan* (*LSB1*, 42), in which all three poems were published. Revisions were relatively heavy, although by no means so extensive as in the case of 'Hell Crane . . .' / 'To My Daughter' (q.v.), and left the general drift of the poem largely unaffected. The full text of the original version is given in the Appendix.

Notes

1   cf. the measuring in the late play *Catastrophe*.
2–3   recall Mozart's opera based on Beaumarchais's play *The Marriage of Figaro* where the elderly suitor, Bartholo, suddenly joins in with Rosine who has been singing: 'Wilt thou have me / Rosinette?'; Bartholo explains, 'It's Fanchonette in the song, but I sing Rosinette for fun and to make it fit in with us. Ha, ha! Good,

eh?' His song concludes: 'Though I may not look much catch by day / In the dark all cats are grey' (82). Cf. SB's *'Whoroscope' Notebook* extract from Mozart's score for *The Marriage of Figaro* and the words of Cherubino's Act 1 aria ' Non so più cosa son, cosa faccio' and Cherubino's Act II canzone 'Voi che sapete che cosa è amor'. SB, who was not generally fond of opera, attended a performance of *The Marriage of Figaro* in Dresden and wrote to MacGreevy that it was the first opera that he was 'sorry to have over' (16.2.37, *LSB1*, 446).

5 'Thyrsis': a personable shepherd in pastoral poetry from Virgil to Matthew Arnold.

7–10 cf. *Dream*, 55, for a more extended treatment of the Smeraldina's tears, and *Dream*, 106, for a discussion on the subject of soup. The phrase 'the first of the first' refers to New Year's Day.

11 Harvey identifies the gladiator with the dying gladiator in the Capitol museum in Rome (278), but no doubt SB also has an ironic eye to Byron's lines on the statue, 'Butcher'd to make a Roman holiday' (*Childe Harold's Pilgrimage*, Canto IV, stanza 141).

14 'Assumption' where we might expect 'Massacre'. Cf. the 1929 short story 'Assumption'. The Feast of the Holy Innocents falls on 28 December, close in time to the events of the poem.

16–35 refer to Ewald Dülberg's painting of the Last Supper, which is also described in *Dream* (77–80) The painting was lost in the war but a photograph of it is reproduced in *Images of Beckett* (Haynes and Knowlson, 60) and on the cover of Pilling's *A Companion to 'Dream of Fair to Middling Women'. Dream*, 77, describes the picture, including 'John the Divine' as 'the green egg'. In the poem Beckett identifies Christ (**17**), Judas (**21**), Doubting Thomas (**22**) and John (**28**).

20 'scrotum': cf. line **4** of 'it is high time lover'.

22 'cyanosed': in *Dream* (62), Belacqua has been reading Vasari before he looks at the Dülberg painting of the Last Supper, but 'blood-faced' / 'cyanosed' Tom seems to derive from Vasari's description of St Peter in *A Picture of St Peter*, which is thought to be Masaccio's self-portrait: 'St Peter in especial, in his efforts to get the money from the fish's body, has his face quite red from bending' (1. 268). Cf. also note to line **47** of 'For Future Reference', *DN* *1020 [one of a number of entries from section III ('The Intoxications') of Sir William Osler's 1892 book *The Principles and Practice* *of Medicine*, a source identified by Mark Nixon], and the 'cyanosis' of Mr Tough in 'Love and Lethe' (*MPTK*, 85).

24   cf. *Dream*, 80.

30   cf. the Polar Bear and his saliva in *Dream* (151, 209).

30–1   cf. *Dream*, 77, and Chamfort: 'Il faudrait avaler un crapaud tous les matins, pour ne trouver plus rien de dégoûtant le reste de la journée, quand on doit la passer dans le monde' (59). ('Swallow a toad in the morning and you will encounter nothing more disgusting the rest of the day when you have to spend it with people.') How well SB knew Chamfort this early remains in doubt; the Chamfort in his personal library was published in 1950, as noted below. There is a single unsourced entry from Chamfort in the *'Whoroscope' Notebook*, fol. 131.

36   for 'Mr Beckett' (not in original version) cf. *Dream*, 69, 141, 186.

38   for 'I want you to cinch up your song' cf. *Dream*, 134 ('cinched'). For 'song' cf. 'carmen' in TM and Aldington versions of 'Serena I'.

44   puns on 'hemistich', a half-line of verse. Cf. also the 'stitch anguish' of 'Return to the Vestry' (Appendix) and Bérard's 'hemistich neuralgia' (SB to TM, [?22.9.31], *LSB1*, 91).

47, 49, 54   cf. 'on Butt Bridge blush for shame', line **5** of 'Serena III'.

48   for 'dud' cf. the 'dud mystic' of *Dream*, 186.

56   'God's pain': cf. 'God's sorrow' in the concluding lines of 'To Be Sung Loud'.

59   'Abfahrt': departure (German).

60   'Platznehmen': take a seat (German); cf. *Dream*, 31.

63   for 'Beauty' see 'crouch of [. . .] beauty' in 'Moly', line **8**, where it occurs in connection with 'preys'; 'Text I', where it is associated with menstruation; 'Tristesse Janale', line **1**; 'Alba', line **12**; 'Serena I', line **5**; 'Serena III', line **1**; 'Seats of Honour', line **7**; and the 'scurf of beauty' in line **24** of 'it is high time lover'. For the turd cf. 'Whoroscope', line **104**; 'Love and Lethe' (*MPTK*, 87); and Nuala Costello's 'étron' of 27.2.34 (*LSB1*, 185).

63–9   Harvey and Calder run the *EC*'s 'Schluss!' and 'Oh Beauty' sections together to form one long section. In her billet doux the Smeraldina refers to 'the "thing" you wrot about my "beauty" (as *you* call it)' (*Dream*, 61). This may refer to 'Casket . . .'. The frequent use of the word in the early poems makes it almost impossible to tie down.

64 and 67 cf. 'sorrow' as in in 'Moly', line **11**; 'To Be Sung Loud', lines **19** and **20**; 'To My Daughter', line **6**; and 'Whoroscope's 'sorrowful cornea', line **69**.

67 cf. 'the very bowels of compassion' (*Dream*, 74).

70 cf. W. H. Drummond's *The Battle of Trafalgar*: 'Mourn, Albion, mourn, thy Nelson is no more'.

71–6 the famous compositor's error in Wordsworth's ode, 'Intimations of Immortality' (there is also a glancing allusion to Wordsworth's 'The Idiot Boy') – of 'sleep' for 'sheep' – is contrived to cast doubt on the possibility of a resurrection for Mantegna's foreshortened dead Christ (in the Brera, Milan). Beckett re-uses the allusion in *Murphy* where the dejected sheep in the Cockpit in Hyde Park make the compositor's error 'seem no longer a jibe at that most excellent man' (64). In the *EC* version Wordsworth is disguised as 'cockerup Willy the idiot boy', an allusion to his place of birth, Cockermouth; cf. 'cock up thy moon' in line **7** of 'Serena III', 'cocks me forth' in line **18** of 'Spring Song', 'cocking up your Old Testament snout' (*Dream*, 100), and 'cock up the other cheek' (from Matthew 5:39) of the parson in 'Draff' (*MPTK*, 178).

77–8 a 'bimbo' or baby, especially if unbaptised, might be expected to dwell in Limbo.

79 cf. the 'milk of human kindness' (*Macbeth* I. v).

81–2 cf. the Gadarene swine. Jesus cast out demons which entered a herd of pigs that rushed into the sea and drowned (Mark 5:11–13 and Luke 8:32–3).

84 'braut': bride in German (cf. *Dream*, 62 and 68; and also 40: 'She ceased to be bride of his soul'). The typescript reads 'Brussells', presumably an error, given that the 'joke' here, such as it is, is all too obvious, with or without a rogue spelling.

To My Daughter

First published as 'Hell Crane to Starling' in *The European Caravan*, 1931 (475–6); cf. the 'starlings' of *Dream*, 36. Reprinted in Harvey and in *Poems 1930–1989*. The Leventhal revision, 'To My Daughter', was first published in *SBT/A* 12 (see below). Although the original title alluded to Dante's *Inferno* (V, 40–51), where the starlings and cranes are emblematic of the adulterous love of Paolo and Francesca, the poem itself is populated by characters from the Old Testament. The revised title leads C. J. Ackerley to suggest that the poem may have been addressed to 'a loved one pregnant to another [*sic*], to whom she has returned' and proposes that this is Mary Manning, the Frica of *Dream* (*SBT/A*, 12, 69). Since Mary Manning's daughter, the poet Susan Howe, was born in 1937, and since the poem was probably revised sometime between August 1932 and April 1933 (and certainly well before the publication of *EBOP* in 1935), Ackerley's suggestion is clearly mistaken.

Although both the original and this revision can be read as poems *in persona* addressed by Lot to his daughter, the idea that there might be a more personal investment in the latter is difficult to resist. With more than 70 per cent of a short poem revised, it seems very likely that circumstances different from those which prompted the original (published in 1931) have occurred in the meanwhile. The very presence of Belacqua (line **6**) – dead in 'Yellow', revived in the jettisoned story 'Echo's Bones' – suggests a Beckettian thumbprint not readily visible in 'Hell Crane to Starling'. The subject of daughters (cf. 'the precious' in line **7** of the revised 'Casket . . .' and the 'putid pute' of line **70** of 'Spring Song') surfaces more than once in *Dream* (74, 84, 116), and in real life there were two daughters in particular, Peggy Sinclair (died 26 May 1933) and Lucia Joyce, with whom SB had been personally involved. The emergence (later in 1933) of Nuala Costello, a friend of Lucia's, as a potential partner may or may not be figured in the 'cantharides' of line **13** (see note below); 'my blear eyes' (line **1**) may or may not signal the ventriloquised presence of Joyce. All that can be said with any certainty of 'To My Daughter' is that the voice of the poem is closer to speakable speech than the exceptionally allusive 'Hell Crane to Starling'. The last line of this revision is perhaps an oblique underlining of the fact that very significant changes have wrought a strikingly different outcome, even if they obviously cannot now be reconstructed in precise detail.

The revised version excises the extrinsic references (for which see Harvey, 304 etc.) to focus more tightly on the whore Aholibah. 'Hell Crane to Starling' is printed in the Appendix.

The starting point for 'Hell Crane to Starling', and thus for 'To My Daughter', appears to have been SB's reading of Voltaire's *Lettres d'Amebad*, especially the thirteenth letter which includes many examples of scandalous behaviour in the Bible. SB marked these references in his Italian Bible. (Our thanks to Dirk van Hulle and Mark Nixon for making their researches in SB's private library available to us in this connection.)

1 and 2 in Ezekiel 23, Jerusalem is figured as a whore with the name Aholiba*h* (Ooliba in the *Lettres d'Amabed*). Zoar is the cave where Lot lay with his daughters (Genesis 19: 30–5, marked by SB 'L d'A'); the spelling of Zoar follows that of the King James English Bible. The proper names Oholiba and Tsoar (as found in 'Hell Crane to Starling') are the forms used in SB's Italian Bible. One of the many striking instances of how 'Hell Crane to Starling' and 'To My Daughter' differ from one another is that the latter uses the English forms of these names. Perhaps SB had Zoar in mind, as a Biblical place of drunkenness and lubricious behaviour, in adopting the Gaelic name for the Irish Free State in the title of his summer 1934 essay 'Censorship in the Saorstat' (*Disjecta*), but it is not possible to say whether this has any bearing on the date of 'To My Daughter'.

3 and 12 cf. Ezekiel 23:20: 'For she doted upon their paramours whose flesh is as the flesh of asses, and whose issue is like the issue of horses. Marginalia in SB's Italian Bible: 'Elle a recherché ceux qui ont le membre d'un âne, et déchargent comme des chevaux (L d'A)'. Cf. also *DN* *912: 'a generous mare insists on a great horse' (from Burton, III, 234, which concludes 'when her tail was cut off and mane shorn close [. . .] she was content to be covered by an ass'). Cf. also *Dream*, 23.

6 'child of my sorrow Belacqua': this replaces the Benoni figure ('Ben-Oni' is underlined in SB's Italian Bible; Genesis 35:18) of 'Hell Crane to Starling' but substitutes in his stead what the name means in Hebrew. SB's Teachers' Bible (still in his library at the time of his death) gives in a marginal gloss 'child of my sorrow' as the English equivalent; his copy of the *Sainte Bible*, which also remains in the library, has 'fils de ma douleur' within an explanatory parenthesis in the body of the text, as the King James version and the Italian Bible do not. (The name 'Bilha' [Bilhah in the King James version] in line 5 of 'Hell Crane to Starling' is also derived from Voltaire, cf. Genesis 35:22; the 'Bilha [. . .] Benoni' sequence reverses the order in which these figures are mentioned in Genesis.)

7   cf. Ezekiel 23:14: 'And that she increased her whoredoms: for when she saw men pourtrayed upon the wall, the images of the Chaldeans pourtrayed with vermilion'.

8   for 'glabrous cod' cf. *Dream*, 157, *DN* *454,*485, 'Hairy Quin' (who is bald) in *MPTK*, and the bald Lord Gall of the story 'Echo's Bones'. Issues of impotence and/or fertility are implied.

9   cf. Ezekiel 23:15: 'Girded with girdles upon their loins, exceeding in dyed attire upon their heads, all of them princes to look to, after the manner of the Babylonians of Chaldea, the land of their nativity'. Cf. the wall and the scarlet torches in 'Spring Song'.

13   'lepping' ('leaping'), the only Irishism to be retained from 'Hell Crane...', is also applied to the lobster in 'Dante and the Lobster' and to the unborn child in 'First Love' ; 'cantharides': Spanish fly, an aphrodisiac, cf. *DN* *460 and *893, and SB's letter to Nuala Costello (27.2.34, *LRB*, 186–7).

Text 1

First published as 'Text' in *The New Review*, II, April 1932, 57 (hereafter *NR*), and incorporated into *Dream*, 83. There are transcriptions of the *NR* version in Cohn's *The Comic Gamut* (in a letter of 24.4.62 [UoR] SB told Cohn 'I have no recollection of "Text"'), and in Harvey, and there is a 'corrected version' in Gontarski's edition of SB's *Collected Short Prose* (17). The source for many of the 'hard words', which at first sight may seem like Joycean neologisms, is the Mermaid edition of the plays of John Ford, edited by Havelock Ellis (cf. Pilling 1999b). SB's composition, a kind of prose poem, gives the borrowed terms a suggestive sexual flavour which they do not have in Ford.

Variants

1   *NR* begins 'Come come and cull me'; *NR* reads 'doublebed' (hyphenated in *Dream*).

3   *NR* has 'Kerry' for 'Wicklow'.

5 'newest news' in *NR*.

6 *NR* and *Dream* read 'rather' for 'liefer'.

7 *NR* and *Dream* read 'coalcave'.

8 *NR* 'goldy veins', *Dream* reads 'golden veins'.

10 *NR* 'beauty day'.

11 *NR* 'and struck'. The Leventhal typescript has a deletion 'xxxx' before 'struck' restoring the *Dream* version.

11–12 *NR* typos 'all of a galimaufry or a salady salmafundi' corrected in Gontarski.

14 *Dream* reads 'cuckooed' for 'cornuted'.

15 'toing' in *NR*; Harvey and Gontarski correct to 'toeing'; *NR* 'Taubchen': Cohn has 'Tabchen', Harvey 'Taübchen' and Gontarski 'Taubchen'; *NR* and *Dream* read 'padlock' for 'lock'.

16–17 *NR* 'before' for 'ere'; *NR* 'hope' for 'hopes'.

Notes

1 'cull': embrace (*The Broken Heart*, II, 1).

2 'cony', cf. 'cony-berry': a rabbit warren (*'Tis Pity She's a Whore* IV, 3); 'springal': young person (*The Broken Heart*, II, 1)

3 'twingle-twangler': 'hotch-potch of Scotch and Irish twingle-twangles', i.e. Gaelic harps (*Perkin Warbeck*, III, 2).

4 'week of redness': menstrual period. For other occurrences of the word 'beauty' in SB's poems see the note to line **63** of 'Casket . . .'.

6 'lust-be-lepered', cf. *'Tis Pity She's a Whore* IV, 3, and DN *65.

7 'puckfisted': a 'puck-fist' is an empty boaster in *Love's Sacrifice* (II, 1); 'coxcomb', a fool's cap, is also in *Love's Sacrifice*, III, 1; 'cave of coal with veins of gold', cf. 'I was ill-advised to dig for gold in a coalpit' (*Love's Sacrifice*, III, 1).

8 'potystick' : 'a slender rod of bone or steel, for cutting plaits of ruffs, cuffs, etc., after starching' according to Havelock Ellis's Mermaid edition of Ford (*Love's Sacrifice*, IV, 1); 'besom': a broom.

9 'hartshorn': Baker's ammonia (ammonium carbonate), a leavening ingredient; 'hartshorn', 'cowslip wine' and 'lettuce' are soporifics:

> You could not do a worse thing for your life.
> Why, if the nights seem tedious – take a wife:
> Or rather truly, if your point be rest,
> Lettuce and cowslip wine: *Probatum est.*

But talk with *Celsus*, *Celsus* will advise
Hartshorn, or something that shall close your eyes.
(Pope, *The First Satire of the Second Book of Horace Imitated*).

11 'gallimaufry': odds and ends, a hodgepodge (*'Tis Pity She's a Whore*, IV, 3).

12 'salmagundi': another word for hodgepodge, but also a sixteenth-century salad of cooked meat, seafood and vegetables, applied by SB to an attempt to clarify his confused sentiments in a letter to TM of 18.8.32; *LSB1*, 119; 'singly and single to bed': cf. 'thus singly I adventure to my bed' and 'Long since I vowed to live a single life' (*'Tis Pity She's a Whore*, II, 2 and I, 2).

13–14 'quab': an unfledged bird (*The Lover's Melancholy*, III, 3); 'cornuted': having horns, cuckolded, cf. *Dream*, 68 (*Love's Sacrifice*, IV, 1).

14 'landloper': wanderer or vagrant (*Perkin Warbeck*, V, 3); 'Täubchen': little dove (German, term of endearment).

16 'galligaskins': wide hose or breeches.

17 'go snacks': to share or divide (slang).

18 'clapdish and foreshop', cf. 'shut up your fore-shop [. . .] come, stop your clap-dish', an attempt to silence someone who is about to broadcast unpleasant truths (*Love's Sacrifice*, III, 1). A clap-dish was a wooden begging bowl with a lid that could be 'clapped' to attract attention.

Text 2

An untitled earlier version is published in *Dream* (21) in a 'rather unpleasant' letter where the poem is described as making itself in the depths of the closed eyes ('au fond des yeux clos le poème se fait'). It thus fits the criterion of 'blank unsighted kind of thing' as SB described 'Serena I' (13.[9.32], *LSB1*, 121). Cf. also Rimbaud's 'eye suicide' in 'Les Poètes de sept ans' (11.3.31, *LSB1*, 73). In a letter to Nuala Costello of 27.2.34 SB mentions 'the celebrated pelicans that really have a most charitable expression' (*LSB1*, 189). The contrast between pity and purity derives from Alfred du Musset's 'Allégorie de Pélican' ('Musset's prayer' in a letter to Mary Manning Howe of 22.5.37 [not in *LSB1*]), which Beckett drew on to describe 'At last I find . . .' as a 'Night of May hiccupsob' (*Dream*, 70), and the poem also references Baudelaire's sphinx ('l'égyptienne') in 'La Beauté'. There is a later, garbled version, probably recalled from memory, also untitled, in a letter to George Reavey of 9 January 1936 (*LSB1*, 296). The initial letter of each line is capitalised in this version and a final stop added. The Leventhal revision is published here for the first time.

Variants in Dream	Variants in Reavey
1 C'n'est au Pelican	Ce n'est pas au pélican
3 ni à l'Egyptienne	Ni à Marie
5 mais à ma Lucie	Mais à Lucie
6	Egyptienne oui et peaussière aussi
7 qui n'm'a pas guéri	(lines 7 and 8 are run together)
9 mais à Jude	(8) Et à Jude
10 dont j'ai adororé la dépouille	(9) Dont j'ai adororé la dépouille
11 qu'j'adresse la cause désespérée	(11) Qu'on dirait la mienne.

Notes

5–6   refer to St Lucy of Syracuse, patron saint of eye conditions, whose name is adapted as the Syra-Cusa in *Dream*, a character modelled on Lucia Joyce (cf. *DN* *774). Her description in the poem as 'peaussière' or skin-dresser may refer to St Lucy's condemnation by the Roman authorities to work as a prostitute and links her to Jude whose hide ('dépouille') the poet rather adores.
9–11   St Jude is the patron saint of lost causes. Line **11** also refers back to the Musset poem which contains the line 'les plus désespérés sont les chants les plus beaux'. Cf. *Dream*, 73: 'Lucy and Jude are kept going pretty well from dawn to dark', and *The Unnamable*, 77: 'their thoughts wander as they call on Jude'.
Reavey line 3   The allusion to Marie is unexplained, perhaps the 'Miss Cordon' to whom Beckett pays homage at the end of the 9.1.36 letter.

Text 3

First published as 'Text' in *The European Caravan*, 1931 (478–80), and reprinted in *The New Review* (I, Winter 1931–2, 338–9), with the addition of the word 'by' to line **54**: 'as they slouch by unnamed'. As Federman and Fletcher point out, this may have been a printer's error (11). Republished in Harvey, and in *Poems 1930–1989*. Harvey and Calder both follow *NR* and include the word 'by'. Harvey and Calder also introduce a section break between lines **55** and **56** of 'Text', which was not present in the *EC* version. The poem is a lengthy disquisition on compassion and the lack of it, which commences with a recollection of Marcel's cook Françoise, detours to the Old Testament and culminates in a bravura recollection of one of Dante's 'rare movements of compassion' (cf. *MPTK*, 11). 'Text' was very probably written while Beckett was working on his *Proust* for Chatto and Windus, and may well be the poem referred to (in a phrase that synecdochally elides the Baron de Charlus and Proust, and the opening section for the entire poem) as the 'baronial nausea' (7.8.30, *LSB1*, 40). There is a tendency to give a rather more personal coloration to the material in the revised version, in which almost half the lines of the original are altered. It is published here for the first time. The original version may be found in the Appendix.

Notes

1–2 as well as being a call for mercy, 'miserere' is also another name for 'ileus' or 'ileac passion', a morbid condition due to intestinal obstruction characterised by complete constipation, with griping pains in the abdomen and, in the later stages, by vomiting of faecal matter. Dante's first spoken word in the *Inferno* (I, 65) is 'Miserere'.

2 SB confuses the 'ilium', or upper part of the bony pelvis which forms the receptacle for the head of the femurs at the hipjoint, with 'ileus'.

3 i.e. as in setting the tuning for an orchestra. Cf. the same phrase in *Dream*, 65, where it is applied to 'the waning lust affair', which is part of the subject matter here.

5–14 retell the story of Françoise's indifference (cf. *Proust, PTD*, 20) to the sufferings of the kitchen maid in *Remembrance of Things Past* (I, 133). Swann had dubbed the girl 'Giotto's Charity' because of her resemblance to the Virtue on the Arena chapel in Padua (I, 87). Marcel is especially keen on asparagus (I, 131).

14 Leventhal's 'teeth her' has been corrected here.

17 'calabash': a bottle gourd, here describing the breasts or 'milch mammae' on which the infant sucks. The word 'buxom' is reflected in numerous instances of the word 'fat' (line 3 of 'Serena II'; the 'fat queen' and 'fat boy' of 'Spring Song', etc.). The phrase 'take a good pull' is in *Dream* (36, 62, 63).

18 'Is it not a mercy': echoed in *Dream*, 26.

19 'mammae': cf. 'Serena III', line 6.

20 the Alba applies this Spanish term of endearment and/or disdain to Belacqua in *Dream*, 233.

21 cf. the Wife of Bath's motto, *amor vincit omnia* (love conquers all) in the *Canterbury Tales*. SB's version is repeated in the short story *Echo's Bones* (18).

22 quotes Psalm 51, verse 15.

25 cf. 'Hast thou eyes of flesh? Or seest thou as man seeth?' (Job 10: 4). SB remembered he had used the phrase 'in an old poem 30 years ago' in a letter of 15.5.59 (HRHRC) to Richard Seaver – it appears in their joint translation of 'The Expelled' (11) – and he used it again in his own translations of *The Lost Ones* (*Texts for Nothing*, 109) and *Ill Seen Ill Said* (*Company*, etc., 59)

31 cf., of Behemoth, 'He moveth his tale like a cedar' and 'His bones are as strong pieces of brass' (Job 40:17 and 18).

34 alludes to Dante's mother's dream in Boccaccio's *Trattatello in laude di Dante*. She 'dreamt that she was giving birth to a child who, feeding himself on laurel berries, became a shepherd and then transformed himself into a peacock' (Caselli, 17). Boccaccio explains that the peacock is an allegory of the *Divine Comedy*: the beauty of Dante's journey is like the beauty of the peacock's feathers; the awful cry of the peacock is like Dante's voice berating sinners living and dead; the dirty feet of the peacock support the bird just as it is Dante's use of the vulgar language which renders his story apt for contemporary minds. SB applies the dirty feet metaphor to Joyce's language in *Work in Progress*: 'Boccaccio did not jeer at the "*piedi sozzi*" of the peacock that Signora Aligheri dreamed about' (*Disjecta*, 19).

35 Asdente, the soothsaying poor cobbler of Parma, shares the fourth *bolgia* of the Inferno with Tiresias and his daughter Manto (cf. *Inf.*, XX, 118–20, *Disjecta*, 125, and an entry in the '*Whoroscope*' *Notebook*).

36–7 cf. 'il pianto delli occhi / le natiche bagnava per lo fesso' ('the tears from the eyes bathed the buttocks at the cleft', *Inf.*, XX, 23–4). The image recurs in *All That Fall* (*Complete Dramatic Works*, 191). These are the lines which provoke Dante's own tears and Virgil's stern rejoinder (XX, 28).

39 cf. 'Text 2' (Ce n'est au Pélican) and Musset's 'Allégorie de Pélican'.

42 'quick tip losers' refers to a joke prevalent in Dublin at the time and the belief that premature circumcision leads to inversion. 'Take a tip from me – as the Jew said to the Rabbi' (Harvey, 293 and 297); cf. 'Home Olga''s 'tip of a friendly yiddophile' (line 6), and SB later objecting that Seumas O'Sullivan had 'circumcised' the poem 'Cascando' for the *Dublin Magazine*. The phrase 'and be made happy for ever' is adapted from the Kempis entry in *DN**579.

43 i.e. Tiresias, who twice changed sex by striking copulating snakes with his staff. 'Bode' is an archaic imperative meaning 'prophesy'. Jove compensated Tiresias with the gift of premonition after Juno blinded him for his answer to the question whether sex was more enjoyable for men or women (cf. lines **42–50**).

50 'ratio at peroration', i.e. the ratio of conclusion to argument in classical rhetoric: at one-to-ten it is in the same proportion as the pleasure to be derived from sex by men and women (see above).

51–60 are a lyrical reworking of another of Dante's 'rare movements of compassion' ('Dante and the Lobster') in Canto III of the *Inferno* (see especially lines 49–50, 67–9 and 124–6).

61 another Old Testament whore, used by the prophet Hosea to personify Jerusalem (cf. Rahab in 'To Be Sung Loud' and, more particularly, Aholiba in 'To My Daughter'). SB marked the relevant passage (Osea 1:2) '*Lettres d'Amabed*' in his Italian Bible, indicating Voltaire as his source. The words Lo-Ruhama (Italian spelling) and Ruhama are underlined at Osea 1:6 and 2:1 in SB's Italian Bible. The name Lo-Ruhama means 'not having obtained mercy' and, as Dirk van Hulle and Mark Nixon point out, the Dantean 'pity is quick with death' is foreshadowed in Hosea 1:6–7: 'Call her name Lo-ruhamah: for I will no more have mercy upon the house of Israel; but I will utterly take them away. But I will have mercy upon the house of Judah [. . .]'.

62 in 'Dante and the Lobster' Belacqua ponders how to translate Dante's 'qui vive la pietà quando è ben morta', i.e. 'there piety lives when pity is dead' (*Inf.*, XX, 28). This may have been the phrase SB and TM were looking for in connection with the latter's poem 'Fragments' (*LSB1*, 35).

63   Dante's pity is a presumption. Virgil accuses Dante of being 'sciocchi' or 'witless' since his 'passion comporta' subjects divine counsel to his own will (*Inf.*, 20, 27 and 30). Cf., for another instance of the word 'pity', 'Casket . . .', **68**.

63–5   cf. Cain banished to the moon 'seared with the first stigma of God's pity, that an outcast might not die quickly' (*MPTK*, 5, drawing on Genesis 4:1–15 and *Par.*, 2, 51). Cain is also invoked in line **52** of 'Spring Song' (q.v.). The spelling error in the Leventhal typescript, 'Presumptious' for 'Presumptuous', has been corrected here.

Whoroscope

There are four extant variants: the holograph on Hotel Bristol paper (HRHRC) (Holo); the version published by Nancy Cunard's Hours Press (HP) and subsequently republished by Harvey and Calder; a copy of the Hours Press publication with SB's holograph corrections in the collection of Georges Belmont (GB) and the revised version in the Leventhal papers in Texas, which includes the Belmont corrections and further revisions (AJL). The Hours Press edition was published in 1930, Beckett having won the prize for best poem on the subject of time in fewer than 100 lines. The holograph runs to 123 lines, with indications for running lines together so as to bring the number within the stipulated length. The AJL version splits many of the lines that have been run together in the HP publication and has 118 lines.

Long after publication SB claimed in a letter to 'Bien chère Nancy [Cunard]': 'I knew nothing about it till afternoon of last day of entry, wrote first half before dinner, had a guzzle of salad and Chambertin at the Cochon de Lait, went back to the Ecole and finished it about three in the morning. Then walked down to the Rue Guénégaud and put it in your box. That's how it was and them were the days.' (26.1.59, Lake, *8, 12; cf. line **27** of the revised text adopted here). Some scholars have doubted this version of events, but with the number of lines the major discrepancy between the Hours Press and holograph versions, it is at least plausible, although the appearance of the sonnet 'At last I find . . .', with its echo of the short story 'Assumption', on the reverse of the last sheet of the Hotel Bristol holograph (HRHRC) may suggest that 'Whoroscope' was written earlier, rather than overnight on 14–15 June 1930.

The title of the poem (used again by SB to give a name to the notebook in which he made plans for the novel *Murphy*; UoR MS 3000) puns on 'whore' (the supposed lubriciousness of Queen Christina of Sweden) and the 'horoscope' successfully kept at bay by Descartes's simple expedient of trying to keep his birthdays a secret. It is a poem on the subject of Time – as it had to be (the Hours Press advertisement for their prize stipulated this, leaving competitors free to adopt an attitude 'for or against') – and SB's numerous anachronisms effectively straddle both the negative and the positive aspects of the topic.

The poem is unique in SB's *oeuvre* as his only attempt at writing a sustained Browningesque poem *in persona*. It is presumably the 'long poem [. . .] waiting to be written about hens and eggs' of *Dream*, 192, which SB had of course already written. Beckett told Harvey that the details of Descartes' life, on which the poem is built, derived from Adrien Baillet's *La Vie de Monsieur Descartes*, (Paris, 1691) and Charles Adam's and Paul Tannery's multivolume *Oeuvres de Descartes* (Paris, 1897–1910). In a 1992 essay, however, Francis Doherty demonstrated that most of the material could be sourced to J. P. Mahaffy's *Descartes*, a popular introduction to the life and works of the philosopher, which contains material, judgements and turns of phrase not to be found in de Baillet. More recently, Matthew Feldman has shown that Beckett may well have read Descartes in Debricon's *Descartes: Choix de textes*, which was still in SB's library at his death. These discoveries lend a little weight to the proposition that the poem was written at the last moment, as do the post-publication revisions.

The revised version for the projected *POEMS* from the Leventhal collection is published here for the first time as representing SB's last, best thoughts on the poem. Indeed, in an inscription on Leventhal's copy of the Hours Press 'Whoroscope' SB wrote: 'un mauvais poème à celui qui comprend que les mauvais poèmes ne sont pas précisément les derniers' ('a bad poem for him who understands that bad poems are not exactly the last', with the implication, perhaps, that bad poems can always be improved), quoted in James Knowlson, *Samuel Beckett: an exhibition* (*37, 30).

In a letter to TM of 9.10.31 (not in *LSB1*) SB told him: '[Francis] Stuart said he liked Whoroscope'. It is not known whether it was the 'pome' sent to 'Boss' Sinclair in Kassel (TM letter of ?17.7.30; *LSB1*, 26), around the time 'Whoroscope' was printed (cf. the notes to 'Casket . . .' above), but it was certainly sent to 'the Penman' [Joyce] (TM letter of *c.*18 to 25.7.30; *LSB1*, 32), perhaps as a kind of peace offering after the good relations between the two men had been affected by issues surrounding Joyce's daughter Lucia.

The last section of 'Whoroscope' as published by the Hours Press (beginning 'Are you ripe at last') was read by A. J. Leventhal in a Third Programme broadcast 'Samuel Beckett: Poet and Pessimist' (30.4.57), the text of which was subsequently published in *The Listener*, LVII (9.5.57), 746–7 (F&F *3006, *1299; [307], 180).

'Whoroscope' was the first item in the running order for the BBC broadcast 'Poems by Samuel Beckett' (8.3.66; the BBC Written Archives at Caversham contain a memorandum relative to this broadcast dated 8.11.65), followed by 'Enueg I'; 'Serena II'; 'Malacoda'; 'Alba'; 'Cascando'; 'Saint-Lô'; 'my way is in the sand . . .'; 'what would I do . . .; and 'I would like . . .' (qq.v). It was the sixth selection for the BBC re-run on 14.4.76, which also included 'Serena II', 'Alba', 'Saint-Lô', 'what would I do . . .' and 'I would like . . .' from the original programme.

Variants

The well-known Hours Press version of 'Whoroscope' is given in full in the Appendix, together with the notes added at Richard Aldington and Nancy Cunard's request. We print here for the first time the Leventhal (AJL) typescript version, which seems to be later than the unnumbered Hours Press copy corrected by hand by SB, and many years later inscribed by him 'pour / Georges et Josée [Belmont] / affectueusement / Sam /Paris avril 66' (Knowlson Collection, UoR, JEK A/3/68). This corrected and inscribed copy is designated GB in the notes below. In what follows 'holo' designates the holograph HRHRC version.

7   'vile old': holo.

9   'ferryman': GB. In holo line **9** is expanded to four lines, the last three of which are deleted: 'The way a boatswain would be / The prince and his charger, the charging pretender of Brigadier General Lindberg [*sic*] / Equilibrium imperilled'. In GB the line ends: 'a clockwork hare'.

13   'ovaries': holo; 'ova': GB.

18–19   holo has annotation to indicate line merge. 'Gassendi's' is a superscript addition in holo over cancelled 'the'; 'crystalline': GB.

20   line break after 'all' in holo, with annotation to indicate line merge.

22   'To think he was my own brother, / Peter the Bruiser', with annotation to indicate line merge. 'Battling Peter': GB.

23   'syllogism': holo.

27–8   two lines in holo, with annotation to indicate line merge. Capital at start of second line in holo. GB indicates the restoration of two lines.

29–30   as single line in previous versions; cf. *LSB2*, 660.

32   'squinty': holo; 'doty' in holo and GB.

34   in holo line break between 'fruit of' and 'a house-and-parlour', with annotation to indicate line merge.

37   'Her little flayed epidermis / and her scarlet tonsils,': holo, with annotation to indicate line merge.

38   'one': superscript addition to holo.

39   'lashed': holo, with a superscript addition of 'stagnant' before 'murky'.

40   full stop after 'murky blood': holo and GB; a new line in GB.

41   'Blood!': holo.

42   'Oh Harvey beloved': holo; 'Oh Harvey sir': GB.

43–5   holo has 'How' and 'the many in the few' as separate line, with annotation to indicate line merge; 'the many and the few': GB, replacing the deleted 'the many in the few' at the start of the line above.

46–7   holo (line **41**) has line break after 'came', with annotation to indicate line merge.

48   'What is that?': holo.

51   'A wind of evil': holo, with 'my despair of ease' marked to be moved up a line.

52–3   'sharp spires': holo [cf. 'the red spire of sanctuary' in line **2** of 'Dortmunder']. Two lines in holo, with annotation to indicate line merge.

53   'douce': GB.

54   comma replaces the colon found in holo.

55   three suspension points in holo.

56   'Kip of Christ, hatch it!': holo, with deletion of 'God' and substitution of 'Christ'; '(hatch it curse you!)' : GB.

58–9   '(Jesuitasters, please copy).': holo.

60   three lines in holo (with addition, 'What am I saying. The gentle canvas', to the right of the text): 'So on with the silk hose / Over the knitted / And the morbid leather', but with annotations to indicate they should be merged into one line; 'worsted': GB.

61   GB also ends with a comma.

62   two lines in holo, with annotation to indicate line merge.

63   'farewell for a space': holo, which has three lines here, with line breaks after 'space' and 'key'. In the holo the key is first 'red', then 'purple', and finally 'yellow'.

67   line break after 'touched' in holo; 'nares throb to': GB.

68   'throne / of the faecal inlet': holo; 'throne of the strange palate': GB.

69   'and the eyes by its zig-zags': holo; 'and the sorrowful cornea': GB.

73–80   holo: five lines extended to eight with annotations to show where lines merge, and with additional line breaks after 'Beaune', 'far', and 'lively'. The holo originally read 'eat him + drink him', with corrections reversing the verbs and capitalising the first but not the second 'him'. GB [at the foot of page 3] reads: 'Thus it, as it has been asserted with rapid reverence / we eat Him bread / and drink Him wine, / Him personally / it is simply that he has the knack / that he has mastered the art of jigging [line deleted] / as far from his Jigging Self or as near [line deleted] / as the Orphists [line deleted]'. At the foot of page 2 of GB: 'of jigging as near to his jigging Doppelganger [*sic*], / or as far from same, /

and as sad or as lively [AJL: 'gay'] / as the atomic frequencies of these species require [line deleted, and replaced by 'as required by atomic tempo of species'].

82 'In the name of': holo, with 'me' as a superscript addition, and with no question mark at the end of the line; 'For the love of': GB.

83 'Guzzle of cave-phantoms': holo; 'gorge': GB.

85 'Moses': holo; '(her love is crucified)' on separate line in holo, with annotation to merge lines.

86 comma also removed in GB.

87 'the pale ['abusive' in a superscript addition] parakeet,' in holo, where it is given a line to itself, with the next line marked to be moved up to join it.

88 'No I believe I assure you' [cf. lines 21 and 29 of 'Enueg II']; comma also added in GB.

89 line also added in GB.

92 'The coy old frôleur': holo; 'The coy lecher!': GB [cf. 'the lecherous laypriest' of line 6 of 'Return to the Vestry'].

93–5 holo reads: 'Tolling + legging [deleted] He tolle'd and legge'd / and put on [deleted] buttoned on his ['Christ Jesus' deleted] redemptorist waistcoat. / Anyhow [deleted] However, let it pass.'; 'a redemptorist cardigan': GB.

96 comma also added in GB.

98 'if I were': holo; 'supposing': GB.

100 'that's': holo.

101 'the lonely petal of a high bright rose': holo.

102–5 holo reads: 'Are you ripe at last, / my slim pale double-breasted turd? / How rich she smells, / this abortion of a fledgling?', with the last phrase corrected from the deleted 'the feathery abortion'; GB lacks an exclamation mark in the final line, and reads: 'Art thou'.

106 'I will eat her': holo; 'I will eat it': GB.

107 'yoke' and 'feathers': holo; 'down': GB.

108–13 holo reads: 'Then I will rise and move moving / to [the Swedish brothel toward the: deleted] ward Rahab [cf. 'To Be Sung Loud' / 'From the only Poet . . .'] of the snows, / the murdering matinal pope-confessed Amazon / Christina the [illegible word deleted] ripper.'

110–13 GB [foot of page 4] reads: 'to the whore [replacing

'toward Rahab', deleted] of the snows, / the homicidal harpy, / [two words deleted] the pope the puke he bleached her soul [cf. *MPTK*, 90]; SB seems to have originally thought of the lines as running something like 'she paged the pope the puke to bleach her soul / her hands are red with sunrise [last word replacing deleted 'break'] / Christina the ripper. / Do you know her?'
115 'bitter steps': holo, replacing the deleted words 'bitter blood'.
116 no suspension points in holo.

Notes

At the suggestion of Richard Aldington, Beckett himself provided notes for the Hours Press edition, reprinted by Harvey and Calder but omitted by Nancy Cunard when she reproduced the poem in her memoir *These Were The Hours* (118–22). In a letter from Paris of 18.1.[30] to Allen Lane of John Lane/The Bodley Head Ltd. in London, Nancy Cunard told him of a 'very surprising find and, author willing, I am going to do it, with notes, as it is very allusive and condensed, by itself, pamphlet form' (UoR Publishers' Archive); cf. also *LSB1*, 28. Beckett did not include notes in the AJL revision.
SB's notes are given in the Appendix with the Hours Press version of the poem.
7 'penny Copernican': in the predecimal currency a penny was often referred to as a copper (cf. line **25**); 'lead-swinging': another pun on Galileo's pendulum and time-wasting; 'son of a sutler': Descartes described Voët thus; a sutler was a provisions merchant to the army.
8–10 an image of relative motion from Descartes' *Principles*. Descartes argued contra Galileo that the earth does not move but is moved. Beckett uses the image in *Dream* (134) and most elaborately in *Molloy*: 'I who loved the image of old Geulincx, dead young, who left me free, on the black boat of Ulysses, to crawl toward the East, along the deck' (*Molloy*, 50). 'That's not moving, that's *moving*' (cf. 'move moving' in line **90** of the published text) restates Descartes' disagreement in Galileo's own *sotto voce* reservation at the moment of his recantation '*eppur si muove*'; cf. Chas in 'A Wet Night' (*MPTK*, 45): "'The poem moves, eppure'" (cf. *Dream*, 203).

13   Descartes famously liked his eggs semi-hatched. Cf. *Dream* (192): 'There is a long poem [. . .] waiting to be written about hens and eggs', and the letter of 27.2.34 to Nuala Costello (*LSB1*, 189). Note the pun on prostitute/prosciutto.

17–21   Descartes' work on the avalanche (Mahaffy, 34), and Gassendi's on the parhelia or false suns, observed at Rome on 20 March 1629 (Mahaffy, 53–4), are here combined in a poetic metaphor to evoke the memory of the three mathematicians. The avalanche and the suns establish the white and red contrast that will colour the poem, as Harvey's white and red corpuscles, bread and wine, Christ's body and blood and finally, the Swedish snow and the letting of Descartes' own blood.

18   'come now': cf. line **63** of 'Text 3'.

22–6   as Doherty points out, there is an anachronism in drawing on the French slang *brétailleur* (a rowdy, rough and disorderly person) for Descartes' brother's punning soubriquet, since the term was not used before 1752. The replacement of 'syllogism' by 'premise' allows for another mild pun, since Descartes' dispute with his brother over his inheritance involved property. Mahaffy reports that Descartes attributed his early love of war to 'a certain animal heat in his liver, which cooled down in the course of time' (20). Descartes sat in his 'airing cupboard', *le poêle*, in October and November 1619 and experienced his 'night of dreams', which led eventually to the publication of his *Method*. However, it was not until many years later, in 1640, that he actually considered it necessary to join battle with the Jesuits (Mahaffy, 83). 'Jesuitaster' is a Mahaffyism.

30   Hals's portrait of Descartes is not thought to have survived, but was probably painted just before Descartes departure for Sweden to the court of Queen Christina.

34–41   Descartes' daughter died aged 5. Details of Descartes' liaison are unknown but it is thought to have been with a servant ('house and parlour' maid). 'Foetus' alludes to Descartes' *De Homine et de Foetu* in which Descartes develops a theory of the circulation of the blood similar to William Harvey's (Mahaffy, 62).

51–65   the substitution of Ancona for Loretto, which is the place Descartes actually visited, may be explained by the proximity of two entries in the *'Dream' Notebook*: 'The Ancona Madonna shedding beads by clockwork' and 'Mary runs a holy house / a little holy house in brick / lighter than air / tired of Nazareth / sacked at Loretto' (*DN* *20 and 21).

51 'A gale of evil' blends an allusion to the 'impetuous' wind that whirls Descartes about in the first of the three dreams which cause him to ask himself what path he should follow in life (Baillet), and to Dante (cf. 'driven by a wind, like the accidiosi' in a letter of [?17.7.30], apparently confusing Cantos V and VII of the *Inferno*; *LSB1*, 25).

60 cf. 'In Holland he affected plain black cloth, though always adhering to the use of silk hose' (Doherty, 40). The phrase 'Au plaisir' is used with reference to Belacqua in 'Yellow', *MPTK*, 156.

66–80 'Descartes' answer to Arnauld insists firmly on the principle that all our senses are modifications of touch – a doctrine asserted plainly by Aristotle'. Mahaffy (118–19) explains: 'If this be so, then it must be the surface and the surface only, of the elements, which produces on our minds the sensations of bread and wine.'

67 'nares': nostrils. The 'sweet air' is from 'l'aere dolce' (Dante, *Inf.*, VII, 122; cf. *'Whoroscope'* Notebook).

68 'strange palate': cf. note to line **75** of 'For Future Reference'.

82–3 Mahaffy discusses Francis Bacon's use of 'phantoms of the cave' in the *Novum Organum* to describe the characteristic errors which vary from individual to individual, arising from culture rather than nature (Doherty, 42).

85 Schurman learnt Hebrew to read the Old Testament in the original. The irony of this devout Protestant adopting the 'touching motto' of St Ignatius Loyola, the founder of the Jesuits, 'amor meus crucifixus est', as she took her vow of virginity must have appealed to Beckett (Mahaffy, 85).

86 'Leider! Leider!': 'Alas! Alas!' (German); cf. *Dream*, 95.

91–4 line **91** combines Descartes' famous 'cogito ergo sum' with St Augustine's 'si enim fallor, sum' from near the beginning of *The City of God*, while line **93** plays on the turning point in Augustine's life, when hearing children recite 'tolle, legge' ('take up and read' (*Confessions*, 8. 12, 28–3) he turned to Romans 13:14 and reformed his life. Line **94** is exuberantly anachronistic. The cardigan was not invented until the 1850s and the Redemptorist order was founded in 1732.

95–101 after Descartes had attempted to prove the existence of

God by the logic of his *Method* he produced an analogy 'in case this proof should be considered too abstract' that 'we are created by ourselves, or by our parents, or by some other less perfect than God'. Beckett disparages the second of these options. Line **98**: Hedberg (1972, 30) parses 'concierge' – a central figure in the poetics of 'Tristesse Janale' (q.v.) and in 'Le Concentrisme'– as a 'hermaphrodite' pun on French slang 'con' (cunt) and 'cierge' (prick). Line **102** may recall Dante's vision of Heaven as a Celestial Rose (*Par.*, XXX–XXXII); the word 'petal' translates 'foglia' (*Par.*, XXXII, 15).

99   'Joachim' presumably refers to the mystical Trinitarian philosopher Joachim of Fiore (*c.*1135–1202), in whose writings the Son figures as Grace, the Father as Law and the Holy Ghost as Spiritual Understanding.

106   the use of a fishfork parodies disputes about the stage in an egg's gestation when it becomes meat and so is not to be eaten on Friday (Hedberg, 1972, 30).

109–13   while Descartes was at the Swedish court (1648–50), Christina was still a Protestant. She was not formally converted to Catholicism until December 1654 and her conversion was not made public until November 1655. On 23 December that year, she went to Rome where the Pope confirmed her in his own name, Alexandra, after hearing her confession. Two years later she earned the epithet 'murdering' when she had her former lover, the Marquis Monaldeschi, killed. All these events happened after Descartes' death. In the poem, it is as if, at the hour of his death, he foresees the future for this 'whore of the snows', so that the poem really does justify its punning title. Line **112** is quoted (from SB's unpublished revision of his poem!) by Ruby Tough in 'Love and Lethe' (*MPTK*, 90).

114   Mahaffy gives Descartes' actual words 'Messieurs, épargnez le sang français!' (136).

115–16   pun on 'Perron': Descartes' title 'Seigneur du Perron' (Mahaffy, 9) and a flight of stairs in front of a building.

117–18   this image of escaping death as a rebirth alludes to the legend that Descartes kept his birthday a secret to prevent his horoscope being cast. Cf. the TM letter of 8.10.35 regarding Jung: 'He insists on patients having their horoscopes cast!' (*LSB1*, 282; 285–6 fn 7).

Tristesse Janale

'Tristesse Janale' is unpublished. It is given in the Leventhal Contents list as 'Lamentation Janale', corrected by hand to 'Tristesse Janale', also the title on the typescript. It is set out in sonnet form but with a rogue fifth line after the opening quatrain. The fourth line reads 'Qui sabres ma détresse en sections coniques,' and the fifth line of the typescript ('Qui centres mes désirs d'un trait antithétique.'), which is set out on its own between the two quatrains of the octave, reads like a variant, as though SB was undecided about which line to choose. The editors have selected SB's fifth line for line 4 in this edition partly because of its echo of 'Le Concentrisme' (see below), partly because of the fuller rhyme with 'bilitique', and partly because it makes explicit the notion of desire which underpins the poem.

In November 1930 SB gave a spoof lecture on the life and works of the fictitious poet Jean du Chas ('Le Concentrisme'; *Disjecta*, 35–42). SB told TM (14.11.30; *LSB1*, 55): '[I] wrote his poetry myself and that amused me for a couple of days.' Du Chas reappears as a character in *Dream* (first mentioned on page 11, he completes a line of Racine's on page 144 and recites a poem, not his own, at the Frica's party (211; and 'A Wet Night', *MPTK*, 68), but in the spoof lecture is said to have adopted the concierge as the aesthetic cornerstone of all his work (*Disjecta*, 36). Hedberg proposes that this is a hybridised version of French slang for the cunt and the cock, which may help to account for the development of a series of antithetical pairings (cf. Du Chas's work as a '*reductio ad obscenum*'; *Disjecta*, 42) in the poem. These antithetical pairings may be intended to operate in dynamic tension with 'Conjoined' in the last line of the sonnet 'At last I find . . .'. (Cf., in this connection, the 'Bouddha biconvexe' of *Disjecta*, 42, the 'succulent bivalve' of *DN* *639, the 'succulent oysters' – compare the 'huîtres' of the 'Le Concentrisme' lecture – of the story 'Echo's Bones', 17, and the 'oyster kisses' of *DN* *922, *Dream*, 17, *Murphy*, 75, German Diaries 13.11.36, and *Malone Dies*, 91).

The poem seems to have been influenced by the many sonnets of Baudelaire and Mallarmé, for both of whom it is the preferred form.

Notes

Title   cf. the 'Janal, trinal agile monster of Divinity: Time' (*Proust*; *PTD*, 35). Janus was the two-headed Roman god looking back to the old year and forward to the new (hence January). He was also the god of doors, very aptly for Du Chas in doorman mode, as imagined in 'Le Concentrisme'.

2   'chose' is overtyped with a capital replacing lower case; 'kanti-enne' lower case. 'Le Concentrisme' mentions 'la Chose de Kant' (*Disjecta*, 42), whose 'Thing in Itself' SB refers to in an August 1930 letter to TM (*LSB1*, 43). The phrase 'icone bilitique' alludes to Pierre Louÿs's supposedly Greek heroine Bilitis (an inspiration for a famous group of melodies by Debussy), who, as a very different kind of Thing in Herself, here becomes iconic of the bisexual or 'Sapphic' subtext of the poem. There is a reference to Bilitis in *Dream* (162).

3   the forgetful virgins brought insufficient oil for their lamps (Matthew 25:6).

5   for 'carquois' cf. 'carquois', meaning quiver, in Baudelaire's sonnet 'La Mort des artistes'; for 'flèches de Télèphe' cf. *Proust* (*PTD*, 11).

6   SB's typescript omits the acute accent required for 'Corrélatif'.

7   cf. 'gouffre interdit de nos sondes' (from Baudelaire's sonnet 'Le Balcon'), quoted in *Proust* (*PTD*, 31), and the 'gouffre des murmures' of line 6 of 'que ferais-je . . .' (q.v.).

8   SB quotes this line in *Dream* (22), Belacqua's French friend 'Lucien' quoting it back to him at the end of his letter ('really a rather unpleasant letter', *Dream*, 19). His letter also includes 'Text 2'/'C'n'est au Pélican' (q.v.).

9–10   presumably 'Mallarméene' (cf. *Dream*, 39) because 'palais' (which means both palace and palate; cf. the last line of 'For Future Reference') has been adopted from the phrase 'le palais de cette étrange bouche' in Mallarmé's 'La Négresse'. In *DN**412 SB describes Mallarmé as 'Un Baudelaire coupé en morceaux', a description presumably deriving from *DN**411, a note taken from Mario Praz, who is himself quoting Sainte-Beuve.

13   cf. 'lacustrines [lake-dwellers] & troglodytes [cave-dwellers]', *DN**657, from Nordau, 198.

Spring Song

'Spring Song' is a dream poem written in the spring of 1932, at about the time that Beckett was translating Rimbaud's 'Le Bateau ivre', and also trying to bring his novel *Dream of Fair to Middling Women* to some kind of conclusion. The title is possibly an allusion to Mendelssohn's 'Spring Song', the thirtieth of the forty-eight piano pieces which make up his 'Songs Without Words' (Book V, op. 62, no 6 in A major), a very popular piece with pianists of all abilities since its publication in 1842. Either Mendelssohn's equally famous and popular 'On Wings of Song' or Keats's 'Ode to a Nightingale', or most probably both, are reduced to 'on the usual wings' in 'What A Misfortune', as Thelma's thoughts turn to her forthcoming honeymoon in Galway (*MPTK*, 118). As in 'Sanies II', which was also written at about this time, a troubled sexuality prevails. While the subject matter of the short story 'Ding-Dong', which was probably written a few months after 'Spring Song', is very different, not only the title of the story, but also some peculiarities of phrasing, notably 'the just and the unjust' *(MPTK*, 38), echo the poem. 'Spring Song' is published here for the first time, and it is difficult to believe it gave Beckett much satisfaction.

'Spring Song' is perhaps SB at his most obscure, employing coded motifs which only he himself could ever have understood. This said, there seems little doubt that all three of the 'fair to middling women' of *Dream* are lurking somewhere in it, together with women of a less fair to middling reputation. SB is presumably attempting to turn the Freudian idea of a 'family romance' into a decidedly unromantic series of either real or imagined encounters with 'death-bed and whoral foras' (letter to A. J. Leventhal of 7.8.35; not in *LSB1*), and appears to be trying to splice this kind of material together with his own modern version of ancient Greek tragedy, with imaginary siblings ('the beacon my sister's'; line 22) playing alongside such real people as Lucia Joyce, 'that putid pute of a daughter of mine' (line 70), the 'Anna Livia' or 'Amnisty Ann' of *Work in Progress* (*Finnegans Wake*, 207). However, the welter of literary reference and wild ideas 'throttle[s]' (line 80) a mind active and alert whilst actually asleep, supplying it with a 'bolster' in lieu of anything more restful, comfortable, or fit for purpose. Like Malone writing some sixteen years later, the 'I' and its projections are 'being given [. . .] birth to into death' (*Malone Dies*, 114). Adrift in a sea of confusion, this drunken boat (much like Rimbaud's) is unable to 'cast all over and moor', leaving 'nothing but death to be desired' (*Dream*, 3), other desires having been entertained, and quite possibly acted upon, but not resolved.

'Spring Song' may have been in SB's mind when he sent Samuel Putnam, editor of *The New Review*, 'the latest, positively the latest hallucinations' (28.6.32; *LSB1* 108), the prose poem 'Text' – extracted from *Dream* – having been published in the previous and, as it turned out, final edition of the magazine (publication date being given as 'April 1932'). In his preface to George Reavey's *Faust's Metamorphoses*, 'Foreword to a Sunken Continent' (The New Review Editions, 1932, 7–9), Putnam writes: 'Beckett is the closest of the ['three or four young after-Joyce Irishmen who have some significance and some promise to offer'], perhaps as yet too close, to Joyce; but then, he sees a task for himself in poetry which Joyce has left untouched, – the task perhaps of expressing, as Rimbaud expressed, passionate nihilism, and transcendental vision at one and the same time' (7–8, *LSB1*, 108–9). In the letter of 28.6.32 SB thanks Putnam for 'nice things in [your] preface' to Reevey [for Reavey] vowing 'I will get over J J ere I die. Yes-sir' (*LSB1*, 108). The acrostic poem 'Home Olga', also written in mid-1932, is more obviously about Joyce and, like 'Spring Song', is something of an attempt on SB's part to get beyond him, or at least to liberate himself from Joyce's influence, and to speak in his own voice.

'Spring Song' was, with the unknown 'Alba 2' and 'Happy Land' ('Sanies II'), referred to in Charles Prentice's letter to SB (27.7.32), which speaks of the 'beauty and terror of "Spring Song"' (UoR; cf. *LSB1*, 113 and 116 fn17). SB had hoped to be in a position to include 'For Future Reference' with them (letter to TM of 14.7.32, not in *LSB1*). Presumably most, or all, of these poems were in due course put before Edgell Rickword at Wishart (letter to TM of 30.8.32, not in *LSB1*), SB's ultimately fruitless enquiries on their behalf having apparently begun with the Hogarth Press (*LSB1*, 111).

Variants

The only known text of 'Spring Song' that differs from the Leventhal typescript printed here (AJL) was faxed shortly before his death in 2002 by the bookseller Alan Clodd to James Knowlson, and is headed 'Georges Belmont's copy' in the Knowlson Collection at UoR (GB below). Belmont's incomplete text (64 lines), which also lacks some material (three line-ends in the 'Cain' section of the poem) which failed to survive the faxing process, can probably best be presumed, on the basis of what is omitted and added in AJL, an earlier unrevised version. Line numbers below refer to AJL.

3   not in GB.

4   lines **3–4** in GB read: 'I shall shriek that in German with / limp hands and shriek that at her'.

10   'die ganze' is repeated in GB.

15   'do nip' in GB.

18   'forth' in GB; 'algor' is an addition to AJL.

23   'bright speck suddenly' in GB.

28   three suspension points in GB.

32   'a silver fizz of angels' in GB.

36   'and suddenly' in GB.

38   'fang of her tongue' in GB.

52   'Cain nonchalant bowed' in GB.

63   'yet dripping from' in GB.

Notes

1   the river in *Inf.*, VIII, first mentioned in VII, 106, that separates the circles of upper Hell, where sins of weakness are punished, from the deeper Hell of wilful sin. It is guarded by Phlegyas, the spirit of intemperate anger, and a fitting guardian spirit for 'Spring Song'. If 'shrieked' in German, Styx might suggest *stich*, a sting, and *stichelei*, jibe, taunt.

6   this is the first of several echoes of SB's translation of 'Drunken Boat': 'Pumping over the blues in sudden stains' for Rimbaud's 'teignant tout à coup les bleuités' (literally 'suddenly dyeing the bluenesses', line 27). The 'bloated angels' of line **59** recall 'I am bloated with the stagnant fumes of acrid loving' ('L'âcre amour m'a gonflé de torpeurs enivrantes', 'Drunken Boat', line **91**). Bab-

bo 'reeking for a bloodslide' (line **61**) recalls '. . . reeking and free in a fume of purple spray' ('Libre, fumant, monté de brumes violettes', 'Drunken Boat', line **73**) and 'The calm sea disembowelled in waterslides' ('Des écroulements d'eaux au milieu des bonaces', 'Drunken Boat', line **51**). Rimbaud's 'eye suicide' is also recalled (see note to line **46** below) and, perhaps, the 'petits caillots de marne rousse' ('little clots of red marl'; cf. the late 'tittle-tattle' squib) of the third *Les stupra* sonnet in the 'loud clot' of line **73** (cf. line **30** of the TM version of 'Serena II' in the Appendix).

7 cf. 'Ich habe Heute die ganze Nacht gehasst (Bismarck)' (*DN* *1089): 'the whole night ("the livelong night") hated'. Bismarck was a chronic insomniac. (Cf. also 'la nuit noire pleine de haines' ('les joues rouges', line **12**).

11 music is frequently a metaphor for sex, especially sex with a prostitute, in early Beckett, most notably in *Murphy* (e.g. 'music, music, music', 147) but also, significantly, in 'Alba' and 'Dortmunder' and in the reworking of 'From the only Poet to a shining Whore' as 'To Be Sung Loud'; cf. also 'cadence', line **30**, and, as the poem draws to a close, 'now the music is over the loud music' (line **87**).

13 'stirabout': 'porridge' (Irish).

14 cf. the 'feet in marmalade' of 'Sanies II' and the 'ruined feet' of 'Enueg I' (line **16**) and *Dream* (8, 129–132 and 237). SB is probably thinking not only of the painful hammer-toe removed later that year (Knowlson, 1996, 166), but also of the shoes worn a size too small in emulation of James Joyce. Cf. also: 'all this livelong way' ('Sanies I', line **1**); the asthmatic in 'Yellow' who sleeps '[d]uring the day, the livelong day . . .' (*MPTK*, 153), and twice in 'Three Novels': 'And yet how often I have implored night to fall, all the livelong day, with all my feeble strength and how often day to break, all the livelong night', and '[. . .] all that livelong time when there was nothing for it but to get to the end [. . .]' (*Malone Dies*, 47; *The Unnamable*, 86).

15 cf. the 'windy prow' of *Dream*, 134. Belacqua leans over the rail of the boat that is bringing him home to Ireland ('after a very dark night in Altona') and raises his eyes to the beacons (cf. line **22**). The 'silver fizz of angels from her scabs' in the Belmont version also recalls 'the seethe of flowers, the silver fizz of flowers, scored by the prow' in the *Dream* passage.

17 cf. 'victory' in line **12** of 'To Be Sung Loud' and 'foaming' in line **49** of 'For Future Reference'.

18 'algor': Latin, coldness; 'rigor' recurs in line **78** and again in 'The Calmative' (*The Expelled*, etc., 27). Cf. 'the shingle that sweats already for the algor of Bilitis' (*Dream*, 84, cf. 73, 162).

19–20 cf. 'smoke more fruit / the old heart . . .' of 'Enueg II', the 'thud of the old plunger' in 'Cascando', and Belacqua's 'bitch of a heart [which] knocks hell out of his bosom three or four nights in the week' (*Dream*, 73; cf. the 'palpitations' mentioned in a letter to TM of 18.10.32; *LSB1*, 136). In *Dream* this is a watery passage ('drowns not in ken of shore'; 'He dared to go off the deep end with his shadowy love and he watered by daily littles . . .'; 'down the drain' and 'deathsweat'), adapting material from St Augustine.

21 The familiar address to Anna Livia Plurabelle, but cf. also note to line **72** for a possible reference to Anne Hathaway and the 'prying into the family life of a great man'.

23 in 'Walking Out' Belacqua hears 'with a pang' the first corncrake of the season, '[w]ith a pang, because he had not yet heard the first cuckoo,' (*MPTK*, 103); cf. also 'the pangs of light began on the foothills' ('Draff', *MPTK*, 173). 'presto': quick, swift (Italian). Swift appears under one of his pen names as 'little fat Presto' in 'Fingal' (*MPTK*, 26). Dante meets Medusa in Canto IX of the *Inferno*, shortly after crossing the Styx. The nurse who starts out Miranda in 'Yellow' ends up 'a granite Medusa' when, having forgotten herself and giggled at Belacqua's long toe, she fails to get his poor joke at the expense of her Scots accent (*MPTK*, 160). Zaborovna Privet in the short story 'Echo's Bones' (6) tosses back 'the hissing vipers of her hair' and turns into 'this Gorgon!'; cf. 'a slush of vigilant gulls' in line **71** of 'Enueg I'.

25 cf. 'Alba', line **13**: 'the tempest of emblems'.

29 cf. the 'royal hulk' of 'Dortmunder' but it is also applied, indirectly, to the Alba as the 'derelict daughter of kings' (*Dream*, 54; cf. also 'royal', 177).

30 cf. 'The lips of her desire are grey' in 'Moly' / 'Yoke of Liberty'. Line **57** conflates this opening line with the 'pitiful crescent' of its close in the phrase 'the cresset the grey jaws the rictus'. Cf. 'her grey throat' later in the poem, 'the stress of her hour' in 'Serena II', line **14**, and the 'affable rictus' in *MPTK*, 176.

32 cf. the 'grey shoals of angels' (spirits of the dead) in the short story 'Echo's Bones' (2), and, perhaps, the 'noirs séraphins' of Musset's 'Allégorie du Pélican', a familiar point of reference for Beckett at this time. Cf. also 'scratching off the scabs of lust' (*Dream*, 73).

35 'stuprum': pollution by lust, rape; hence 'stuprum of biding', the violation of tarrying too long in the brothel. Cf. '<u>Stuprum</u>: illicita virginis defloratio', i.e. the illicit deflowering of a virgin (*DN* *433) and 'the stuprum and illicit defloration, the raptus, frankly violentiae . . .' which the Smeraldina-Rima commits on Belacqua (*Dream*, 114). Cf. also Rimbaud's adoption of the term for his *Les Stupra* sonnets. For 'biding', cf. *Dream* (26, 74) and 'Sanies I', line **37**.

39 cf. 'Enueg II', lines **21** and **29**. SB seems to have understood the Grock tag 'Nicht möglich', used in *Dream* and *MPTK*, as meaning something like 'I assure you'. For the slightly antiquated 'thee' cf. the note to lines **15–17** of 'To Be Sung Loud'.

40 'sordes': the foul matter that collects on the teeth and tongue in low fevers ; cf. also the 'clot of sordes' (*Dream*, 85).

41 singular of *rendez-vous*, correctly 'rends-toi' as in *Dream* where the Alba looks forward to her 'rends-toi' with Jem Higgins (151; cf. 32); cf. also 'The spot I'll seek if the hour you'll find' (*Finnegans Wake*, 215).

43 the first of several references to Aeschylus' *Agamemnon* where (in the Philip Vellacott translation) a stage direction (90) reads: '*The palace doors open, revealing* Clytemnestra. *At her feet* Agamemnon *lies dead, in a silver bath, and wrapped in a voluminous purple robe. On his body lies* Cassandra, *also dead.*' Line **45** echoes Cassandra's 'There is a smell of murder. The walls drip with blood' (88) and 'inviolate carrion' (line **61**) echoes the accusation of the Chorus against Clytemnestra, 'Spirit of hate,' of '[s]tanding like crow on carrion' over the dead body of Agamemnon (93) who was murdered in his bath (cf. line **63**). (line **69**). The Syra-Cusa is identified with Clytemnestra (*Dream*, 50).

46 cf. 'like Job – I made a covenant with my eyes' (*DN**884, based on Burton III, 196; from Job 31:1). The notion of voluntary blindness is developed in the following lines, which combine the eye-suicide of Rimbaud's 'Les Poètes de sept ans' with St Bernard's 'shine in jewels and stink in conditions:/ have purple robes and a torn conscience' (*DN* *857, from Burton, III, 98). The trope is revised at the end of the poem in the line: 'quiet your eyes brother blind them on her grey throat'. Cf. SB's description later that year of 'Serena I' as 'a blank unsighted kind of thing' (?13.9.32, *LSB1*, 121).

50   cf. *Dream*, 45, 136 for this exclamation.

55   a very similar line occurs in *Dream*, 130. In 'Draff': 'That was what [the undertaker] was there for, that was what he was paid for' (*MPTK*, 175), while in *Dream*, 220 listening is 'not what [the Professor of Bullscrit and Comparative Ovoidology] was paid for'. In 'Dante and the Lobster' Cain is 'fallen and branded, seared with the first stigma of God's pity, that an outcast might not die quickly'.

56   a passage in *Dream* (129–30) has much in common with this section of 'Spring Song' and completes the phrase: 'unjust'; cf. *Purg.*, XVI, 75: 'Lume v'e dato a bene ed malizia' ('light is given on good and evil'). Cf. also 'Ding-Dong', *MPTK*, 38.

57   Belacqua, 'the prognathous Commendatore', grinds his 'bicuspids in a rictus' (*Dream*, 84), and the features of the Frica, 'as though the hand of an unattractive ravisher were knotted in her chevelure, were all set at half-cock and locked in a rictus' (215). In 'Draff' Hairy Quin shrinks away from the 'affable rictus' of Scarmiglione (*MPTK*, 176). Cf. also 'A rictus of cruel malignity lit up greyly their old bony faces' (Joyce, *A Portrait of the Artist as a Young Man*, 149).

61   'babbo': colloquial Italian: 'daddy'. Lucia and Giorgio called Joyce 'babbo'.

63   Agamemnon, dead in his bath, proves the truth of St Augustine's observation: 'The Greek bath drives sadness from the mind' (*DN* *178; *Confessions*, 9, 12, cf. *Dream*, 86).

67   an ovariotomy is a surgical incision in the ovary.

69   cf. 'klepsydra', from Burnet (*Greek Philosophy*, 72), underlined in the TCD Philosophy Notes. The clepsydra is an ancient Greek water-clock.

70   'putid': 'now rare: stinking, rotten' (*OED*). Beckett found the word in Burton: 'putid songsters and their *carmina quae legunt cacantes*' ('poems which are read shitting', *DN* *727). The Smeraldina is a 'lil pute' (*Dream*, 84), obviously almost a reflex in SB's mind when it comes to fathers describing daughters. Rahab, the shining whore, is 'Puttanina mia' ('From the only Poet to a shining Whore'); cf. 'puttanina', of 'the Syra-Cusa' (i.e. Lucia Joyce), in *Dream*, 51.

72 'Grisild': a Beckettian variant of the patient Griselda of Boc-caccio's final story in the *Decameron* and Chaucer's *Clerk's Tale*. Griselda is sorely tried by her husband who pretends he has had their children killed. There is a whiff of incest in the dénoue-ment when he presents their missing daughter as his future wife. 'Princess [. . .] of Denmark' elides Griselda's patience with Ham-let's indecisiveness. Both references tie in with allusions to Joyce whose daughter, Lucia, was the model for Issy in *Finnegans Wake*, the object of the incestuous desires of her father Tom Finnegan; while in *Ulysses* Stephen Dedalus 'prying into the family life of a great man' has Shakespeare in the role of Hamlet's ghost address his own dead son, Hamnet, in the following terms: 'you are the dispossessed son: I am the murdered father: your mother is the guilty queen. Ann Shakespeare, born Hathaway' (241).

73 SB's father died (like Otto Olaf in the short story 'What a Misfortune') of a 'clot' (*MPTK*, 130), in 1933. But the 'clot' here is a kind of gloss on 'clot of anger' in line **13** of 'Enueg I'.

74 cf. the Polar Bear's 'high red cacklebelch of duty done', *Dream*, 151, and, for other odd compounds, 'randygasp of ruthi-larity' (*Dream*, 73) and 'snotgasp of reliefhilarity' (*Dream*, 67), both (perhaps as here) 'in honour of private joke'. The (literally) private joke is presumably predicated on 'the jewels' in the previ-ous line being genitalia (as in Diderot's *Les Bijoux indiscrets* of 1748).

75 the 'peacostrich' is an obviously hybrid bird which relies, in part, on Dante's mother's peacock dream recounted in Bocca-cio's *Trattatello in laude di Dante* (see Caselli, 16–19, for the best discussion in English), and SB's own musings on the ostrich. Both birds are, in their different ways, prophetic. The peacock foretells Dante's success in the vulgar tongue, whereas 'who knows what the ostrich sees in the sand?' (*Murphy*, 111). The peacock foretells some sort of truth in a dream, but the ostrich? – the hybrid as-serts this ambiguity. The word 'wunnerful' occurs twice in *Dream* (24, 74).

77 in the short story 'Echo's Bones' (25) Belacqua recollects his life 'prior to Thanatos' (for Thanatos, cf. *Dream*, 146). In *Beyond the Pleasure Principle*, Freud developed the idea of the death drive, or Thanatos, in contrast with the libido or sex-drive, Eros. Freud offered a surprising redefinition of pleasure and unpleasure to describe these drives, with unpleasure describing the stimulus that the body receives (e.g. excessive friction on the skin produces a burning sensation) while pleasure results from a decrease in stimuli. So, if pleasure increases as stimuli decrease, then the ultimate experience of pleasure would be zero stimulus, or death. Hence the resolution in 'Spring Song' of the extreme stimulation of the opening with the appearance of Thanatos. Cf. also the 'fatal pleasure principle' (*Molloy*, 102).

78   a clear, if suitably coded, indication that this is a dream poem: 'Tread softly for you tread on my dreams' ('He Wishes for the Cloths of Heaven', W. B. Yeats); cf. also the post-prandial tiger of Riga (or Niger) in 'Sanies I'.

79   dusk as the placenta of the departed day. Cf. in Lucien's French letter, 'le placenta de l'aurorore' and 'the livid strands of placenta praevia' (*Dream*, 21 and 31). Cf. also the Rimbaldian 'banner of meat bleeding' in 'Enueg I', line **73**, and the 'nasty birth' of dawn in 'Yellow' (*MPTK*, 152).

80   for 'haply', cf. *Dream*, 198; for the 'fatboy', cf. the 'overfed child' of *Dream*, 1.

82   reminiscent of a form of address used in the *Divine Comedy*; cf. Belacqua: 'O frate, andar in sù che porta?' ('O brother, what is the use of going up?'), *Purg.*, IV, 127 (misquoted in *Dream*, 141). It is often used when an error is being corrected, cf. e.g. *Purg.*, XVI, 65: Marco Lombardo's address on free will begins 'Frate'.

85   the Smeraldina's colour, but cf. Beckett to MacGreevy of Ethna MacCarthy, 18.10.32: 'Occasionally it happens that I remember her and then, presto! I had nothing up my sleeve nor she in her amethyst bodice' (*LSB1*, 135).

87   cf. the title of 'To Be Sung Loud'.

89   like 'Sanies I', 'Spring Song' ends with a sad going home (for 'slink', cf. line **18** of 'Serena III'), and both poems are therefore in accord with the 'laetus exitus' tag from Kempis to which SB was so attached (cf., among many instances, 'Ding-Dong', *MPTK*, 32, which ironises it).

it is high time lover

This is the only poem in the Leventhal papers that is untitled in the typescript, although its title is given as 'it is high time lover' in the contents list. It is a much reworked and reduced version of 'Return to the Vestry', which was published in *The New Review*, Aug.-Sept.-Oct., 1931, [98]–99. In an undated letter of either late August or early September 1931 SB wrote to Samuel Putnam 'Many thanks for N.[ew] R.[eview] and for including my lovely lovely poem', referring to 'Return to the Vestry' (*LSB1*, 86). Perhaps seeing his 'lovely lovely poem' in print prompted SB to set about improving it at some later date. The revision reduces the original from 47 lines to 29 and only three lines remain unaltered. The earlier version was written at some point after SB's visit to the sadly neglected tomb of the great French poet Pierre Ronsard at Saint Cosme during his Loire holiday of 1926. Judging from the position it occupies in the Leventhal contents list SB may have undertaken the revision between November 1932 and May 1933 (the month in which Peggy Sinclair died).

Both poems rewrite Ronsard's 'Magie, ou délivrance d'amour', a poem alluded to in the first line of 'Dortmunder', where it is linked with Bérard's *Odyssée*. In *Dream* (175) the Alba mentions Ronsard's poem and describes him as 'a comic old lecher', after which remark Belacqua 'had no excuse for prolonging his visit'. The revision tightens up the poem considerably and helps focus it by a new division into three sections. The opening address, which expands a single word in 'Return to the Vestry' to seven intemperate ones in 'high time', may well represent SB's recognition that any romantic or sexual attachment between himself and Ethna MacCarthy has ceased to be a possibility, as (more obliquely) does 'Serena III', and it is this bitterness that gives the poem its edge. The 'Anteros' sections which conclude the two poems both have their merits, but while the concluding lines of 'Return to the Vestry' bear comparison with 'Moly', in 'it is high time lover', if Belacqua cannot have the Alba (or some other loved one), then, imaginatively at least, no one can. (Belacqua addresses the Alba as 'Spirit of the Moon' [*Dream*, 175] and it is the moon that Anteros 'lays'.)

Notes

2   'hochzeit': 'wedding' in German (with a capital letter), but literally 'high time'.

3–5 paraphrase the opening quatrains of Ronsard's ode as the poet strips off the bonds of love; 'priapean bard': i.e. Ronsard who had a reputation as the 'Great Pan' of the Renaissance. For the use of 'thy' in line 3, cf. the note to lines **15–17** of 'To Be Sung Loud'.

8 'his chapel', i.e. the Prieuré de Saint-Cosme where Ronsard is buried.

15 SB re-used the phrase 'all risks are covered' in his revision of Ralph Manheim's translation of George Duthuit's 'toutes garanties de sécurité' in *The Fauvist Painters*, 58; cf. page 248 of the French text.

16 like the good tourist he is, Beckett takes a photograph. A motif ostensibly derived from photography is later found in 'Rue de Vaugirard'.

18 'brimstone [. . .] fire': a common biblical combination, found in Genesis, Psalms, Ezekiel, Luke and Revelation. The comparable lines in 'Return to the Vestry' are less biblical in diction, although conceptually similar.

20 'spinning-jenny': cf. W. B. Yeats, 'The Words Upon The Window Pane': 'Locke sank into a swoon / The Garden died / God took the spinning-jenny / Out of his side'. Yeats translated Ronsard's 'Quand vous serez bien vieille' as 'When You Are Old', omitting the phrase 'dévidant et filant'. Perhaps SB wishes to make good this omission.

21 'vermuth': derived from 'Wermuth' (German for 'wormwood'; cf. line **28** of 'Return to the Vestry' in the Appendix).

23 for 'bric-à-brac', cf. *Dream*, 123.

27 Anteros, brother of Eros. For Ovid, the Cupid who extinguishes the flames of love. In *Dream*, Beckett remembers a poem he has written to Anteros 'cogged from the liquorish laypriest's Magic Ode' (68). Later, Belacqua imagines himself in Limbo where 'Eros was as null as Anteros and Night had no daughters' (121), with Beckett probably thinking of 'Dortmunder' and 'Casket . . .'. Cf. 'an anterotic' in the letter of 27.2.34 to Nuala Costello (*LSB1*, 186).

28 two deletions in the typescript: '~~like a~~ cloud of ~~the~~ latter rain'. 'latter rain' symbolises in the Old Testament (notably in Proverbs 16:15) new life and fertility for the land of Israel, so that the image of Anteros as a cloud of latter rain laying the moon finally subverts the anti-erotic ambitions of the poem (cf. 'a cloud of randy pollen' in the 1933 story 'Echo's Bones', 1). SB had noted that the phrase meant '(Grateful)' in *DN* *555, and had used the phrase less effectively in *Dream* (200) and again in 'A Wet Night' in *MPTK* (see introductory note to 'Calvary by Night').

UNCOLLECTED POEMS

At last I find

'At last I find' exists in three versions, all of which are untitled, in holograph with the 'Whoroscope' ms. (1930?), as part of 'Sedendo and Quiescendo' (*transition*, 21, March 1932, 13–20) and in *Dream* (70–1). There are no section breaks in either the holo or 'S&Q' versions. It is not included in the contents list for *POEMS* (Leventhal papers, HRHRC, Austin, Texas). The *Dream* version was republished in Harvey (untitled, but referred to elsewhere as 'Sonnet to the Smeraldina') and in *Poems 1930–1989*, where it is called 'Sonnet'. Harvey adds that SB 'did in fact write three sonnets to the girl he knew in Germany' (283). We have preferred to refer to it by its opening words to avoid confusion with *Tristesse Janale* which is also in sonnet form. The poem shares its ambiguous mystical impulse with, and borrows phrases from, the short story 'Assumption' (*transition*, 16–17, June 1929, 268–71) in which the protagonist 'hungered to be irretrievably engulfed in the light of eternity, one with the birdless, cloudless skies, in infinite fulfillment'. The mystical dimension suggests that it may have been the 'pome [. . .] the nice little whimper' sent to George Russell (AE) at the *Irish Statesman* (*LSB1*, 19). SB's control of his material is exemplary as the sonnet unfolds in one long sentence, but almost all the elements in it can be seen being subverted or parodied in other uncollected poems.

Variants

1   'confused' in holo.
2   'cypress' in holo.
3   'Tis' in holo.
5   'consumed', superscript correction for absorbed [?] in holo.
9   definite article, superscript insertion in holo.
11   'of', presumably in error, in the typescript of *Dream*.

12 'A strange exalted death' in holo and 'S&Q'.
13 and **14** 'Like two merged stars, sublimely bright, / Conjoined in one + in the infinite' (holo), 'Like two merged stars, intolerably bright, / Conjoined in One and in the Infinite!' in 'S&Q' and in the typesript of *Dream*.

Notes

13 'syzygetic' is a technical term in astronomy to describe the alignment of three celestial bodies such as the sun, the earth and the moon or one of the planets.
14 presumably the possibility of an obscene pun (cf. the 'concierge' conjunction in line **1** of 'Tristesse Janale') cannot be entirely ruled out, even in a poem so ostensibly spiritual in tendency.

Calvary by Night

'Calvary by Night' appears in *Dream* (213–14), where it is 'given' to the Poet and, ironically, dubbed a 'strong composition'. The *Dream* typescript version was republished in Harvey and in *Poems 1930–1989*, where the typing error 'kingfished' (line **12**, corrected in the Black Cat edition) is retained. It was revised for inclusion in *MPTK* but not included in the contents list for *POEMS*. In *MPTK* there is a pre-echo of the poem in the second of Belacqua's requirements of a public house: 'the solitary shawly like a cloud of latter rain in a waste of poets and politicians' (48; cf. a 'cloud of randy pollen' in the 1933 story 'Echo's Bones', 1). In *Dream* the latter rain (from Proverbs 16: 15; found in DN *555, and again in the penultimate line of 'it is high time lover' [q.v.]) was 'after the sands of poets and politicians' (200), as if wishing them washed away courtesy of Ireland's rainy climate. (There is almost continual rain in *Mercier and Camier*, and it rains almost all day in *From an abandoned work*. But 'What would Ireland be [. . .] without this rain of hers. Rain is part of her charm': *Dream*, 239.) The poem is clearly a parody of the 'Middle West gravity that is like an ogle-ful of tears' (*MPTK*, 53) but it is also, in its way, a crooked sort of *hommage* to Joyce, like 'Home Olga' and perhaps other jettisoned poems also.

Variants

11 'an untroubled bow of petal and fragrance' in *Dream*.
14 'Lamb of my insustenance' in *Dream*.

Notes

2 cf. Joyce's poem 'Flood': 'A waste of water ruthlessly / sways and uplifts its weedy mane' (*Pomes Penyeach* (1927); *Poems* and *Exiles*, 49).

4 cf. the etymology of 'pansy' in the French 'une pensée', a thought.

5 recalls Leopold Bloom's voyeuristic encounter with Gertie MacDowell on the beach, which culminates in onanistic wetness as the fireworks explode, in the 'Nausicaa' episode in *Ulysses* (477), no doubt also with some recollection of the 'limp father of thousands' of Bloom in the bath in the 'Lotos-Eaters' episode.

14 cf. the Lamb of God and Bloom's Eucharistic musings (*Ulysses*, 99), but also the final quatrain of Joyce's poem 'Flood' of which this is a truncated and perverted version: 'Lambent and vast and ruthless as is thine / Incertitude'.

15 cf. the blue flower of Novalis [*Heinrich von Ofterdingen*] in the short story 'Assumption' (1929).

17–18 cf. 'the waste of waters' (*Dream*, 134).

Home Olga

First published in *Contempo* (Chapel Hill, N.C.), III, no. 13 (15 Feb. 1934). Republished in Ellmann (1982), Harvey and Calder. The Calvin Israel typescript does not include accents on 'sarà sarà' but has a section break between 'JAMES' and 'JOYCE'. There is no section break in any published version. Calder substitutes full stops for semi-colons in lines **7** and **8**.

Offered ostensibly as a homage to Joyce in the form of an acrostic of 10 lines, but in many ways a mirror that SB is holding up to himself and, as Harvey (296) says, 'an admirer's farewell to the master'. This is a kind of 'precipitate' (a term that SB appears to have adopted only in 1934), and was probably written in the spring of 1932, after Joyce's fiftieth birthday on 2 February and before the Bloomsday anniversary of 16 June. The '[m]odo' is an imitation, or pastiche, of Joyce's manner in *Work in Progress*, but the 'forma' is more like Dante, with two complete sections of *terza rima* (aba/bcb/cdc/d) at the centre of the poem. The content is a cavalier attempt to repeat the argument of the 1929 essay 'Dante...Bruno.Vico..Joyce' in a much more condensed space. SB leaves sufficient room in his long lines, however, to allude to Vico's *ricorsi* in line **9** and Bruno's coincidence of opposites in line **8** (and perhaps also in line **10**), and also to include Homer (line **9**; the 'father' of Joyce's *Ulysses*)and a hint of Shakespeare's Hamlet and the ghost of *his* father in line **7**. There is perhaps also a suggestion that SB has in mind Rimbaud's 'Voyelles' sonnet (he was working on a translation of Rimbaud's 'Le Bateau ivre' at about the same time). This is a poem in which everything seems to point to everything else (as in *Work in Progress*), but also to gesture beyond itself to something which it stands in place of (as in allegory, although there is no attempt at fourfold allegory of the kind practised by Dante).

Two letters to TM (4.8.32 [*LSB1*, 112] and ?27.8.32 [not in *LSB1*]) register 'nothing from [Stuart] Gilbert', to whom SB had sent the poem. Its appearance in print was delayed until February 1934 (*Contempo*), but for a number of reasons SB remained concerned as to the poem's fate after he had sent it to Gilbert. In a later letter to TM of 22.6.[33] SB asks: 'Did you ever hear did Home Olga appear or come to the ears of Stephen?' [i.e. Joyce as 'Stephen Dedalus'](not in *LSB1*). The Leventhal contents list for *POEMS* includes 'Home Olga', but it remained uncollected until the Calder *Collected Poems* of 1977.

The title adopts an idiom used by Tom MacGreevy and his friends in the late 1920s and early 1930s, roughly equivalent to modern-day phrases like 'let's get the hell out of here'.

Notes

1 the green of jade (cf. line **6** of 'Dortmunder') gives the second of the three theological virtues, hope, just as the red of erythrite gives the third, charity or love, in line **4** and the white of opal the first, faith, in line **7**. These last two stones are decidedly off-colour and play a similar trick to the Bovril sign at the beginning of 'A Wet Night' where the theological virtues are subsequently reimagined as 'Doubt, Despair and Scrounging (*MPTK*, 43). For 'jade' cf. *DN**496 (from Louis Laloy). The word 'exile' is equally applicable to Dante and Joyce, but is here principally to generate 'silence'(lines **4** and **5**) and 'cunning' (line **7**) to reflect the trinity of choices made by Stephen Dedalus in *A Portrait of the Artist as a Young Man*.

2 'haemorrhoidal' for the Emerald Isle. SB adapts this to 'Haemorrhaldia' to refer again to Ireland with disdain in a 29.11.58 letter to Barbara Bray.

3 Joyce, who apparently found nothing to object to in the poem, thought 'tickled' would be an improvement on 'giggled' (Ellmann, 701 fn.).

4 'sweet noo style' is a 'translation' of *dolce stil nuovo* (Dante, *Purgatorio*, XXIV,57), a phrase often used to describe Italian lyric poetry of the second half of the thirteenth century that combines sincerity of feeling with musicality of expression. Just as Dante changed the history of Italian poetry, Joyce has changed the course of modern literature, not only by writing *Ulysses* but more especially in his *Work in Progress*.

5 for the 'mew' cf. the opening of *Murphy*, but 'Swoops' at the beginning of the line suggests a bird (of divination, prophecy or annunciation) similar to the one seen or imagined by Stephen Dedalus from the steps of the library in committing himself to his literary vocation.

6 'Juvante Jah and a Jain' nods in the direction of the opening of what became *Finnegans Wake*, III.2 ('Jaunty Jaun . . .', 429; part of the 'passing hence' [427] of Shaun the Post), first published as an extract from *Work in Progress* in *transition* 13 (summer 1928). The 'tip of a friendly Yiddophile' looks back to Bloom and the horse Throwaway in *Ulysses*, and perhaps also to God seen in *Ulysses* as a collector of foreskins. Harvey points out a reference to an Irish joke: 'Take a tip from me – as the Jew said to the Rabbi' (297 fn77).

7 the word 'winking' picks up from 'tip' in the line above by way of the slang phrase 'to tip the wink', to signal to someone to convey a warning or to keep something secret. The line ends with a triple farewell (cf. line 1 of poem XI in Joyce's *Chamber Music*;

Harvey, 297 fn78), with perhaps a kind of farewell to Joyce hidden in it (cf. Harvey, 296). Joyce apparently quite liked the poem (letter of 22.7.32), but Eugene Jolas thought it 'acid and not funny' (F & F, 12).

8 'Latin me that' occurs in the Anna Livia Plurabelle section of *Finnegans Wake* (215; Harvey, 297 fn80). SB uses 'riddle me that' at least twice in letters to Barbara Bray of April and December 1962, in the first linking the phrase to Lawrence Harvey, who had been visiting Paris to acquire material for his *Poet and Critic* book.

9 'Homer . . . spew': Homer because Joyce has moved far beyond *Ulysses*, but also because of 'Homer spews . . .' from Robert Burton (*DN* *729), with the latter part of the quotation adapted in *Dream* (120) to attack Balzac. The '[s]hameful spewing' motif recurs on page 17 of the typescript of the short story 'Echo's Bones' at Dartmouth.

10 thanking Joyce for being an example, and perhaps specifically for having supplied SB with examples for 'Dante...Bruno. Vico..Joyce'. The phrase 'ecce himself' recalls 'the prospect of self-extension' in the first paragraph of SB's 1929 essay (*Disjecta*, 19; with 'Behold Belacqua' from section 'ONE' of *Dream* also in mind), but also reflects SB's recognition that even in *Work in Progress* Joyce is writing autobiographically. Joyce's poem 'Ecce Homo' was written in February 1932 on the death of his father and the birth of his first grandson, and he recited it shortly after its composition to SB, who remembered it (almost) off by heart until the end of his life (Knowlson, 157–8). The 'pickthank agnus' (cf. *DN* *966) can be 'translated' as a fawning or sycophantic lamb ('agnus dei'= Lamb of God, i.e. Jesus), envious of Joyce's God-like creative powers. But there is presumably some sense here of SB himself, also on display, or at least partly visible here, in the guise of a 'sacrificial lamb' once again undertaking something on behalf of Joyce at the expense of doing something for himself, hence perhaps 'e.o.o.e', errors or omissions excepted (an abbreviation also used by SB in his 1934 essay 'Censorship in the Saorstat'; *Disjecta*, 86). SB may well have thought of the poem, or the writing of it, as an error that perhaps ought to have been omitted, as some members of the Joyce circle certainly did.

Seats of Honour

Identified by the editors from the letter to Nuala Costello of 24 February 1934 as a likely candidate for the missing poem 'Seats of Honour' in the Leventhal contents list. Published as part of that letter but without this identification in *LSB1* (187–8). The poem, consisting of two quatrains, was written at a time when SB was showing a fondness for this form (cf. 'Gnome', 'Up He Went', which was also sent to Nuala, and 'Da Tagte Es'). It may not be wholly coincidental that letters of 7.5.34 (to A. J. Leventhal; not in *LSB1*) and Nuala Costello (10.5.34; *LSB1*, 209) mention SB visiting Stoke Poges in Buckinghamshire; Thomas Gray's 'Elegy Written in a Country Churchyard' is in quatrains.

Notes

Title   cf. DN *354: 'a claque on the seat of honour'. In *Dream* (97) the Smeraldina 'waggled her seat of honour' (and in so doing provokes a learned discussion) as she dances with the glider champion on New Year's Eve. A flagellatory frenzy of phrases (largely derived from Cooper) follows (*Dream*, 98), very different in character from this much cooler and more contemplative poem, which is led up to in the Nuala Costello letter by a number of psychoanalytic references (to Naomi Klein, Karin Stephens and, by implication at least, Sigmund Freud).
1   cf. 'mammon' in the last line of 'Serena I'; reheard as 'maman' in the mother of line 4.
2   referring to the French vaudeville star Louise Weber immortalised by the painter Toulouse-Lautrec, called 'The Glutton' from her habit of helping herself to customers' drinks. During her cancan she is reported to have shown the seat of her drawers embroidered with a heart.
2   'a cob's': cf. the horse in *Dream*, 1. Freud's Wolf Man derived 'an uncanny feeling from witnessing horses being beaten' (*The Standard Edition of the Complete Psychological Works of Sigmund Freud*, XVII, 16). SB may also have known the story of Nietzsche going mad in Turin on seeing a horse being beaten. Mrs Rooney expresses ambivalent feelings seeing a 'hinny' being beaten at the beginning of *All That Fall*. She, like Dr Nye in the short story 'A Case in a Thousand', has an obsession with horses' buttocks

(Complete Short Prose, 19). There is a horse apparently in some distress towards the end of 'Dante and the Lobster', but it is not clear whether it has been beaten (*MPTK*, 13).

5   Freud's Wolf Man asked his 'Nanya' whether God has a bottom.
6   proverbial instances of licentiousness and stupidity.

Gnome

A pithy farewell to academe and intellectualism generally, interestingly and ironically in tension with the review (entitled 'Caviare to the General') of SB's *More Pricks Than Kicks* by 'NH' ('a book that glitters and will make holiday for the highbrows') which appeared in the same issue of the *Dublin Magazine* in which 'Gnome' was first published (IX, n.s., July–September 1934, 8). Influenced, in spirit if not in form, by the Goethe/Schiller Xenien which SB took notes from probably early in 1934 (*'College' Notebook*, UoR Ms 5002). The suggestion in *LSB1*, 107, that 'Gnome' may have been the 'short' poem sent to Samuel Putnam on 3.4.[32] is incorrect (see the introductory note to 'Dortmunder'). Cf. Watt's 'tenth rate xenium' (*Watt*, 112).

'Gnome' was republished in Harvey, in *The Lace Curtain*, 4, Summer 1971, 7, and in *The Faber Book of Irish Verse*, edited by John Montague, 1974, 295. It was first collected by Calder in 1977. Calder (1977 and 2002) introduces what looks like an error in line 3 ('a world'), but this accords with Jack MacGowran's reading of the poem (untitled, and then uncollected) in the 24.11.66 ('More Poems . . .') BBC broadcast, in which the poem is described as 'unpublished', SB having apparently forgotten its appearance in the *Dublin Magazine* more than thirty years earlier! Still untitled, it was the last of the eleven selections in the 14.4.76 broadcast compiled from the 'Poems . . .' (8.3.66) and 'More Poems . . .' broadcasts. In the BBC Written Archives at Caversham the poem is recurrently given the 'title' 'Span [*sic*] the years of learning', obviously an administrative error, since MacGowran very clearly says 'Spend'.

Note

The '-ing' ending upon which this poem depends is part of a

prevailing participial tendency in SB's pre-war poems in English, which contain more than 150 examples of the form. It seems likely that Beckett favoured the form because it leavened his 'statemental' tendency, and left the greater precision of more specific tenses suspended in a kind of limbo. The form also reinforces his 'keep on the move' impulse (cf. 'Serena III') as an index of life continuing. Cf. also 'I grow gnomic' in the next entry.

Up he went

Included in a letter to Nuala Costello dated 10 May 1934 and published as such in *LSB1* (209), which omits 'it' after 'rue' in the version transcribed by Knowlson (UoR). Like 'Gnome', this is another farewell to academe. In the Nuala Costello letter Beckett comments: 'I grow gnomic. It is the last phase.' Included here principally because it is presumably one of the two 'quatschrains' (with 'Gnome' being the other) that Beckett mentions in his letter to Leventhal of 7 May 1934 (HRHRC; not in *LSB1*). We have replaced SB's ampersands with 'and' in lines 1 and 2.

Cascando

Midway through the *'Whoroscope' Notebook*, sandwiched between two entries in German, SB writes and underlines: 'Cascando: praesectum decies ad unciam', (i.e. 'pruned down by a tenth to an ounce') with the last word doubly underlined. This is an adaptation (although no source is given) of line 294 of Horace's 'Art of Poetry' (Epistola ad Pisones): 'praesectum decies [some texts read 'deciens'] non castigavit ad unguem'. Horace's line describes how the poet's tenfold labour to attain accuracy has not been despised, whereas SB is no doubt reflecting on the labour he has expended on several versions of 'Cascando' to bring it to some kind of finality, while suspecting that, despite his efforts, it may not be well received ['castigavit']. Under the heading 'Surrealism' later in the *'Whoroscope' Notebook* SB quotes the opening lines of the 'Art of Poetry' in Latin, giving the source as 'Epistola ad Pisones'. SB had owned a polyglot Horace, bought in London, since the summer of 1932, and borrowed phrases from it for *MPTK*, and for his 1980 Riverside production of *Endgame* (*The Theatrical Notebooks*, vol. 2, ed. S. E. Gontarski, Faber, 1992, [195], 197).

The earlier entry (*'Whoroscope' Notebook*) was either made shortly before SB left for Germany in late September 1936, when he was practising his German, or shortly after his arrival there in October. In August 1936 SB attempted to translate 'Cascando' into German (a language he had never been formally taught) on his own, partly just for practice and perhaps also in the hope of interesting any literary contact whom he might meet while away. In Germany, occasionally having sought the help of others, he made changes to this version on 2.11.36, 15.11.36, 18.11.36 and 30.3.37, sending a copy of his 'final' revised version to the novelist Paul Alverdes (*German Diaries*). The German version ('Mancando', q.v.) is anything but a diminution, numbering 62 lines, where the English numbers 37 (32 in its *Dublin Magazine* version; DM in the notes).

A letter to TM of 15.7.36 (not in *LSB1*) establishes the date of composition as early July 1936 (immediately after the completion of *Murphy*, which contains the phrase 'a slow cascando of pellucid yellows' in the penultimate paragraph of chapter 12), at which point SB seems to have thought of 'Cascando' as two poems (a follow-up letter of 17.7.36 twice refers to 'poems' [*LSB1*, 358, 359], and the two-poem idea gives extra foundation for 'saying again' at the head of the second section), sections one and two as published. The line that comprises the third section (with an upper case 'Unless') was sent in a later letter to TM of 26.7.36 (*LSB1*, 360); TM had queried the opening section, which was in any event later to be omitted by Seumas O'Sullivan, the editor of *Dublin Magazine*, when he published it for the first time (O'Sullivan registered it as 'Two Poems'; *LSB1*, 357). A letter of 18.1.37 registers SB's relief that TM had liked it (*LSB1*, 428), and describes the poem as 'the last echo of feeling' (a curiously apt phrase in the circumstances: see below); an earlier letter of 19.9.36 registers regret at its 'circumcision' (cf. the 'tip' note to 'Home Olga', above) by O'Sullivan (*LSB1*, 376): 'I think I told you about S O'S's request for an inch off the poem. Circumcised accordingly, it now begins with the abortion dilemma' (*LSB1*, 370).

SB had told TM on 7.8.36 that the poem had been 'accepted' (*LSB1*, 365), but he wrote again on 9.9.36 to say that: 'Seumas O'S[ullivan] sent another proof with request to make one line of two somewhere, anywhere, in the interests of his pagination' (*LSB1* 371–2 fn3). In his *German Diary* entry for 5.10.36 SB ruefully remembers that there was 'no reason at all for him to have made me cut it'.

'Cascando' was first published in the *Dublin Magazine*, XI, n.s. (Oct.–Dec. 1936), 3–4. It was first published in book form in *Gedichte* in June 1959, and reprinted in August 1961 in *Poems in English* under the rubric 'Two Poems' (with 'Saint-Lô'). Cronin (235) reprints the MacGreevy version but introduces errors in transcription and section division, and omits the numbers 1 and 2. *LSB1* reprints the SOS version. A typescript of the revised version is in the Calvin Israel collection (Burns Library, Boston College). A carbon typescript copy of the poem, sent to George Reavey at his European Literary Bureau, presents it in four sections (as in the German version, 'Mancando'), rather than three (HRHRC; Lake, *54, 36).] A typescript of SB's own German version is in the Lawrence Harvey collection at Dartmouth College. Harvey discusses a few of the German phrases in his treatment of 'Cascando' (176–7). Hunkeler (1999, 31–3) reprints this German version; it is reprinted here in the Appendix. There are apparently other variant versions of 'Cascando' still in private hands.

The 'occasion' prompting the poem was SB meeting, and thinking he had fallen in love with, an American friend of Mary Manning Howe, Betty Stockton Farley, who did not reciprocate SB's feelings, although soon 'wordshed' (cf. 'writing-shed', TM 18.10.32; *LSB1* 134) seems to have taken over from those feelings. SB later remembered his feelings as a marker ('the Farley episode', *German Diaries* 7.2.37, when he was struggling unsuccessfully with another poem), but it was the poem that mattered. It looks back to 'Serena II' with the 'bones' of line **8** and to *EBOP* more generally – perhaps especially in *Gedichte*, which does nothing to indicate that it is not part of the *Echo's Bones* section that the book opens with – since its practice of 'saying again' generates the 'bare bones' of an echo; cf. 'the last echo of feeling' (TM 18.1.37;

LSB1, 428). The second section echoes and expands the opening of TM's poem 'Dechtire': 'I do not love you as I have loved / The loves I have loved – / As I may love others'.

The term 'cascando' is (rarely) used in music to distinguish a diminuendo in volume and/or tempo. SB uses the word 'cascando' with reference to *Waiting for Godot* in a letter to Peter Hall of 14.12.55 (Harmon, 3), and titled his 1961 radio play (originally written in French), which is not obviously about love and much more concerned with writing, *Cascando* (also the English title), with music by Marcel Mihailovici.

The BBC plan to broadcast 'Cascando', 'Malacoda' and 'Dieppe II' (i.e. 'my way is in the sand . . .') as verbal interludes on the 'Music Programme', first mooted on 4.12.67, had to wait until 28.7.68 to occur (BBC Written Archives, Caversham; cf. the headnote to 'Alba' above). The poems were read on the Third Programme by Denys Hawthorne at 5.00 p.m. under the title *Words and Music*.

Variants

[1]

1–3 Three lines as first published in book form in *Gedichte* with lines **2** and **3** run together in the TM and SOS to read: 'Why / why were you not simply what I despaired for / an occasion of word-shed' omitted in DM. In TM and SOS line break here.

4 'is it better to abort than be barren' in TM and SOS; 'is it better abort than be barren' in DM.

5 lower case 'the' in TM; upper case in SOS.

9 'once filled' in TM and SOS.

10 'is it' omitted in TM and SOS.

[2]

25 TM and SOS read: 'the churn of old words in the heart again'.

26 TM reads 'love love love old thud of the plunger' and SOS 'love love love thud of the old plunger'.

32 'of being unloved' in TM, SOS and DM.

[3]

There is no third section in TM or SOS. Harvey says that Beckett's 'original typescript' read 'unless of course they love you' (178).

Notes

17–18   Cf. a letter to Barbara Bray of 17.2.59, although the specific point of reference there is 'Dieppe': 'enough of lasts that are never', effectively a way of saying (again) 'a last even of last times'. For 'barren' cf. 2 Peter 1:8.

Ooftish

First published in *transition* 27, the tenth anniversary number, April–May 1938, 33. A 19-line squib treating conventional religious consolations in the face of mortality with savage irony. Probably written early in August 1937; sent in letters to TM and to Cissie Sinclair (*LSB1*, 534–7) of 14 August 1937 with the title 'Whiting', thinking of the 'whited sepulchre' of Matthew 23:27. (In 1937 Whitsun was on 16 May.) On 5 June 1936 [*recte* 1937] SB told TM: 'Apparently Denis Devlin wants me to give Ria Mooney a poem to read on the wireless. I think that is almost sufficient incentive to write a new one' (*LSB1*, 503), and the phrase 'the new prostitution' in a letter to Mary Manning Howe of 22.5.37 (not in *LSB1*) may suggest that SB had already tried to write one. SB told TM (19.8.37; *LSB1*, 544) that Brian Coffey had liked 'Ooftish', adding: 'Of course I can't ventilate it anywhere, except perhaps in *transition*', which may perhaps explain why he considered trying to interest *Ireland To-day* in publishing it (*LSB1*, 555). Presumably Edward Sheehy turned it down, which may explain why SB was later unsure of whether to send him 'they come' (q.v.) (*LSB1*, 596), even though he eventually did so (*LSB1*, 597 fn11). (Neither of the two poems appeared in *Ireland To-Day*.) SB may have been thinking back to 'Ooftish' when he told Mary Manning (30.8.37): 'I write the odd poem when it is there, that is the only thing worth doing' (*LSB1*, 546). On 20.6.38 SB told George Reavey that *transition* had printed the poem 'all wrong' (*LSB1*, 634), although there are actually very few variants.

The neologism 'Ooftish' is derived from Yiddish 'auf dem Tisch', i.e. 'put it [your money] on the table, show your hand, commit yourself', which is reflected in line **1**. (SB uses a number of German words in a letter of 5.6.36 to TM, just as he had done in a letter of 14.3.34 to Arland Ussher, now in the Leventhal collection at HRHRC; neither of these is in *LSB1*.) Beckett told Harvey that the poem was prompted by a sermon he had heard in Ireland. The preacher described his reaction when visiting the sick: 'What gets me down is pain. The only thing I can tell them is that crucifixion was only the beginning. You must contribute to the kitty' (156). The *transition* version was reprinted by Cohn (*The Comic Gamut*) and by Harvey. Calder (1977) prints a variant of the *transition* version. The Sinclair variant 'Whiting' is given in *LSB1* (536–7). We have followed Calder 1977, since Beckett reluctantly allowed three early poems which had not been collected in Calder's 1961 edition to be included: 'Gnome', 'Home Olga' and 'Ooftish'. In a letter to the late Ruby Cohn after the Calder publication of *Poems in English* (16.2.62) SB told her 'I chose the poems', and explained that it was his decision to omit 'Ooftish'. In a letter to Richard Seaver of 5.4.62, ahead of the Grove Press *Poems in English*, SB wrote: 'I am against [the inclusion of a number of unspecified poems], with possible exception of "Ooftish". I leave it to you. Put it in if you like'. On 16.8.62 SB told Seaver: 'Set up of poems [Seaver having omitted 'Ooftish'] fine. Go ahead.' SB's feelings about the poem are perhaps in part reflected in a letter to George Reavey of 9.11.61 which, after mentioning 'Whoroscope' and *EBOP* by name, describes the other selections in the Calder volume as 'odds and ends'.

Variants

1   Sinclair has a capital O; lower case in TM. In the handwritten Sinclair there is some suggestion that lines 10 and 17 also begin with a capital letter although this is not apparent in *LSB1*.
7   TM and Sinclair have 'toga virilis' (cf. *MPTK*, 68, where it is given in italics).
13   TM and Sinclair have 'can't' for 'won't'; *transition* has 'you-you won't'.
19   *transition* has 'the blood of the lamb'.

Notes

2   'potegg': 'British: a dummy nest egg for a fowl' (Harvey, 156).
7   cf. 'syphilis; toga virilis' (*DN* *486). This adapts one of more

than sixty entries from Garnier's *Onanisme seul et à deux*, and SB later adapted it again to describe 'Chas' in 'A Wet Night' (*MPTK*, 68). Garnier treats of syphilis in his opening pages but does not apply the term 'toga virilis' to it. The toga virilis or toga pura was worn by Roman citizens on their assumption of manhood. In a letter of 8.10.32 to TM Beckett writes: 'the faithful impetigo: toga mollis' (a phrase omitted from the *LSB1* printing of the letter).

19 cf. Revelation 7:14.

TRANSLATIONS

Eugenio Montale: Delta

Eugenio Montale's 'Delta' first appeared in an Italian literary magazine in November-December 1926, written too late for inclusion in Montale's subsequently famous and ground-breaking *Ossi di Seppia* (*Bones of Cuttlefish*), which first appeared in 1925 (Milan: Gobetti) and was reprinted in an augmented edition, including 'Delta' in section 'III' of the collection, in 1928 (Turin: Ribet).

The *This Quarter* printing (II, April–May–June, 1930, 630) gives the translator as 'S B Beckett' (SB's preferred signature in the late 1920s and early 1930s). SB had been asked, by Samuel Putnam, who was guest editing a special issue of Edward Titus's magazine devoted to modern Italian writing (1930), to choose some texts he wished, or was able, to translate, some of which Putnam himself may have supplied, and not all of which had yet been published in the original Italian. Presumably SB considered 'Delta' as 'by far and away the best of a bad lot' (letter to Putnam of 14.5.30; *LSB1*, 24–5) but, since the letter makes no specific mention of the poem, SB's estimation of Montale remains a matter for speculation.

As some commentators on SB's version have pointed out, he is more successful at the level of vocabulary than in dealing with Montale's awkward and sinuous syntax; but he conveys the troubled and internalised mood of the original well, and at times could even be said to have intensified it by bringing it close to his own mood and spirit in the late 1920s and early 1930s, especially when paraphrasing the original. Of Leishman's Rilke SB says, 'The numerous deviations are unwarrantable, that is to say, ineffective' (*Disjecta*, 67), but SB's 'deviations' here create much of the interest of his version, and need not be considered 'ineffective' unless strict translation is the acid test.

Twenty lines of Montale become twenty-four in SB's version. Montale's chiasmic or 'mirror' form (4+6+6+4) is lost, but SB compensates by introducing formal echoes of his own ('Of thee', lines 12, 20; 'only', lines 13, 22), often uses gerunds or present participles (six in stanza 3 alone) where the original employs simple present indicative forms, and introduces several alliterative consonants for what has to be lost by way of assonances in the original. SB's slightly antique vocabulary (e.g. 'thee', lines 1, 12, 20; 'forth', line 24; he also uses 'thy' and 'thee' in translating from French, e.g. Eluard and, if they are by SB, in the unsigned translations of Tristan Tzara for *This Quarter* in 1932; q.v.) ignores the fact that there is nothing distinctively antique in the original, and SB's rhythm, as created by the placement of commas, also differs from Montale's. All Montale's (irregular) rhymes, whether internal or end-rhymes, are omitted, with only the ghosts of them left in lines 1+4, 2+3, in a first stanza which becomes more of a paraphrase than a strict translation as it proceeds. SB's 'tidings' very cleverly adapts Montale's 'messaggio' to the real or imagined circumstances, and is part of the pervasive melody of '-ing' in the vicinity. There is no 'bright gulf' (line 24) in line 20 of the original, only a 'golfo'. The 'dighe' ('dykes', as in line 5 of SB's version) may have contributed to an episode, no doubt one of many personally experienced by SB, of engulfment early in *Dream* (26), in a scene depicting the sense of fragile barriers having collapsed, or having caved in, to leave the self either more nakedly exposed, or more confused, or even more doomed and confined than was the case before the influx. For 'sanctuary' in line 9 cf. 'dark sanctuary' (*Dream*, 40).

For detailed, and for the most part positive, discussions of SB's version, see essays by Laura Visconti (1997; adapted from an Italian original), Marco Sonzogni (2005, 2006; in Italian) and Norma Bouchard (2008, 145–59), but there is still room for a fuller and more informed assessment of SB's Montale, certainly one of the most interesting of all his many translations, the earliest known, and obviously his only serious published attempt at translating a great modern Italian poet.

Arthur Rimbaud: Drunken Boat

Beckett's well-known and much admired version of one of the most famous of all French poems ('Le Bateau ivre'; SB's only comparable enterprise of this magnitude was his translation of Apollinaire's 'Zone' [q.v.]) was undertaken in the early months of 1932, probably principally for financial reasons (Edward Titus of *This Quarter* was prepared to pay 700 FF, although SB was hoping for 1,000 FF), although SB's admiration for Rimbaud had deepened sufficiently during his brief time teaching at TCD for him to 'amuse' (cf. 11.3.31; *LSB1*, 73) his students with quotations from the poet. In his introduction to the 1976 Whitenights Press edition and to Ronald Pickup's 1977 broadcast of a reading of SB's translation for the BBC in the same year, James Knowlson contextualises SB's financial needs with respect to him being without a *carte de séjour* in the wake of the assassination of the French president Paul Doumer, and without sufficient funds to return home (in the event, via London). Knowlson mentions the good offices of the painter Jean Lurçat and his apartment at the Villa Seurat as an intermediate stopover prior to SB receiving payment from Titus, and presumes that a translation which he had already worked on was finalised there. Of the three copies SB typically made of his work, no original typescript (nor any manuscript) survives, only the partly fire-damaged top copy given to Nuala Costello (see below).

The copy text for Beckett's translation was the 1929 Mercure de France reprint of the *Oeuvres de Arthur Rimbaud: Vers et Prose*, edited by Paterne Berrichon, first published in 1912. This edition has since been superseded by the 1939 critical edition. As Felix Leakey points out in his critical essay, Berrichon's errors occasionally give rise to '"magical" translations' (13). *This Quarter* folded in December 1932, and presumably room could not be found for SB's version in the intervening months. SB obviously retained some affection for it, as is indicated by a letter to George Reavey of 27.12.36 (*LSB1*, 406; cf. 393 fn20), in which SB enquires as to whether it would be appearing in another ephemeral magazine (*Contemporary Poetry and Prose*) or had been 'sidelined'. In the event it was displaced there by an Ezra Pound piece ('The Coward Surrealists' in no. 7, November 1936, 136).

SB seems thereafter to have lost interest in it. *Drunken Boat* was long presumed to be irretrievably lost until it was miraculously found in the possession of Nuala Costello, in a very slightly damaged typescript which had survived a fire because it was folded into a copy of *The Oxford Book of French Verse*, by Felix Leakey, and in due course published, with introductory essays by Leakey and James Knowlson, in a de luxe limited edition by the White-knights Press of the University of Reading (1976). It was reprinted, without the essays, in Calder's 1977 *Collected Poems* with Rimbaud's French *en face*. This was a modified version of the Berrichon text published by Leakey and Knowlson which incorporated much of the punctuation from Verlaine's original transcription, but retaining the errors which give rise to Beckett's apparent mistranslations (cf. lines **59** and **81**). The modified French text is reproduced in Faber's *Selected Poems 1930–1989*.

There were few published translations of Rimbaud's poem in 1932, but SB's version still stands up well against what are now many competitors. The fullest and most judicious assessment of it is Gerald M. Macklin's essay in *Studies in 20th Century Literature*, 27:1, Winter 2003, 141–66, and Macklin is very sensitive to both its 'intermittent literalness' (145) and the many occasions in it where SB has 'gone beyond translation [. . .] to create a transformation'. But as early as 1932 Samuel Putnam, in his foreword to George Reavey's *Faust's Metamorphoses*, had the foresight to identify in SB 'the task perhaps of expressing, as Rimbaud expressed, passionate nihilism, and transcendental vision at one and the same time' (8; *LSB1*, 108; cf. the headnote to 'Spring Song').

See *LSB1*, 73, 93, 135, 218, 319, etc., for SB references to Rimbaud in his correspondence. The middle section ('UND') of *Dream* is a kind of prose equivalent of 'Le Bateau ivre', and a tacit *hommage* to Rimbaud. In *DN* *1075 SB tells himself 'Translating Rimbaud I had great trouble mitigating the chevilles' (the 'padding'; cf. *Dream*, 47, 122). The original typescript of *Dream* (122; Lawrence Harvey archive, Dartmouth College) has 'did him into the eye', a phrase SB often used for inaccurate translation or otherwise dishonest dealings, whereas the editors of the published text (137) have substituted 'pat', as if to suggest that this might be distinctively Irish English.

DN *1075, *1078 and *1079 show that SB was also familiar with Rimbaud's letters. 'Enueg I' and *Dream*, 172 adapt phrases from 'Barbare' (*Les Illuminations*), and motifs derived from 'Les Poètes de sept ans' are frequent in the 1933 story 'Echo's Bones'. It seems likely that in later life Mallarmé, earlier much less of an enthusiasm than Rimbaud, proved of greater creative value for SB. But in a letter to TM of 21.11.32 (not in *LSB1*) Beckett quotes from Rimbaud's poem 'Bonheur' (as earlier in 'The Possessed' of 1931; *Disjecta*, 100: 'O saisons! O chateaux!') to demonstrate how superior he is to Paul Valéry, and as late as 1953, in an undated 'mardi' letter to Mania Péron, SB quotes four lines from Rimbaud's 'Comédie en trois baisers' (*LSB2*, 558–9).

'Drunken Boat' was read by Ronald Pickup on BBC Radio 3 on 12.3.77.

Notes

1 'impassive' for 'impassibles'; in translating 'impassible' from *Premier amour* (1946; Minuit, 52) SB preferred to keep the same word in English (*First Love*, 58; in *The Expelled*, etc., 'corrected' to 'impassable', 78).
6–7 cf. *Dream* (140–1): 'all its freights, crew and cargo'.
14 'Nine nights' translates 'Dix nuits'; cf. 'nine days never floated the loved' in 'Cascando'.
60 Berrichon misread 'ont béni mes dérades' for 'ont bercé mes dérades', i.e. 'blessed' for 'rocked'; 'canticles of wind' for 'ineffables vents'. Cf. 'canticle of the ring-doves' in 'What a Misfortune' (*MPTK*, 122).
67 cf. 'à reculons, like one of Rimbaud's drowned' (9.10.33; excised from *LSB1*, 166).

81 cf. the 'waste of waters' in *Dream* (134), a phrase which echoes the poem 'Calvary by Night' (q.v.).

82 cf. 'strom' in *Dream* (1, 119, 139, 199), and line **18** of 'Serena I'.

85 travestied in the story 'Echo's Bones', 14, with an oblique allusion to the penultimate quatrain of Rimbaud's poem immediately afterwards.

92 cf. the late English poem: 'bail bail till better/founder'. 'Founder' translates 'Oh! que j'aille à la mer'.

95–6 for 'un papillon de mai'; cf. *Dream*, 22, 129, 138.

98 typescript begins 'No more [absorb]', which is crossed out, and replaced by 'Absorb no more', the only correction of any significance.

99 for 'drapeaux': cf. the 'banner' of 'Enueg I'.

SURREALIST TRANSLATIONS

SB's translations, which included several prose pieces in addition to the poems republished here, were first published in *This Quarter*, *Surrealist Number* (volume 5.1, September 1932, 72–5, 86–98), guest edited by André Breton. The works which SB translated were selected by the Surrealist Committee and then assigned to him by the editor and publisher of *This Quarter*, Edward W. Titus (SB to James Knowlson, 8.1.71, quoted in James Knowlson, *Samuel Beckett: an exhibition*, *64, 39). In his introduction Titus remarked: 'We shall not speak of the difficulties experienced in putting the material placed at our disposal into English, but we cannot refrain from singling out Mr Samuel Beckett's work for special acknowledgement. His rendering of the Eluard and Breton poems in particular is characterizable only in superlatives' (cf. *LSB1*, 128). The skill and accomplishment of SB's Eluard translations is attested by their frequent reprinting in anthologies of twentieth-century French poetry in translation. The *Surrealist Number* of *This Quarter* was reprinted in 1969 by Arno Press and the *New York Times*.

Beckett seems to have enjoyed working on Breton and Eluard. In a letter written shortly after the translations appeared, Beckett told Thomas MacGreevy that Nancy Cunard had asked him to translate some Eluard and Breton and that he had written to her saying it was always a pleasure to translate the two Surrealist poets (18.10.32; *LSB1*, 135). There is no evidence that anything came of this. A year later the poet Denis Devlin wrote to MacGreevy about a meeting he and Brian Coffey had had with Beckett reporting that Breton had impressed Beckett and that 'Eluard inspires affection' (23.9.33; *LSB1*, 169). However, when George Reavey asked Beckett to undertake further translation (the poem 'La Personnalité toujours neuve' from Eluard's *La Rose Publique*, 1934) for *Thorns of Thunder* (Europa Press and Stanley Nott, 1936), Beckett declined regretfully since he was busy with his novel *Murphy* (2.5.36; *LSB1*, 330, and 6.5.36; *LSB1*, 332).

SB's response to *Thorns of Thunder*, with versions by several hands, was fairly critical (see notes to Eluard's 'Lady Love'). In a letter to TM of 18.1.35 (not in *LSB1*) SB contrasts the real irrationalities of Lucia Joyce with the literary simulations of Breton and Eluard.

André Breton: The Free Union

André Breton (1896–1966) was a founder of the Surrealist movement and its most influential thinker and polemicist.

'L'Union libre' was first published in 1931 and included in *Le Revolver à cheveux blancs* (*The White-Haired Revolver*) in 1932. The title may indicate both free love and the free association of metaphor that characterises the poem. As so often in his translations, Beckett finds highly satisfying English versions for most lines, although the poem gets off to a rather prosaic start in the opening line which translates Breton's 'Ma femme à la chevelure de feu de bois'. Breton's original is 60 lines long, SB's translation 58, since two lines are (inadvertently?) omitted.

Notes

8 'stabbed Host' may allude to a painting by Uccello, the Urbino predella, and is anticipated by Breton's *Nadja* and by Joris-Karl Huysmans (*Là-Bas*, chapter 20).

11 'pothooks' down-strokes' (for French 'bâtons d'écriture d'enfants'); cf. the first line of 'Serena III'.

20 SB reverses 'de martre et de fênes'; 'fêne', more usually 'faine': beech-nut or beech-mast.

21 French: 'De nuit de Saint-Jean'.

22 SB does not translate the final word of this line, 'scalares' in Breton, presumably because he had no idea what it meant. (The term does not appear in *Le Grand Robert*.) Cauvin and Caws assume it is a variant of 'scalaire', an angel-fish or other mollusc (246).

28 of the original is untranslated: 'Ma femme aux pieds d'initiales'.

30 'golden Vale', 'Val d'or' in the original, which Parisian readers would associate with a hilly area of Saint-Cloud, an excursion area outside the city.

31 the sole example in this poem of SB's tendency to resort to biblical or archaic language in his French translations. Breton reads: 'De rendez-vous dans le lit même du torrent'.

35 'spectrum of rose' a (deliberate?) mistranslation of 'spectre de la rose', with its obvious allusion to the famous Diaghilev ballet of 1913.

47 Beckett chooses to Anglicise, rather than translate, French mineralogical 'amiante' (asbestos).

50 'iris' translates 'glaïeul' (gladiolus).

51 'placer' – surface sediment containing particles of gold; 'ornithorynchus' – duck-billed platypus; the following line (line 53 of the original) is untranslated: 'Ma femme aux sexe d'algue et de bonbons anciens'.

56 'water to drink in prison' used in *Dream*, 108 and adapted in *MPTK*: 'dungeon' in 'Fingal' and 'Perrier' in 'A Wet Night' (18; 70).

André Breton: Lethal Relief

First published as 'Le Grand secours meurtrier' in *Le Revolver à cheveux blancs* (*The White-Haired Revolver*) in 1932. The poem is a tribute of sorts to Lautréamont, author of *Les Chants de Maldoror*, regarded as an important precursor by the Surrealists. Indeed, Breton opened his introduction to *This Quarter* with an epithet from Lautréamont: 'At the time of this writing new shivers are running through the intellectual atmosphere: it only needs courage to face them' (7). In his essay 'Poetry's Evidence' later in the volume Eluard quotes Lautréamont some nine times compared with half a dozen quotations from Rimbaud. 'Lethal Relief' was republished in *The Random House Book of Twentieth Century French Poetry*, edited by Paul Auster, in 1984.

Notes

'Le Grand secours meurtrier' has 24 lines, SB's translation 26.
2   'quinine tabloids' translates 'cachets de quinine'.
4   'hiloderm' translates 'héloderm', a type of lizard found in Mexico; SB's 'a shady customer' introduces the trace of a pun absent from the French 'suspect'.
9   Lautréamont was born in Montevideo. There may also be an allusion to the swans at the end of strophe 6 of *Maldoror*. Cf. Beethoven as 'the swan of Bonn' in *Dream* (229), in a passage omitted from 'A Wet Night' (*MPTK*).
10   the laconic 'Should the problem [. . .] arise' translates the crisp 'Lorsque il s'agit'.
15   translates 'se crisperont' from two lines above in the French, adding an extra line to the original.
18   'interversion' translates 'intervertir'; the idea is that the hearts of men and birds are exchanged.
19   'Convulsionary in ordinary' brilliantly translates – and perhaps improves upon – 'en qualité de convulsionnaire'. Cf. the famous last line of *Nadja*, 'La beauté sera CONVULSIVE ou ne sera pas', and *L'Amour fou*, chapter 1: 'Les "beau comme" de Lautréamont constituent le manifeste même de la beauté convulsive' (Chauvin and Caws, 248). Cf. also 'convulsive space', SB's translation of 'espace pantin' in 'what would I do' (q.v.).
25   'squitch' translates 'le chiendent' (couch grass).

Paul Eluard: Lady Love

Paul Eluard (1895–1952) was, with Breton, one of the founders of the Surrealist movement. He is equally celebrated for his love poetry, his political engagement and his poems to painters. He was a close friend of Picasso (cf 'Le Travail du peintre', first published in *Labyrinthe*, 15 juin 1945, no 9; collected in *Poésie ininterrompue*, Paris, Gallimard, 1946 and reproduced with SB's translation in *Transition Forty-Nine* 5, December 1949; q.v.). All of these translations for *This Quarter*, with the sole exception of 'Confections', were reproduced in George Reavey's 1936 Europa Press edition of Eluard's poems, *Thorns of Thunder*, which was published to coincide with The International Surrealist Exhibition in London (11 June–4 July 1936). However, SB expressed strong dissatisfaction with Herbert Read's preface for the book and also with the prospectus which seems to have suggested that Beckett would be reading his translations after Eluard read the originals at Burlington House (9.6.36; *LSB1*, 340). Reavey's edition included translations by several hands. SB commented: '[Eluard] does come through after a fashion, the frailty and nervousness. But no attempt seems to have been made to translate the pauses. Like Beethoven played strictly to time' (17.7.36; *LSB1*, 359). (SB makes several allusions to Beethoven's Seventh Symphony in *Dream* and, in a letter to Axel Kaun, describes it as a 'sound surface torn by enormous pauses' [9.7.37, *LSB1*, 518–19; *Disjecta*, 172].) In 1938, when Beckett had started to write poems in French himself, he considered showing these to Eluard, but there is no evidence that he ever did so. SB's translations are very close to the originals and all the better for that, although, as he told Mac-Greevy, he 'winced' at them (26.7.36; *LSB1*, 362). The *This Quarter* selection (with the exception of 'The Invention') was collected by Calder with, for the first time, the French originals *en face* in the 1977 *CPEF.*

'L'amoureuse' was first published in November 1923 in *Intentions*, no. 19, 23. It was collected in 1924 in *Mourir de ne pas mourir*. Beckett captures the strange simplicity and directness of Eluard's original, occasionally inverting phrases, most notably the third and fourth lines, which read 'Elle a la forme de mes mains, / Elle a la couleur de mes yeux' in the original. David Wheatley in his edition of the *Selected Poems 1930–1989* for Faber (192) is mistaken in saying that 'Lady Love' and 'Out of Sight in the Direction of My Body' were first published in *Thorns of Thunder*.

'Lady Love' was reprinted as part of A. J. Leventhal's essay 'Surrealism or Literary Psycho-Therapy' in the *Dublin Magazine*, XI, n.s. (Oct.–Dec. 1936; the same issue in which 'Cascando' appeared), with the encomium 'Surrealist poetry might be expected to defy translation but Mr. Samuel Beckett has in the following poem caught Paul Eluard's elusiveness'. 'Lady Love' was subsequently reprinted in *The Oxford Book of Verse Translation*, edited by Charles Tomlinson, Oxford University Press, 1980, 496, and *The Random House Book of Twentieth Century French Poetry*, edited by Paul Auster, 1984, 201.

Paul Eluard: Out of Sight in the Direction of My Body

'A perte de vue dans le sens de mon corps' was first published in 'Le Surréalisme au service de la révolution', 1931, no. 4, December 1931, 13, and collected in *La Vie immédiate* the following year. Beckett translates the intimate 'tu' formations in this and other Eluard poems by the archaic 'thine' (line 3) and 'thy' (line 7), but that seems to work well enough here (cf. his translation of 'Delta', undertaken two years earlier). Note, however, that in the eighth line 'Tes idées fixes' is translated as 'The fixed ideas' and subtly alters the sense of the original.

This translation was reprinted in *The Penguin Book of Modern Verse Translation*, 1966, edited by George Steiner, Penguin, 1970, 203, reprinted as *Poem into Poem: World Poetry in Modern Verse Translation* by Penguin in 1970, and in Paul Auster's *The Random House Book of Twentieth Century French Poetry*, 1984, 209.

Paul Eluard: Scarcely Disfigured

'A peine défigurée' also appeared in *La Vie immédiate*. The second line,'Bonjour tristesse', was adopted by Françoise Sagan as the title of her first novel, published in 1954. When the novel appeared in English the French title was retained since any literal translation might appear rather mawkish in English. Hence, perhaps, SB's rather strained 'Greeting sadness' where 'greetings' might have been expected. Eluard's 14 lines are reduced to 13 by

Beckett: 'Puissance de l'amour / Dont l'amabilité surgit / Comme un monstre sans corps' becoming 'Mightiness of love that lovable / Starts up as a bodiless beast'.

This translation was reprinted in *The Penguin Book of Modern Verse Translation*, 1966, edited by George Steiner, Penguin, 1970, 203, reprinted as *Poem into Poem: World Poetry in Modern Verse Translation* by Penguin in 1970.

Paul Eluard: The Invention

'L'invention' first appeared in *L'Invention*, No 1 and *Proverbe*, No 6, 1 July 1921, 3, and was collected in *Répétitions* (*Rehearsals*) published in 1922. 'The Invention' was republished in *The Random House Book of Twentieth Century French Poetry*, edited by Paul Auster, 1984, 199.

Notes

5   translates rather oddly the line 'Tout juste l'agréable durée des moissons'.

8 and **9**   are quoted by Beckett (in French) in his important letter to Thomas MacGreevy (18.10.32; *LSB1*, 134) on the nature of poetry.

Paul Eluard: Second Nature

'Seconde Nature' was the fifth of a series of 25 poems published under that title in *L'Amour la Poésie* (*Love, Poetry*), 1929. Paul Auster adds the Roman numeral 'V' to his reprinting of SB's translation in *The Random House Book of Twentieth Century French Poetry*, 203). SB's version, like Eluard's original, manages without a main verb. The third line is translated somewhat freely from 'Les disparitions du monde sans mystère'.

Paul Eluard: Scene

'La Vue' was first published in *La Vie immédiate*.

Notes

1 'mental viduity': cf. *Krapp's Last Tape* – Krapp's mother's 'long viduity' – 'State – or condition – of being – or remaining – a widow – or widower'. SB jotted down 'vidual' in *DN* *430 and used it in *Dream* (143, 216). In a letter written in French to Jacoba van Velde of late 1958 SB claimed that he had found 'viduity' in Cicero (Cicéron), who uses the word *viduitas* on a number of occasions.

3 'In a most thoroughfare' for 'Dans une rue très passante' introduces a pun absent from the original; cf. also final line, 'In a so thoroughfare' for 'Parmi tant de passants'.

13 cf. the 'dauntless daughter of desires' in 'Sanies I', line 47.

26 'All of a single sudden' translates 'De but en but un seul but nul ne demeure'.

29 'nacre': mother of pearl.

Paul Eluard: Universe-Solitude

When *A toute épreuve* was published as a collection in 1930 it contained a section of fifteen short poems entitled *L'Univers-solitude*. On republication as part of *La vie immédiate* in 1932 Eluard expanded this section to 22 poems. Similarly, *Confections* was also originally part of *A toute épreuve*, where it comprised 14 poems; *Confections* was also republished with additional material (30 poems in total) in *La Vie immédiate* in 1932. SB's *All-Proof* translations should therefore be seen as a selection, although it is unknown whether this selection was made by the editor (Breton), the author (Eluard) or the translator himself. 'All-Proof' is (presumably) SB's rendering of the term *à toute épreuve*, which might more usually and idiomatically be translated as 'foolproof'.

Lake, *52(h), 34, describes Eluard's 6 pp. holograph of the original poem, which is partially reprinted in facsimile on the page facing.

The table following sets out SB's numbering (Arabic numerals) against the numbering in *La Vie immédiate* (Roman) and, where appropriate, *A toute épreuve* (Arabic).

1	II	[1]
2	III	[2]
3	IV	
4	VI	
5	VIII	[5]
6	IX	[6]
7	XI	
8	XIII	
9	XV	
10	XVII	
11	XVIII	

7 'yestersun' translates 'soleil d'hier'.

Paul Eluard: Confections

The table below sets out SB's numbering (Arabic numerals) against the numbering in *La Vie immédiate* (Roman) and, where appropriate, *A toute épreuve* (Arabic).

1	I	[1]	
2	III	[3]	
3	IV	[4]	
4	VIII	[5]	* only poem out of Eluard's sequence
5	VI		
6	VII		
7	XI	[6]	
8	XII		
9	XVIII		
10	XVI		
11	XVII		
12	XIX		
13	XX		
14	XXI	[9]	
15	XXII		
16	XXIV	[10]	
17	XXVI	[11]	
18	XXVIII	[12]	
19	XXIX		

The 'Confections' poems were not included in *Thorns of Thunder*.

Notes

1   'yea' translates 'même'; cf. 'The Free Union', line **31**, and line **35** of 'Sanies I'.
3   SB omits Eluard's fifth line 'Une plage peu fréquentée', reducing this poem from 8 to 7 lines.
9   'rapt' translates 'immobile'; cf. *Dream*, 23: 'rapt, like the spirit of a troubadour, casting no shade, herself shade'. In 1812, Napoleon's army suffered heavy losses at the battle of Beresina on its retreat from Moscow. Since then, 'c'est la bérézina' has been a synonym for catastrophe in French. Cf. 'as though he had just brought an army over the Beresina' (*Dream*, 203, repeated in 'A Wet Night', *MPTK*, 47). Cf. also *Dream*, 23: 'amorously cast open the double-jug dugs'.

Tristan Tzara: [from] The Approximative Man

This and the following poem are unsigned translations from the September 1932 *This Quarter* special Surrealist number which are possibly not SB's, but which leave the strong impression that they might be. SB's 'Tzara next' (TM [9.10.31]; not in *LSB1*) cannot refer to Nancy Cunard's *NEGRO* anthology, which contains no texts by Tzara. The five selections, from which we have made our own selection in the uncertain circumstances, are among the best versions of Tzara (born Sami Rosenstock in Romania in 1896, died in Paris in 1963) in English. From 'L'homme approximatif' (VIII), 1928.

Notes

4   'felons' for 'voleurs'.
6   'haloes' for 'auréoles'.
11   'the fields the eyes had closed' for 'les champs fermés par les yeux'; cf. SB's 'yeux clos' in *Dream*, 21, and his description of a poem as 'unsighted' (letter to TM of 13.[9.32], *LSB1*, 121).
12   'screwing [. . .] screw' for 'se vissant [. . .] l'écrou'; cf. line **40** of 'Serena I'.
16   'mirror' for 'glace'.
25   'grew withered' for 's'est recroquevillée'.

Tristan Tzara: Reminder

From 'The Traveller's Tree', 1930.

Notes

6   'plaintive' for 'douloureux'.
10 'frail' for 'légères'; 'avoids you' for 'vous finit'.
14 'depressing' for 'lourde'.

Ernst Moerman: Louis Armstrong

Ernst Moerman (1879–1944) is now perhaps best remembered (if at all) for his 1937 Surrealist film *Monsieur Fantômas*. SB's translation of this poem was first published in Nancy Cunard's massive *NEGRO: an anthology* (London: Wishart & Co, 1934, 295–6), for which Beckett supplied 19 translations now conveniently collected in Alan W. Friedman's *Beckett in Black and Red* (Lewisburg: University Press of Kentucky, 2000). Friedman twice (11, 186–7) gives the poem's title as 'Armstrong', which is reserved by Wheatley, 2009 (122) for the French original; but both in the body of *NEGRO* (which does not print the original French text), and on its contents page, the title is given as 'Louis Armstrong'. Whether SB ever received the £25 he had apparently been promised for his labours on Nancy Cunard's behalf (letter to MacGreevy of 9.10.31) has been questioned (Friedman, xxiii–xxiv), but here, in one of his earliest attempts at translating a poem from French (probably ready at the latest by January 1933, perhaps the product of work done between August and December 1932), there is overwhelming evidence of a virtual recomposition of the rather pallid original (Friedman, 186–7), and considerable ingenuity is employed in making a much more vivid poem out of it. If, as seems likely, SB translated Moerman close in time to making his version of Rimbaud's 'Le Bateau ivre' (early to mid-1932), it would help to explain why Moerman's poem ends up in this version looking a little as if it might have been a Rimbaud cast-off. As Friedman says (xxix, xxx), this is 'jazzlike' and 'slangier'.

Notes

10 'down down down down': a reiteration with no real equivalent in the original French; cf. 'Draff' (of Hairy Quin: 'down, down, down'; *MPTK*, 173), which probably postdates 'Louis Armstrong' by nine months or more.

13 'Narcissus lean and slippered': possesses 'a Shakespearean resonance which is absent from the French original ['un miroir où la douleur se regarde vieillir']', as noted in Lawlor, 2011, 29, who cites the 'lean and slippered pantaloon' from *As You Like It*, Act II, scene vii, Jaques's Seven Ages of Man speech. Beckett studied *As You Like It* at TCD in the Michaelmas Term of 1924 (Frederik N. Smith, *Beckett's Eighteenth Century*, Basingstoke: Palgrave, 2002, 168).

19–20 'the black music it can't be easy / it threshes the old heart': there is no real equivalent in the French original, SB having here adapted phrases from 'Enueg II' (summer 1931) and 'Serena II' (autumn 1932).

34 for 'suck', cf. line **27** of 'Sanies II'; the image is not present in Moerman.

POÈMES 37–39

SB's first published poems in French (*Les Temps modernes*, II, November 1946, 288–93) were written in Paris before the outbreak of the Second World War, but only appeared in print after the cessation of hostilities, in November 1946, in the second issue of Jean-Paul Sartre's magazine, under the title *Poèmes '38–39'*. In *Gedichte* and subsequent collections the dates were changed to '1937 to 1939' to accommodate 'Dieppe'. In *Les Temps modernes*, the twelve poems were numbered I–XIII, but with no number XI. Despite this anomaly, SB wrote to George Reavey on 14.5.47: 'Thirteen poems, old, have appeared in the *Temps modernes*' (*LSB2*, 55). When the poems were republished in *Gedichte* (1959) and subsequently, the numbering was abandoned. They were first collected in France in *Poèmes*, Minuit, 1968, in an edition of 662 copies (plus 100 *hors commerce*) [with notes and variants by John Fletcher] (F&F *279, 73–4). SB returned the proofs of this edition to Jérôme Lindon on 13.12.67. In Calder's 1977 *Collected Poems* the order of appearance of 'Dieppe' (untitled in *Les Temps modernes*) and 'Rue de Vaugirard' was reversed, perhaps to facilitate the *en face* English translation which was collected there for the first time, although the English version was in fact the earliest of these poems to appear (in the *Irish Times*, 9.6.45). They were republished in *Poèmes suivi de mirlitonnades*, Minuit, 1978, in *CPEF* and in Calder's 2002 *Poems 1930–1989*.

Two much earlier poems in French, 'Tristesse Janale' (1930) and 'Ce n'est au pélican' (?1931), had apparently never been offered to editors, and had been effectively jettisoned. During the 1930s SB had occasionally written squibs and suchlike (e.g. 'C'est une Dent'; card to GR, 15.2.37; *LSB1*, 442; tried out in SB's *German Diary* a few days earlier; the publisher Dent had recently turned down *Murphy*), and occasionally whole letters in a language in which he had been fluent since TCD days. But it was not until after returning from Germany (March 1937) that SB gave much thought to the possibilities of 'violat[ing] a foreign language' (letter to Axel Kaun of 9.7.37, *LSB1*, 512–20; *Disjecta*, 173). In taking up permanent residence in Paris, SB may have started to write directly into French on some *faute de mieux* basis. But he may also have been prompted to do so by his recent reading, some of it in French (e.g. Jean-Paul Sartre's Husserl-inspired *L'Imagination*, 1936), but much of it in German (e.g the philosophers Kant and Mauthner). It is tempting to think of these French poems, relatively straightforward as they are, as indirectly influenced by the *epoche* (or 'bracketing') of Phenomenology, and more particularly by Mauthner's attack on metaphor, and language generally, in his *Beiträge zu einer Kritik der Sprache*. Most if not all of the extensive notes which SB took from Mauthner's *Beiträge* in the *'Whoroscope' Notebook* were probably entered in the late spring or early summer of 1938 (Pilling, 2006, 162ff.; 2005, 37).

The recondite manner of the *EBOP* collection was well within SB's compass on switching to French (as is evidenced by a number of letters and most extensively by the spoof lecture of 1930, 'Le Concentrisme' [*Disjecta*, 35–42]), but he chose instead to adopt a deliberate simplification and refinement of means and method, reducing (if not wholly abandoning) allusions, exploring the self-sustaining subtleties of syntax without necessarily emphasising the verbal surface and without surrendering unexpected juxtapositions, and contenting himself for the most part with a single and singular focus. Even when the material in these poems expands beyond a dozen or so lines – 'être là sans mâchoires sans dents' has 20 lines; 'Ascension' 18; 'ainsi a-t-on beau' 14 and 'Arènes de Lutèce' 23 – a general terseness creates the tension. In asking GR to change the title of his first collection from *Poems* to *EBOP*, SB had suggested that the alternative was 'plus modeste', and the French poems are indeed more 'modest'. All of them, moreover, read like 'precipitates', whereas only some of the *EBOP* poems do. Along with a difference in language and stance go other differences: whereas all thirteen poems of *EBOP* have titles, only four of the *TM* poems or five of the poems as collected do. It seems likely that SB was trying to 'echo' (cf. 'Cascando'), in this first collection of French poems, his only published collection in English (*EBOP*). The 1935 volume is through-composed, even though it is a collection only assuming a kind of unity after the fact, having been reduced to thirteen poems from the much larger number envisaged for *POEMS*. These twelve French poems – cf. letters to George Reavey of 15.12.46 and 14.5.47 (*LSB2*, 48, 55), which speak of thirteen – are not simply a collection in the sense of having been brought together in one place, but maintain, and in some ways strengthen, the 'theme and variations' pattern of the earlier volume. The same subjects recur and interweave throughout: sexual activity (together with the idea of sameness and otherness), emptiness, and time as a fluid medium in which past, present and future co-exist.

In two letters of 1938, one to TM (15.6; *LSB1*, 630), and the other to GR (undated, and lacking a leaf, but after 24.10 [*LSB1*, 648]), SB writes: 'I enclose the last few poems in French. When I have enough I thought of taking them to Eluard', and 'I have 10 poems in French [. . .]. Mostly short. When I have a few more I shall send them to Eluard. Or get Duchamp to do so.' It seems significant that Beckett was thinking of these two figures, one the epitome of the spirit of Dada, the other a key figure in the history of Surrealism, as possible 'agents' for these poems. In the event, much later (in 1946), the role of agent seems to have fallen to Jacoba van Velde.

[I] they come / elles viennent

First written (it had 'dictated itself'; *LSB1*, 596) in English as 'they come', on SB's discharge from the Hôpital Broussais, as he told TM (mentioning 'the night before last') in a letter of 27.1.38. A few days later (11.2.38; not in *LSB1*) he told him that he had sent the poem to *Ireland To-day*, where it did not appear, and that his friend Alfred Péron had incorrectly translated its lead line '*ils* viennent'. SB's sexual involvements with women at this time (and in particular with Suzanne Deschevaux-Dumesnil, Peggy Guggenheim and Adrienne Bethell) were exceptionally tangled, one reason why, in a letter to Arland Ussher of 12.5.38, he ironically described the new poems as 'French anacreontics', poems in the manner of Anacreon, in praise of love or wine (*LSB1*, 622). The motif of 'absence' sets up resonances with the later poems in the collection, but this is the most 'formal' of these poems, with line-lengths and units of syntax adapted to one another, as if SB's turbulent feelings might yet be brought under aesthetic control, as later they certainly cannot.

The poem was first published in Peggy Guggenheim's *Out of This Century* (1946, 205n; 1979, 175), where the initial letter of each line is capitalised and the final line reads 'With each the absence of life is the same'. F&F comment: 'the variant "life" for "amour" [. . .] is almost certainly a genuine Beckettian variant' (*30, 23). However, given Beckett's declaration that the poem 'dictated itself' in the form we recognise, this may be open to doubt. Peggy Guggenheim writes that Beckett 'never seemed to be able to make up his mind whether or not he was going to have me, but he did not want to give me up. (To replace our sex life, we used to drink wildly and then walk all over Paris until the early morning.).' Peggy further states that Beckett 'said he was dead and had no feelings that were human and that was why he had not been able to fall in love with Joyce's daughter' (175). She prints a poem that she wrote, addressed to Beckett after a sexual fiasco. It includes the lines:

To my void she came much wanting
Shall I chance this fear unending?
[. . .]

Shall I kill her Holy passion?
Destroying life, not taking action? (176)

Peggy's direct, if rhetorical, way of putting things offers a useful insight into the mental state in which Beckett wrote some of
these poems.

[II] à elle l'acte calme

This is the first of these poems to shift the burden of meaning
from structured, repetitive units (as in 'they come') to the play of
syntax across line-ends, and within the lines; and the first to em-
body 'absence' in the poem itself with a break between stanzas.
The early dominance of the definite article weakens to the indefi-
nite in lines **6–7**, and the last word has no article at all, although it
creates a kind of half-rhyme.

Notes

1   'calme': cf. 'Le Calmant' (1946), the last line of 'bon bon il est
un pays' (1947), and what Vladimir and Estragon make of the
word in *Waiting for Godot* (perhaps by way of Verlaine: *The Theatrical Notebooks of Samuel Beckett*, vol. 1, ed. Dougald McMillan and James Knowlson, London: Faber and Faber, 1993, 134).
Coughlan (198) asks: 'Is it he or she who is capable of the "calm
act"?', and suggests the matter is best left undecided. If there is an
ambiguity at the start of the poem, however, the concluding three
lines are a strong indication that the 'calm act' is hers.
2   'bon enfant' qualifying 'le sexe': French slang for 'a very good
sort', perhaps also by analogy 'bonne femme' (simple home-
cooked food).
3–4   cf. poem [I].
5   'l'azur' (cf. line **8** of poem [V]) is a favourite motif of Mallarmé; 'les points [. . .] morts' means 'neutral gears'.
6   cf. 'je voudrais que mon amour meure'.

[III] être là sans mâchoires sans dents

This comes closest (with 'ainsi-a-t-on beau' and 'jusque dans la
caverne' at a further remove) to SB's *EBOP* manner. Although it

in no way resembles any of the *Fêtes Galantes* of Paul Verlaine (who had also been hospitalised in the Broussais), it may be the poem of a 'conversation galante'-type that Brian Coffey had in mind in an essay on *Murphy* ('Memory's Murphy Maker: some notes on Samuel Beckett', *Threshold* [Belfast], 17, 1962, 28–36). If this is indeed the poem Coffey had in mind, it seems probable that the potential (if 'indiscriminate') association of 'death-bed' with 'whoral foras' (SB to AJL, 7.8.35 [not in *LSB1*]) in connection with 'Da Tagte Es') is here being reanimated more discriminatingly, but because of its subject matter more obscurely. Oblique periphrasis, rather than plain or direct statement, serves to keep dark matters dark. There are also, arising out of the situation, more subjunctives ('qu'elle mouille' in lines 10 and 15; 'parfasse tout le superflu' in line 16; and 'et vienne' in line 17), as if to reinforce the effect. Even so, this is perhaps the most sexualised of a group of poems with an unusually large and intense concentration on sexual content by comparison with SB's practice elsewhere.

Notes

1   cf. the opening line of 'Mort de A.D.', a poem much more a matter of 'death-bed' [see the headnote above], and cf. also another very different kind of utterance ('Là/ Go where never before'), written some fifty years later, shortly before SB's own death.

5   Roscelin was a twelfth-century Nominalist tried for, but acquitted of, heresy. Nominalists believed in individuals over species, names rather than things, in contradistinction to Realists, who believed that Universals had a real, objective existence. SB had read about Nominalists and Realists in Windelband, and had opted for the former over the latter in his unsent 1937 letter to Axel Kaun (*Disjecta*, 53, 173). Roscelin is presumably invoked here to emphasise the [Nominalist] particularity of the act, in an attempt to reduce the [Realist] idea of Universals and transform them into merely words (*flatus voci*) or an emission of sound, in a poem in which sounds are given an unusual prominence, e.g. lines 7–8, 20, etc.). This attempt is then brought up short by 'et on attend', a phrase in which the poet's subjectivity is 'objectified' by the use of the impersonal pronoun.

Roscelin is also mentioned in typewritten notes taken from R. P. Gredt, OSB, *Elementia philosophia*[e] *aristotelico-thomistica*[e] (Fribourg: Herder, 7th edition, 1937) (TCD MS 10971/6; SBT/A, 16, 154). This is an unusually recondite source, even for Beckett, and would presumably not have come to his attention without the influence of his friend Brian Coffey – poet, exceptional Latinist, and Thomist scholar – acting as an intermediary. Coffey's apparently close involvement with SB's 1937–9 poems has yet to be fully investigated, but SB's sense of Coffey's early poems as 'another pair of sleeves' (letter to TM of 9.1.35; not in *LSB1*) suggests that Coffey was more an intellectual influence than a poetic one. There does, however, seem to have been some kind of sexual triangle of a rather less highbrow nature involving SB, Coffey and Peggy Guggenheim during the spring and summer months of 1938 (*Other Edens*, 85, 94), with or without Roscelin being called on for guidance as to how best to proceed. Coffey's collection *Third Person* was published in London by Europa Press in 1938.

8   the quotation here, 'identified' by the use of italics, is from a popular 'chanson' of the 'mal mariée' type, in which a female laments the (sexual) inadequacy of a 'petit homme' (cf. 'petit cadeau', French slang for a prostitute's payment [Harvey, 194], and by implication a penis, earlier [line **6**]), where it is imaged as an 'adverbe' (cf. 'accusative' in 'Sanies I', line **44**). The reader has to supply the missing element(s) in a situation in which some failure of gallantry or something like it is almost certainly an issue. The 'elle' figure here seems to have excited herself to no purpose, or at least on her own.

9   'faisant la fleur': SB adapts the expression 'faire une fleur à quelqu'un' which means to do someone a favour, probably unexpected, or to pay them an exceptional compliment. Harvey, presumably prompted by SB, proposes (194) that in this context the phrase refers to an interweaving or interlocking of hands and fingers as in a 'familiar pastime'. The possibility that SB attached this special meaning to the phrase is reinforced by the German translation of the phrase in *Gedichte* (59), by Elmar Tophoven working in collaboration with SB: 'mit den Fingern spielend'. Both Harvey and Tophoven soft-pedal what seems to be more a matter of intimacy than familiarity, with 'qu'elle mouille' so close at hand.

10 and 15 While apparently not sharing his irritation, SB undoubtedly has in mind Jules Renard's 'aussi navrant que le "attendez que je mouille" d'une vierge' ('as irritating as a virgin's "wait till I'm wet"'; undated, 1887, *DN*212*).

12 Les Halles, famous for its market, where the Pompidou Centre now stands, was a well-known area for prostitution.

16 implying: 'would that all the superfluous preliminaries [left 'suitably' unspecified] were over and done with'.

18 'formicante': cf. SB's use of the word 'formication' in line **10** of his translation of Velarde's 'Ants' [q.v.], and in *Happy Days* and *Oh les beaux jours*, where it mingles the sensation of ants crawling on the skin with the sound affinity of 'fornication'.

19 'au bloc cave [. . .]': in the translation by Elmar Tophoven for *Gedichte*, overseen by SB, this becomes 'zum Hohlkopf [. . .]', i.e. to or with an empty head. Wheatley 2009, doubtless with an eye to the dynamic of an innuendo, has: 'to the basement door' (179).

20 the 'ciseaux argentins' is probably a reference to Atropos and the severing of the thread of life by the Fates; cf. the *mirlitonnade* 'noire soeur' (q.v.).

[IV] Ascension

Sent, with what became poems [V] and [VI], to TM, probably as enclosures with the letter of 15.6.38 (a letter of that date speaks of 'the last few French poems' [*LSB1*, 630]), which are presumably what he also has in mind in writing of 'Only a few more French poems' in a letter to George Reavey of 20.6.38 [*LSB1*, 633]). The TM version has a variant last two lines:

en reçoit-il une colombe
aussi souvent que moi

which help to justify the title. The published version makes 'elle' dominant but the message from above is drowned in or by the airwaves ('airs') of the radio, and the cries of the crowd. The contrast between the radio emissions and the deathbed scene makes this a particularly striking, and even shocking, poem.

Notes

1 the 'mince cloison' reflects SB's lifelong interest in the point of contact (and division) between inside and outside, which stretches from as early as *Proust*, through the 'tympanum' of *L'Innommable* (*The Unnamable*, 100), and at least as far as the late poem 'something there' (q.v.). Surprisingly, Coughlan takes the thin partition to be the skull so that the poet is overhearing other parts of himself. This seems clearly mistaken.

2–3 SB varies the biblical 'prodigal son' to 'prodigal child' to embrace the female subject of this poem, his cousin Peggy Sinclair, whose spectral presence is revealed as the poem progresses. This 'enfant prodigue' is also Christ ascending to Heaven on Ascension Thursday having been prodigal with his love of mankind.

5–6 the voice of a commentator on the 1938 World Cup football tournament, held in Paris, won by Italy. In letters to TM of 26.5.38 and 15.6.38 (*LSB1*, 626, 630) SB mentions a noisy 'wireless' (heard through too thin a 'cloison' between himself and an adjoining apartment), probably the more annoying because of his own interest in rugby, and of course cricket. Note also the first occurence of 'voix' – other voices, coming to the poet – which recurs in 'musique de l'indifférence' (line **4**) and the second line of 'jusque dans la caverne'.

8 SB's cousin, and first love, Peggy Sinclair died at the age of 22 from tuberculosis on 3 May 1933. Ascension Day 1938 fell just after the fifth anniversary of her death, on 16 May, and the World Cup about a month later. This line prepares the reader for lines **13–16**.

10 'tout court': directly, through the window, not via the wireless.

13–16 a switch from present to perfect tense as SB borrows an image which he had used to describe the death of his father: '[h]e lay in the bed with sweet pea ['des pois de senteur'] all over his face' (2.7.33; *LSB1*, 165) to imagine the death of Peggy Sinclair; 'mec', simply 'bloke' – Peggy's German fiancé Heiner Starcke was with her when she died. Cf. also Beckett's recollections of the death of his father in the last three poems in *EBOP* and in 'ainsi a-t-on beau'. For another death from tuberculosis, see 'Mort de A.D'.

17 'rôde': all previous publications have 'rode' which is incorrect, as a 1946 'Vendredi' letter (probably from either the second half of October or very early in November; *LSB2*, 46) to Jacoba van Velde makes clear. 'Rôder' means 'to prowl', 'roder' to 'grind or polish'. The poet is entombed in the noises carried across the airwaves while the dead girl is, in some sense, released to prowl lightly above him.

[V] La Mouche

This fly is a kind of cousin to the 'common housefly' who was 'my brother' in the last section of 'Serena I'. Here there are no brotherly feelings, but an extraordinary exercise in close observation, especially in the second section, which ends by paying a kind of compliment to a tiny creature that is nevertheless capable of upsetting the sea and the serene heavens (cf. lines 9 and 10).

Notes

4   'ventre à terre': 'flat out', 'hell for leather'.
5   'sanglée dans ses boyaux': entangled in its own guts.
8   'l'azur': a favourite motif of Mallarmé (cf. line 5 of poem [II]).

[VI] musique de l'indifférence

When he sent this poem to TM in the summer of 1938 SB gave it the title 'Prière' (cf. the 'prayer' reference in a letter to Nuala Costello of 27.2.34; *LSB1*, 188; a similar reference in a letter to TM of 8.8.35, not in *LSB1*; and 'Musset's prayer' in a letter to Mary Manning Howe of 22.5.37, not in *LSB1*), although 'music' in the early works is a 'synecdoche' for sex (e.g. 'To Be Sung Loud'; *Murphy*, 50, etc.). It was in reviewing TM's *Poems* for the *Dublin Magazine* in 1934 (*Disjecta*, 68–9) that SB first made public his belief that 'All poetry is prayer' (an idea of which he reminded himself in his *German Diaries*), and there is a prayer-like aspect in the last three lines here, by way of an imperative (uttered perhaps more in hope than in expectation) and, subsequently, the subjunctive mood of the verb (cf. the three subjunctives in the poem 'être là . . .', and elsewhere in this group). The five substantives of line 2 – heart time air fire sand, a unique succession of monosyllables in this group of poems – seem to define this 'music of indifference' which is immediately restated as a music of silence, engulfer of loves (cf. 'éboulement' or 'landslip' in line 3). The element of prayer is apparent in the invocation to cover their voices (for a similar use of the plural see the first poem of this sequence) and to silence the poet so that he will no longer hear himself. This prayer is apparently unanswered since the 'vieilles voix' are still heard even from beyond the tomb in the last of these poems, 'jusque dans la caverne' (line 2). In a letter to George Reavey of 27.9.38 SB uses the phrase 'handful of sand' (*LSB1*, 642).

[VII] bois seul

A poem which twice emphasises 'seul' (lines 1 and 2), but which nevertheless more often exploits the plural forms which SB may have particularly associated with Rimbaud, whose 'Le Bateau ivre' (with plurals in almost every line) he had translated in the spring of 1932. Abstract plurals are much more common, and much more comfortable, in French than they are in English, but SB's interest seems also to be in contrasting words like 'les absents' and 'les présents' with strikingly physical bodily functions, and in generating a disjunctive tension between monosyllables (seven in the first eight words) and multisyllables, as if rhythm were more important to him than melody, and juxtapositions to be preferred to harmonies.

Notes

3   cf. the absent/present motif of 'elles viennent'.
4   the 'roseaux' (reeds) may owe something to Pascal's sense of man as a 'thinking reed', inventive but frail, in one of his most famous *Pensées*, jotted down in the *'Whoroscope' Notebook*, perhaps close in time to the composition of this poem. Here, however, the sense is of turning away from mankind towards an insentient being (cf. 'Dieppe' and 'the turning away from the local' in a letter to TM of 31.1.38; *LSB1*, 599). W. B. Yeats's 'wind amongst the reeds' may also have been in mind.
5   the 'aïs' are three-toed sloths (cf. the 'mammouth' and 'dinothérium' of poem |VIII|. For 'sors tes yeux', cf. Matthew 5:29. The 'yeux clos' motif in *Dream*, 21, and elsewhere, is adapted from Rimbaud, and is a favourite SB point of reference. But the variation here may be predicated on 'it is useless to close the eyes' ('Serena II', line 45).

7 'veille': wakefulness or, in the sense of vigil, aligning this poem with the 'attente' of 'à elle l'acte calme' (line 3) and the 'attend' of 'être là sans mâchoires sans dents' (line 5). SB uses the phrase 'l'état de vielle' in the *nouvelle* 'La Fin' (*Nouvelles et textes pour rien*, 116), translated in 'The End' as 'waking' (*The Expelled*, etc., 54).

[VIII] ainsi a-t-on beau

This poem adapts details from Ernst Cassirer's study of the life and works of Kant (received from Munich in early 1938; TM 5.1.38, *LSB1*, 581), and from the third of Fritz Mauthner's three-volume *Beiträge zu einer Kritik der Sprache* (1923 Munich edition) – notes from both being found together in the *'Whoroscope' Notebook* – to a meditation upon the death of SB's father five years earlier, in June 1933. The perspective is rendered prehistoric by way of Mauthner, and historical by way of the Lisbon earthquake of 1756, on which subject Voltaire wrote a famous poem. In the *'Sottisier' Notebook* (UoR MS. 2901) is a *mirlitonnade*, 'somme toute' (q.v.; based on Voltaire's 'Poème sur le désastre de Lisbonne'), probably written in late January 1977. Cf. also *Watt*, 35, for 'a man buried alive in Lisbon on Lisbon's great day'.

Notes

4–5 the two extinct creatures are from volume 2, 644 of Mauthner.
5 'les premiers baisers': from Alfred de Musset's poem 'Souvenir' (*DN* *1093), the lovers' first kisses being followed by their first oaths or vows.
9 'générations de chênes': in the *'Whoroscope' Notebook* SB enters the phrase 'a generation of oaks' (in English, translated from volume 2, 648 of Mauthner).
11 'bon': in the *TM* printing 'gentil'.

[IX] Dieppe

'Dieppe', the tenth poem in the *CPEF* sequence, was also the ninth poem in Michael Lonsdale's reading of *Poèmes suivi de mirlitonnades* for the LP Atalect A110. SB told Federman and

Fletcher (F&F* 370, 75) that it was originally written in French, although it first appeared in a variant five-line English version in the *Irish Times* (9.6.45) under the title 'DIEPPE 193?' (*sic*). The use of capitals, a date in the title and the five-line structure of the original publication foreshadow 'SAINT-LO 1945' which would appear a year later in June 1946. As the *Irish Times* printing of 'Dieppe' in 1945 makes clear, the date of composition is impossible to reconstruct exactly, but subsequent printings have ascribed it to 1937. It may well (if first written in English) pre-date 'à elle l'acte calme'. In more than one respect, however, it is German in spirit, like the earlier (1934) quatrain 'Da Tagte Es' (q.v.). The direct inspiration is Hölderlin's 'Der Spaziergang', mentioned and quoted from in SB's review of Denis Devlin's collection *Intercessions*, written in late 1937 (*LSB1*, 549) but not published until the last pre-war number of *transition* in April 1938. SB had apparently been reading Hölderlin in late 1937 (his copy at UoR has the date 24.12.37 in it), and he refers to 'the terrific fragments of the Spätzeit', of which 'Der Spaziergang' is one, in a letter of 14.6.[39] to Arland Ussher (*LSB1*, 665); but other inspirations were more personal. The words 'encore' and 'dernier' in line 1 echo (across the language divide) SB's own poem 'Cascando' (itself echoic), and it was in late 1937 that SB took the Newhaven–Dieppe ferry on his return to France from Dublin (where, having left it only a few weeks earlier, he had gone back to testify on behalf of Harry Sinclair in a libel trial). There was every reason, then, whether looking backwards or forwards, to think of the 'vieilles lumières', or lights of old. These 'vieilles *lumi*ères', which are elements in an 'invocation of the unsaid by the said', are perhaps an index of 'a mind aware of its *lumi*naries' (*Disjecta*, 94), one of whom was (for SB) Hölderlin.

Denis Devlin's translation of Hölderlin's 'Dem Sonnengott' as 'To the Sun God' was first published in his posthumous *Translations into English*, ed. Roger Little, Dublin: Dedalus Press, 1992, 301, which also includes 32 selections from René Char (q.v.), and two from Alain Bosquet (q.v.). Devlin's *Collected Poems*, ed. J. C. C. Mays, Dublin: Dedalus Press, 1989, contains 'Congratulations on your edition of Denis Devlin's "Collected Poems". / Amends at last. // Samuel Beckett' [7], but in 1933 and 1937 his feelings about Devlin's poems were more mixed (letters to TM of 9.10.33 and 21.9.37; *LSB1*, 166 and 549): 'Amends [. . .]' may suggest that SB felt he had not supported Devlin sufficiently wholeheartedly fifty years earlier. (Cf. in this connection, the quotations from TM's October 1937 essay contrasting SB and Devlin, as quoted in the notes to 'Alba' and 'Serena II' above, some of the terms of which may perhaps have rankled with SB at the time, however faint they had become across the years.)

It was presumably a four-line version of this poem (in English) that Beckett sent to Blanaid Salkeld for her projected 'Dublin Poets and Artists' broadsheets at her Gayfield Press (letters of 6.6.39 to TM, and to Mary Manning Howe, the latter in *LSB1*, 659, and see 661 fn8), where it did not appear. SB wrote the English version of 'Dieppe' (and 'Saint-Lô', q.v.) into Eugene Jolas's copy of *EBOP* (xerox in UoR), although it is unclear when he did so. A typescript of the poem in English and French with corrections in Beckett's hand is in the Calvin Israel collection, Burns Library, Boston College. (There never was a comparable collection at SUNY, Geneseo, New York, *contra* Admussen, 40). In a letter to Barbara Bray of 17.2.59 (TCD) SB quotes the French text of this poem (with an overwritten capital 'E' in the first line), from which he considered using 'The Last Ebb' as the title for the radio play which in due course became *Embers*. But in the same letter he rejects his own suggestion, as if (after 'Cascando') it were too much of a cliché: 'enough of lasts that are never'. On 11.3.59, in a letter to the same correspondent, he reiterated: '*The Last Ebb* alone will not do', after telling her, 'The real title is the first line of the little poem *Again the Last Ebb*'. In a letter of 24.7.60 SB tried to dissuade John Calder from reprinting 'Dieppe' and the other three of the 'Quatre poèmes' (q.v.), because Lindon and Minuit had prior claims over them, and the permission rights (UoR). The French texts were, however, reprinted *en face* in Calder's 1961 *Poems in English*.

Variants

Untitled in *TM*, titled 'DIEPPE 193?' in *Irish Times*.
Five lines in *Irish Times*: 'again/the last ebb/the dead shingle/the turning then the steps/to the lighted town'. This is reduced to four lines in Jolas.

4 'to the lighted town' in *Irish Times* and Jolas; 'towards the lighted town' in *Poems in English* (1961); 'towards the lights of old' in *CPEF* (1977) and subsequently. Cf. *Watt*: 'on the dark shingle the turning for the last time again to the lights of the little town' (32), an echo slightly obscured in the French translation, on which SB worked with Ludovic and Agnès Janvier: 'sur les galets nocturnes chaque fois pour la dernière le demi-tour vers les feux du bourg' (Minuit, 40).

Notes

3 the 'demi-tour' is, in English, 'the turning'; cf. 'the turning away from the local' in a letter to TM of 31.1.38 (*LSB1*, 581). Whenever SB discussed this poem (as, for example, with Lawrence Harvey in person, or with Barbara Bray in a letter of 17.2.59), he emphasised that 'puis' ('then') – the word which, as it were, 'does' the turning – was the key word; he associated it with Hölderlin's 'Dann' in 'Der Spaziergang'.

[**X**; ninth in the *CPEF* sequence] **Rue de Vaugirard**

A short poem, a kind of snapshot, 'taken' (as if found) on the longest street in Paris, which begins close to where SB had his apartment in the rue des Favorites. The 'je' figure is apparently not, as might be supposed, riding a bicycle, but walking (Harvey notes; Dartmouth College). In a letter to George Reavey of 27.9.38 (*LSB1*, 643) SB comments, after imparting the news of the impending wedding of Brian Coffey and Bridget Baynes in London: 'Here there is a great afflux of tenderness, even in the commune of Vaugirard', raising the possibility that this poem is intended as a sort of wedding photograph!

Notes

1 cf. the note to line 3 of 'Dieppe' (above), and also perhaps 'Nel mezzo del cammin di nostra vita' at the beginning of *Inferno* in Dante's *Divina Commedia*. In 1938 SB was 32, almost halfway through his allotted 'three score years and ten'.
2 'je me débraye' in the *TM* printing.
3 the word 'expose', in combination with 'débraye' (line **2**, a

word associated with changing gear, although SB emphasised to Harvey that the idea was of a walker metaphorically going into neutral), and 'négatif' (line 5) represents the opening and closing of the poet's eye of 'candeur' as if it were the shutter of a camera (cf. 'Return to the Vestry' of 1929; q.v.), or as if some disengagement were occurring.

[XII] Arènes de Lutèce

The most expansive of the *TM* poems, and the only one with punctuation. The Arènes – of 1st-century Roman origin, but only rediscovered when the rue Monge was being built in the 1860s – are in the 5th *arrondissement* of Paris (in Latin 'Lutetia'), a tidy walk from the rue des Favorites but fairly close to the Ecole Normale Supérieure where Beckett lived from 1928–30. Whose 'triste visage' we are left with at the end of the poem is unclear in a poem where some splitting of the self between ego and others (including a dog) seems to have occurred. The 'triste visage' may look back to the face-to-face encounter with Mr Endon in *Murphy*, which prefigures the death of the eponymous 'hero' in that novel. In its way it anticipates the face of the TV play . . . *but the clouds* . . ., and the *mirlitonnade* with the title (the only one with a title) 'rentrer'.

Variant

2   'je vous vois' in the *TM* printing.

Notes

4   'le sable sombre': cf. line 17, and 'like dust of sand, on the arena, after the massacres' (*The Unnamable*, 92).
6   green is an unusual colour for a dog. There is a dog in Kensington Gardens in *Murphy*, where only the love of biscuits seems to matter, but in *Krapp's Last Tape* and in part I of *Comment c'est/How it is* a dog and questions of love are combined. There are several dogs (one of the most important being called Teddy!) in *Molloy*.
10   Gabriel de Mortillet (1821–98) was a palaeontologist and palaeoethnologist. Coughlan (200–1) sees the statue – which does not represent de Mortillet but is dedicated to him (it was sculpted

by A. Le Penne in 1905 and looks down over the amphitheatre) – combined with the title of the poem, as establishing, as effectively underwritten by the title of the poem, 'a long perspective which is reminiscent of the poem "ainsi a-t-on beau"'; an even longer perspective is implied in poem [XIII].

17   'la bruine': fine drizzling rain.

18   'un cerceau': a child's hoop.

20–21   cf. the end of 'Enueg II': 'the overtone the face / too late to brighten the sky'.

[XIII] jusque dans la caverne ciel et sol

Old voices again, Classical (Ovid, *Metamorphoses*, Book V: Proserpine, raped and spirited off to Hades from the plains of Enna, where she was picking flowers); Atropos, one of the three female Fates, the one who shears off the threads of life and death, cf. 'noire soeur' and the final line of 'être là sans mâchoires' (with also perhaps some thought of Plato's cave), Romantic (Chateaubriand's *Mémoires d'outre-tombe*; line **3**) and Symbolist (if there is an allusion to Verlaine's 'Jadis et Naguère' in lines **6** and **8**). Here everything is in shadow (cf. 'casting no shade, herself shade' in *Dream*, 23), as in SB's favourite stanza of Keats's 'Ode to a Nightingale' ('I cannot see what flowers are at my feet . . .'). The situation is similar to what 'Dieppe' calls a 'reflux' (line **1**), and there may be some further influence here of Yeats's play *Purgatory*, which SB had seen during its first run in Dublin in August 1938. (Yeats died in France, at Roquebrune, in January 1939.)

All these echoes, or at least some of them, are occurring in a projection by the poet of what it might be like actually to be dead, rather than merely metaphorically so. With everything the same ('même', line **4**; 'mêmes', line **7**), it seems there may be no real difference between death-in-life and life-in-death (a Yeatsian concern, also found in his 'Byzantium'). One thinks back to 'pareil' and 'autre' in poem ['I'] ('they come'), but the mood here is very different, at the end rather than the beginning of a season, in hell or out of it.

PART 2   Post-War

Saint-Lô

One of the most widely admired of SB's poems, often described
as his 'masterpiece' (Mahon 1984, 53; cf. Fletcher 1967, 3; Hedberg
1974, 17; Harvey, 179), but sufficiently enigmatic to leave few commentators confident as to its meaning, with some (e.g. Cohn 2001,
124, anticipated by Harvey) seeing it as falling into two halves
because of its 'difficult' syntax, a view others (notably Wheatley
1999, 275) have attempted to counter. As 'SAINT-LO 1945' [*sic*]
it was first published in a five-line version in the *Irish Times* of
24.6.46. The use of capitals, a date in the title and the five- line
structure of the original publication might have reminded readers
with very good memories of 'DIEPPE 193?', which had appeared a
year earlier (in a five-line version) in June 1945. An unauthorised
reprint in the magazine *Rhinozeros* in 1960 (Lake, *250, 113) was
entitled 'Saint-Lô 1945'. It was, surprisingly, omitted from *Gedichte*
and first collected in *Poems in English* (1961) in its final four-line
version, with the third and fourth lines of the original conflated
and 'ghost-forsaken' replacing 'ghost-abandoned'. The Jolas autograph copy of *EBOP* transcribes the poem in its original five-line
version and reads 'ghost-abandoned' in the fourth line.

Saint-Lô, as Beckett puts it in 'The Capital of the Ruins', 'was
bombed out of existence in one night' (*As The Story Was Told*,
Calder, 1990, 25) by the Allies. As a product of SB's brief time at
the Irish Red Cross Hospital in the devastated Normandy town
(35 kilometres south-west of Bayeux), it seems natural to want to
compare the poem with other Saint-Lô texts (the squib 'Antipepsis' [q.v.], and the radio broadcast 'The Capital of the Ruins' and
'Mort de A.D'. [q.v.]). But it is quite different in character, perhaps
primarily as a consequence of SB registering, and publicly par-
ticipating in, the trauma of a situation newly encountered face
to face; Cronin, 355, seems to assume that it was written *after* SB
had left Saint-Lô, but offers no evidence for his assumption, and
on the balance of probabilities an earlier date is to be preferred.

Here any personal feelings are absorbed into an impersonal (but heavily freighted) manner, a remarkable outcome given the essentially subjective mood, which leaves almost all the few details elusive and intangible. The local Dublin response to the poem can be judged from the fact that the *Irish Times* published three letters about '*St.-Lô-1945*' on 27 June, 3 July and 4 July 1946 (F&F *1927–1929, 239). In the first of these letters 'Bewildered' asks for the help of the newspaper's 'able correspondents' to explain the meaning of the poem. His pseudonym, which recurs in the two following letters, may have prompted line 23 of 'Antipepsis' (q.v.; cf. also the headnote to *EBOP*). 'Bewildered' offers a paraphrase, having looked up 'vire' in Chambers Dictionary. This draws a stinging response from Professor H. O. White of TCD who suggests 'Bewildered' should have turned to an atlas rather than a dictionary and explains that 'the subject of Mr Beckett's strange and moving poem is clearly stated in its title'. SB's own feelings for the poem can be seen in a much later letter to White: 'Ever since your defence of "Saint-Lô" which so moved me at the time, you have been the truest of friends' (3.2.59; TCD). SB seems never to have attempted to translate this eminently 'French' poem into his second language, although a French translation reading 'Les méandres de la Vire charrieront d'autres ombres / à venir qui vacillent encore dans la lumière des chemins / et le vieux crâne vide de ses spectres / se noiera dans son propre chaos' is now carved in stone – a tribute paid to no other of Beckett's poems – on the entrance to the town's municipal cultural centre (Gaffney, 1999a, 76), arguably a more appropriate response than the poem received in Dublin in 1946.

Notes

1   the 'Vire' is the river which flows through Saint-Lô. The French verb *virer* means 'to turn' or 'to wind' (cf. line 12 of 'que ferais-je . . .', 'eddying' in SB's English translation), and the pronunciation approximates the English verb 'veer'; hence 'wind' supplies a sort of multilingual pun. The word 'will' is a prophetic, future tense which, presumably, also governs 'tremble' (line 2) and 'sink' (line 4), with the expectation of rebirth from the ruins of war in tension with the prospect of renewed 'havoc'. The 'shadows' are perhaps, as Harvey suggests, the new buildings that will

arise. SB may also be thinking of the new shades or ghosts created by the thousands killed in the blitz of Saint-Lô in June 1944 (cf. 'ghost-forsaken' in line 3).

2   the word 'unborn' is separated from, but qualifies, the 'shadows' in line 1. In 'tremble' there may also be some thought of 'the trembling of the veil' (cf. 'a veil that must be torn apart . . .', 'Letter to Axel Kaun', *Disjecta*, 52, 171), a religio-aesthetic idea prevalent in French Symbolist poetry, Mallarmé especially, addressing the possibility or impossibility of expressing a revelation only dimly intuited.

3   'and' is not merely the neutral connective it might seem to be, but in its 'weak' way reinforces the feeling of one thing necessarily following hard upon another in a consequential chain impossible to break or escape from.

3   the 'mind' in question is perhaps not just SB's, on being confronted by the 'ruins' of Saint-Lô, but also Europe's after World War Two, faced with the difficulties of reconstruction and rehabilitation with a 'wind' of change, or changelessness, imperviously blowing.

3   'ghost-forsaken' is preferred over 'ghost-abandoned' for the 'k' sound which in part prepares for 'sink' and 'havoc' in line 4, but also because it shifts the emphasis from the figure left without a ghost to an active force no longer present.

4   probably with some thought of 'Cry havoc! And let slip the dogs of war' (from Shakespeare's *Julius Caesar*, which SB had studied in the summer term of 1924 at TCD), but SB subsequently associated the word (in his English translation of 'Le Calmant' [1946], 'The Calmative') with a dispersal or dissolution of mental and physical images in a broken mirror (*The Expelled*, etc., 21; the 1991 French reprint of the 1955 original has 'fracas', Minuit, 44).

Antipepsis

A squib written in (irregular) octosyllabics, the typical form for satirical poems from Samuel Butler's 'Hudibras' through Swift to James Joyce's 'The Holy Office' (1904), and quite different in character from 'Saint-Lô'. The issues raised here are less exclusively ecclesiastical than in Joyce's poem, although there are hints of this in 'pia/Mater' and 'Purissima Virgo' (lines 9–10, 22), but the subject matter is Irish in origin, as best demonstrated by Phyllis Gaffney (in an essay in *Irish University Review*, vol. 29, no. 2, Autumn/Winter 1999, 256–80, esp. 270ff; hereafter 'Gaffney'), which effectively demolishes any lingering doubt – as left in Wheatley's note in the Faber *Selected Poems 1930–89* (189) – that 'Antipepsis' was 'possibly written in response to the banning of *More Pricks Than Kicks*'. In donating the typescript of the poem to the BIF (UoR MS 2906) SB added a handwritten note specifying '1946 After St Lô', and almost all the details in it can be correlated with SB's dealings with the Irish Red Cross Hospital both before and after his six or seven months employment with them at Saint-Lô between August 1945 and January 1946, having attended (Gaffney, 271) a preliminary committee meeting at their offices in St Stephen's Green in Dublin on 12 July 1945. The picture here is not so much of 'a universe become provisional' ('The Capital of the Ruins'), but rather of 'a world turned upside down' (Gaffney, 273).

The poem was first published posthumously in *Metre: a magazine of international poetry* (no. 3, Autumn 1997, Lilliput Press: Dublin, 5) and subsequently collected in *Poems 1930–1989* (2002) and in *Selected Poems* (Faber, 2009).

Notes

Title   'Indigestion', SB's own coinage, from the Greek 'pepsis', 'digestion', presumably by way of 'antisepsis', the medical discipline of remedies for infection.

1 and 2   21 St Stephen's Green: the headquarters of the Irish Red Cross.

3   referring to 'the two components of the hospital: its personnel and its material equipment' (Gaffney, 271).

4   the first of the many passive forms (cf. lines **5, 11, 13, 20, 22, 23**; as noted by Gaffney, 272) in the poem.

6   'design' is the first of many words 'denoting the processes of the mind' (e.g. lines **8, 9–10, 13, 18, 20, 21**; Gaffney, 273).

8   Wheatley points out (*Selected Poems 1930–1989*, 189) that the error 'The ass was the more intelligent' is corrected to 'The cart' on the typescript.

13–15   'the mind [. . .] amok': cf. lines **3** and **4** of 'Saint-Lô'.

16   for the activities of some at least of the Irish at Saint-Lô cf.

Knowlson, 348–9, which describes trips to the local brothel in the Red Cross ambulance, and Gaffney, *Healing Amid the Ruins*, 55, which quotes SB to TM on the atmosphere of 'promiscuity' and 'intemperance among the ruins' at Saint-Lô.

21 a Gaelic cry of lamentation and woe, habitually used by SB (often with 'dead and not gone' added) in the last years of his life, in letters to Barbara Bray (undated [1987]), and in late letters to Ruby Cohn (4.11.87; UoR), John Beckett (5.12.87; UoR), Kay Boyle (2.1.89; HRHRC) and Mary Manning Howe (7.1.89; HRHRC). Cf. 'ochone' below.

23 a travesty of the refrain in the well-known Rodgers and Hart song 'Bewitched' (*Pal Joey*, 1940). Cf. also the correspondence from 'Bewildered' regarding 'Saint-Lô' in the headnote to that poem.

24 a variation on the traditional cry heard in times of plague. The possibility of references either to Manzoni's novel *The Betrothed* (Gaffney, 273–4) or to a coded Resistance warning issued on the eve of the D-Day invasion (Gordon, 162) can probably be discounted.

POEMS FROM NOVELS AND PLAYS

The first poem from a novel to be included in an anthology was 'To Nelly' (*Watt*, 7) as 'Song from Watt' in *Modern Irish Poetry*, edited by Derek Mahon (London: Sphere Books, 1972, 111), where it is described as a 'furious and delightful love song'. Mahon also included a 'lyrical passage' from *Waiting For Godot*, under the title 'All the Dead Voices' – the passage, less the final line, which is reproduced on the back cover of the 2010 Faber edition. The only bona fide poem reprinted by Mahon was 'what would I do' (q.v.).

who may tell the tale

The fourth of the 37 'Addenda' to the novel *Watt* (in the '*Watt*' Notebooks at HRHRC, SB adds 'Isaiah 40.12' in the margin), adapted to SB's own condition after coming out of a course of treatment at a Paris nursing home in a late letter to Jocelyn Herbert (5.12.88; UoR). It was included in the BBC's 70th-birthday SB tribute of poems (14.4.76) in the Jack MacGowran reading taken from the broadcast of 24.11.66, but appeared (as 'Tailpiece') in a collection for the first time in Calder's 1999 *Beckett Short No 12: Selected Poems* and in *Poems 1930–1989* (2002). It was recorded by SB for Lawrence Harvey, as was 'Watt will not' (see below). In the '*Watt*' Notebooks (2.40–41) and typescript (119) the poem is associated with a lady called 'Pompette' (cf. *Malone meurt*, 147, and 'Poupée Pompette'), and followed by: 'One gallon of gravel-water, bottled at the cemetery, offered and with the help of God given for the correct solution', thus providing a link also to the other, cemetery-bound, poem in *Malone meurt*, 148/*Malone Dies*, 92: 'C'est l'amour qui nous conduit'/'To the lifelong promised land'.

Beckett's fondness for the quatrain form – here a double quatrain – is evident in 'Da Tagte Es', 'Gnome', 'Dieppe', 'Saint-Lô' and, as indicated above, in the 'brief rimes of curious structure' composed by Macmann, which take a quatrain form in English but are six lines in their French originals (*Malone Meurt*, 91–2, with 'rimes' restored as SB's preferred spelling; *Malone meurt*, 147–8; cf. Appendix 1 for *en face* French and English versions).

Watt will not

The 23rd of the 37 'Addenda' to *Watt*, traced back by Ackerley (2006b, 208) through the HRHRC notebooks and typescript, and compared by him to a Milton sonnet (XXII) to Cyriack Skinner. It originally appeared in a meeting between 'Johnny' (later 'Watt') and Arsene at the house of 'Quin' (later 'Knott'). SB recorded this poem for Lawrence Harvey; with 'who may tell the tale' it is one of the few recordings of SB's voice in existence. In line **26** we have adopted the reading 'tot', following C. J. Ackerley's 'decision [. . .] to retain the apparent "error"', as noted in his 'Preface' to *Watt* (xiv).

Age is when to a man

From the radio play *Words and Music*, first attempts at which date from early 1961, although for the most part it was composed in late November 1961. The play was first published in the November/December 1962 issue of *Evergreen Review*, and first broadcast on the Third Programme of the BBC on 13 November 1962. The play's first appearance in book form was in *Play, and two short pieces for radio* (*Cascando* being the other) from Faber in March 1963. In *Words and Music* Words is presented as composing the poem on the spot, making numerous false starts as he does so, and its two halves (lines 1–14, 15–24) remain textually separate. Lines 15–24, omitted from subsequent reprintings of 'Age is when . . .' as a poem in its own right, read: 'Then down a little way / Through the trash / Towards where / All dark no begging / No giving no words / No sense no need / Through the scum / Down a little way / To whence one glimpse / Of that wellhead.' It was included in the 24.11.66 broadcast selection, but as a poem its first appearance in book form was in *The Faber Book of Irish Verse*, edited by John Montague, 1974, 296; it was reprinted (with the title 'Song') and first collected in Calder's 1999 *Beckett Short No 12 Selected Poems* (22), and subsequently in *Poems 1930–1989* (2002, 40) and in Wheatley (63). It was not included in the BBC 70th-birthday tribute broadcast of SB's poems of 14.4.76, where it would have perhaps seemed too equivocal for a celebration, but would certainly have possessed a certain wry aptness.

SIX POÈMES

bon bon il est un pays

For this and the following two poems, see *LSB2*, 229–30, letter of 22.3.51 to Marcel Bisiaux. '[B]on bon', originally entitled 'Accul' ('at bay'), was written for Geer van Velde in February 1947 and published with 'Mort de A.D.' and 'vive morte' initially in the *Cahiers des Saisons*, and subsequently in the 1959 *Gedichte*, the 1968 Minuit *Poèmes* and the 1977 *CPEF.* In 1959 it was reassigned to Avigdor Arikha and published in the catalogue *Paintings, Gouaches, Drawings* to accompany an exhibition at the Matthiesen Gallery, London (8 April–2 May). The poem dramatises the internal monologue of the creative artist who 'believes painting should mind its own business', as Beckett put it in the catalogue for Geer van Velde's 1938 exhibition at Peggy Guggenheim's London gallery (*Disjecta*, 117), hence (in line **18** of the poem) 'ne me posez plus de questions'.

Variants

The title and the initial capitalisation at line 18 ('Qu'est-ce que c'est') was dropped when the poem was collected for the first time in *Gedichte*, Wiesbaden, Limes Verlag, 1959. The first drafts of the poem are in the second *'Eleutheria'* notebook (HRHRC). A photocopy of them was given to Calvin Israel and is now in Boston. It consists of three sheets, all of which are so difficult to read that transcription is uncertain. The first begins with three lines in which the poet appears to see a face: 'visage ça un visage si vous voulez'. The image of the face invites comparison with 'Enueg II', written some 16 years earlier, and the more recent 'Arènes de Lutèce', and this may have prompted 'ciel' to come. These are crossed through and a second attempt follows: 'face ça une face mon [image]'. A pair of lines then places the poet: 'souvent devant la mer sous le ciel / moi aussi mais je suis innocent innocent'. A heavily deleted third line is illegible and the draft is cancelled with a large cross. There is an uncancelled section of five lines set out in two pairs and a single line beginning 'ces histoires ne finiront jamais' and concluding 'les vers d'occasion ça ne fait que commencer', a reference presumably to the fact that Geer had asked Beckett to write something for him. Finally there is a ten-line section, the eighth line of which is crossed through, which is close to the opening of the finished poem. It begins: 'ceci dit il y a un pays'. It includes a reference to 'l'oubli' and concludes:

> on la tait la tête est muette
> on sait non on ne sait rien
> [~~ni la forme on sait ni le sens~~]
> on n'y chante pas non plus
> et il n'y a rien à pleurer

This section is also crossed through.

The second page is a further development of the 'ces histoires ne finiront jamais' section, worked up to seven lines, with a single line following which reads: 'ceci [imaginé] il est un pays'. The first nine lines of the second stanza of Shelley's 'Ode to the West Wind', end-

ing 'The <u>locks</u> of the approaching storm' (original emphasis) are
written upside down from the foot of the page in a different hand.

At the top of the third page, SB has written: '37.38.39 [*sic*] rough
draft / poem in French → Poèmes', and vertically in the right
margin: 'bon bon il est un pays / written for Geer van Velde'. This
is substantially 'bon bon il est un pays' except that the poem begins with what is the second section as published ('ma solitude je
la connais allez je la connais mal'), has a middle section of eight
lines, corresponding to the final section of the poem as published, but starting with two lines later deleted: 'je vous demande
donc d'avoir pitié de moi / je ne veux pas de votre pitié mais ayez
pitié de moi' (almost certainly a verbal echo of Apollinaire's 'La
jolie rousse'). The poem concludes with the section which opens
the published version, 'ceci dit il est un pays', although Beckett
has not yet found the phrase 'bon bon' to open with.

Notes

As Harvey has remarked, the poem reads like a sonnet with two
sestets (425). It proposes 'ignorance, silence and *l'azur immobile*
as the solution to the riddle, the final solution' (cf. 'Le monde et le
pantalon', *Disjecta*, 125).
1   'bon bon' ['O.K. O.K.'] indicates that this poem is part way to
being a dialogue. But the poet is also conceding a point by implying that he has decided to comply with a request to which he has
only reluctantly acceded.
3   'innommés' anticipates *L'Innommable*, and, like that novel
(begun in 1949), the poem has many internal questions, apparent
improvisations, repetitions, cancellations and self-contradictions.
6   James Knowlson has suggested (private communication) that
'le chant des bouches mortes' may echo Paul Verlaine's 'Colloque
sentimental': 'Leurs yeux sont morts et leurs lèvres sont molles, /
Et l'on entend à peine leurs paroles' but with a quasi-inversion of
eyes and mouth. If so, there may also be a relationship between
Verlaine's 'Qu'il était bleu, le ciel, et grand l'espoir! / L'espoir a fui,
vaincu, vers le ciel noir' and lines 12 and 13.
7   Cf. Du Bellay's 'Heureux qui, comme Ulysse, a fait un beau
voyage'.
9   'ma solitude': cf. 'cette peinture solitaire, solitaire de la

solitude' (of Bram rather than of Geer) in 'Le monde et le pantalon' (*Disjecta*, 132, written earlier, in January 1945).

10–11   rely on 'temps' meaning both time and weather in French; 'un temps de chien' means 'filthy weather'.

12   'grain' in the nautical sense of a squall or storm at sea.

13   'ocellé' from the Latin 'ocellus' ('little eye'): either the simple eye of insects and some other invertebrates consisting of light-sensitive cells, or eye-like markings such as the tail feathers of a peacock (cf. 'Zone', line **64**). Here the sense seems to be of a ray of light piercing the darkness of the past.

20   cf., of Geer in 'Le monde et le pantalon': '. . . c'est une peinture d'un calme et d'une douceur extraordinaire' (*Disjecta*, 129).

Mort de A.D.

First published (with 'bon bon il est un pays' and 'vive morte') in the magazine *Cahiers des Saisons* in October 1955); first collected in book form in England in the Calder 1977 *CPEF*.

The 'AD' of the title is Arthur Darley, a doctor colleague of SB's at the Irish Red Cross Hospital at Saint-Lô in 1946, who died in Dublin of tuberculosis, aged 40, on 30.12.48. Darley was an accomplished musician, playing violin, piano and guitar, and former patients remember '*le grand Sam*' on piano accompanying Darley on the violin (Gaffney, *Healing Amid the Ruins*, 24, 55). The two men (as Phyllis Gaffney's studies of life at the hospital have shown) inevitably often spent their leisure time together. While they are not otherwise known to have been particularly close, SB refers to Darley as 'mon ami' in line **7**. As Knowlson points out, the poem 'touchingly evokes both Darley's physical appearance and the turbulence of his divided inner life' (349). However, the poem can also be read as something more than a response to the death of a friend, as a desperate reaction to the fact of death itself, which is underlined by the use of Darley's initials in the title to give us the English word 'dead' and the redundancy of 'mort'/'dead'. Arthur Darley had been in charge of the tuberculosis ward at the Irish Hospital and it was this disease, prevalent in the Ireland of the time, which killed him. Perhaps SB was struck by the cruel irony of a doctor unable to cure himself, like Dr Nye, a 'sad man' in the 1934 story 'A Case in a Thousand', who thinks ruefully 'Myself I cannot save' (*Complete Short Prose*, 18). Yet for Beckett this death of Arthur – which may have inspired some thought of the legendary 'once and future' king of ancient Wessex who is set to return one day (cf. 'témoin des retours' and 'd'Arthur' below) – definitely seems to have been a distinct marker in the sand. Elements referring back to 'Mort de A.D.' recur in sentence 225 (Dartmouth College typescript, 17) of a text written on the way to *Pour finir encore* and sent to Ruby Cohn in the early 1970s: SB first typed out 'manière de support mais moins la vieille planche [cf line 2] de la mort d'A.D. témoin des départs d'alors', with 'd'A.D.' replaced by 'd'Arthur' and 'd'alors' with 'd'antan' in holograph corrections. It is referred to again as late as the first section of *Stirrings Still*, where the real name of the real man is replaced by a near-homonym in the sentence 'The same place and table as when Darly for example died and left him' (*Company*, etc., 108). Neither of these later instances clarifies whether 'Mort de A.D.' was written in memory of, and in mourning for, a sometime friend, or rather in response to an occasion prompting thoughts more specific to SB who, after leaving the Irish Red Cross Hospital at Saint-Lô, did not return there.

Variant

14   begins 'vieux bois grêlé . . .' in the *Cahiers des Saisons* printing; 'grêlé' omitted in *Gedichte* and subsequently.

Notes

1   cf. 'être là sans mâchoires sans dents'. However, this is not so much a yearning to be dead as to 'be again', as Krapp will later put it.
2   for 'vieille planche' cf. also 'vieux bois' of penultimate line. The word 'vérolée' ('poxed') is perhaps a recollection of brothel-going in Saint-Lô.
3   cf. the later play on day and night in lines 9 and 10.
5   'aveu' (confession) is the first of several terms that acknowledge Darley's Roman Catholicism. Cf. lines 9 and 10 and 13–15.
7   'mort hier' (and again in line 11): there is no need to suppose that this poem was literally written the day after Arthur Darley's death, although of course it may have been. The time frame of

the poem (which in some ways resembles that of 'que ferais-je
. . .'; q.v.) is 'set' by 'être là encore là' in line 1 and the 'temps'
which is 'mourant' in line 5 and 'irrémissible' in line 13, as well
as by the 'départs' / 'retours' at the end. SB may have spent the
New Year period of 1948–9 in Dublin, i.e. at precisely the time that
Darley's death was announced, but how much of Darley SB saw
after Saint-Lô has not been satisfactorily established.

9–10   these lines may indicate that SB had visited Darley in Our
Lady's Hospice in Harold's Cross, to which he was admitted in
1947 after a final visit to Saint-Lô, and where he died in December
1948. SB's assistant storeman, Tommy Dunne, certainly did (Gaffney, *Healing Amid the Ruins*, 73).

13   'coulpe': a grave fault only remitted by contrition and confession.

14   cf. 'un vieux bout de bois', *Nouvelles et Textes pour rien*, 1969,
80–1; *The Expelled*, etc., 38.

vive morte

Assigned on the perhaps sketchy basis of SB's memory to the
subsection 'Six Poèmes (1947–1949)' – which would align it, quite
plausibly, with the composition (November 1947–May 1948) of
Malone meurt – and therefore always appearing in association
with 'bon bon il est un pays' and 'Mort de A.D.' (as on the first
appearance of these three poems in the Minuit magazine *Cahiers
des Saisons* in October 1955). Although these three poems differ in
character, it is possible to see them as a kind of 'trilogy', the first
being concerned with a living friend, the second with a dead one,
and the third with a self that is 'living dead'.

In a letter of 28.2.85 SB thanks Kay Boyle for remembering a
poem (not otherwise known) 'written 1954, in my brother's house
near Dublin', when Frank Beckett was dying, a poem which may
have been misdated in the letter, if SB had 'vive morte' in mind.
In a letter to Pamela Mitchell (5.6.54; not in *LSB2*), written when
SB was caring for Frank, he speaks (by way of the first novel in
Sartre's *Roads to Freedom* sequence, first published in 1949) of 'la
mort dans l'âme'. Irrespective of when it was written, 'vive morte'
was still sufficiently close to the forefront of SB's mind to be

echoed in *Comment c'est*, begun in December 1958 (see two of the notes below); but if SB had written it in 1954 he would presumably have remembered that the '47–49' heading for the *Cahiers des Saisons* in 1955 would have to be altered. A translation of the poem into English appeared in the Paris magazine *Frank* in 1992.

Notes

1 cf. 'my only season' (*How It Is*, 53), and lines 10–11 of Villon's 'Le Lais', with perhaps some thought also of Rimbaud's 'Une saison en enfer'. But presumably the dominant allusion here is to Ecclesiastes 3:1, promising a season to everything. Given this poem's first line, its appearance in the ephemeral magazine *Cahiers des Saisons* looks very appropriate.

2 chysanthemums bloom in the autumn and, like white lilies, are typically associated with deaths and funerals, as for example in D. H. Lawrence's short story 'Odour of Chrysanthemums'. But chrysanthemums occur twice in *Malone meurt* (27 and 99) / *Malone dies* (16 and 61), where the associations are with Michaelmas and All Saints' Day. Cf. 'daffodils' and '[M]arch' in 'thither' (q.v.).

4 for the 'boue' cf. *Comment c'est, passim*. SB's birthday was 13 April. A possible context is supplied by a letter from SB to Pamela Mitchell from Killiney (6.8.54): 'Soon the leaves will be turning, it'll be winter before I'm home', an idea repeated in a letter to the same correspondent of 7.9.54 and again towards the end of *From an abandoned work*, probably written in 1954. A 30.6.54 letter to Pamela Mitchell refers to flowers, perhaps with this poem in mind.

5 for 'beaux jours' cf. 'Elle n'est part au bout de ses beaux jours, la crise sujet-objet' in SB's January 1952 *hommage* for Henri Hayden (*Disjecta*, 146) and of course the 1961 play *Happy Days*. For 'gris de givre' cf. *Comment c'est*, 122: 'branches noires grises de givre' and *How It Is*, 67: 'grey with hoar'.

TROIS POÈMES / THREE POEMS
je suis ce cours de sable qui glisse / may way is in the sand
que ferais-je / what would I do
je voudrais que mon amour meure / I would like my love to die

These three poems were first published in *Transition* 48.2, June

1948, 96–7. They are unique in SB's *oeuvre* as the only example of the first publication of his works with English and French versions set out, as they have been subsequently, on facing pages. No manuscript of the French originals survives, but there is an undated holograph of SB's first attempts to translate the poems into English. It breaks off at the beginning of the final line of the third poem with the word 'mourning'. This is particularly interesting, because there are three variant conclusions to this line in published editions of SB's poems. The three poems were republished with 'Dieppe' under the heading *Four Poems* in *Stand: a quarterly Review of Literature and the Arts*, vol. 5.1 (with the misleading claim that 'these are the first poems of Beckett's to be published in this country') ahead of John Calder's 1961 edition, where they appeared as *Quatre Poèmes/Four Poems.* The English translations were reprinted under the heading '*FOUR POEMS Translated from the French by the author*' in *The Guinness Book of Poetry 1960/61*, London: Putnam, 1962 (F&F*255.13, 52). They were published under the heading *Six Poèmes 1947–1949* with the French poems 'bon bon il est un pays', 'Mort de A.D.' and 'vive morte ma seule saison' in 1977 in Calder's *CPEF* and in *Poems 1930–1989.* These six poems were republished in Faber's *Selected Poems 1930–1989* under the bracketed subheading '[Poems in French, 1947–1949]'. The poems, whether in English or French, are very skilful, as the late Ruby Cohn puts it, in 'the quiet enfolding of sound into sense' (*A Beckett Canon*, 158).

The English version of 'what would I do . . .' was reprinted in *Modern Irish Poetry*, edited by Derek Mahon, London: Sphere Books, 1972, 112; English versions of 'my way is in the sand . . .', 'what would I do . . .', and 'I would like . . .' were reprinted in *The Penguin Book of Irish Poetry*, (ed.) Patrick Crotty (Harmondsworth, 2010), 647–8.

Variants

my way is in the sand flowing
7   MS has 'cease to' erased and corrected to 'cease from [tread] ing'.
The second section of the English version has four lines rather than five as in the French original.

que ferais-je
1   'visages' (plural) in *Transition* (*T*) altered to 'visage' (singular)
in *Gedichte* (*G*) and subsequent editions.
10   'avant hier' in *T*; 'aujourd'hui' in *G* and subsequently.

what would I do
Published versions are identical; MS variants given below.
1 and 6   'become of me' deleted and replaced by 'would I do'.
3   'into the void' for 'in the void'.
4   'what lasts' deleted and replaced by 'in the end'.
7   'and' deleted before 'pantings' and before 'frenzies'.
10   'become of me what has become of me' deleted and replaced by 'I do what I did'.
11   'to see' deleted and replaced by 'looking'.
12   'wandering with me [?waivering] far from the living'.
13   not 'convulsive', but it is unclear what SB's first choice was
[?'cracked'].
14/15   'voiceless among the voices / locked up with me'.

je voudrais que mon amour meure
3   *T* reads 'rues' for 'ruelles'.
4   *T* reads 'qui m'ait aimé' for 'qui crut m'aimé'.

I would like my love to die
1   'love' for 'like' in MS and in broadcast anthology 'Poems
by Samuel Beckett', BBC Third Programme, 8 March 1966. This
change – apparently introduced by SB at rehearsals (F&F 'note' to
*255, 52; a BBC memo dated 8.11.65 has 'like' in the proposed run-
ning order) – was not adopted in subsequent publications.
2   'falling' in MS.; in *T*; and in the 1961 *Poems in English*; 'raining'
in BBC (F&F, 52), *CPEF* and subsequently.
4   MS has single word 'mourning', SB apparently finding it
too problematic to continue; *T* and 1961 *Poems in English* have
'mourning the first and last to love me'. Kay Boyle's copy of the
1963 Grove edition in the Winthrop Palmer Collection of French
and Irish Rare Books (Long Island University) has the final line
'mourning the first and last to love me' crossed out and the revised
version 'mourning her who thought she loved me' (cf. F&F, 52)
written in SB's hand and initialled by him. In an accompanying

note, written by Kay Boyle on 16 August 1999, she explains that she sent the book back to Beckett asking him 'to be more accurate in his translating of his own work from French into English' and he obliged. Beckett had inscribed the copy to Kay Boyle and dated it 'Paris April, 1963', so presumably the change was made shortly after this date, some three years before the first public appearance of the final version of the line in the 1966 BBC radio broadcast. The publisher's note in the 1977 Calder and Grove editions claiming that the original last line 'was varied in later editions' to 'mourning her who sought to love me' is incorrect. No such version was ever published, although it is clearly an elegant and accurate version of the original French 'qui m' ait aimé' and one which, no doubt, Beckett had at some point considered.

Notes

je suis ce cours de sable qui glisse
Probably written in the summer of 1947, which seems to have been an exceptionally wet one, even for Ireland. This makes it at least plausible that the short poem that Beckett was pleased MacGreevy had liked (SB to TM, 4.1.48; *LSB2*, 71) was 'je suis ce cours'. It may, however, have been 'je voudrais que mon amour meure', with the latter addressing the subject of his sick mother in Ireland, and with the rain falling on his father's grave down at Greystones.
1   cf. 'Gliss' in *Watt*, 35, preceded by Arsene's 'I was . . .', etc. (34; cf. 'je suis' here).
2   cf. 'Dieppe', line 2.
9–10   Cf. *Purg.*, IX, 121–6; and the 1976 prose text *neither*.

que ferais-je / what would I do
5   cf. Eluard's 'Elle s'engloutit dans mon ombre' which Beckett translated as 'In my shade she is engulfed' ('L'amoureuse' / 'Lady Love', *This Quarter*, 5.1, September 1932).
6   cf. linc 7 of 'Tristesse Janale', and the Baudelaire quotation in *Proust* (*PTD*, 31).
8–9   cf. the sky of line 1 of 'The Vulture' and the 'spirale poussière d'instants' of 'bon bon il est un pays'.
10   'aujourd'hui' in French; 'the day before' in English [translating the *Transition* text; see above].

15   cf. 'ainsi a-t-on beau', lines 3 and 14: 'enfermé chez soi enfermé chez eux'.

A setting of this poem for soprano solo appears in the last movement of Marcel Mihalovici's 5th Symphony, published by Heugel
in Paris in 1972, with the text printed separately from the music.

je voudrais que mon amour meure
Ruby Cohn in *A Beckett Canon* believes that the poem is 'a
response to Yeats's thirteen-line sonnet "He wishes his Beloved
were Dead"' (157). In a letter of 17.2.55 (UoR) SB told Pamela
Mitchell: 'Bill [Stanley William] Hayter asked me for a text [for a
projected 'engravings to poems' exhibition], and I gave him the
following, written a couple of years ago [quotes all four lines of
'je voudrais . . .']. Haven't yet seen what he has made of it.' In 1955
there was no printing of the poem in book form.
2   cf. the repetition 'the rain to be raining' with 'the summer rain
rains' of 'my way is in the sand flowing'.
2 and 4   Cohn (*A Beckett Canon*, 157) compares the alliteration of
'pleuve' and 'pleurant' with Verlaine's 'Il pleure dans mon cœur/
Comme il pleut dans la ville' (*Romances sans paroles*, 'Ariette
oubliées', III).
4   the shift of tense from the present subjunctive, 'qui m' ait
aimé', to the *passé simple* (past historic), 'qui crut m'aimer',
strengthens the feeling of completion. Harvey tells us that
Beckett associated the tense of 'crut' with Racine's 'Ariane, ma
soeur! de quel amour blessée/Vous mourûtes aux bords où vous
fûtes laissée' ('Ariadne, sister, wounded by what love/You died
on the shores where you were abandoned', *Phèdre*, I, iii, 253–4).
Chas completes the quotation in *Dream* (144) after Belacqua
has introduced it with the observation: '[. . .] the preterites and
past subjunctives have never since Racine, it seems to me, been
exploited poetically to the extent they merit to be' – until now!
Beckett had used the tag in his lectures on Racine at Trinity in
1930–1 and recalled the quotation in his *German Diary* (19.12.36)
when, in the Kronprinzenpalais in Berlin, he was captivated by
Munch's *Umarmung* (*Embrace*), part of the *Linde Frieze* series,
and, in particular, by *Einsamkeit* (*Solitude*) where he rhapsodised
about the 'woman on empty shore. "Elle mourût aux bords . . .",

last exquisite'. This *German Diary* entry enacts SB's grammatical error. He uses the past subjunctive for Racine's *passé simple*.

Reprinted as 'Poem' in *The Penguin Book of Irish Verse*, edited by Brendan Kennelly, 1970, 345, and in *The Faber Book of Irish Verse*, edited by John Montague, 1974, 295.

TRANSLATIONS

SB'S TRANSLATIONS FOR *Transition*

The mission of post-war *Transition* was 'to assemble for the English-speaking world the best of French art and thought, whatever the style and whatever the application'. This included SB's own work: the bilingual publication of 'Trois poèmes' / 'Three Poems' in *Transition* 48.2, the celebrated 'Three Dialogues' with Georges Duthuit, the owner, publisher and editor of the magazine, in 49.5 and 'Two Fragments' (extracts from *Molloy* and *Malone Meurt* in SB's English translation before publication of the original French versions) in 50.6. In addition to these signed appearances, Beckett had a hand in some thirty uncredited pieces, including translating a number of poems, a selection of which are republished here, some of them for the first time in fifty years.

Henri Pichette: Apoem 4

SB also checked another Pichette text ('Letter Red') (cf. the invoice sent to Duthuit dated 27.5.48; *LSB2*, 79); both Pichette texts were published in *Transition* 48.2. SB's translation of 'Apoem 4' is unsigned, but even if he had not acknowledged it to Federman and Fletcher, there is ample textual evidence to reveal his hand. (See *LSB2*, 94, 96.)

SB's opening sentence is a reasonably close but idiomatic version of Pichette's: 'J'appartiens à la Terre. Je suis un rendez-vous: plusieurs personnages ayant planté leurs tentes sur ma langue ou emménagé dans mon poing droit (car désormais l'écrivain *man*oeuvrera ainsi du poing, et depuis c'est le Réveillon de la

Colère).' (Our transcription corrects two typos in the English and follows the original in italicising 'man' in 'manoeuvre'.)

If the first sentence had its opportunities, they were as nothing compared to the challenges that multiplied half a dozen pages later as Pichette began to put into practice his theory of 'Man counterbalanced by the Human, itself intimately mingled with the machine' ('Letter Red', 14) in an extended 'sense-reorganised' description of the sexual act. Pichette writes in a Verticalist idiom that would not have been out of place in Eugene Jolas's pre-war *transition*: 'Je vronpile à mimo le sire, et vide mon sac'. Beckett responds with gusto: 'I whizbang awhistwhack his highness and do my stuff'. This woman-machine is also a panther with 'sa tanière de fauve-de-lid' or her 'lidojungle lair'. Later she is transformed into 'L'une déesse ligide et sofome arquée sur le glaïeul, avec son bengal à zob, et ses chats qui me gâtaient L'autre, comme une suite dans les pensées, moins violente que le miel' or in SB's English: 'The one goddess ligid and sofomous arched over the iris with bengal cock, and her pussies that spoiled me'.

Beckett is equally good at fracturing English sayings and adding Irish idioms, to render Pichette's broken French: 'Il fait dimanche le jeudi, son amour est la semaine de quatres jours' becomes 'It's Sunday on Thursday, her love is the week of Sundays'; 'an Irish virgin's siding' (cf. *Murphy* on rounds completed ahead of time) translates 'la voie de garage d'une demi-vierge'. SB frequently adopts a riddle-me-ree strategy reminiscent of his pre-war manner, notably by introducing Laurel and Hardy, Nahum Tate and the Marquis de Sade into his version of: 'En souvenir de ce dernier amour je plaide non coupable : car le Monde-à principes-ridicules à mariages-de-raison à-lyrisme-ecclésiastique passages-à-tabac le Monde bouché à l'émeri et le très-pur Pourceau que je fusse devenu si j'avais respecté les lois nous mourûmes de concert'. Occasionally Beckett transposes or anglicises French words rather than translating them, for example 'no osmose' for 'aucune osmose' (osmosis), 'schlitters' for 'les schlitteurs' (lumberjacks) and 'borborygmous' for 'borborygmes' (rumblings of the bowels). Occasionally, however, the translation is even more obscure than the original. For example, SB renders Pichette's 'je me fraie un violon dans les villes mortes', apparently a portmanteau phrase combining the ideas of 'scraping' a violin and of clearing a way for oneself, as 'I olebulldoze through the dead towns'. In general, however, the translation is lively, quirky and readable, and was obviously calculated to whet the appetite of a public for whom Pichette was almost entirely unknown, as indeed he is now.

Henri Michaux: To Right Nor Left

Just as in *Transition* 50.6 extracts from *Molloy* and *Malone meurt* would be published in translation before the original French appeared, so Michaux's 'A hui ni à dia' appeared in SB's English translation (in *Transition* 48.4) before Michaux's original French was published in the magazine *K* in May 1949. When he collected the piece for inclusion in the second edition of *Passages* in 1963, Michaux altered the title to the correct French expression 'A hui *et* à dia', the original title, as the editors of the Pléïade edition point out, giving the impression that the piece was translated from English! Michaux made a number of changes to the text as published in *K* including the deletion of a preamble which assigns the piece to a character called Solpliquet – he occurs in SB's text as Solpliguet (perhaps a typo), and the deletion of the opening and closing paragraphs of the *K* text proper, the latter having been in-corporated into *Face aux verrues* in 1954. (See *LSB2*, 95, 97, 99–104.)

Although Michaux's editors comment that SB's translation is imaginative rather than literal, it is in fact much closer to the original than his rendering of 'Apoem 4'. Michaux's subject mat-ter would seem, on the face of it, to strike more of a chord with SB's preoccupations at the time, and SB's English imparts an almost biblical sonority to Michaux's sparse, workaday French. Michaux's text is a meditation on the meaning of reality, ana-lysed in terms of the weight of words, relations between young and old and the passage of time. Its climax is a splendid elabora-tion of the power of the word 'merde!' (The exclamation mark is SB's, who does not translate the French expletive, as much as it is Michaux's.) An indication of the magisterial transformation effected by Beckett may be seen in the passage beginning 'Many a weighty word . . .', which translates: 'Souvent on dit une grande parole, pour empêcher une petite de venir. Cette grande parole toutefois ne vient pas seule. Comme elle n'est bonne à rien, non réchauffée par pression environnante, il en faut des mille, des mille, pour dresser une surface et obscurer la personne derrière cette surface.' Here SB's English elevates the tone of Michaux's French. By contrast, elsewhere Beckett makes good use of English colloquialisms: '[. . .] les jeunes ne peuvent pas les souffrir': 'the young cannot bear the sight of them'; '[. . .] ils tiennent le bon bout. Nenni': 'the old have got hold of the right end of the stick. Alas, such is not the case'. SB handles the occasional obscenities in Michaux (toned down when these texts were collected) adroitly, and there is at least one good joke added when 'Monsieur Racine illisible à la canaille' becomes 'Monsieur Racine unreadable incidentally for foreigners'.

Michaux's discourse on the inexorability of time takes on rather more of the coloration of 'que ferais-je' in SB's translation than it had in the original French: 'cette existence qui fuit sans jamais se laisser punaiser' becomes 'this galloping, unpinnable existence', 'le tombeau commun' becomes 'the dust and refuse' and 'son petit coin' becomes 'a tiny space'.

Stéphane Mallarmé: Édouard Manet

An unsigned translation, perhaps one of the most interesting of the many that Beckett did for post-war *Transition*, published in a special issue focused on modern painting and its representation in modern poetry (49.5). Confirmed as SB's by a letter to Duthuit of 1.3.49 (*LSB2*, 120, 122) in which Beckett suggests 'Edouard Manet' as more amenable to translation than another of Mallarmé's *Divagations* ('De même'), highlights its 'eye' and 'hand' motifs (cf. 'For Avigdor Arikha'; *Disjecta*, 152), and reflects on its 'charming stammers' ('pittoresques balbutiements'). A little-known SB text in this connection is the abandoned prose work 'On le tortura bien' of February 1952 (almost illegible in the HRHRC manuscript, quoted here from the UoR typescript MS 1656/3/9), where one of the imagined characters ('Nat') is described as being interested ('sans conviction') only in the poet Mallarmé, 'whose *Divagations* never leave him'.

In a letter to MacGreevy of 18.10.32 (*LSB1*, 134), Beckett says he has been rereading Mallarmé and trying to like him, but unable to respond to his 'Jesuitical poetry'. In a letter of 20.7.51 (*LSB2*, 266–7) SB said that he was leaving the Mallarmé quotations in his translation of Georges Duthuit's essay ('Vuillard and the Poets of Decadence', *ARTnews*, 53, March 1954) in the original French. But Beckett alludes to Mallarmé's 'Adieu' in *Dream* (3, 12), where he borrows a phrase from 'Hérodiade' (68) and misquotes (148) the opening line of the sonnet 'Le vierge, le vivace . . .' ('The Swan' of the MacGreevy letter, which also mentions 'Hérodiade'), and Mallarmé may have been an influence in the background of SB's first poems in French (see notes on these). Much later in life, according to Anne Atik (122; '2 November 1985'), Beckett was much more positive about Mallarmé's poems, if not his prose poems. In the '*Sottisier*' *Notebook* (with entries between 1976 and 1982) Beckett jotted down a line and a half from Mallarmé's poem 'Brise marine' (cf. the note to line 2 of 'Da Tagte Es') describing a lamp shining on an empty sheet of paper 'que la blancheur défend', as if thinking back to his interest in whiteness as a focus for creative expression in such texts as *All Strange Away*, *Imagination morte imaginez*, and *Bing* (1964–6). A letter to Barbara Bray of November 1960 (TCD) speaks of 'the half-forgotten Mallarmé line' ('Calme bloc ici-bas chu d'un désastre obscur', line 12 of the sonnet 'Le Tombeau d'Edgar Poë'), which Beckett goes on to quote perfectly accurately. In a later letter to her he describes 'Marine' [? 'Brise marine'] as 'stubborn' (16.2.78).

Paul Eluard: The Work of the Painter

SB had translated several earlier Eluard poems (q.v.) for the special Surrealist issue of *This Quarter* (May 1932), prompting its editor, Edward Titus, to say that SB's versions were characterisable 'only by superlatives', an opinion with which posterity has been largely disposed to agree, as the many reprints of them confirm. SB remained interested in Eluard throughout the 1930s, but this sequence seems to have been his only creative encounter with the later, post-war Eluard – he had turned down the opportunity of translating 'new' poems by Eluard for a projected 'American luxury edition' with illustrations by Chagall (letter to George Reavey of 15.12.46; *LSB2*, 48) – and these versions are perhaps more workmanlike than truly inspired. They are reprinted here from *Transition* 49.5, December 1949, 6–13, because SB told Duthuit in a letter of 17.1.[49] (*LSB2*, 114–15) that he thought highly of them and considered them superior to Prévert's Picasso poem (q.v.). Eluard's suite of 7 poems was first published under the title 'Le Travail du Peintre' in the famous collection *Poésie ininterrompue* (1946). It is one of many Eluard *hommages* to a friend and fellow artist of long standing, with whom he collaborated closely and creatively from the mid-1930s onwards, until his death in 1952. In poem I of the sequence SB responds well to the hand/lids distinction which always attracted him, and no doubt Eluard's interest in the play of light and shadows (I, II, III), in madness (IV, V), in the issue of 'images' (IV) and in difference and sameness (V; cf. 'they come'/'elles viennent') also touched a chord. The word 'bourns' in poem V (T49, 11) has here been corrected to 'bourn*e*s'. As in his earlier Eluard translations, SB is very effective at finding convincing English idioms for idiomatic French, e.g. 'A question of true friends/Kindred down the ages / Creation every day / In the careless day' for 'Une affaire d'amis sincères / A travers les âges parents / La création quotidienne / Dans le bonjour indifférent' (VI, lines **82–5**).

René Char: Courbet: the Stone-Breakers

An unsigned translation for *Transition* 49.5, 49, identified as SB's by a private communication from Tina Jolas (Char's partner from 1957 to 1970; Char was born in 1907 and died in 1988) to Rémi Labrusse. Tina Jolas was one of the two daughters of Eugene and Maria Jolas and SB knew all the Jolases well, but his relations with Char (and with his patron, the Baroness Marguerite Caetani, founder and proprietor of the prestigious magazine *Botteghe Oscure* [25 issues between 1948 and 1960]) were much more distant, as seen in a letter to Duthuit (3.1.52; *LSB2*, 310–11). Tina Jolas claimed that SB had translated Char more than once, but no other translation has yet been identified, and despite the relative success of this translation (compare Mary Ann Caws's in her 1976 Char selection for Princeton University Press), SB obviously did not find Char's poems all that attractive or sympathetic.

Char's poem first appeared in the collection *Dehors la nuit est gouvernée* (1938) and was written 1937–8; it was reprinted in Christian Zervos's de luxe magazine *Cahiers d'Art*. Gustave Courbet's famous 1849 canvas 'Les Casseurs de Cailloux' was destroyed in 1945 in the Allied bombings of Dresden. The painting was in the Alte Akademie, which SB visited early in 1937, noting in his *German Diaries* (14.2.37) that Courbet was 'very uninteresting'. SB's version is one of the very earliest attempts at conveying Char in English, a language to which his vision is not notably well-attuned. But it has been praised by Mary Ann Caws in an essay (*Samuel Beckett Today/Aujourd'hui*, 8, 43–59, esp. 54–6), who has drawn attention to SB's use of sibilants and his preference for commands (55), and to his transposition of plurals in the last stanza (56). SB does his best to physicalise ('aching', line 12) what in the French tends to be either abstract or neutral, and adds an imperative ('Drink' in line 6). Char uses the word 'l'oubli' in line 11 of his poem (translated by SB as 'forgetfulness'), a word which governs the first section of SB's 1947 poem 'bon bon il est un pays'.

Jacques Prévert: Picasso Goes for a Walk

An unsigned translation for *Transition* 49.5, 50–3, with the original *en face*, identified as SB's by a reference in a letter to Duthuit of 17.1.[49] (*LSB2*, 114–15), comparing Prévert unfavourably with Eluard (q.v.) in their responses to Picasso.

Prévert's poem was first published in Christian Zervos's de luxe magazine *Cahiers d'Art*, the 1944 issue covering the five years of Nazi Occupation in Paris, and duly collected subsequently in the poet's famous *Paroles* volume, the first of the numerous (later frequently augmented) editions of which appeared in 1946. Prévert was probably too popular, and too populist, a poet to have appealed to SB at any point in his writing career, but this is perhaps one of the most successful of the versions he undertook on behalf of Duthuit and his magazine. SB was obviously not sufficiently engaged by Prévert to make many changes or imaginative adaptations indicating some investment of effort or re-creative intent, and his version is suitably straightforward and plain, but with some nice touches, e.g. 'having none [of it]', line

8, for 'elle ne se laisse pas', line 7 of the original) and 'before you can say knife' (line **13**, for 'sournoisement', line 14 of the original). There is no literal or implicit equivalent in the original for 'invincibly' (line **46**).

Alfred Jarry: [selections from] The Painting Machine

A letter to Georges Duthuit (17.1.49; *LSB2*, 114–16) shows that SB was involved (possibly only in a supervisory capacity) in the translation of the 15 prose poems by Jarry published in *Transition* 49.5, 38–42, with the title 'The Painting Machine'. This was the title given to chapters 33 and 34 of part six ('A Visit to Lucullus') of Jarry's posthumously published *Gestes et opinions du docteur Faustroll, pataphysique (roman néo-scientifique)*, Paris: Fasquelle, 1911, a section which greatly influenced the Surrealists. Jarry had finished his bizarre so-called 'roman' in 1898, nine years before his death in 1907.

We have selected four of these translations ('The River and the Meadow'; 'Love'; 'The Jester'; 'A Mere Witch'), all of which (like a number of the other prose poems not here selected) employ colour motifs. Instances of grotesquerie or of a proto-Surrealist confusion of mind and world are frequent. In 'Love' 'changing like the skies' translates 'couleur du temps'. In 'The Jester' 'sprinkler' translates 'goupillon', literally an aspergillum or sprinkler for holy water. In 'A Mere Witch' 'heaven's' translates 'du ciel', 'forefingers' translates 'les index' and 'broom' (i.e. broomstick) translates 'balai'. The clearest index of SB's hand in these Jarry translations is the use in 'The River and the Meadow' of the word 'lanugo' (cf. 'pubic lanugo', i.e. pubic hair, in *Dream*, 66) to translate 'au duvet vert'.

Guillaume Apollinaire: Zone

SB mentions Guillaume Apollinaire (1880–1918) in *Dream* (171, where there are oblique references to the poems 'Zone' and 'La jolie rousse'), and invokes 'La Chanson du mal-aimé' in his 'review' of Denis Devlin's *Intercessions* for the last pre-war issue of *transition* (no. 27, April–May 1938, 289–94; *Disjecta*, 93–4). SB's translation of 'Zone', perhaps the most successful he ever attempted, and very nearly the longest, was first published, unsigned, in the last issue of post-war *Transition* 50.6, October 1950, 126–31. See *LSB2*, 146.

Apollinaire's 'Zone' was first published in *Les Soirées de Paris* (no. 11, December 1912), and was the most recently written poem included in his subsequently famous collection *Alcools* (1913), where it is given pride of place as the first poem. Letters to the editor and proprietor of post-war *Transition*, Georges Duthuit (17.3.49; *LSB2*, 146), and to SB's friend Thomas MacGreevy (27.3.49; *LSB2*, 144–6) show when the bulk of the work on the translation was done, i.e. some 18 months before publication, which may suggest that it was undertaken as much to satisfy a personal impulse as to provide material for Duthuit.

At SB's death, copies of *Le Poète assassiné* (1927 edition), of the Pléïade *Oeuvres poétiques*, and of the two volumes of Apollinaire's translation of the works of Aretino were still in his library, and as he told George Reavey (letter of 24.8.72), he had once possessed Apollinaire's essay on and selections from Sade for the Bibliothèque des Curieux, which in fact he still did possess. Anne Atik refers frequently (7, 40, 48–9, 91) to SB's love of Apollinaire, and suggests (7) that lines 9–10 of the jettisoned poem 'les joues rouges' (reproduced in facsimile in *How It Was*; 10) refer to the first stanza of the fifth poem in Apollinaire's sequence 'A la Santé' (*Alcools*). SB's special fondness for this stanza is reflected in his quotation of it in a letter to Kay Boyle (HRHRC) of January 1983 (with the comment 'Wish I could translate that'); a follow-up February letter quotes the last stanza of the sixth poem in the 'A la Santé' sequence. Apollinaire was briefly imprisoned in the Santé prison on the Boulevard Arago on the grounds of his supposed involvement in the theft of the Mona Lisa from the Louvre, a charge subsequently dropped. SB's apartment in the Boulevard St Jacques later gave him a spectacular view of the Santé and its courtyard. SB adapts the refrain from Apollinaire's poem 'Le Pont Mirabeau' – 'Les jours s'en vont je demeure' – for use in *Comment c'est* (*How It Is*, 27: 'time passes I remain').

SB had decided to forgo rhyme in translating Rimbaud's great 'Le Bateau ivre' early in 1932, but in 'Zone' – SB's only other comparable attempt at a 'classic' of French literature – he very resourcefully matches the assonantal rhymes and half-rhymes of Apollinaire's original. SB's decision inevitably necessitated some transpositions within and across lines (e.g. **13–14**; **38–9**; etc.), but surprisingly few of them look awkward or forced even with the original *en face*. Some relatively unimportant loss of material occurs (e.g. the fact that the peehees are Chinese; line **69** – although we should remember this from lines **61–2**), and the last line (**155**) of the translation cannot really catch or match Apollinaire's brilliant and enigmatic 'Soleil cou coupé'. But comparing SB's version with any of the many translations of 'Zone' confirms this as a quite exceptional achievement, in spite of one or two questionable interpretations (in line **2**, for example, should not the 'oh' attach to the Eiffel Tower rather than to the 'herd', which itself should surely ideally be 'shepherdess'?), and at least one desperate remedy to save a rhyme ('a/Nimitation [. . .] Judea'; lines **45–6**).

SB's translation of 'Zone' remained uncollected until *CPEF* in 1977, but in 1972 the Dolmen Press of Dublin, in association with Calder and Boyars, republished it *en face* in a trade edition as well as a de luxe signed, numbered and limited (250) edition, noting that this was the first time the poem had been published separately. Liam Miller of the Dolmen Press took a great deal of trouble with the edition and recognised the difficulty of respecting Apollinaire's single-line section breaks in a bilingual edition. (No attempt had been made to do so in *Transition* 50.6, where SB's translation was published without the French text.) Since, as Beckett pointed out, both original and translation were 155 lines long, corrected spacing should result in exactly corresponding pages. This meant that, for the most part, French and English were exactly aligned, but there were many instances where run-ons threw the versions out of kilter so that one or other would end with a double line break to compensate. Given this limitation, Apollinaire's breaks were respected as well as they could be in a bilingual edition, with facing sections beginning opposite each other. This begins to slip in *CPEF* which introduced double line spacing between the breaks and where the smaller format leads to more run-ons, so that, for example, the second sections on pages 108–9 start two line spaces apart although they come together by the end of the pages. By the end of the poem, where Apollinaire is firing off his brief *aperçus*, the misalignment of the French and English texts is irritating and unnecessary, and exacerbated by the use of double spacing between sections.

Beckett's translation was reprinted in *The Random House Book of Twentieth Century French Poetry*, ed. Paul Auster, 1984, 3–11.

Variants

8   *Transition* 50.6 (hereafter '*T50*') has a 'stanza' break not found in Dolmen or *CPEF*.

14   the number is in italics in *T50*.

24–5   no break in *T50*, which introduces erroneous breaks after line **26**, **29**, **34**, **38**.

25–8   quoted in the Picabia article with the following variants: (25) You are but a small child (26) Your mother [etc.].

34–5   only found separated in *T50*.

38–9   only found separated in *T50*.

41–2   no break in *T50*.

43   'it is no novice' replaces 'he is no novice' in *T50*.

47   reads 'If it can fly let flyer be its name they cry' in *T50*.

48–9   Beckett omitted these lines accidentally from *T50*, adding them for the Dolmen revision.

56   'Flamingoes' replaces 'Flamingos' in *T50*.

81   Beckett corrected 'bloodred' in *T50*.

82–3   no break in *T50*.

83   'Our Lady beheld you' in *T50*.

92   'One is Nissard one is from Menton and two from La Turbie' in *T50*.

93   'polypuses' ('poulpes') is rendered as 'octopuses' in *Poems 1930–1989*.

106   'Marseille' in *T50*.

118   'Your life was folly and your days in vain' in *T50*.

119   'your eyes' in *T50*.

147   'Fernine the false' in *T50*, in error for 'Ferdine la fausse', corrected in Dolmen.

151   'fetiches' in *T50*, corrected to 'fetishes' for Dolmen.

Notes

Transition 50.6 (hereafter '*T50*') includes an article – almost certainly translated by Beckett – by Gabrielle Buffet-Picabia on Apollinaire. She describes an occasion in October 1912 when the poet travelled with her and her then husband, the painter Francis Picabia, and Marcel Duchamp to Etival, a little village in the Jura, the borderland of which is 'known as "the Zone"'. According to Gabrielle Picabia he was extremely familiar with the history of the Zone. He recited a couple of extracts from the poem (see notes below), declaring when asked for the title: 'It is not finished and I have not yet given it a name.' Then, suddenly: 'I shall call it "Zone".'

12 'So much for' (translating 'Voilà'; at line **25** translated 'There') anticipates the end of the first paragraph of *Assez/Enough* ('So much for the art and craft', the last word being used in a different sense, twice, in line **47** here).

62 Apollinaire had displayed his considerable erudition by discoursing on 'the one-winged bird [. . .] and equally parabolic matters' (*T50*, 118). He also revealed 'the exact recipe of the soja sauce used in China to garnish baby girls'.

64 cf. 'ocellé' in 'bon bon il est un pays' (1947).

71–4 quoted by Picabia as translated by Beckett.

75 cf. *Hamlet* III, i: 'Get thee to a nunnery'.

76 'paternoster' (cf. SB's *German Diary* entry for 27.11.36) translates 'prière', perhaps the point of origin for SB's persistent equation of poetry and prayer.

99 St Vitus Cathedral in Prague has agates and other semi-precious stones encrusted in its walls.

104 Hradchin (usually 'Hradschin'): the castle in Prague.

119 'your eyes' in *T50*. Beckett seems to have shared Apollinaire's own uncertainty about the appropriate form of self-address. Although SB could not have known it, at the proof stage for *Alcools* Apollinaire corrected 'je' to the definitive 'tu' in lines 119 (*Je* n'ose), 121 (*Je* regarde), 135–7 (*Je* suis . . . *Je* prends . . . *Je* suis); cf. Apollinaire, *Oeuvres poétiques*, Bibliothèque de la Pléïade, 1042.

130 Le Marais is still a centre of Orthodox Jewish life in Paris.

Gabriela Mistral: Message from Earth

Gabriela Mistral (born Lucila Godoy y Alcayaga; 1889–1957) was a Chilean poet and prose writer who gained international recognition in 1945 with the award of the Nobel Prize for Literature, the first Latin American figure to be thus honoured. Her Goethe poem first appeared in Spanish (untitled) with SB's English version, titled 'Message from Earth', *en face* in a 1949 UNESCO volume celebrating the two hundredth anniversary of Goethe's birth (76–81). Mistral's poem acquired the title 'Recado terrestre' on being collected in her 1954 volume *Lagar* [Wine-Press] published by Del Pacifico Editions of Santiago de Chile, which also contains another *hommage* to Goethe ('Recado sobre un copa'). Beckett had been asked to revise a number of translations for the Goethe volume. However, as far as the Mistral was concerned, he 'was obliged to translate this poem with the help of a scholar specialised in Spanish and some friends' (F&F *496, 98), perhaps Ethna MacCarthy and Gerald Brenan. However difficult he may have found it to share Mistral's (and, for that matter, Goethe's) vision, SB's 'retranslation' often produces striking results, notably in the last few lines. (On 'Recado terrestre' in *Lagar* see an essay by the Mistral expert Cedomil Goic in the Santiago de Chile magazine *Taller de Letras*, 27, November 1999, 9–22.)

No other version of this Mistral poem in English is known to the editors, and this must have been one of her earliest appearances before an English-speaking audience. The translator(s) has or have been obliged to sacrifice some of the acoustic subtleties of 'Recado terrestre', but this is lessened by some very adroit transformations, alliterations and assonances, suggestive of a very experienced literary hand. The last stanza of Mistral's poem is rendered particularly well.

The Goethe volume was printed in Switzerland and poorly proofread. The editors have corrected obvious errors in the original publication. The Spanish text is itself by no means error-free, containing about a dozen mistakes.

2: 'among'   correcting 'Among' in 1949.

3: 'watch [...] astare'   translating 'vigilas', deliberately used in the original to maintain the religious/sacrilegious aspects of the opening.

12: 'immemorial'   a word Mistral could have chosen, but the original simply reads 'vieja'.

15: 'Prakriti'   correcting 'Pakriti' in 1949; Mistral's original reads 'Prakriti', a Sanskrit word denoting 'Nature' in the *Bhagavad-Gita*.

21: 'sun'   correcting 'sum' in 1949.

26: 'visionary jest'   referring to Goethe's *Faust*.

27: 'cloven tongue'   translating 'lengua bífida' in line 28 of the original; 'forked tongue' might perhaps have been expected.

28: 'with yes and no'   Mistral also has 'un s[í]-es no-es' in line 56 of her original in 1949, which the translation makes no attempt to render.

30: 'still'   the first of three uses of the word over the next seven lines, blurring the distinctions between 'aun' and 'Todavía' in the original, and in the third instance spelling out what the original only leaves implicit.

32: 'cave'   translating 'gruta', more literally 'grotto' or 'sanctuary', with an implicitly religious connotation lacking in the translation; cf. SB's hesitations over 'gruta' in the Urbina translation.

39: 'livid'   a favourite SB word (cf., for example, the notes to 'Enueg I'), but here translating 'lívida' in the original.

45: 'dead men'   correcting 'deed men' in 1949.

50: 'What time'   a favourite SB archaism for 'meanwhile' (cf. its use in 'What A Misfortune', *MPTK*, 122), here used to translate 'Como que . . .'.

50: 'the earth'   in 1949 the Mistral original has 'la Tierra'.

51: 'stricken like a beast'   an ingenious attempt to convey 'sajada en res' in the original, referring to the slicing up of meat.

55: 'a quiver of good news'   correcting 'goods news' in introducing a passage of considerable complexity in the original, which becomes a very free but very imaginative adaptation of Mistral.

58: 'nought'   probably in part chosen to convey some idea of the seven words (out of fifteen) ending in '-o' in the original; 'whispering' correcting 'wispering' in 1949.

SELECTIONS FROM *Anthology of Mexican Poetry*

The *Anthology of Mexican Poetry* (hereafter *Anth*; mentioned in *LSB2*, 177, 181, 184, 192, 195, 197, 200–1, 439, 510, 530, 665–7), compiled by Octavio Paz with a preface by C. M. Bowra, was published in late 1958 by Indiana University Press, and in early 1959 by Thames and Hudson, neither of which print the original poems, which makes the *Anthology* look more self-standing than it really is. It had been preceded by *Anthologie de la poésie Méxicaine*, with a preface supplied by the poet and dramatist Paul Claudel and with the original poems in Spanish printed *en face*, which was published in November 1952 by Les Editions Nagel of Paris. Paz selected more than 100 poems of which only about one-seventh are reprinted here, in order not to overbalance this book with material which SB was only ever (with the exceptions noted below) dismissive about, and even more so than was habitual with him. Typical in this regard is the judgement in a letter of 21.7.58 to Richard Seaver, which emphasises that it was 'an alimentary job [. . .] rather handicapped by my ignorance of Spanish. But most of the poems chosen by Octavio Paz are so extremely bad that not much is lost.' For other similar comments see undated (1950) letters to Georges Duthuit (*LSB1*, 181–2, 194, 200) and letters to Mary Hutchinson (6.2.59), Aidan Higgins (23.3.59), Hugh Kenner (14.1.60), Kay Boyle (20.11.60) and George Reavey (9.11.61).

The HRHRC materials relative to the whole project – which have been largely ignored on the supposition that any autograph hand on them is not SB's – have been convincingly assessed by Maria José Carrera (in an essay unpublished at the time of writing) as being in fact almost all by Beckett. There are four further poems in the HRHRC typescript which, in the event, were omitted from the published texts in 1958.

The bulk of SB's work on the *Anthology* was almost certainly largely conducted over quite a short period, early in 1950, although it is possible that it dragged on a little longer, perhaps more than a year longer, as Paz and SB found the time and the will to agree on what was to be included, and what excluded, and as the two men found it either possible or expedient to make up their minds about other ancillary issues. In the '*Sam Francis*'

Notebook (UoR), which contains vocabulary and drafts towards the translations (see below, especially under the entries for Urbina and Reyes), there is a draft letter to Paz regarding the 'poèmes supplémentaires' which had been added to the selection, which may help to explain SB's irritation in a letter to MacGreevy of 19.9.52 (not in *LSB2*) regarding work for UNESCO.

SB's very considerable commitment to the project, and his achievement, were rewarded by Gerald Brenan (thanked in the 'Translator's Note'), after he had read the whole book, finding almost nothing that needed correcting, in spite of SB's professed deficiencies in Spanish, as almost always emphasised in his later and invariably rueful correspondence on the subject. But this does not supply grounds enough to endorse the view of Nobel Prize-winning novelist J. M. Coetzee in his introduction to volume IV of the *Grove Samuel Beckett Centenary Edition* – 'His most enduring contribution to poetic art is probably contained in his translations, particularly in the volume of Mexican poetry he translated into English in 1958 [*sic*] under the auspices of UNESCO' ([ix]) – with which almost anyone sympathetic to SB as a poet will find it difficult, if not impossible, to agree. The more modest claim of Glauco Cambon to the effect that 'Many of [Beckett's] translations are English poems in their own right' (380) is more easily endorsed, as is Boyd Carter's judgement of Beckett possessing 'the rather rare talent of being able not only to transfer nuances but also to maintain patterns of consistency in rhythmic expression' (357).

Francisco de Terrazas (1525–1600): Sonnet

The original (untitled, as in the facing French translation) rhymes abba abba cdc cdc, a pattern SB makes no attempt to emulate, although this translation is one of the most successful in the whole *Anth*, with a good deal of evidence of personal input. Throughout *Anth* SB ignores rhymes, preferring assonantal and alliterative effects.

2 'will' translates 'querer' (literally, 'heart'; 'cœur' in the French version), SB being more interested in the former than the latter.
7 the original reads: 'y el filo de una espada la una asía', which

in the French becomes 'et l'une saisissait le tranchant d'une épée'; SB's 'trenchant' is probably a multilingual joke, but may suggest that he had seen Guy Lévis Mano's version, which repeats 'tranchant' in line 11.

8 'little herb' (in French 'une herbe frêle') translates 'yerbazuela', which is shortened to 'yerba' in the next line; SB's 'Little and little' at the beginning of line 9 ties the sestet more securely to the octave.

10 'ever sorer vexed' translates 'deshaciendo'.

12 'from self estranged' translates 'mal me entiendo' (in French: 'pauvre entendement!'), both of which are much less forceful and much less Beckettian, emphasising the 'understanding' rather than the estrangement. Cf. a letter to TM of 18.10.56 (*LSB2*, 663) embodying the idea in its very syntax: 'It is not easy to get through the ages from self so estranged . . .'

Miguel de Guevara (1585?-1646?): [1] **I am not moved**
[2] **Time demands** [*Anth* 61; 63]

One of only two poets SB specifically excluded (the other being Juana de Asbaje) from his general condemnation of the poems that Paz had selected in a letter to Kay Boyle of 20.11.60, in which SB raises doubt as to Guevara's authorship of 'I am not moved to love thee . . .'. Two of the four Guevara sonnets (the first and the fourth as published in the *Anthology*) appeared in variant and revised versions (as '1' and '2' under the title 'Kottabistae') in the TCD magazine *Hermathena* (no. CXXXIII), whose assistant editor was A. J. Leventhal, in May 1954. SB sent these to Jérôme Lindon at Minuit on 26.7.54 (IMEC archive). These are the versions reprinted here in accordance with the principle adopted elsewhere (cf. especially the Leventhal revisions) of collecting SB's final thoughts, where these can be reasonably inferred, on his poems and translations. F&F, in their note to *501 (102), speak of them as 'early versions', perhaps as advised by A. J. Leventhal, but the dates and the research of Maria José Carrera seem to be against this.

Both Guevara sonnets rhyme abba/abba/cdc/dcd in the original ('No me mueve, mi Dios'), the second ('El tiempo y la cuenta') using only two rhyme words ('tiempo' and 'cuenta'). SB makes no attempt to rhyme the first, but preserves the two-word rhyme pattern in the second.

[1]
1   *Anth* has 'my Lord God'.
2   *Anth* has 'By'.
6   *Anth* has 'at' as the first word.
7   *Anth* reads: 'I am moved by thy body all over wounds'.
8   *Anth* reads: 'I am moved by thy dishonor and thy death'.
11   *Anth* reads: 'and though there were no hell I should still fear thee.'
13   *Anth* reads: 'for though my present hope were all despair,'.

[2]
1–2   *Anth* reads: 'Time requires me to give account; /The account, if I would give it, requires time:'.
6   *Anth* begins the line: 'for the account . . .'.
9–11   *Anth* reads:
What account shall suffice for so much time?
What time suffice for so great an account?
Life careless of account is shorn of time.

Matías de Bocanegra (1612–68): [from] Song on Beholding an Enlightenment

[Verse paragraphs selected from *Anth* 66 and 69–70; original title: 'Canción a la vista de un desengaño']

[1] 29 lines in the original (13 couplets and 1 triplet); here 30 (unrhymed).
8   'is assailed' translates a past tense in the original (respected in Guy Lévis Mano's French version).
12   'profane tumult' translates 'tumulto civíl'.
24   'close rig of pain' translates 'la pena los cordoles'.
30   'dead life' translates 'vida muerte'. The words (cf. the original title of the Martínez poem below) must have struck a chord with SB if, as is more than likely, he had recently written 'vive morte' (q.v.).

[2] 34 lines of rhyming couplets in the original; here, unrhymed.

10 'vertiginous' translates 'veloz' (in the French version 'rapide').

21–2 'poising,/stoops boltlike' translates 'se prepara/ y rayo'. For 'stoops' compare 'The Vulture' and 'Alba'.

31 'baneful' (here, as in the second Asbaje selection) translates 'funesta'; 'flowers' translates 'la foresta'.

Luis de Sandoval y Zapata (mid-17th century): To a Dead Actress

The original ('A un cómica difunta') rhymes abba/abba/cde/cde.

3 'dulcitude' translates 'dulzura'.

6 'sonorous . . . summons' translates 'el clarín'.

13–14 in the original the lines end with the words 'muerta' and 'viva'.

Juana de Asbaje (1651–95): [1] Diuturnal infirmity [2] First Dream

[1] The fourth Asbaje/Sor Juana poem selected for *Anth.* In the original ('Diuturna enfermedad . . .') a sonnet rhyming abba/abba/cdc/dcd.

1 'Diuturnal' translates 'Diuturna' (in the French version 'Interminable').

2 'fainting' translates 'cansados'.

5 the repeat of 'forever' is not in the original.

11 'deluded' translates 'entretenida'.

12 'lot' translates 'suerte'. Christopher Ricks (*Beckett's Dying Words*, Oxford: Clarendon Press, 1993, 17) suggests SB treats the word with 'suspect respect'.

[2] The twelfth Asbaje/Sor Juana poem selected (an extract from a 975-line original, 'Primero Sueño') for *Anth.* (In the French edition this is the thirteenth selection; presumably SB forgot to translate the twelfth selection; cf. the note to Tablada below.) In a letter to Kay Boyle (20.11.60) SB describes the poem as 'extraordinary and untranslatable', Juana de Asbaje being one of only two of these poets who seem to have really moved him (cf.

Guevara, above). Irregular rhyme scheme, five sentence units in the original, six here.

3 'dayspring', a Miltonism, translates 'arbor primero' (in French: 'blancheur première'). SB uses the word again in a late revision of his English translation of *L'Innommable* (*The Unnamable*, 119: 'it's the dayspring [. . .] I call that the dayspring').

4 'Tithonus's' translates 'Tritón' (in French: 'Triton'); two different figures in mythology, with Tithonus arguably the more apt since he was the lover of Eos, the goddess of dawn.

14 'tiro' translates 'bisoñas' (in French: 'novices').

27 'clarions' translates 'clarines'.

28 'their featly artless' translates 'diestros – aunque sin arte –' (French version: 'habiles, encore que naturelles'). Dr Johnson gives 'featly' as occurring in Shakespeare's *The Tempest*, which SB studied at TCD, and 'feat' (later to be found in *Footfalls*) from Shakespeare's *Cymbeline*. Atik (*How It Was*, 54) says 'feat' was one of the rare and/or recondite items of vocabulary she discussed with SB.

54 'cerulean' translates 'cerúlea'.

56 'baneful' translates 'funesta' (as in Bocanegra, above).

64 translating 'en su mismo despeño recobrada'.

70 'what time' (a Miltonism and, later, a deliberately archaic Victorianism for 'meanwhile', found in the 'Love and Lethe' and 'What a Misfortune' stories in *More Pricks Than Kicks*) translates 'mientras' (in French: 'tandis que'). The locution 'What time' is also put to use in the Mistral translation (see note above), and in the Acuña poem (see below).

Both poems were included in *The Oxford Book of Latin American Poetry: A Bilingual Anthology* (eds. Cecilia Vicuña and Ernesto Livon-Grossman), Oxford: Oxford University Press, 2009, 32 and 28–30.) The anthology also reprints SB's translation of the Juana de Asbaje sonnet 'This coloured counterfeit that thou beholdest' (31), not included in this selection.

Ignacio Rodríguez Galván (1816–42): [from] The Prophecy of Cuauhtémoc

In the French edition given the title 'Fragment' in both languages, with a note at the end indicating that it is selected from 'The Prophecy of Guatimoc'; SB's Mexican spelling suggests that Paz may have intervened.

2 'azure' ('azúl', blue, in the original, occurs only once): SB probably has Mallarmé in mind.

5 'restlessness' translates 'volubles'.

8 'bleeds slow away' translates 'destila' (distils).

9 'abyss' translates 'cavidad'.

16 'cheek' translates 'faz'.

18 'blandishment ' translates 'halago' (in French 'caresse'); SB avoids 'caress' because he has used it two lines earlier to translate 'acarició'.

24 is followed by a section break, as in the original, there introduced by '. . .'

25 'Make haste' translates 'Venid'.

27 Ricks (*Beckett's Dying Words*, 79) sees a 'galvanised' cliché here.

29 'fed' / 'felt' introduces a wordplay not present in the original, which does not repeat 'felt' in the next line.

31–2 one line in the original, 'end' here conveying what there is simply the passage through life; Weinberger (*Fulcrum*, 618) quotes the last three lines in a more literal translation, noting that they are clipped in SB's version, with God removed, but the removal occurs in the French edition also.

Vicente Riva Palacio (1832–1896): To the Wind

In the original ('Al viento') a sonnet rhyming abba/abba/cdc/dcd.

2 'at my door' translates 'las puertas [. . .] de mi aposento'.

5 'tumult' translates 'rumor'.

9 'hear' translates 'siento'.

10 'incoercible prison-bars' translates 'prisión las fuentes rejas'.

13 'wind', a repetition not in the original.

Manuel Acuña (1849–1873): Before a Corpse

Terza rima ending in a quatrain in the original ('Ante un cadáver'). Paz (*Fulcrum*, 623) claims that SB was 'intrigued' by this poem, and sees it as exploring 'a kind of disguised cannibalism or a religious communion . . .': 'A strange idea, and we laughed at that.'

3   'and darkens' is added.

15   'enouncement' translates 'enunciado'.

21   'the bonds' translates 'la carcél'.

23–4   are a very free translation.

25   in the original: 'Miseria y nada más' with double (Spanish) exclamation marks.

45   'source' translates 'foco'.

51   'alchemy' is not explicitly present in the original.

54   in a loose leaf in the HRHRC materials SB tries out 'breadless' for the original's 'sin encontrar un pan', an experiment normalised as 'wanting for bread' in the published text.

55   'What time' (cf. the Mistral translation and the second Asbaje translation, above) here translates 'En tanto que . . .'.

59   'love' translates 'amores'.

63   no repetition in the original.

69   'cloister' translates 'encerrada'.

80   'body' translates 'máquina'.

83   'being' translates 'organismo'.

85   'unforgiving' translates 'justiciera'.

93   'substance' translates 'alimentándose'.

95   'solicitude' translates 'afán'.

96–7   'endowed/with other semblances' translates 'cambía de formas'.

Manuel José Othón (1858–1906): Envoy (from 'Wild Idyll')

An 'Envoi' sonnet (entitled 'Envoi' in the French edition) ending a six-poem sequence, rhyming abab abab cdc ede in the original ('Idilio Salvaje').

6   'wildering' translates 'andar'; highlighted by Weinberger (2007, 619), who cannot find the English word in the *OED*, although it is there.

14   the phrase in the original reads: 'horrible disgusto de mi mismo'; so nothing specifically Beckettian here.

Francisco A. de Icaza (1863–1925): Golden

Two quatrains, rhyming abab baba in the original, entitled 'De
oro' with the location 'En los Trigos' specified at the head of the
poem (in the French version 'Dans les blés').

1   'gold' translates 'oro'.
2 (and 5)   'golden' translates 'dorada'.
7   'earth' translates 'camino' (literally a road).

Luis G. Urbina (1868–1934): The Ancient Tear

In the original entitled 'Vieja Lágrima', irregularly rhymed. The
MS version of this poem in the *'Sam Francis' Notebook* (UoR; MS
2912), where its title is given as 'Ancient Tear', offers remarkable
evidence of how in some cases SB gave intense commitment to
these translations in spite of his expressed dissatisfaction with
every aspect of the enterprise. Lines 10–12 and most of the lines
from 40 onwards seem to have posed particular difficulty. A fully
detailed record of the MS variants is not attempted here, but
significant variants are, however, noted.

1   'cavern' was originally 'grot' in MS and the word left unrevised; the original reads 'gruta' ('grotte' in the French version)
which SB had translated as 'cave' in Mistral's 'Message from
Earth', see note above.
2   'lost': SB originally wrote 'hidden' in MS, and then crossed it
through.
3   'these centuries' translates 'desde hace', used again by Urbina
a few lines later (in SB's line 7 he renders it 'this long time past').
12   'consigned' was originally 'despatched' in MS and subsequently corrected. The original reads: 'me la manda'.
18   in the MS SB originally wrote 'they were a snowfall' and then
crossed it out; the original reads 'mi llanto fué nevasca'. A tearful-
looking doodle is in the right margin opposite these lines in MS.
19   'Now I weep no more': SB first tried out 'Now I have no more
tears' and crossed it through; in the original 'Hoy no llaro'.
22   'tear by tear' in MS; SB moves this phrase to line 39 of the
published version; hence the change here. Urbina writes 'lágrima

a lágrima' in both instances.

23 'exhaustless' translates 'inagotable'.

24 'indefatigable' translates 'que no se acaba'.

31 in the MS the line originally read 'fraught' (replaced by 'sudden and' above) and 'unbridled' is left unrevised as 'uninvolved'. The original reads: 'bruscas y salvajes'.

32 'ineffectual': in MS 'impotent' is crossed out ('impotentes' in the original).

40 'day': 'time' in MS ('día' in the original).

41 'seemly' translates 'pudoroso'.

42 'made': added to the ms. version above the line.

44 'desk' was originally 'work-table' in MS ('mesa de trabajo' in the original).

44–5 SB's first attempt at these untypically short single units shows him still in some doubt as to whether 'tarde' in the original designates afternoon or evening, and how best to translate 'linda'.

47 'singing' was originally 'song' in MS (crossed through and altered). The original employs a verb form.

49 'hour of your frolic' in MS; Urbina writes 'vuestra alegre corazón' in his original poem.

50 'seeps' translates 'filtra'; 'unknown to you' translates 'sin daros cuenta' in the original (i.e. without you giving any account [of it]).

Amado Nervo (1870–1919): An Old Burden

In the original, quatrains (apart from stanza three, which has five lines) rhyming abab, with a short final line repeating the first half of the previous line as in SB's translation. The original title is 'Vieja estribillo' (in French: 'Vieux refrain').

An untitled draft version of this poem in the *'Sam Francis' Notebook* begins with a false start (half a line, deleted) and has crossings out in all five stanzas. The third stanza is crossed out and has a clean version (identical to the published version) at the foot of the page, bracketed and marked with an arrow for substitution. In the deleted third stanza the phrase 'evening's divine fire' was originally 'divine fire of the evening'. The fifth stanza, and particularly its second line (a variant version of the published text is scored through), seems to have given SB a good deal of difficulty. This draft offers the best evidence of how hard SB worked at what he obviously considered a thankless task, later (to George Reavey; 9.11.61) described as 'an alimentary chore'. (Weinberger, 2007, 616, quotes SB's description of UNESCO as 'that inexhaustible cheese'.) SB repeatedly emphasised in his 1959–61 correspondence, after which the subject not unnaturally only intermittently reappeared, that he had undertaken the UNESCO commission in desperate need of money; but it probably did not make much, and in the same letter to Reavey SB added, with as little emotion as he could muster or conceal: 'I just got paid for the job [. . .] No royalties.'

Weinberger (2007, 619) offers a literal translation of the first two lines, and comments: 'The poem in SB's version sings, as it doesn't in Spanish.'

José Juan Tablada (1871–1945): Haiku of the Flowerpot

The second of six selections in *Anth*, not strictly a haiku by Japanese standards, whether in Spanish, English or French. Paz (2007, 623) claims that SB particularly admired Tablada. The French edition of the *Anthology* reversed the order of appearance of Tablada and Martínez, as it did Léon (not included in this selection) and Nervo.
6   ends in a question mark in the original, and to conform to Spanish practice the stanza has begun with one; not a question in the French version.
7   'crawling' is added.
14   line 13 in the original.
20–1   reverses the order of the original lines.
25–6   also two lines in the original.
27   'feast' is added to the original.

SB omits, or neglects, to translate stanzas 11 and 13 of the original, as Guy Lévis Mano does not. In an undated (early 1950) letter to Georges Duthuit SB writes: 'J'ai du me taper une revision. J'avais sauté, sans le vouloir, des vers, des strophes et même des poèmes entiers! Et le peu d'Espagnol que j'avais appris à ce moment-là est bien parti. Si leurs [Mexican] plasticiens ressemblent même de loin à leurs poètes, je me dispenserai d'y aller' (*LSB2*, 200). SB is not known to have visited Mexico.

Enrique González Martínez (1871–1952): Romance of the Living Corpse

Verse paragraphs of 14, 16 and 14 lines in the original ('Romance del muerto vivo'; cf. SB's 'vive morte') as here. The French edition of the *Anthology* reversed the order of appearance of Martínez and Tablada.

4 'wound' translates 'amortajados'.
21 'ramp' translates 'encrespan'.
23 repeats 'here', as the original does not.

Ramón López Velarde (1888–1921): [1] My Cousin Agueda; [2] Ants

[1] 'My Cousin Agueda' ('Mi primo Agueda'), the first of eleven selections for *Anth*. In 1994 Paz (2007, 623) said: 'SB's translations of López Velarde are masterpieces, and he clearly loved these poems.' Perhaps so, but he never afterwards referred to them. The 'Agueda' poem does, however, manifest a great deal of loving care.

11 ends '. . .' in the original.
19 'morbid' translates 'insana' ('folle' in the French version).
30 'ancient' translates 'añoso'.

This translation was reprinted in *The Oxford Book of Verse in English Translation*, edited by Charles Tomlinson, Oxford University Press, 1980, 493.

[2] 'Ants' ('Hormigas') is the eighth selection in *Anth*.
10 'formication' translates 'hormigueo'; compare 'à la main formicante' in 'être là sans mâchoires sans dents' [q.v.] and *Happy Days*. The French version has: 'fourmilière'. SB restructures this stanza; in the original it is line 6 that reads: 'Fustigan el desmán del perenne hormigueo'.
13 'bagasse' translates 'bagazo' (in the French version:

'bagasse'); in French one meaning of 'bagasse' is 'sugar cane pulp from which the juice has been extracted'.

Alfonso Reyes (1889–1959): To-and-Fro of Saint Theresa

The fourth of six selections for *Anth*. Eleven quatrains with no obvious rhyme scheme. A loose leaf in the *'Sam Francis' Notebook* (UoR),which contains items of Spanish vocabulary with English equivalents, shows SB trying out two versions of the second quatrain of this poem ('Vaivén de Santa Teresa' in the original; 'Va-et-vient de Saint Thérèse' in the French version). The first reads:

caught among eyelashes
in their tiptoe flight,
captive and free the eyes
sue in peace and ['wage war' crossed out] give battle

The second follows closer to the word order of the original than the published text:

The eyes in tiptoe flight
caught among the lashes,
free and captive give
battle and sue for peace

Anth substitutes 'sparkling' for 'tiptoe' ('en pavesas' in the original; literally 'in ashes'), coming a little closer to the original. Maria José Carrera has demonstrated, in an unpublished essay, that 'sparkling', adopted for the published text and present in the UoR *'Sam Francis' Notebook*, indicates a late revision of the typescript of the English translations at the HRHRC, where it does not occur.

3 'hitherandthithering' translates 'corretona' (French version: 'trotteuse'); Jean-Michel Rabaté, who considers this translation one in which SB has 'réussit pleinement' (*SBT/A* 8, 78), hears a Joycean echo: 'un clin d'oeil au motif d'Anna Livia dans *Finnegans Wake*' (79).

9 'darky' translates 'negrito'.

22 'hales' translates 'entrega'.

41 'Flying quiet' translates '– Voladora y quieta' (in the French version '– Mouvante et immobile').

Jean Wahl: The Word Is Graven: Illustrations for The Bible by Marc Chagall

Jean Wahl (1888–1974) was an important French philosopher and professor at the Sorbonne from 1936 to 1967. While in the USA from 1942 to 1945, he and others established a 'university in exile' to facilitate meetings between French and American intellectuals. As well as writing and publishing his own poetry, he translated Wallace Stevens into French. He published widely on philosophy and many of these works have been translated into English. He also wrote on literature, including D. H. Lawrence, Sartre's *La Nausée* and William Blake's 'Tiger' and the poetry of Hölderlin. Wahl translated the second hypothesis of the *Parmenides* of Plato as 'Il y a de l'Un', which Lacan adopted as the central point or existential sentence of psychoanalytic discourse, its negation being 'Il n'y a pas de rapport sexuel' – 'there is no such thing as a sexual relationship'. Wahl was a member of Georges Duthuit's advisory board for *Transition*, and it is likely that this is how he and Beckett became acquainted. He contributed a 'Note on Metaphysics' to *Transition* 48.1, and 'Introduction to Léon Brunschvicg's "The Toil Towards the Truth"' in T 48.3. (Wahl is mentioned in *LSB2*, 213, 251–2, 263, 276–7, 342, 353–4, 590.)

The poems were first published in French under the title 'L'Écriture est Gravure' in 'VERVE, Vol VIII No 33–34', Printed in France by Draeger Frères, 10.9.56. The English translation, distributed by A. Zwemmer Ltd, carries a superscription on the title page 'Verve, Vol IX No 33/34' – the volume number being, no doubt, an error. It was written to accompany 105 etchings by Chagall, reproduced in heliogravure, illustrating the Old Testament. The poem is signed 'Jean WAHL' at the foot above a note which reads: 'The poems have been translated from the french [*sic*] original by the author with the kind assistance of Samuel BECKET [*sic*]'. The extent of SB's input is not clear. Wahl, who spent the war years in the USA, was fluent in English but he clearly saw the advantage of working with a native speaker. The translation includes a strong element of revision, which may suggest the contribution of another hand. For example, many of the poems read like someone pointing out what the reader can see illustrated on the page, but, in the second section, the consistent translation of various French formulations – 'est là', 'Ce sont' and 'Voici' – by 'are there' gives greater rhythm and weight to the lines. The English version tends to name biblical figures where the French does not (cf. Samson, line **89**, Abraham, **97**, 'the prophetesses', **128**, 'Jacob towards Egypt', **138**; 'Jeremiah', **161**, 'David', **205**). There are many examples of felicitous Englishing where it is tempting to see SB's hand at work, e.g. lines **3–5** which render 'le baladin paladin balladeur / aux yeux étonnée fraîche / à la couleur étonnée fraîche' as 'The lordly wandering playboy / with his fresh wondering eyes / Fresh wondering colour'. Other examples are given in the line notes. The number of lines in each section and breaks between sections do not correspond exactly with the French. Care has been taken to reproduce the somewhat erratic punctuation accurately.

Notes

First section: initial words of each line in the French original of this section start with lower case except line **1** and third line from end of section, with full stops at line **4** from end and final line. For the rest of the poem English punctuation follows the original.

11–12 translate 'ouvre ses yeux et sa boîte à couleurs et son coeur' (one line in French, omitting the last phrase in that line 'à la création' and the following four lines, 'que l'autre / peintre / ouvrant ses yeux, sa boîte à couleurs et son coeur / a créé'.

25 'herd' translates 'berger' as it does 'bergère' in SB's translation of 'Zone'.

47 this line not in French original although it may translate and transpose 'De nouveau la douleur' which occurs before 'Prédecesseur de Job' ('Job's harbinger', line **57**) but is otherwise absent in the English. Cf. 'David weeps for Absalom. / All suffering is in an eye-shielding hand' (lines **188–9**) which translates 'Toute la douleur est vue dans une main qui couvre les yeux'.

59 translates 'le départ tumultueux et gai' and recalls SB's favourite exitus/redditus tag from Thomas à Kempis, first used by him in *Dream* (16) but later used to characterise his own poem 'Sanies I' (q.v.).

74 'oriflamme of the wings' translates 'l'oriflamme des ailes'. This rare English word was used by Beckett to translate 'flammes' in *Drunken Boat*, **99**.

86 translates 'colonne de lumière'.

88 Samson's 'stubborn-headedness' is untranslated ('Ah! tête butée sur pierres écroulées').

112 Not in French.

124–32 condense three sections in French:
Rebecca, première des idylles
Trois règnes trois signes
La femme est une palme au-dessus des palmiers

Entre les palmes et le roi forment cercles
Les beaux cercles de Bethsabée

La jupe est un torrent arrêté sous le vent
Tombé de pitié, de pitié , Joseph
The translation of 'pitié' as both 'piety' and 'pity' recalls the play on pity and piety (*Inf.*, XX, 28) which so exercised Belacqua in 'Dante and the Lobster' (*MPTK*, 11) and is a strong indication of SB's hand in this part of the poem.

140 translates 'Et voit tout passée'.

146–9 expands 'Le manteau de Noé: il est calme / monté sur les tréteaux'.

Alain Bosquet: Six Poems

The first three poems, 'In me, civil war', 'Fresh sighs for sale' and 'Knife', were first published *en face* with the French originals in the 1963 Bosquet selection published by New Directions of New York, all taken from the poet's second collection (*Deuxième Testament*, Paris: Gallimard, 1959), and these are presumably the three poems that SB tells Barbara Bray he has translated 'too freely' (although apparently to Bosquet's satisfaction) in a letter to her of 27.10.59 (TCD), at about the time he was moving on from a major revision of part II of *Comment c'est* to begin the difficult composition of part III. They were reprinted, 'traduits en anglais', without the French originals, in the Brussels magazine *Marginales*, 24, April 1969, 45. The other three versions, 'He can only live in shivers', 'Why must the day' and 'Now that he has drained', presumably undertaken later, are also from *Deuxième Testament*, and all six appear *en face* ('copyright Samuel Beckett 1972') in the Ohio State University Press *Selected Poems of Alain Bosquet* published

in 1972–3, and again in the expanded and slightly revised New
Directions volume of 1988, *No matter no fact*, but without the
French originals. These three additional Bosquet translations
were first published in England in *PN Review* 4:3, 1977, 48–50. All
six of Beckett's Bosquet translations are presented *en face* with
the originals in *No More Me*, a selection edited by Roger Little for
the Dedalus imprint in Dublin (1995), the copy text here. 'Fresh
sighs for sale' with the original *en face* was reprinted in *Poems
1930–1989*.

Alain Bosquet (born Anatoly Bisk in Odessa in 1919, died Paris
1998) published more than a dozen poetry collections with Gallimard, and more than a dozen novels, and was a significant
literary figure in Paris after the war, becoming Literary Editor
of *Le Monde* and writing hundreds of pieces for magazines like
Combat (it was in *Combat* that he reviewed SB's *Le Dépeupleur*,
29.3.71; *Critical Heritage*, 316–20), but he never acquired a very
wide readership outside France. SB knew Bosquet well enough
to be invited to his literary gatherings in the mid-1950s (his first
significant encounter with the painter Avigdor Arikha took place
at one of these on 2.7.56; Atik 15–16), and in a letter to Ruby Cohn
of 10.6.67 SB mentions a recent meeting with Alain Bosquet and
Tom Bishop. Relations between SB and Bosquet seem to have remained cordial without ever becoming especially close, and there
is no record of them collaborating beyond 1972–3.

'Knife', 'He can only live' and 'Why must the day' have the same
number of lines as the French originals, and in the other three
cases only vary by a single line less or more. None of the first
three versions published (1963) is especially 'free', except perhaps
the first ('stertorous', line 5, for 'ronfle'; 'crammed', line 7, for
'remplie'; 'throttled', also line 7, for 'pendus'), and the third makes
somewhat awkward use of the English equivalent of the subjunctive mood. In the second poem, 'Fresh sighs for sale', SB makes
good use of traditional-sounding street cries, which perhaps accounts for the archaisms in lines 8 and 11, and in line 13 he finds
a brilliant equivalent wordplay on reason/season rendering Bosquet's 'le marchand des quatres raisons' as 'Bargains, bargains, in
and out of reason'.

'He can only live', 'Why must the day?' and 'Now that he has drained' stay close to Bosquet's originals (although the last borrows 'drained' from SB's 1930 translation of Montale's 'Delta'), and are perhaps the more successful for doing so. In 'Now that he has drained' SB's translation of 'l'imaginaire' as 'fancy' (line 2) reflects an interest given more emphasis in *All Strange Away* (provisionally entitled *Fancy Dying*) and *Imagination morte imaginez* (1963–5).

LATER POEMS

Long after Chamfort

Nicholas-Sébastien Roch Chamfort (1741–94) served the aristocracy before the French Revolution and joined the Jacobin club after it. Despite his Jacobin enthusiasm, his aristocratic pretensions led to his denunciation and a bungled suicide attempt in September 1793. He succumbed to his wounds seven months later on 13 April [SB's birthday!] 1794. His *Maximes* were published posthumously.

On 12 May 1967 Beckett told Ruby Cohn he had found a 'good thing about "Hope" in Chamfort'. At around the same time he inscribed a version of Chamfort's 'Hope' maxim (see below) on the half-title of a copy (no. 14) of the fifty in the Minuit 1957 limited edition of *Fin de Partie* (on 'vélin pur fil du Marais', F&F *265, 65). This copy forms part of the Henry Wenning collection of Beckettiana at Washington University, St Louis. In a letter of 3.6.67 written to William Matheson, Chief, Rare Book Department, Washington University Libraries (now in the Lilly Library, Bloomington, Indiana), Wenning describes how this occurred. He had been discussing *Fin de Partie* with SB. Wenning said that he did not see the 'affirmations or expressions of hope' that some of his friends saw in the play. 'The author then said, in substance, "oh those hope fellows. I was reading Chamfort the other day and he had a memorable comment to make on the subject of hope. Here, give me that book and I will put it in as closely as I can from memory".'

SB's memory was good, if not word-perfect. The autograph reads:

'"L'espoir est un charlatan / qui nous trompe sans cesse[.] / Et pour ma part je n'ai trouvé / le bonheur que longue je l'ai eu / perdu. Je mettrais volontiers / sur la porte du Paradis les vers / que le Dante a mis sur celle / des Enfers: Lasciate ogni speranza . . ." // Chamfort'.

It was Chamfort's 'Hope' maxim that SB first attempted to translate into English, and it too first appeared in association with *Endgame*, the English version of *Fin de Partie*, where it is inscribed on the title page of the Kobler copy and dated April 1969 (Lake *218, 101;see 'Hope' below). The fact that SB associated this particular Chamfort maxim with the play on two distinct occasions seems to have been ignored by most commentators.

'Hope is a Knave' was also the first maxim to be published (in *Hermathena*, Summer 1973). The first six appeared in *The Blue Guitar*, Facoltà di Magistero, Università degli Studi di Messina, Vol. I, No. 1, December 1975. All eight, which were written before 12 November 1973, first appeared in Calder's 1977 *CPEF*. The title under which they are published, *Long After Chamfort*, suggests not only that Chamfort has been dead a long time, but also that they are very free versions. The eighth poem, in fact, is not from Chamfort but from Pascal.

The 'Hope' maxim, which characteristically translates Chamfort's prose into rhymed verse, is, uncharacteristically, a quatrain in iambic pentameter. Most of the other versions are in couplet form (SB's letter of 15 March 1972 to Professor E. J. Furlong, editor of *Hermathena*, refers to 'riming' some of Chamfort's *Maxims*). Elsewhere SB described this process as 'doggereliz[ing]' ('The trouble with tragedy' and 'Live and clean forget') and the poems as 'doggerel' ('Hope') and 'doggerelisable' ('how hollow heart').

Wit in fools
On 12 November 1973 Beckett sent Barbara Bray a handwritten copy of the first five poems beginning with 'Wit in fools' and continuing in the order of publication, providing French and English texts of the first five and referring her to *Hermathena* for the sixth.

The trouble with tragedy
Sent to Kay Boyle on 22 August 1973, with 'Live and clean forget'.

Live and clean forget
Sent to George Reavey from Ussy on a card postmarked 7 August 1972, with the message 'Have disimproved some hours dog-gerelizing Chamfort's *Maxims*. Here is one may divert you.' The maxim was sent to Kay Boyle a year later (22.8.73), introduced by the reflection 'Time gets like a last oozing [cf. Keats 'To Autumn'], so precious and worthless together. Here's a Chamfort maxim may amuse you, doggerelized.' After telling Boyle that he had finally finished translating *Mercier et Camier*, Beckett added 'Here's another' ('The trouble with tragedy'). SB's letters to Barbara Bray also find him describing his versions of Chamfort as 'doggerel'.

Ask of all-healing
Like the other poems which opt for a pentameter line and those that constitute themselves as a couplet (six of the eight), 'Ask of all-healing' has an eighteenth-century 'feel' about it, and it is possible that SB had Swift and Pope in mind as useful models for what he himself might be able to achieve in a similar mode.

Hope is a knave
First version, inscribed on the title page of *Endgame* 'for John and Evelyn [Kobler] / affectionately / Sam / Ussy April 1969' reads: 'Hope is a fraud that fools us evermore / Which till I lost no happiness was mine / I take from Hell and write on Heaven's door / All hope abandon ye who enter in / (Apologies to Chamfort)'. Three weeks later Beckett told Kobler, 'In the third line of doggerel for "take" read "strike" '. 'Hope is a knave' was published under the title 'Kottabista' (cf. the two 'Kottabistae' Guevara poems in *Hermathena* in 1954) with 'strike' in line 3 in *Hermathena: A Dublin University Review*, number CXV, Summer 1973 (19). *Hermathena* prints two letters from Beckett to Professor E. J. Furlong ('Dr Furlong') of 15.6 and 28.6, in the first of which in line 3 the phrase 'and grave' occurs, corrected in the second to 'to grave'. Furlong comments on SB's 'typically positive response' to requests from 'his *alma mater*'. These *Hermathena* readings are retained in the 1975 publication of six Chamfort maxims in *The Blue Guitar*. Cf.

also 'And perhaps [Sisyphus] thinks each journey is the first. This would keep hope alive, would it not, hellish hope' (*Molloy*, 139).

sleep till death
For the last line, cf. 'this long disease, my life', line 132 of Pope's 'An Epistle to Dr Arbuthnot'. Sent to Barbara Bray on 10 September 1973 with the initial letter of each line capitalised. On the other side of the card sent to Bray, Beckett included an unpublished maxim ('In fear not / Of God / But of Man / Wisdom began.'; cf. Genetti, 178). However, in a subsequent letter (30.9.73) he commented: 'Glad you liked two extra Chamfort. The sleep one is O.K. I think, the other tame.' A variant reading 'In fear/Not of God/But of Man/Wisdom began' occurs in UoR MS 2929 with its French original ('L'Ecriture a dit que le commencement de la sagesse était la crainte de Dieu; moi, je crois que c'est la crainte des hommes'). The same sheet contains six other selections from Chamfort in French and untranslated, indicating that SB may have considered a longer suite of doggerelising.

how hollow heart
Not Chamfort, but Pascal, as Beckett well knew. He wrote to Barbara Bray from Marrakesh on 12.9.73: 'Wondered about Pascal's Pensées doggerelised', and then from Tangiers on 10.10.73: 'Found a 2nd hand Pascal annotated in Arab hand. Nothing doggerelisable so far.' However, a version of this pensée was sent to Patrick Magee on the following day (11.10.73) and to Ruby Cohn twelve days later (23.10.73), Beckett noting, 'did a couple more Chamfort and one Pensée (Pascal)'. It may be that Beckett was dissatisfied with his first attempts because holograph drafts of 'how hollow heart' are found on a single page among the working papers for 'dread nay' (earliest draft of which is dated '31.1.74'). Here the first complete version of the Pascal reads 'How empty / Heart / how full / of muck thou art.' Beckett tries out a three-line version before settling on the couplet form and final wording. Beckett sent Barbara Bray a version in a letter of 31 March 1974 from Tangiers. It reads: 'How empty heart and full / of muck thou art', as does the penultimate version in the 'dread nay' manuscript. The final version in the 'dread nay' manuscript is the same as the published version.

Chamfort makes one uncomplimentary mention of Pascal in his *Maximes*: 'Le Jansénisme des chrétiens, c'est le Stoicisme des païens, dégradé de figure et mis à la portée d'une populace chrétienne, et cette secte a eu des Pascal et des Arnauld pour défenseurs!' ('The Jansenism of the Christians is the Stoicism of the pagans, disfigured and discarded, and this sect has Pascals and Arnaulds [the Jansenist opponent of Descartes, cf. 'Whoroscope'] for its champions!')

hors crâne
something there
dread nay

The manuscripts of 'hors crâne' and 'dread nay' (Burns Library, Boston College) provide an unusual, perhaps unique, insight into Beckett at work on parallel composition in French and English from the same starting point: a striking visual image from Dante. Beckett commenced work on 'hors crâne' on 1 January 1974, a bitterly cold day, which may have called to mind the chattering head of Bocca degli Abati frozen in the ice of Antenora, the deepest pit of hell. The first draft, which looks more like prose jottings than the beginnings of a poem, opens with a phrase, 'Là quelque-chose' ('something there'), which encapsulates the essence of the three poems that follow. In the fifth draft, signed and dated 4 January 1974, the prose fragments were organised for the first time as a twelve-line poem in four sections of three lines each. This is recognisably the poem as published, but it went through five more drafts (two of which are dated, draft 7: 28.2.74 and draft 9, the penultimate draft: 4.3.74) before finding its final form.

Beckett told Kay Boyle that he had written a twelve-line poem ('hors crâne') on 1.3.74. On 7.3.74 he passed on more details to George Reavey: 'One little poem in French, 12 lines and a rather dimmer companion in English ('something there')'. A handwritten copy of the final version which SB had copied for Josette Hayden on to the back of a Craven 'A' packet was sold at Sotheby's on 13 July 2006. Josette, a heavy smoker, favoured Craven 'A'. She added SB's name and the date 'mars 74' underneath the poem. Four *mirlitonnades* ('rentrer', 'nuit qui fais tant', 'imagine' and 'qu'à lever la tête', q.v.), also copied on the back of Craven 'A' cigarette packets, were sold at the same sale. On the Boston College copy Beckett wrote: 'forget where if ever poem was published'. (It was first published in *Minuit*, 21, in 1976 and subsequently collected as the last poem in the 'Poèmes' section of Minuit's 1978 *Poèmes suivi de mirlitonnades*.) In *CPEF* it is titled 'Poème 1974'.

On 16 January 1974 Beckett sent Barbara Bray the manuscript of 'something there' with a corrected typescript corresponding to the published text. Since 'something there' is a version 'after' 'hors crâne', this means that Beckett probably worked either from draft 5 (4.1.74) or the undated draft 6. However, the opening of 'something there' remembers the previous drafts of 'hors crâne' which all begin 'là quelque chose', while the holograph (which has a couple of false starts and two versions for each of the three sections of the poem) suggests that the English version gave Beckett less trouble than the French original.

There is a photocopy of the typescipt sent to Bray in the BIF (UoR MS 2924/1) with minor corrections in SB's hand bringing the poem into line with the published version: 'outside' at start of line 9 moved to end line 8; line 11 'whole' inserted before 'globe'; line 12 'all' deleted before 'bare'; line 13 'at it' deleted before 'the eye'. The typescript sent to Michael Horovitz, editor of *New Departures*, where the poem was first published in 1975, has a gnomic handwritten note which reads, in part, 'If you think above worth having for No. 15 it's yours with three hearts over two' (reproduced in *Samuel Beckett Today/Aujourd'hui* 8, 205, where the editors explain that three hearts in response to a strong opening bid of two hearts in a game of Bridge would represent minimal encouragement).

A month after beginning 'hors crâne' (31.1.74), Beckett set to work methodically on 'dread nay'. The first draft, like 'hors crâne', consists of notes, but here they are organised under four numbered headings: '1. Head'; '2. Position of Head'; '3. Argument'; '4. Inside of Head'. In the section on 'Position of Head' Bocca is named again and precise reference made to the *Inferno* (XXXII, 44–5 and XXXIII, 1–2). There is a further elaboration below which sets out the eight-part structure of the poem: 'A. Statement embracing all 4'; 'B. Head alone'; 'C. Without alone'; 'D. Position of head in without with ref to *Inf.*, XXXII, XXXIII'; 'E. Stir alone'; 'F. Eye alone'; 'G. Inside of head normally / Inside of head eye open'; 'H. Restatement (varied) embracing all'.These are bracketed together 'Any order'. Underneath Beckett has written 'First prose. Then', followed by two words too heavily cancelled to read. It is not until draft 5 that 'dread nay' is set out as a poem (in quatrains) but with three workings of the fourth and lacking the last three stanzas. In drafts 7 and 8 the poem takes on the short eight-line structure almost complete but for the penultimate stanza, which is still missing. SB then produces four versions of this section under the heading 'stir dread'. The last of these is close to the published version:

at ray
in latibule
long dark
stir of dread
till long after
breach stopped
dark again
still again

Beckett's correspondence with Barbara Bray may indicate that he was 'stuck' in drafts 5–6 in March and April. On 28 March he wrote: 'Had a look at outstanding *Fizzles*, also quatrain 3. Unsuccessfully.' On the 31st he complained that he was '[s]till stuck in poem'. (This letter also included a version of 'how hollow heart' [q.v.], manuscript drafts of which are found among the 'dread nay' papers.) On 3 April SB told Barbara Bray that he was 'bogged down in these silly verses'; on the 5th he announced that he was 'still bogged down in poem' and a letter later that same month, 16 or 18 April, announced: 'Poem abandoned'. The penultimate draft (draft 10) was not completed until 3 June.

hors crâne
First published in November 1976 in *Minuit*, 21, 13–22, with eighteen other poems, i.e. *Poèmes 37–39* and *Poèmes 47–49*.

The triplet form may be a tribute to Dante's *terza rima*.

6   at the battle of Montaperti in 1260, Bocca, a Ghibelline fighting in the Guelf ranks, cut off the hand of the Guelf standard bearer and caused a panic. It was Bocca's treason that brought long-remembered disaster on Florence when 'the rout and great slaughter stained the Arbia red' (*Inf.*, X, 86). Dante does not know whether it was will or fate or chance, but he encounters Bocca by stumbling over his head and kicking him in the face (*Inf.*, XXXII, 77–8). Bocca refuses to give his name, but Dante, recognising him, pulls out his hair by the handful, so that Bocca barks like a dog.

something there
First published, dated 'jan. 1974', in *New Departures 7/8 10/11*, 1975, 27.

dread nay
First published with 'hors crâne' and 'something there' in Calder's *CPEF* in 1977. Sections 5–8 appeared in the Paris magazine *Frank* in 1992 under the misleading title 'Roundelay'.
13   cf. the constrained movement of the damned in *Inferno*, XXXII, 44–5, who 'bent back their necks; and [. . .] raised their faces to me', and Ugolino, 'that sinner' who 'lifted his mouth from the savage meal, wiping it on the hair of the head he had wasted behind' (*Inf.*, XXXIII, 1–3).
25–9   cf. 'their eyes, which before were moist only within, gushed over at the lids, and the frost bound the tears between and locked them up again, never did clamp bind beam on beam so hard' (*Inf.*, XXXII, 46–50).
30–2   cf. 'the suffering shades in the ice, setting their teeth to the note of the stork' (*Inf.*, XXXII, 35–6).
49   cf. the unpublished 'Long Observation of the Ray' (UoR) which Beckett worked on in November 1976 and in 1977.
50   the Latin word 'latibulum', a hiding place, usually an animal's lair, occurs as early as the very brief section G of the second draft: 'Within all dark + still till when + while eye gapes stir of dread at faint light in latibulum.' The 'um' is crossed out to make an English word: 'latibule'. If Beckett had a Latin source for the word, it is probably from the Psalms, e.g. 'repleta sunt latibula terrae tentoriis violentiae' ('the dark places of the earth are full of the habitations of cruelty', Psalm 74:20) but cf. also the 'furibunda

latibula' of Catullus, Poem 63, 'Super alta uectus Attis celeri rate maria' ('Borne in his swift bark over deep seas').

Roundelay

First published in *Modern Drama*, 19, September 1976, 223. Beckett sent this poem, as published but untitled, to Barbara Bray from Tangier on 1.2.76, with the message 'a rondeau for your return'. When he sent the text to Calder for publication it was marked 'Paris, 14.11.76'. UoR MS 2913 consists of two sheets with two copies of the poem; both have title in lower case and reverse lines 7 and 8. The first sheet is dated '1976' in SB's hand. The version sent to Bray has the lines in published order. The poem recalls 'Dieppe' with its seaside location and turning motif, and the play *Footfalls* with its counted paces and turning.

A 'roundelay' is a song in which a line or phrase is repeated as a refrain, a role played here by 'on all that strand'. A 'rondeau' is, more technically, a poem of ten or thirteen lines with two rhymes and having the opening words of the first line used as an un-rhymed refrain. 'Strand' is a particularly Irish usage, cf. 'je suis ce cours de sable qui glisse' which, according to Harvey, was written on Killiney Strand, County Dublin, during one of SB's summer visits to his mother.

thither

'thither' appears to be another experiment in the manner of 'Roundelay'. Just as the first five lines of that poem lead up to a point of stillness (four lines) and then a movement away from stasis (4 lines), so the three sections of 'thither' ('thither', 'there' and 'thence') mark a similar epiphany but with the third or 'then thence' section containing within it the sense of recurrence (note the threefold repetition of 'again' qualifying, or so it would seem, the three elements which balance the first and third sections: 'daffodils', 'march' and 'a far cry/for one/so little').

The Downs

'The Downs' has a similar quality to 'Roundelay' and 'thither', albeit over a more extended form. The first four sections, set in summer on the Downs, use 'hand in hand' as a refrain; the last three, set in Winter on a bridge, and therefore in town, use 'foaming on' and foam'. These two settings are united by similarities of phrasing, although only 'no thought' and 'gazing down' are actually carried across the seasons.

'The Downs' was first published in the *Sunday Times* on 8 January 1989. According to *Poems 1930–1989*, Beckett could not remember when he had written the poem, but said that it came to him when looking down at the Thames from Waterloo Bridge. From this Calder offers the suggestion that the poem might have been written in 1964 when Beckett attended rehearsals for *Play* with Billie Whitelaw at the National Theatre. However, manuscript evidence suggests that the poem was written later than this, since two earlier drafts – both with amusing misreadings of 'the downs' in the descriptions of them given in the Sotheby's catalogues – are dated 1981, although clearly written earlier, and 1977. The published version consists of 55 lines (an opening section of seven lines and six further sections of eight lines each). An earlier draft of 183 lines in SB's hand with extensive autograph revisions was sold for £400 at Sotheby's on 17 December 1981. This was signed and dated 'Paris 1981'. The date and authenticating signature indicate when SB donated the manuscript to Oxfam rather than when it was written since Beckett told Knowlson in a letter of 12.12.81 that he had 'no memory of the Oxfam poem' (UoR MS 2911/1). What little of the manuscript is reproduced in facsimile in the Sotheby's sales catalogue contains almost all the elements of the final poem, which suggests an oddly recursive process of composition. The catalogue mistranscribes the opening words as 'The worms' and Beckett is quoted as calling it a 'quick miscarriage' of a poem. Almost exactly a year later to the day, 15 December 1982, Sotheby's sold for £220 another version of the poem, described in the following terms: 'Beckett (Samuel) Autograph mss of an unfinished, 55-line poem beginning "The Lovers / Summer days on the downs", signed, marked "unfinished" and dated 1977, 1 page from a quarto notepad with an autograph envelope postmarked 1981'.

The poem may conceivably involve a partial recollection of SB's 1938 visit to Peggy Guggenheim's Yew Tree Cottage near Petersfield, from which the South Downs are very visible, although Knowlson indicates that they spent little time alone together (1996, 286–7). The present whereabouts of the manuscripts sold at auction are unknown. There is a typescript of the poem (as published) in the BIF (UoR MS 2911/1) but with the final two lines added by hand.

6–7   cf. the *mirlitonnade* beginning 'rentrer à la nuit / au logis' (written 24.11.76). The draft reproduced in the Sotheby's catalogue reads 'tent' for 'hut'.

one dead of night

Written in Stuttgart (26.6.77), where Beckett had gone to direct his two new television plays *Ghost Trio* and . . . *but the clouds* . . .; and entered into his *'Sottisier' Notebook*. Beckett gave the poem to his cameraman Jim Lewis. It has an intimation about it of the 1980 play *Ohio Impromptu* and SB's final prose piece *Stirrings Still*. First published in *Poetry Review*, 86.3, Autumn 1996, 9. The UoR holograph presents the poem as seven separated sections, with dividing marks between them.

MIRLITONNADES

In French a 'mirliton' is a toy flute and 'vers de mirliton' doggerel or trashy verse. Beckett wrote these scraps of verse originally on scraps of paper and cardboard – and even a beer mat! – between 24.11.76 ('rentrer') and June 1980 ('qu'à lever la tête' and the previously uncollected 'minuit mille ans d'ici'). Most, however, were written between February and July 1977 in Paris (P), Ussy (U) or Tangiers (T) (UoR MS 2460). Some of these scraps include several drafts of a poem, often crossed through as SB reworks them. He entered the final version of these poems into his *'Sottisier'*

Notebook (hereafter *Sott*; UoR MS 2901), which also contains extraneous material. Beckett numbered the poems as he entered them, although his numbers do not correspond exactly with the published order. Various titles for the collection were tried out inside the front cover of the notebook: 'Rimailles', 'Rhymeries', 'Versicule(t)s', while the typescript that Beckett prepared for publication was originally entitled 'Poèmes courts 77', which is deleted and replaced by '*MIRLITONNADES*'. In the back of the notebook he lists people to whom some of the poems were sent for publication, although he also sent copies privately to friends. *Poèmes suivi de mirlitonnades* was published by Minuit on 28 August 1978 (*achevé d'imprimer*). This suite of 35 *mirlitonnades*, beginning with 'en face' and ending with 'noire soeur', was included in Calder's 1984 edition of the *Collected Poems*. Two new *mirlitonnades*, 'le nain nonagénaire' and 'à bout de songes', appeared in *Minuit 33*, March 1979, under the title *Deux Poèmes*. They were included on pages 26 and 27 of an augmented impression of *Poèmes suivi de mirlitonnades* (*achevé d'imprimer* 20 March 1979), mistakenly placed at the end of the *Poèmes* rather than with the other *mirlitonnades*. (There was a trade edition on ordinary paper and a limited edition of 99 copies on alfamousse.) It was not until 1984 that 'le nain nonagénaire' and 'à bout de songes' found their rightful place on page 45 as the last poems in the *mirlitonnades* section (second augmented impression, *achevé d'imprimer* 21 February 1984). A third augmented impression including 'Comment dire' (imprint dated 29 June) was published in 1992. (Our warm thanks to Breon Mitchell for his help with the Minuit chronology.) *Poems 1930–1989* (Calder 2002) published a further six poems, one of which was, in fact, a variant. This edition was marred by a number of transcription errors. We have printed the *mirlitonnades* in the same order as Minuit 1988, followed by six additional poems, which appear in the order in which they were written. Five of these latter poems appeared in *Poems 1930–1989*. Errors in transcription in that edition are corrected.

The commercial LP recording by Michael Lonsdale of *Poèmes suivi de mirlitonnades* (Atalect A 110), which also includes 'Imagination morte imaginez' and 'Bing', places 'le nain nonagénaire'

and 'à bout de songes' at the end of the *Poèmes*, which accords
with the 1979 printing. Lonsdale's performance naturally enough
renders the relatively regular rhythms of these poems, and the
frequent rhymes and half-rhymes, with an emphasis not always
apparent in the silent act of reading them to oneself.

en face

Dated P[aris] 12.11.77 in *Sott*; the scrap has some eight draft versions which trace the development of the poem from its beginnings as a simple couplet, 'mauvais oeil / veille sur la sépulture',
which is immediately complicated by the conversion of the eye
into the mystical-sounding third eye. SB works through another
four versions until he produces: 'du tiers oeil revenu sur terre / il
fixe son tombeau jusqu'à ce / qu'en soit perdue toute trace / puis
clos sa tierce paupière'; this version is dated (U[ssy] 5.11.77 and
entered into *Sott*, and subsequently cancelled. However, Beckett
carried on working on the poem, losing first the eye but retaining
the eyelid: 'face la / misère / la pire / jusqu'à ce / qu'il en fasse /
sourire / et bas la / paupière'. The unpublished version was the
29th entry in *Sott*, where it is dated 'P. 12.11.77', although given
pride of place in the published collection as the epitome *mirlitonnade*, not only for what it is saying, but also for its idiosyncratic
rhyming. It is hard to imagine a native French speaker akwardly
separating 'ce que' ('it') like this, so that it straddles two lines
to draw attention to the rhyme, and it is impossible to find an
equivalent for an English version. (The use of rhyme is a strong
element in the *mirlitonnades*, which is not much in evidence
elsewhere in SB's poems.)

The poem was sent to Barbara Bray and is reproduced in the
Centre Pompidou centenary catalogue *Object Beckett,* plate 95
(hereafter *CPOB*). On the same undated card is 'de pied ferme'
(TCD MS 10948/2/119). The poem was anticipated in the idea of
worsening in 'ce qu'a de pis' (31.3.77) and itself anticipates a trio
of quotations from *King Lear* entered in *Sott* between 28.12.80
and 23.3.81: 'The lamentable change is from the best, / The worst
returns to laughter –', 'Who is't can say, I am at the worst –' and
'The worst is not/ So long as one can say, This is the worst'. Anne

Atik, in a diary entry for 24 August 1983, has SB remembering the third of these quotations. She says that he sent it to Jocelyn Herbert on the death of George Devine (January 1966). While no such letter is preserved among the correspondence at the University of Reading, Beckett did use the quote in a letter to Herbert of 12.12.87 in relation to a poor production of *Godot*, adding 'To myself as Edgar to the Fool' (cf. Atik, 117). There is also a letter to Barbara Bray of 31.8.67 in which SB discusses quotations from *King Lear*.

The five-line version in a letter to John Beckett (9.3.89; UoR) is probably a rearrangement due to failing memory.

rentrer

The first, undated and cancelled scrap, entitled 'Eteindre pour voir', has a note against it, reading 'Vers Octave'. A scrap dated 24.11.76 and entitled 'Retard' has variant lines **2** ('le visage à la nuit') and **6** ('la nuit'). A copy made for Josette Hayden on the back of a Craven 'A' packet, and dated by her '3 déc 1976' is entitled 'Octave'. It was the first of the *mirlitonnades* SB wrote and the only one he attempted to find a title for. It is the first (untitled) entry in *Sott*, where SB notes that it was sent to 'Hans Meyer 76'. The face pressed against the glass ('vitre') may recall the fly against the glass in 'La Mouche'.

somme toute

The scrap, dated 13.2.77, is reproduced in *CPOB*, plate 97. The calculation that Beckett performed to arrive at 'a quarter million quarters of an hour' shows through from the other side of the page. SB begins by calculating the number of days a man lives based on the biblical three score years and ten (365 by 70 = 25,550), then calculates the number of hours (rounds up to 26,000 by 24, = 624,000), then starts to draft a poem in English before moving to French and concluding with a pun on 'temps morts' ('slack time', but also here the long time in which we are all dead):

Some 26000 days
and nights
600 000 hours
3 and 1/2 million minutes
~~d'attente~~
chiffres ronds
~~d'attente~~ d'instance
chiffre rond sauf erreur
vingt-six mille jours
et nuits
six cent mille heures
~~trois millions et demi de minutes~~
d'~~attente~~ d'instance
sans compter
les temps morts

This was not SB's first attempt to calculate the length of his life in small units, as he approached his birthday. (He would be 71 the following month.) On 12 March 1956, he wrote to Pamela Mitchell: 'Shall be fifty in a month's time and can well believe it. 18,000 days and not much to show for them' (*LSB2*, 606). The *Sott* entry, of which the second line reads 'bon poids', is dated 2.2.77. There is a slightly earlier undated version, which has as its second line 'peu s'en faut', which is followed by a quotation from the Book of Job – 'moaning that the sparks fly upward' (also given in French) – and a quotation from Voltaire: 'Tristes calculateurs des misères humaines / Ne me consolez point, vous aigrissez mes peines' ('Poème sur le désastre de Lisbonne': 'Sad calculators of human misery / You do not console me at all, you aggravate my pains'. Cf. 'ainsi-a-t-on beau').

fin fond du néant

Sott 9.2.77. The original scrap, which begins 'loin dans le néant', is reproduced in *CPOB*, plate 96. The poem reprises and combines the 'something there' trope of 'dread nay' and 'hors crâne'. Beckett had used the 'fin fond' idiom, meaning 'deep in', in a thank-you poem addressed to Maria Jolas on 1 April 1940, after she had afforded him the shelter that is here denied. The poem, 'Au fin fond du blanc Bourbonnais', is reproduced in *LSB1*, 677.

silence tel que ce qui fut

Dated 18.2.77 both in *Sott* and on scrap. The first of the *mirliton-nades* to be published in the aptly named *Cahiers du Silence Ar-rabal* (Paris: Kesselring, 1977, 172). SB's typed contribution, dated 19.3.77, which is reproduced in facsimile, bears the message: 'Voi-ci, si vous en voulez, un petit inédit pour votre Cahiers du Silence Arrabal'. On the same page there is a newspaper report of Arra-bal's appearance before the Public Order Tribunal in Madrid in 1966 on charges of blasphemy and insulting his homeland, which includes extracts from the letter that Beckett wrote in his defence in 1966. This is the first example of the words-for-company motif in the *mirlitonnades*. The second line of the *Sott* version reads 'auparavant ne sera plus', which is corrected to 'avant jamais ne sera plus' in the published version.

For 'taire' cf. 'musique de l'indifférence'.

écoute-les

Dated 20.2.77 both in *Sott* and on scrap. Cf. Clov's 'Grain upon grain, one by one, and one day, suddenly, there's a heap' in *End-game*. For 'pas' cf. *Pas*, SB's translation into French of the play *Footfalls*.

lueurs lisières

The penultimate scrap (22.2.77) and final undated scrap have a variant sixth line ('dos aux deux'), as does *Sott* (21.2.77), which is corrected to the published version. The first draft works up the image of a shuttle ('navette') plying to and fro between two gleams of light ('entre deux lueurs') finishing halfway ('mi-chemin') and somehow incomplete without itself or another:
     navette entre deux lueurs
     les atteindre les éteint

s'endétourner [*sic*] les allume
halte en fin mi-chemin
sans soi sans l'autre

In successive drafts SB complicates the image by associating the glimmers of light with 'lisières', and characterising the final halfway halt of the shuttle as a homecoming ('chez-soi') despite the contradictory absence of the self. David Wheatley (*Selected Poems*, 182) translates 'lisières' as 'edgings', from the finished, non-fraying edges of a length of woven fabric, which is the first meaning given for the word in Robert ('selvedges' would be a more technical English term). However, other meanings of the word would seem to make better sense: 'lisières' as the guiding reins used on small children or, better still, as a border, extremity or limit. 'Nous sommes des enfants qui essayons de faire quelques pas sans lisières' as Voltaire says in *Le Philosophe ignorant*, XIV. In fact, the poem reworks the prose text 'neither', which Beckett sent to Morton Feldman on 1 October 1976 nearly five months earlier, so that 'neither' might provide a suitable lexicon for a translation of 'lueurs lisières'.

Charles Juliet described a meeting with Beckett on 11 November 1977 (*Conversations with Samuel Beckett and Bram van Velde*, 166) in which SB said that he had been writing some short poems in regular verse called *mirlitonnades*. (It seems unlikely that Beckett would have hit upon this term as early as November 1977, since the typescript, which was certainly not prepared until 1978, is headed 'poèmes courts 1977', amended to '*Mirlitonnades*'). Juliet asked him if he would send one to a friend who was launching a literary magazine. Beckett agreed and a few days later sent 'lueurs lisières' to Yves Peyré. The poem duly appeared in the review *L'ire des vents*, no. 1, 1978, 67 (*achevé d'imprimer*, 12.5.78). At the same meeting with Juliet, Beckett mentioned that he had been reading the late poems of Heine. One of these, 'Es sitzen am Kreuzweg drei Frauen', is a depiction of the three Fates which may possibly have influenced 'lueurs lisières' and 'noire sœur', whereas the 'ciseaux argentins' of 'jusque dans la caverne' are probably taken from classical mythology by way of Lemprière's Dictionary (purchased 1936).

There is a similar wordplay, 'chez soi [. . .] chez eux', in the last line of 'ainsi a-t-on beau'. Cf. also the 'demi-tour' of 'Dieppe'.

imagine si ceci

'imagine' was published in *Hand and Eye*, a limited edition *hommage* to Sacheverell Sitwell (Geoffrey Elborn, Edinburgh: Tragara Press), in November 1977. We have reinstated line **7** 'si ceci', as published in *Hand and Eye* and as it appears in both the *Sott* (Ussy 26.2.77) and final scrap versions (26/27.2.77) and in the copy SB made for Josette Hayden on the back of a cigarette packet (dated by her '15 [mars 77]'. Line **7**, 'si ceci', was omitted (in error?) from the typescript that SB produced for Minuit, thus ensuring it did not appear in subsequent editions. Cf. *Imagination morte imaginez*. In SB's penultimate version 'pouvait / s'atténuer' occurs in place of 'si ceci / cessait' (lines **7–8**).

d'abord

Sott (2) and scrap (10) versions both dated U[ssy]. 26 and 27.2.77. The earliest scrap gives a little more away, revealing that right (droite) and left (gauche) refer to a hand: 'd'abord une main / à plat sur la table / ensuite la seconde / à plat sur la première / enfin sur l'appui le tout / ainsi constitué / le front cette tête la tête'. This seems to reflect the same impulse as the late English *mirlitonnade* 'head on hands' (26.5.81; q.v.).

flux cause

'flux cause' and 'samedi répit' (both completed U[ssy] 7 March 1977) and 'chaque jour' (U[ssy] 9 and 10 March) draw on SB's philosophical readings. In his reading notes on the pre-Socratic philosopher, Heraclitus of Ephesus (*c*.500 BC), SB writes: 'Primacy of flux in his cosmos. <u>All things flow</u>.' and 'The "flux of things" is a ceaseless strife of opposites and this strife the father of all things'. The advice that everything that is in being is best not spoken of may derive from another of SB's notes on Heraclitus: 'We cannot say of things that they are; they only become, and pass away in the ever-changing play of cosmic flow' (TCD MS 10967). In a series of undated jottings on the reverse of the 'flux cause' scrap, Beckett refers to the pre-Socratic philosopher as 'qui fut le fou / / l'optimiste / [vécu] / 6 siècles avant Christ' and tries out a series of brief encapsulations of his philosophy, the most developed of which reads: 'qui dit à / propos de tout /qu'il est et du / même coup / n'est plus'.

The *Sott* draft is reproduced in *CPOB*, plate 99, dated 'U[ssy]. 7.3.77' and numbered '9'. Number '10', 'samedi répit', is on the same sheet (6) with the same date.

samedi répit

Beckett revised 'plus pleurer', which is how the final scrap version reads, to 'pas pleurer' in *Sott* and in the typescript, and this is how the poem appears in the Minuit edition. However, Calder 2002 reverted to 'plus pleurer'.

Once again, the scraps reveal the development of a line of thought, from 'samedi / trop tard pour rire / trop tôt pour pleurer' (verso 'chaque jour') to 'samedi / trop tard pour vivre / trop tôt pour pleurer', playing with the familiar notion of laughing till you cry and Donne's paradox: 'Now among our wise men, I doubt not but many would be found, who would laugh at Heraclitus weeping, none which would weep at Democritus laughing', quoted in 'Yellow', *MPTK*, 154–5. The two philosophers are also side by side in a letter to Nuala Costello of February 1934, *LSB1*, 185, threaten to become confused in *The Unnamable* (127: 'hee hee, that's the Abderite [i.e. Democritus], no, the other'), and reappear as 'Hemocritus et Deraclitus, philosophes muets' in a jotting at the back of SB's Schiller-Theater Werkstatt Berlin production notebook for the 1975 production of *Das letzte Band* [*Krapp's Last Tape*], as reproduced in facsimile in *The Theatrical Notebooks of Samuel Beckett*, vol. 3, ed. James Knowlson [247]. It has been further suggested that SB's hesitation over the final line of this *mirlitonnade* may owe something to Spinoza's 'non ridere, non lugere, sed intellegere' (Clément, 2009, 100).

The date of the final scrap and *Sott* versions, 7.3.77, was in fact a Monday.

chaque jour envie

Beckett had long taken to heart what Geulincx had taught him: 'The best status of all is not to be born. The most similar status to this is to reach death as soon as possible' (TCD MS 10967/6/32). He revisited the sentiment in *A Piece of Monologue*'s opening line 'Birth was the death of him', which he found impossible to translate into French (cf. *Solo*), and perhaps more closely in Chamfort's 'Indian' proverb (cf. 'Better on your arse'). 'chaque jour', however, seems to be a neat encapsulation of related ideas from Geulincx's Proposition 11, which concludes with the phrase beloved of Murphy 'ubi nihil vales ibi nihil velis' ('wherein you have no power, therein you should not will', as Beckett translates it in his Philosophy Notes). Before coming to his famous conclusion, Geulincx had argued, 'I was brought to this condition (that is, to use the common way of speaking I was born), without my consent, and without knowing anything about it . . . I shall also depart from this condition (that is, I shall die) as ignorant as ever: but also (to my shame) against my will' (TCD 10971/6/2–3). Final scrap and *Sott* versions are dated U[ssy]. 10.3.77; an earlier version, dated U[ssy]. 9.3.77, lacks 'certes'.

nuit qui fais tant
rien nul

'nuit qui fais tant' (*Sott* P[aris] 19.3.77) and 'rien nul' (scrap 21.3.77) develop the philosophical train of thought of the previous three *mirlitonnades*. They also seem to remember the end of *Fin de Partie* and Hamm's recollection of Baudelaire's 'Tu réclamais le soir; il descend; le voici' (expanded in *Endgame* to 'You cried for night; it falls: now cry in darkness') and his chilling summary of his own life as 'instants nul, toujours nuls, mais qui font le compte' (also expanded in *Endgame*: 'Moments for nothing, now as always, time was never and time is over'). A copy of 'nuit qui fait tant' for Josette Hayden on the back of a Craven 'A' cigarette packet, and dated by her '6 avril 77', presumably the date when SB made the copy, corresponds to the published text.

à peine à bien mené

Scrap 28.3.77; *Sott* 29.3.77. Earlier scraps show how concerned SB was with the subtle rhyme scheme and overall shape of the poem, marking the lines ending 'attendant', 'autant', l'avant' and 'présent' with 2, the lines ending 'l'usage' with 3 and, curiously, the single line ending 'faix' with 1. Another version divides the poem thus: 3+3+4.

ce qu'ont les yeux
ce qu'a de pis

'ce qu'ont les yeux' and 'ce qu'a de pis' (*Sott* 31.3.77; no scrap versions of either) comprise another linked pair of *mirlitonnades*, both commencing with a 'what' statement ('ce qu'ont' and 'ce qu'a') and ending with even-handed comparatives, 'le bien revient en mieux' / 'le pis revient en pire'. 'mal vu', line 2 of 'ce qu'ont les yeux' anticipates the title, at least, of *Mal vu mal dit*, commenced October 1979. 'ce qu'a de pis' anticipates and offers a French rendering of the quotations from *King Lear* in *Sott* quoted in full in the note to 'en face'. An earlier version of 'ce qu'ont les yeux' (*Sott* U[ssy]. 30.3.77) reads 'les mains' for 'les doigts' and 'de bien échapper' for 'de bien filer'.

ne manquez pas à Tanger
plus loin un autre commémore
ne manquez pas à Stuttgart

Three related *mirlitonnades*; the first two were written after Beckett visited the Anglican churchyard of St Andrew's parish church in Tangiers, 'stuffed with Brits', as he noted (see below: 'bourré de britanniques'), the third, by analogy, in Stuttgart.

'ne manquez pas à Tanger' (*Sott* 1.5.77); the scrap (2.5.77) is clearly earlier than *Sott*; in it, for example, Beckett adjusts 'ensevelis' (buried or shrouded) to 'surensevelis' (superenshrouded?). Sent to Bray in a letter of 1.8.77.

The first three attempts were more expansive: 'aux 3/4 mort / le quart qui reste / de fatigue d'avoir / tant grimpe [*sic*] // connais-tu à T. / le cimetière St. André // ne manquez pas à Tanger / le cimetière St. André / ~~bourré de britanniques~~ / le banc à la mémoire / du cher Arthur Keyser assis dessus un zigue / mort seulement de fatigue / mort seulement de fatigue // Leurs tombes sous un fouillis / de fleurs ensevelis / Arthur Keyser'.

'plus loin un autre commémore' was written on a subsequent visit to Tangiers (25 July–25 August 1977). Beckett sent Bray the following lines, which he had found on another seat in the cemetery in loving memory of Caroline Hay Taylor: 'One who never turned her back but marched breast forward / Never doubted clouds would break. / Never dreamed though right were worsted wrong would triumph. / Held we fall to rise, are baffled to fight better, sleep to wake'. (SB contracted 'would' and wrote 'thought' for 'though'.) The lines were published as Beckett's in Calder 2002 (45) but Calder was in good company in his error, since in the letter to Bray (9.7.77) SB attributes them to Caroline Hay Taylor's daughter! On 19 August Beckett wrote to Bray: 'Struggling feebly with poem on Caroline Hay Taylor. I can't get it.' The *Sott* entry is dated simply 'Tanger août 77'; scrap versions are undated.

'ne manquez pas à Stuttgart' was the next *mirlitonnade* to be written after 'ne manquez pas à Tanger' (scrap and *Sott* both dated 20.6.77). Beckett had gone to Stuttgart to direct his two new television plays *Ghost Trio* and . . . *but the clouds* . . . . While there Beckett also wrote 'one dead of night' (26.6.77; q.v.), which he gave to his cameraman Jim Lewis.

In the final line, Beckett reverses the originally juridical and now journalistic catchphrase 'd'ores et déjà' ('now' / 'henceforth') not only for the sake of the rhyme, but also to restore some sense of 'déjà vu'.

vieil aller

Also written in Stuttgart (*Sott* 25 and 26.6.77), it conveys, in stripped-down form, a similar 'ghost-forsaken' (cf. 'Saint-Lô') experience to 'ne manquez pas à Stuttgart'. The last line of *Sott* has '(s)'arrêter'. The first version had 'vieux ~~chemin~~ trajet' and 'absent' twice replacing 'en songe'.

fous qui disiez
pas à pas
rêve

Drafts of these three *mirlitonnades* appear on the same scrap, with the earliest draft of 'fous qui disiez', which reads 'mots qui disent / silence / vite dite', dated simply 'Ussy juillet 77'. Versions of 'fous qui disiez' and 'pas à pas', dated 6.7.77, were entered, unnumbered, in *Sott*, cancelled, redrafted and numbered 21 and 22, but not dated.

'fous qui disiez' is in part a kind of gloss on 'The fool hath said in his heart, there is no God' (Psalm 14); 'pas à pas' revisits the pacing motif of *Footfalls* and 'écoute-les'.

'pas à pas' was dedicated to the philosopher Herbert Marcuse on his 80th birthday and first published in the German literature magazine *Akzente*, June 1978 (227), in a supplement celebrating Marcuse's birthday.

The *Sott* draft of 'rêve', numbered 23, appears in *CPOB*. plate 99, dated 'U[ssy]. 14.7.77' on the same sheet as 'morte parmi', number 24, dated 'P[aris] 17.7.77' and 'D'où', number 25, 'P[aris] 18.7.77'.

In 2006 the 'NB' section of the *Times Literary Supplement* ran a series (beginning with the 9 June issue, continued in later issues) that demonstrated the 'untranslatability' of SB's *mirlitonnades*, with 'rêve' figuring prominently.

morte parmi

Sott 17.7.77. A poem of haiku-like perfection and simplicity. After the frenzied flies of 'Serena I' and 'La Mouche', these flies are finally at rest about their predator. Beckett animates the scene by transforming a 'vent coulis' or draught into a 'souffle coulis' (a draught of breath?) which rocks the dead spider like a baby in a cradle. This breath is very different from the vagitus in *Breath* or the panting in *How It Is*.

d'où

The first line of the final draft (*Sott* P. 18.7.77) retains the opening phrase of the scrap versions, 'd'où vient', but with 'vient' cancelled. An undated scrap draft reading 'd'où vient / la voix qui dit / vis / elle vient / d'une autre vie' makes it clear that, initially at least, SB saw the final line as answering the opening question.

mots survivants

The original scrap draft was entitled 'comédie' and, while it contained the governing idea of words for company, as in *Company* (which Beckett began a couple of months earlier, on 5 May after the breakdown of *Long Observation of the Ray*), it was very different from the final poem: 'finie / peu s'en faut / la vie les mots / pour compagnie'. Intermediate versions have words dying ('mourant') rather than surviving. The *Sott* entry, dated 'Tanger 27.7.77', a later scrap (août 77), and the versions sent to Barbara Bray contain a variant last line: 'tenez-nous compagnie'. Beckett sent this version twice to Bray, adding in his letter of 30 July 'Finally!' and 'For better or worse'. He sent it again on 1 August, saying 'Got on a little with *Company*. Another piece of doggerel may have sent it in last.' However, Beckett altered the final line from 'tenez-nous compagnie' to 'tenez-lui compagnie' in the typescript.

fleuves et océans

Scrap and *Sott* dated Ussy Toussaint 77, i.e. 1 November. On the verso of the scrap are notes apparently towards *A Piece of Monologue*.

Perhaps a version of Rimbaud's epic voyage in his *Drunken Boat* in miniature. This *mirlitonnade* starts, like Rimbaud, with rivers and oceans but ends by the brook, the ru [or brook] de Courtablon, which winds its way through the field at the end of the rue de la Dehors in Ussy where Beckett and Suzanne first rented a house in 1948. The now drained marsh, the Mare-Chaudron, was within sight of the house that Beckett had had built in 1953 and serves as the cold, black puddle on which the sad child looses his boat at the end of *Le Bateau ivre*.

de pied ferme

Scrap, three drafts, third dated 'P[aris]. 13.11.77' and entered into *Sott.* Cancelled in *Sott* and final version entered 'P[aris]. 21.11.77'. There are significant variants in the versions in *Sott*, line 1 'tout attente tout en' becoming 'de pied ferme tout en'.

A poem card, sent to Barbara Bray, is reproduced in *CPOB* (plate 95). On the same card is 'en face / le pire' (TCD MS 10948/2/119).

sitôt sorti de l'ermitage

Sott P. 22.12.77; no scrap. Sent to Cohn 26.12.77 and recited to the Arikhas 30.12.77 (Atik, 94). This *mirlitonnade*, which reverses the familiar notion of the calm *before* the storm, seems to express relief from 'the siege in the room' which writing represented for Beckett. (Beckett is more than halfway through *Company*.)

à l'instant de s'entendre dire

The scrap which tries out various versions of the opening word ('le jour', 'la nuit', 'pas plutôt') is dated P[aris]. 13.1.78 and U[ssy]. 17.1.78, but does not contain the final version entered in *Sott* and dated P[aris]. 13.1.78.

la nuit venue

An earlier version of this *mirlitonnade* ('ne verra-t-il jamais / finir la nuit / où l'âme lui / sera réclamée') was entered in *Sott* (numbered 33 but undated; an earlier version on facing page is also numbered 33 and dated U[ssy]. 18.1.78). It is followed by 'pas davantage', a number of jottings ('on le prognostiqua mort', several lines from Eugenio Camerini to the effect that it could be said that Dante's life ended when his poem ended, the famous quotation from Dante's letter to Can Grande 'fiorentino di nazione non di costumi' and 'Wriggle on all fours through rock gradient 1 in 1 to first cornice where Belacqua'), another poem, 'son ombre une nuit' (dated 'P[aris]. 11.6.78'), and then 'la nuit venue', with a question mark where one might expect the date, as if Beckett were unsure which version he preferred. Calder (2002) printed 'ne verra-t-il' as an uncollected *mirlitonnade*, but with errors. 'ne verra-t-il' is the penultimate title on SB's handwritten list of *mirlitonnades* on the brown envelope which contains the scraps (UoR MS 2460). 'pas davantage' is the final entry, and indeed the last entry to be numbered (34) in *Sott*. This indicates that Beckett prepared 34 *mirlitonnades* for publication between 8 February 1978 and 11 June 1978, adding the thirty-fifth ('son ombre une nuit') soon after it was written, since Minuit published the *mirlitonnades* on 28 August 1978.

pas davantage

Sott dated T[angiers] 8.2.78 (mistakenly dated 77) and sent to Bray 9.2.78. SB's birthday was in April (Good Friday the 13th, 1906). For 'avril' cf. 'ma seule saison' of 'vive morte' with its April leaf mud.

son ombre

Sott 11.6.78 (late on in the composition of *Company*). The original scrap, dated 'Paris 10.6.78', with two cancelled drafts, is reproduced in *CPOB*, plate 98. This poem anticipates one of the themes of *Ohio Impromptu* (cf. 'one dead of night').

noire sœur

The last poem in the *mirlitonnades* as first published by Minuit in 1978, although written in Tangiers at the beginning of the holiday in 1977 which produced 'ne manquez pas à Tanger'. Both scrap and *Sott* dated 'Tanger 21. 4.77'. Earlier that month Beckett had written to the director Alan Schneider saying that he wished he could 'do an Atropos all in black – with her scissors' (10.4.77; Harmon, 355). Eleven days before writing the poem Beckett told James Knowlson that his attempts to get going on a play about the Fates had been in vain.

The *Sott* entry is followed by a helpful gloss, which confirms the identity of this 'dark sister' as the third Fate, Atropos:

Clotho (youngest)   – birth – distaff
Lachesis   – life – spindle
Atropos   – death – scissors
          dressed in black
ministers of Pluto, sitting
at foot of his throne
a clew of thread (yarn)
Proserpine

[An arrow links Atropos to the line 'dressed in black'.] At a meeting with Charles Juliet on 11.11.77, Beckett described an idea for a one-minute play in which a solitary figure is asked '– Are you waiting for someone? The figure shakes its head. – Something? Same response'. He also told Juliet that he had been reading Heine's late poems. Heine's 'Es sitzen am Kreuzweg drei Frauen' ends with the poet's imploration: 'Oh speed the wheel, and sever / This thread for me, / And set me free / From this life's frightful affliction forever!' (tr. Hal Draper, *The Complete Poems of Heinrich Heine*, Oxford University Press, 1982). The final question in SB's poem, 'what are you waiting for?', has much the same force as Heine's. Atropos had made an earlier appearance (with Pluto's bride, Persephone) in 'jusque dans la caverne' and, unnamed, via the 'ciseaux argentins' of 'être là sans mâchoires sans dents', but presumably via Lemprière rather than by way of Heine. Cf. 'great shears of the black old hag older than the world born of night' (*How it is*, 92).

2   echoes the opening of the Lord's Prayer.

3   the second draft reads: 'coupant à tort', which becomes 'à tort coupant' in subsequent drafts and in the *Sott*: 'à tort ~~impasse~~ [?] tranchant'; finding the right word to rupture the French idiom 'à tort et à travers' seems to have given Beckett some trouble. Its nearest English equivalent might be 'without rhyme or reason'. Beckett sent the poem to Barbara Bray on 24.4.77. He also sent it to Harold Pinter on 14.5.77, thanking him for the poems he had sent, presumably those published as *Harold Pinter, Poems and Plays, 1949–1977*, Eyre Methuen, 1978. Beckett wrote: '"Message" bang in the eye. Bravo. Verso one for you.'

'noire sœur' was first published in *Littack Supplement* 5, October 1978: 1, an ephemeral magazine edited by William Oxley, a friend of the poet Hugo Manning.

le nain nonagénaire

The scrap seems to begin with a series of notes or ideas towards this *mirlitonnade*: 'nain / bière / cercueil / lit de mort / avant d'expirer / agonie'. The second draft introduces the idea of the full-sized coffin the dwarf desires, '[. . .] / que l'on m'enterre / si l'on veut bien / dans une grande bière / le nain octogénaire / [. . .]'. The dwarf then ages by a decade in the next draft .The final scrap draft is dated 'Paris 9.9.78'. It corresponds to the version entered in *Sott* ('P[aris]. Sept 78') in which line 2 reads 'd'un ultime murmure' corrected first to 'suprême', then to 'dans un dernier' and back again to 'd'un suprême'. SB reverted to 'dans un murmure' for the published version.

Both 'le nain' and 'à bout de songes' were first published in *Minuit*, 33, in March 1979 (2–3) and later that month in a new edition of *Poèmes suivi de mirlitonnades* among the *Poèmes*. 'le nain' was also published in an article by John Calder in *Frank: An International Journal of Contemporary Writing and Art*, Paris, 14, 1992, with an (uncredited) English translation: 'the dwarf in his last / nonagenarian gasp / for mercy's sake at least / a full-sized coffin'. Published in Calder 2002, reversing their order of appearance in *Minuit*, which is also the order in which they were written.

Two sepulchral, litter-bearing dwarfs appear in *For to End Yet Again/Pour finir encore* where they carry a 'civière', which Beckett translates as 'litter', but which could mean the bier on which a coffin is carried. On the way to *Pour finir encore*, SB wrote a short prose piece with the title *La civière* which he sent to Ruby Cohn in 1971 (shortly after he had begun what would become *Pour finir encore* some three years later), and on 10.1.72 wrote to tell her: 'I'm struggling to extract a *caput mortuum* from the Dwarves' (UoR).

à bout de songes un bouquin

Beckett was even more hesitant about the final shape of this poem, producing three different dated (which generally means finished) versions. The earliest (Ussy 5.11.78) reads 'à bout de songes un bouquin / sans autre forme de procès / à évacuer son gîte astreint / oublia le chandelier'. The second dated version (*Sott*, Paris, November 78) is as finally published but for the second line which reads: 'du gîte à déguerpir contraint'. This is superseded by a scrap (Tanger 12.12.78) and another *Sott* entry (27.12.78) reading as published.

SB gives a clue to the source, at least, of this puzzling four-liner in La Fontaine's fable of the Hare and the Frogs. (SB refers to the same poet's fable 'The Rat who withdrew from the world' in *Dream*, 9.) It comes as a great surprise to the timid hare that he is capable of frightening the frogs in their pond. Beckett quotes the following lines in *Sott*: 'Car que faire en un gîte / à moins que l'on n'y songe'. It seems rather bizarre that a hare should have a 'candlestick' in his form but a 'bouquin' can also mean an old book.

Calder 2002 follows 'le nain' and à bout de songes' with four previously unpublished *mirlitonnades*, the first of which, 'ne-verra-t-il', as explained above, is an earlier draft of 'la nuit venue'. The other three were written before 'le nain nonagénaire'.

c'est l'heure

Both scrap and *Sott* dated 2.8.78. SB initially put a question mark, subsequently crossed out. Published in Calder 2002 with a transcription error in the second line.

'c'est l'heure' and the following six *mirlitonnades* were not included by SB in those published by Minuit in his lifetime.

comme au berceau

Four scrap drafts dated 'Tanger 28.8.78'; *Sott* version dated 'Tanger ~~Paris~~ août 78'. The *Sott* version is uncancelled. Published in Calder 2002 with a transcription error in the final line.

lui

This *mirlitonnade* (dated Ussy November 1978 in *Sott*) was written around the time that Beckett was finishing *Company*. The sacral or vertebral canal runs throughout the sacrum or largest bone at the base of the spine. SB may well have a pun in mind, thinking ironically of the 'blessed' tear canal. Elsewhere in *Sott*, SB quotes Kierkegaard's 'My sorrow is my castle', followed by 'Nulla dies sine lacryma (K)', from his 1840 *Journal* (Fontana edn, 1958, 67). First published in *Poems 1930–1989*.

par une faille dans l'inexistence

There are four complete scrap drafts of this *mirlitonnade*, written after the suite was published by Minuit, one of which is dated 'Ussy 5.7.79'. The *Sott* version is dated simply 'Ussy juillet 79'. Calder published 'par une faille' in *Poems 1930–1989*, reading the last line as 'pour bonheur à peine'. Beckett, however, has written 'par bonheur à peine', since he clearly considers the noxious whiff of oxygen piercing the void and portending the start of life is scarcely a stroke of good fortune.

minuit mille ans d'ici

Published here for the first time. Scrap dated 'Courmayeur Juin

80'; in a letter to Bray of 24.6.80 SB wrote: 'started a doggerel "d'ici mille ans il sera minuit"'. Also in the letter are four lines, probably quoted from memory, by the medieval French poet Alain Chartier (c.1392–c.1430): 'Désormais est temps de me taire/Car de dire je suis lassé/Je veux laisser aux autres faire/Leur temps, car le mien est passé'. Beckett reverses 'suis-je' and omits 'est' ('Leur temps est') in the fourth line. These are lines 41–4 of Chartier's 'La Belle Dame Sans Merci', the source for the title of John Keats's much later and much more famous poem.

silence vide nue

On the same scrap as 'rien nul', dated 'P[aris] 21.3.77'. Not in *Sott*. Published here for the first time.

qu'à lever la tête

On the same scrap as 'minuit mille ans'. It shares the fascination of 'dread nay' and 'hors crâne' with the gesture of raising the head, finally used to good effect in *Catastrophe*. Sent to Bray 4.7.80 and to the Arikhas 7.7.80. Reproduced in Atik (103), with her own translation: 'Just to raise the head / that is the beauty / just to raise / it'. A copy for Josette Hayden on the back of a cigarette packet was sold at Sotheby's on 13 July 2006. First published in *Poems 1930–1989*.

MIRLITONNADES IN ENGLISH

'[P]ar une faille dans l'existence' is the last of the French short poems in *Sott*. Beckett did, however, go on to compose a number of short English *mirlitonnade*-like poems which are collected together here for the first time.

there

The poem answers Petruchio's question from *The Taming of the Shrew* (Act IV, sc i, [Petruchio's song]): 'Where is the life that late I led?', which Beckett had copied into *Sott*. The poem is dated

'23.3.1981'. 'there', 'again gone' and 'head on hands' were first published in *New Departures* 14, 1982, 64, under the collective title *pss*, and republished thus in *Obra poética completa*, ed. Jenaro Talens, Madrid: Hiperion, 2000, 126 with a facing Spanish translation. Beckett sent a handwritten copy of the poems to *New Departures* dated 17.9.81, signing off 'above recent croaks'. Republished in *Selected Poems 1930–1989*, Faber, 2009.

ceiling

Sott 9.4.81. Later that year Beckett wrote a prose text (written between 10 and 26 July, but not considered complete until September 1981) for Avigdor Arikha with the same title (published in *Avigdor Arikha*, Paris: Hermann, 1985). The poem 'ceiling' was reprinted in Dirk Van Hulle's preface to the 2009 Faber edition of *Company/Ill Seen Ill Said/Worstward Ho/Stirrings Still*.

bail

First published in *Selected Poems 1930–1989*, Faber, 2009. *Sott* 11.4.81, with an arrow placing 'better' on the line with 'founder'. Sent to Jocelyn Herbert in a letter dated simply 'May day' [1981] with the following superscription: 'I dedicate to us both the following elegy', but earlier sent to Ruby Cohn (20.4.81).

away

The day before writing this poem, Beckett wrote to Ruby Cohn: 'Only desire peace to dream all away' (20.4.81). A poem card sent to Barbara Bray, setting out the poem in two lines, is reproduced in *CPOB*, plate 95. Andra Samelson, writing in *Boulevard* (Fall 2000, 237), says that at her last meeting with SB he told her he was not able to write; he 'could only come up with the same words again and again: "Always dream all away"'. While this may be a genuine variant, it seems more likely that the first word was misheard or misremembered.

Published in a book of one-line poems, *Orange Export Ltd*

1969–86, Paris: Flammarion, 1986, and reprinted in volume IV of *The Grove Samuel Beckett Centenary Edition* (General Editor, Paul Auster, New York: Grove Press, 2006, 49).

head on hands

Sott 26.5.81. *New Departures* (cf. 'there' and 'again gone') misprints the first line as 'head oh hands'. Published in Atik (107) with initial capital. SB had attempted a short prose piece in *Sott* (28.12.80) beginning: 'That head. In those hands. His? No. Mine. Those eyes. On the sheet. His? No. Mine'. SB considered a variant third line 'untwine' in brackets in *Sott.*

again gone

Uniquely for the English *mirlitonnades*, there is a 'scrap' version of this poem, from which the published version is considerably reduced: 'Gone with what / left to tell // or gone / wherewith to tell // or / retell // or again gone / wherewith to tell // or again / retell // Or gone again all / wherewith to tell / or again all / retell'. This version and a four-line version, with corrections, in *Sott* are dated 9.9.81. A second, undated four-line version, corrected to the published version, was published with 'there' and 'head on hands' as *pss* in *New Departures* 14 (1982). SB notes erroneously that it was sent to *New Directions* on 17.9.81. Republished in *Selected Poems 1930–1989*, Faber, 2009.

let ill alone

A fairly obvious play on the old saw 'leave well alone'. *Sott*, Stuttgart, June 1981.

nothing blest

A similar reworking of 'sweet fuck all'. *Sott, ib* [i.e. Stuttgart, June 1981].

ashes burning

Sott 'Courmayeur June 81'. An identical draft is on verso 18 of the draft of *Worstward Ho* (UoR MS 2602/1). In a letter to Bray of 4.7.81 SB wrote: 'Poem feebly tagging on "ashes more burning than flames"'. A few days later SB sent her this version.

on whence

Also on verso 18 of the draft of *Worstward Ho* (but not copied into *Sott*). The poem appears first in a six-line version, the sixth line of which is cancelled: 'on whence / no sense / but on / to whence / no sense / ~~but back~~'. The second version has a cancelled line between lines 7 and 8: '~~with whence~~'.The beginning of 'on whence' is printed in Dirk Van Hulle's preface to the 2009 Faber edition of *Company/Ill Seen Ill Said/Worstward Ho/Stirrings Still*.

poetic miscalculation

The draft reveals several hesitations; originally entitled 'Poetic calculation', 'mis' is added in superscript. The first word was originally 'indifferent', SB's uncertainty marked by the question mark he added before the word. A circle around the 1 in 95.1 suggests this may not have seemed the dearest decimal after all.

The dictionary definition of 'incalescent' gives 'the action or process of growing warm' and adds 'now rare'. Lines 2–5 of 'poetic miscalculation' were printed for the first time in Dirk Van Hulle's preface to the 2009 Faber edition of *Company/Ill Seen Ill Said/Worstward Ho/Stirrings Still*.

look in thine arse and write

Sott P[aris]. 8.81. A travesty of Sir Philip Sidney's '"Fool", said my Muse to me, "look in thy heart and write!"', the last line in the first sonnet of the sequence *Astrophel and Stella*.

tittle-tattle

Sott 11.3.82. The word 'marl' refers to a sort of clay (cf. Rimbaud's 'petits caillots de marne rousse' in the third of his *Les Stupra* sonnets), or poetically to 'the world'.

Là / go where never before

'Là' was written on 17.9.87 and sent to James Knowlson on 21.9.87. The card contains two drafts, the first reading 'aller ailleurs où jamais avant / à peine là que jamais ailleurs / où qu'ailleurs où jamais avant / qu'à peine là que jamais ailleurs'. The second draft is as published except that the last line read 'qu'à peine là là toujours'. On 24.9.87 SB sent Knowlson the translation with a note to say 'In French last line change "qu'à" to "à"'. 'go where never before' was published in *Het Beckett Blad*, Number 1, 1990 in facsimile. Both poems were published in *Journal of Beckett Studies*, (n.s.) 1.1&2, 1992, 1–2, with a variant version of the French original. 'go where never before' was first collected in Calder's 1999 *Beckett Short No 12 Selected Poems* (28). Both poems were collected in Calder's *Poems 1930–1989* (2002),46, and appeared in facsimile in the University of Reading *Research Review*, issue 8, Summer 2009.

Brief Dream

First published in the Irish press on SB's 83rd birthday, with his permission (13.4.89), but first given wider currency on its publication in *Journal of Beckett Studies* (n.s.) 1.1 & 2, 1992, [3] – where it is dated '1987' – and on its appearance in facsimile in May 1992 in the Paris-based magazine *Frank*. Sent to Bray in a letter misdated 'Jan 87' for January 1988. First collected in Calder's 1999 *Beckett Short No. 12: Selected Poems* (29) and in *Poems 1930–1989* (2002, 46).

In a letter postmarked 25.7.82, to Jocelyn Herbert, SB told her: 'Wrote a piece for Stuttgart TV a dreamer and his brief dream'. The TV 'piece' was *Nacht und Träume*, a title from one of Schubert's best-loved lieder (D.827). The last seven bars of the song are the only sounds in an otherwise silent text consisting solely of fade-outs and fade-ups. The poem effectively 'translates' the exclusively visual shifts of its predecessor into six variable three-beat strophes, rhyming abcbac, and could easily be set to music. A holograph version of the poem is found in the UoR 'Super conquérant' notebook (MS 2934) between *Stirrings Still* and an unpublished play fragment ('Bare Room'), suggesting that SB was working on it at some point between August 1984 and September 1985, closer in time to *Nacht und Träume* than to its publication date. But the poem and the play (some of the motifs in which anticipate *Stirrings Still*) remain generically separate and consequently generate different effects.

EPITAPHS

il ne sait plus

Sent to Bray (with 'ochone') in an undated [1987] letter.

ochone

A favourite SB tag (cf. 'Antipepsis', line **21**) derived from an old Irish Gaelic saying that he probably often heard in his youth, which was sent to Barbara Bray in an undated [1987] letter, and also used in late letters to Ruby Cohn (4.11.87; UoR), John Beckett (5.12.87; UoR), Kay Boyle (2.1.89; HRHRC) and Mary Manning Howe (7.1.89; HRHRC). In the Kay Boyle letter SB introduces it with: '"Time gentlemen please", as they used to say in the Dublin pubs coming up to 10 p.m.'.

In its way this is a kind of footnote to a conversation in SB's short story 'Draff' (*MPTK*):
'Now in Gaelic' said Hairy on the way home 'they could not say that'.

'What could they not say?' said the parson. He would not rest until he knew.

'O Death where is thy sting?' replied Hairy. 'They have no words for these big ideas. [. . .] They can't say it once and for all. A spalpeen's babble'. (177)

Le médecin

As SB's life was drawing to a close he composed this brief punning epigram on his physician's name (Dr Coulamy) and his own situation (11.12.89; Atik, 127). SB may have also had in mind the famous dictum of Heraclitus to the effect that 'All things flow' (cf. 'flux cause' and 'samedi répit' in the *mirlitonnades* above), and consequently 'it is not possible to step down twice into the same stream' (Philosophy Notes; TCD), as alluded to in the first paragraph of the story 'Echo's Bones' (1) and again in 'Le Monde et le Pantalon' (*Disjecta*, 128).

Ci-gît / Hereunder

On 28.12.38 SB wrote to Arland Ussher: 'I have begun a primer of the higher French syntax. It takes the form of Xenien. Here is one.' 'Ci-gît' follows. This squib is not strictly like Xenien in form (distich composed of hexameter and pentameter), but is closer to the form than 'Gnome' (q.v.) written some four years earlier; *LSB1* (648) gives 'Xenian', and fails to point out here that SB had been aware of the Goethe-Schiller *Xenien* for some time (but cf. *LSB1*, 107). Cf. Watt's 'tenth rate xenium' (*Watt*, 130), translated rather nicely as 'cet aphorisme de dixième ordre' (Minuit, 136). On 31.3.60 SB found one of Goethe's 'Zahme Xenien' which he sent in letters to Barbara Bray and Avigdor Arikha. Atik (65) translates the lines as 'The world is falling apart / Like a rotten fish, / We will not / Embalm it'. 'Ci-gît' was incorporated into the post-war short story *Premier amour* (Minuit, 1970, 10). Its rather longer and more complex English translation appears in *The Expelled*, etc., 62. Although the Grove 1974 edition (and what Gerry Dukes calls 'Ts 2') have 'survived' for 'lived on' in the second line of the 'Hereunder' epitaph, Dukes proposes, very plausibly, that this is not SB's final version and that 'Beckett revised the text again prior to first British publication' (*First Love and other novellas*, edited by Gerry Dukes, Penguin, 2000, 95). It is his and our copy text.

It seems a fitting item to conclude this collection of Samuel Beckett's poems, but we are respecting SB's wishes by finishing with 'Comment dire' and 'what is the word'.

Comment dire / what is the word

This was Samuel SB's final written work. The original French holograph, dated 29.10.88, was published in a limited edition facsimile to celebrate the 30th anniversary of La Librairie Compagnie, which takes its name from another work of Beckett's, on 4 May 1989. *Libération* published 'Comment dire' on 1.6.89. The English translation first appeared posthumously in the *Irish Times* (25–7.12.89) and the *Sunday Correspondent* (31.12.89). A version 'for Joe Chaikin' appeared in *Grand Street*, vol. 9, no. 2 (Winter 1990). (See Dirk Van Hulle's 2009 Faber edition of the late prose for these details.) 'Comment dire' was published in the third augmented impression of *Poèmes suivi de mirlitonnades* (imprint dated 29 June 1992). The English version is reprinted in Christopher Ricks's edition of the *Oxford Book of English Verse* (OUP, 1999, 600) and in Calder's *Beckett Short no 11 Stirrings Still* (1999) (25–8). French and English versions appear in Calder 2002. For a detailed reading, see Van Hulle, 2011, 99–104, with facsimiles on 100–1.

Notes

Beckett wrote at the top of his autograph 'Keep! for end' as if to assert that 'what is the word' would be his final word.
SB called these dashes – or hyphens (in French 'traits d'union') – 'traits de désunion'.
'afaint afar away': cf. the final words of Joyce's *Finnegans Wake*.

In the case of eight poems in Part 1 of this edition we have chosen unpublished versions over versions which were published for the first time in various formats more than eighty years ago:

- – 'Whoroscope' (SB's first separately published work, in a limited edition by the Hours Press in 1930)
- – 'From the only Poet . . .' (published by the same press in the same year in *Henry-Music*)
- – Four poems ('Hell Crane to Starling', 'Casket . . .', 'Text' and 'Yoke of Liberty' [otherwise known as 'Moly']' in *The European Caravan* in 1931, of which only the first three were subsequently revised in such a way as to make our choice of a copy text a matter of any real significance.
- – Two other poems, 'For Future Reference' and 'Return to the Vestry', both first published in 1931, the first in *transition*, the second in *The New Review*.

In the body of the book we have placed the revised versions of these poems in the 'Leventhal' section. Here we print the unrevised texts, 'framing' the *European Caravan* poems, 'Whoroscope' and 'From the only poet . . .', with the 'twice round & pointed ones' of SB's letter to TM of 25.8.[30] (*LSB1*, 43): 'For Future Reference' and 'Return to the Vestry'.

Also included here is the complete unrevised version of 'Serena II', which helps to show how SB arrived at the final *EBOP* version.

The Appendix also includes the only known example of SB trying to write a poem in German, and two 'rimes' which SB 'gives' to the character Mahood in the novel *Malone meurt / Malone Dies*, a practice apparently first adopted in respect of (and no doubt also in disrespect of) the Poet in SB's first, jettisoned, novel *Dream of Fair to Middling Women*.

The running order of the poems in this Appendix corresponds to that followed in Part 1, and is not intended to be in any way precise in terms of their chronology, beyond observing certain obvious groupings.

There is no 'danger' of any 'neatness' in any edition of SB's poetry, whether a 'critical' one or not, and it would be idle to pretend that there could be. But in order that a slightly clearer picture of a very tangled web might emerge we have thought it best to supply this extra material in a place easily located and equally easily sidelined should readers choose to disregard it. There is of course no suggestion that, as suggested in the 'Addenda' to the novel *Watt*, it was '[o]nly fatigue and disgust which prevented its incorporation' (215) in Parts 1 and 2 of this edition.

For detailed readings of the early and jettisoned poems, with very extensive annotation (much of which has obviously been supplied by SB himself), see Harvey, as follows: 'For Future Reference' (298–301); 'From the only Poet to a shining Whore' (305–7); 'Casket of Pralinen . . .' (277–96); 'Hell Crane to Starling' (302–5); 'Text' (287–96); 'Whoroscope' (3–66); 'Return to the Vestry' (307–13)

Additional note to 'Casket of Pralinen . . .'
On page 477 of the *EC* printing 'memory' is misprinted as 'momery' (Harvey notes, but not mentioned in his book).

Additional note to 'Text'
67   for the 'sad maimed shades': cf. *Inf.*, XXIX, 6: 'l'ombre triste smozzicate'.

Additional notes to 'Return to the Vestry'
Title   for a suitor (or lover) as 'vestryman', see *Dream*, 78, 121.
25   for the 'Singer' (sewing-machine and poet), cf. the onanistic seamstresses from Garnier (*DN* *475).
29   for 'it stinks of breeding', cf. 'he stinks eternal' in line **36** of the *EC* 'Text', and SB's letter to Charles Prentice on the subject of 'Sedendo et Quiescendo' (*LSB1*, 81).
34   for Miranda, cf. *Proust* (*PTD*, 45), *Dream*, 10, and the name given to a nurse in 'Yellow'.
43   for the 'grey tilt of silk', cf. the 'silk loop' of line **2** of 'Yoke of Liberty' / 'Moly', *Dream*, 181 ('a blade of silk'), and *DN* *509: 'like the melancholy royal Chinese concubine who loved the sound of rent silk' (echoed in the story 'Echo's Bones', 6).
46   for 'impurity', cf. 'impurée' in 'Hell Crane to Starling'.

'Mancando'

For a discussion of 'Mancando', see Thomas Hunkeler's essay '"Cascando" de Samuel Beckett', *Samuel Beckett Today/Aujourd'hui*, 8, 1999, 27–42.

'Poupée Pompette' / 'Hairy Mac and Sucky Moll'

In the French original Macmann composes 'courts écrits curieusement rimés pour les offrir à son amie' (*Malone meurt*, 147), which are directly addressed to his 'Poupée Pompette', Moll. The English translation takes the form of a statement in the third person, although these too are described as 'brief [rimes] of curious structure, to offer to his mistress' (*Malone Dies*, 91; with the original reading here, as in the note to poem 70, restored in preference to 'rhymes' [Faber, 2009, 'Preface', xiii, 91], given SB's usage elsewhere). The structure of the French poem is, perhaps, more 'curious' than its stronger English translation (abba/aa), with the half lines (**5** and **6**) repeating line **4**. The English translation, in SB's favoured quatrain form (cf. note to 'who may tell the tale'), varies the rhyme scheme to abab, with a nice rhyme on 'Molly/melancholy' and a pleasing play on 'ending/unending' which is not present in the French.

1 'Poupée Pompette': literally something like 'funeral parlourmaid dolly' is how Macmann's lover signs herself in *Malone meurt*. C. J. Ackerley explains that 'Pompette' is short for 'Madame Pompedur de Videlay-Chémoy' in the second '*Watt*' Notebook (2006b, 202; cf. note to 'who may tell the tale'). Beckett translates as 'Sucky Moll' (*Malone meurt*, 147; *Malone Dies*, 91).

'C'est l'amour qui nous conduit' / 'To the lifelong promised land'

These two poems are in the same format as their respective predecessors, with the French in six lines and the English in quatrain form and the rhyme scheme varied as noted above.

2 'Glasnevin': SB notes, 'Nom de cimetière très estimé' (*Malone meurt*, 148). One of Dublin's largest cemeteries, and the resting place of, among others, the Great Liberator, Daniel O'Connell (O'Brien, 104). The original of the so-called 'Church of Saint Tamar/Glasnevin' at which Belacqua marries Thelma (*MPTK*, 115) is near the cemetery.

Select Bibliography

STUDIES OF BECKETT'S POETRY

Ackerley, C. J. 2006a. 'Fairy-tales and Flagellation: Samuel Beckett's "Sanies II"', in: Philip Nicolayev (ed.), *Fulcrum: an annual of poetry and aesthetics*, 6, Cambridge, MA, 2007, 500–6.

– 2002. '*Lassata Sed*: Samuel Beckett's Portraits of His Fair to Middling Women', *Samuel Beckett Today/Aujourd'hui*, 12, 55–70.

– 1993. 'Beckett's "Malacoda", or: Dante's devil plays Beethoven', *Journal of Beckett Studies*, (n.s.) 3:1, 59–65.

– 1992. 'The Cartesian Hen-and-a-Half', *Journal of Beckett Studies*, (n.s) 2:1, 117.

Albright, Daniel. 2006. 'Beckett's Poems as Plays', in: Philip Nicolayev (ed.), *Fulcrum: an annual of poetry and aesthetics*, 6, Cambridge, MA, 2007, 522–9.

Alphant, Marianne and Nathalie Léger (eds.). 2007. *Objet Beckett*, Paris: Centre Pompidou/IMEC.

Anon. 1936. Review of *Echo's Bones and Other Precipitates*. *Dublin Magazine*, n.s. XI (April–June): 78.

– 1936. Review of *Transition*. (Includes reference to *Echo's Bones and Other Precipitates*.) *Irish Times* (25 July), 7.

Bouchard, Norma. 2008. 'Recovering Beckett's Italian Translations', *Journal of Beckett Studies*, (n.s.) 15: 1 & 2, 145–59.

Burghardt, Lori Hall. 1976. 'The Bawds of Euphony: images of women in Beckett's early poems', in: Edouard Morot-Sir, Howard Harper and Dougald McMillan (eds.), *Samuel Beckett: the art of rhetoric*, Chapel Hill, NC: University of North Carolina Press, 151–6.

Cambon, Glauco. 1960. 'Immediacies and Distances' (review of *Anthology of Mexican Poetry*), *Poetry*, XCV, 379–81.

Carter, Boyd. 1959. 'Mexican Poetry in English Translation', *Prairie Schooner*, XXXIII, Winter 1959–60, 355–61.

Caws, Mary Ann. 1999. 'Beckett Translating', *Samuel Beckett Today/Aujourd'hui*, 8, 43–58.

Clarke, Austin. 1962. 'Three Irish Poets' (review of *Poems in English*), *Irish Times*, 3.2.1962, 8.

Clément, Bruno. 2009. 'Rire du Pire', *Samuel Beckett Today/Aujourd'hui*, 21, 89–102.

Connors, Patricia. 1978. 'Samuel Beckett's "Whoroscope" as a Dramatic Monologue', *Ball State University Forum*, 19:2, 26–32.

Coughlan, Patricia. 1995. '"The Poetry is Another Pair of Sleeves": Beckett, Ireland and Modernist Lyric Poetry', in: Patricia Coughlan and Alex Davis (eds.), *Modernism and Ireland: the poetry of the 1930s*, Cork: Cork University Press, 173–208.

Davie, Donald. 1962. 'Nightingales, Anangke' (review of *Poems in English*), *New Statesman*, LXIII, 5.1.62, 20–1.

Doherty, Francis. 1992. 'Mahaffy's "Whoroscope"', *Journal of Beckett Studies*, (n.s.) 2:1, 27–46.

Engelberts, Matthijs. 1998. 'Beckett et le *light verse*: les *Mirlitonnades* et *Long after Chamfort*', *Samuel Beckett Today/Aujourd'hui*, 7, 277–96.

Fletcher, John. 1967. 'The Art of the Poet', in: *Samuel Beckett's Art*, London: Chatto and Windus; reprinted from 'The Private Pain and the Whey of Words: a survey of Beckett's verse', in: *Twentieth Century Views: Samuel Beckett: a collection of critical essays*, ed. Martin Esslin, Englefield Cliffs, NJ: Prentice-Hall Inc., 1965, 23–32.

– 1964. 'Beckett's Verse: Influences and Parallels', *French Review*, 37: 3, 320–31.

Friedman, Melvin J. 1976. 'Introductory Notes to Beckett's Poetry', in: Edouard Morot-Sir, Howard Harper and Dougald McMillan (eds.), *Samuel Beckett: the art of rhetoric*, Chapel Hill, NC: University of North Carolina Press, 143–9.

Furbank, P. N. 1962. (Review of *Poems in English*), *The Listener*, LXVII, 8.2.62, 29.

Gaffney, Phyllis. 1999a. *Healing Amid the Ruins*. Dublin: A & A Farmar.

– 1999b. 'Dante, Manzoni, De Valera, Beckett . . . ? Circumlocutions of a Storekeeper: Beckett and Saint-Lô', *Irish University Review*, 29:2, 256–80.

Gaspar, Laura Monrós. 2006. 'El mito de Eco y la escisión del sujeto: representaciones del silencio en *Echo's Bones* de Samuel Beckett', *Quaderns de Filologia, Estudis Literaris* (University of Valencia), 149–67.

Gavard-Perret, Jean-Louis. 2001. 'Approche théorique de l'oeuvre poétique', and 'Vers la disparition des images: l'oeuvre poétique ou le lieu impracticable', in: *L'imaginaire paradoxal, ou la création absolue dans les oeuvres dernières de Samuel Beckett*, Paris-Caen: Lettres Modernes Minard, 13–47.

Genetti, Stefano. 1994. 'Molto dopo Chamfort, Beckett', *Quaderni di Lingue e Letterature* (University of Verona), 19, 163–79.

Gontarski, S. E. 1982. 'Samuel Beckett, James Joyce's "Illstarred Punster"', in: Bernard Benstock (ed.), *The Seventh of Joyce*, Bloomington, IN: Indiana University Press, 29–36.

Gross, Katherine Travers. 1970. 'In Other Words: Samuel Beckett's Art of Poetry'. Unpublished PhD dissertation, Columbia University, New York.

Hamburger, Michael. 1977. 'The Poetry of Samuel Beckett', *PN Review*, 5:1, 15–16.

Harvey, Lawrence E. 1970. *Samuel Beckett: Poet and Critic*. Princeton, NJ: Princeton University Press.

Hedberg, Johannes. 1974. 'Some Thoughts on Three Poems by Samuel Beckett', *Moderna Språk* (Stockholm), 68, 11–18.

– 1972. *Samuel Beckett's 'Whoroscope': a linguistic-literary interpretation*, Saltsjö-Duvnäs: Moderna Språk Monographs.

Hunkeler, Thomas. 2001. 'La Poésie est-elle Verticale?', *Samuel Beckett Today/Aujourd'hui*, 11, 416–24.

– 1999. ' "Cascando" de Samuel Beckett', *Samuel Beckett Today/ Aujourd'hui*, 8, 27–42.

Jacobsen, Josephine, and William R. Mueller. 1963. 'Beckett as Poet', *Prairie Schooner*, XXXVII, Fall, 196–216.

Katz, Daniel. 1996. ' "Alone in the accusative": Beckett's narcissistic echoes', *Samuel Beckett Today/Aujourd'hui*, 5, 57–71.

– 1992. 'Will in Overplus: a graphic look at Beckett's W/ horoscope', *Interfaces/Samuel Beckett: intertextualités et psychanalyse*, Dijon: Université de Bourgogne, 17–36.

Kinsella, Thomas. 1993. 'Poems of Samuel Beckett', *Journal of Beckett Studies*, (n.s.) 2, 11–18.

Knottenbelt, E. M. 1993. 'Samuel Beckett: poetry as performative act', *Samuel Beckett Today/Aujourd'hui*, 2, 31–40.

Kosters, Onno. 1992. ' "Whey of Words": Beckett's poetry from "Whoroscope" to "What is the Word"', *Samuel Beckett Today/ Aujourd'hui*, 1, 93–105.

Krolow, Karl. 1981. 'Zu Samuel Becketts "Mirlitonnades"', in *Flötentönen*, Frankfurt am Main: Suhrkamp Verlag, 95–101.

Laass, Henner. 1980. 'Exploration of the Non-Feasible: syntactic ambiguity in some poems of Samuel Beckett', in: Ronald Hagenbuchle and Joseph T. Swann (eds.), *Poetic Knowledge: circumference and centre*, Bonn: Bouvier, 100–13.

Lawlor, Seán. 2010. 'The "Dream" Poems: Poems in Personae', in: S. E. Gontarski (ed.), *A Companion to Samuel Beckett*, Oxford: Wiley-Blackwell, 228–43.

– 2009. '"O Death Where Is Thy Sting?": Finding Words for the Big Ideas', in: Steven Barfield, Matthew Feldman and Philip Tew (eds.), *Beckett and Death*, London: Continuum, 50–71.

– 2008. 'Making a Noise to drown an Echo: allusion and quotation in the early poems of Samuel Beckett'. Unpublished PhD dissertation, University of Reading.

– 2007a. ' "Alba" and "Dortmunder": Signposting Paradise and the Balls-aching World', *Samuel Beckett Today/Aujourd'hui*, 18, 227–40.

– 2007b. 'Beckett, MacGreevy and the Stink of Joyce', in: Philip Nicolayev (ed.), *Fulcrum: an annual of poetry and aesthetics*, 6, Cambridge, MA, 484–49.

– 2007c. '"Sanies I": being careful not to take a serious view of their accidents', in: Philip Nicolayev (ed.), *Fulcrum: an annual of poetry and aesthetics*, 6, Cambridge, MA, 565–83.

Lecercle, Ann. 1984. '*Echo's Bones* – la rédoubtable symmétrie de l'oeuf pourri, ou une poétique de la suture', in Jean-Michel Rabaté (ed.), *Beckett avant Beckett: essais sur les premières oeuvres*, Paris: PENS, 47–78.

Little, Roger. 1994. 'Beckett's Poems and Verse Translations, or: Beckett and the limits of poetry', in: John Pilling (ed.), *The Cambridge Companion to Beckett*, Cambridge University Press, 184–95.

Locatelli, Carla. 2009. 'Ways of Beckett's Poems: "il se passé devant/allant sans but" ', in: Daniela Guardamagna and Rossana M. Sebellin (eds.), *The Tragic Comedy of Samuel Beckett*, Roma: Editori Laterza, 177–89.

M., H. L. [H. L. Morton]. 1930. 'Books and Authors: a Prize Poem' [on 'Whoroscope'], *Everyman*, 3.6.30.

Macklin, Gerald M. 2003. '"Drunken Boat": Samuel Beckett's

Translation of Rimbaud's "Le Bateau ivre"', *Studies in 20th Century Literature*, 27:1, 141–66.

Mahon, Derek. 2006. 'Watt is the word: 'the "brief scattered lights" of Beckett's poems', *Times Literary Supplement*, 1 November, 12–14.

– 1984. 'A Noise like Wings: Beckett's poetry', *Irish University Review*, 14:1, 88–92; reprinted in *Journalism: selected prose*, ed. Terence Brown, Dublin: Gallery Books, 1996, 50–4.

McGuire, James. 1990. 'Beckett, the Translator and the Metapoem', *World Literature Today*, 64:2, 258–63.

McMillan, Dougald. 1976. '*Echo's Bones*: starting points for Beckett', in: Edouard Morot-Sir, Howard Harper and Dougald McMillan (eds.), *Samuel Beckett: the art of rhetoric*, Chapel Hill, NC: University of North Carolina Press, 165–87.

McQueeny, Terence. 1987. 'Beckett, Chamfort and the Wastes and Wilds of Self-Translation', *The Literary Review*, 30:3, 407–417.

Morot-Sir, Edouard. 1976. 'Samuel Beckett and Cartesian Emblems', in: Edouard Morot-Sir, Howard Harper and Dougald McMillan (eds.), *Samuel Beckett: the art of rhetoric*, Chapel Hill, NC: University of North Carolina Press, 25–104.

Nixon, Mark. 2007. '"Unutterably Faint": Beckett's Late English Poetry', in: Philip Nicolayev (ed.), *Fulcrum: an annual of poetry and aesthetics*, 6, Cambridge, MA, 507–21.

– 2007. '"the remains of a trace": intra- and intertextual transferences in Beckett's *mirlitonnades* manuscripts', *Journal of Beckett Studies*, (n.s.) 16, 1 & 2, 110–22.

Okamuro, Minako. 2000. 'The Cartesian Egg: alchemical images in Beckett's early writings', *Journal of Beckett Studies*, (n.s.) 9:2, 63–80.

Paz, Octavio, and Eliot Weinberger. 2007. 'Octavio Paz on *An Anthology of Mexican Poetry*', in: Philip Nicolayev (ed.), *Fulcrum: an annual of poetry and aesthetics*, 6, Cambridge, MA, 622–4.

Pilling, John. 2004. 'From the pointed ones to the bones: Beckett's early poems', in: Clare Hutton (ed.), *The Irish Book in the Twentieth Century*, Dublin: Irish Academic Press, 68–83.

– 1999a. 'Beckett and "the itch to make": the early poems in English', *Samuel Beckett Today/Aujourd'hui*, 8, 15–25.

- 1999b. 'A Mermaid Made Over: Beckett's "Text" and John Ford', in: Bruce Stewart (ed.), *Beckett and Beyond*, Gerrards Cross: Colin Smythe, 211–16.
- 1997. 'More poems than precipitates: towards *Echo's Bones* and beyond', in: *Beckett before Godot*, Cambridge: Cambridge University Press, 77–92.
- 1977. 'A Kind of Greatness', *Books and Bookmen*, 22:10, 52–4.
- 1976. 'Beckett's poetry', in: *Samuel Beckett*, London: Routledge and Kegan Paul, 159–83.
Putnam, Samuel. 1932. 'Foreword to a Sunken Continent' [Preface to George Reavey's *Faust's Metamorphoses*] Fontenay-aux-Roses, Seine : The New Review Editions.
Rabaté, Jean-Michel. 2007. 'Formal Brilliance and Indeterminate Purport: The Poetry of Beckett's Philosophemes', in: Philip Nicolayev (ed.), *Fulcrum: an annual of poetry and aesthetics*, 6, Cambridge, MA, 530–50.
- 1999. 'Beckett et la Poésie de la Zone: Dante . . . Apollinaire . . . Céline . . . Levi', *Samuel Beckett Today/Aujourd'hui*, 8, 75–90.
Salisbury, Laura. 2008. ' "What Is The Word": Beckett's aphasic modernism', *Journal of Beckett Studies*, (n.s.) 17: 1 & 2, 78–126, esp. 78–86.
Shadoian, Jack. 1969. 'Samuel Beckett's Poetry', *Research Studies of Washington State University*, 37, 259–73.
Sonzogni, Marco. 2006. 'Debiti e doni della tradizione poetica: Montale tra T S Eliot e Beckett', in: Giancarlo Alfano and Andrea Cortellessa (eds.), *Tegole dal cielo: la letteratura italiana nell'opera di Beckett*, Roma: Antalia/Edup, 139–65.
Stepancher, Stephen. 1963. (Review of *Poems In English*), *New York Herald Tribune*, 11.8.63, 6.
Van Hulle, Dirk. 2011. *The Making of Samuel Beckett's* 'Stirrings still'/'Soubresauts' *and* 'comment dire'/'what is the word', Antwerp: University Press.
Visconti, Laura. 1997. 'The Artist and the Artisan: Beckett as a translator of Italian Poetry', *Samuel Beckett Today/Aujourd'hui*, 6, 387–98.
- 1988. 'Il Purgatorio sferico: la poetica di Samuel Beckett', *Joyce Studies in Italy*, 2, ed. Carla De Petris, Roma: Bulzoni Editore, 55–76.
Weinberger, Eliot. 2007. 'Beckett/Paz', in: Philip Nicolayev (ed.),

Fulcrum: an annual of poetry and aesthetics, 6, Cambridge, MA, 616–21.

Weller, Shane. 2007. '"All the Dead Voices": Beckett and the Ethics of Elegy', *Journal of Beckett Studies*, (n.s.) 16: 1 & 2, 85–96.

– 2000. 'The Word Folly: Samuel Beckett's "Comment dire" ("What is the word")', *Angelaki*, 5:1, 165–80.

Wheatley, David. 2009a. 'The Work of the Abscess', *Dublin Review*, 35, 78–90.

– 2009b. '"That they may be damned": Samuel Beckett and the Poetry of Misogyny', in: Justin Quinn (ed.), *Irish Poetry After Feminism: A Collection of Critical Essays*, Gerrards Cross, Bucks: Colin Smythe, 89–99.

– 2007. '"Labours Unfinished": Beckett's *mirlitonnades* and the Poetics of Incompletion', in: Philip Nicolayev (ed.), *Fulcrum: an annual of poetry and aesthetics*, 6, Cambridge, MA, 2007, 500–6.

– 2005. 'Slippery Sam and Tomtinker Tim: Beckett and MacGreevy's Urban Poetics', *Irish Studies Review*, 13:2, 189–202.

– 1999. 'Occasions of Wordshed: studies in the poetry of Samuel Beckett'. Unpublished PhD dissertation, Trinity College Dublin.

– 1998. '"what is the word": Samuel Beckett as Poet', *The Prague Revue*, 5, 161–6.

– 1995a. 'Samuel Beckett's Pedestrian Poetry: a fresh look', *Wit's End*, 1:1, 26–8.

– 1995b. 'Samuel Beckett's *Mirlitonnades*: a manuscript study', *Journal of Beckett Studies*, (n.s.) 4:2, 47–75.

Zilliacus, Clas. 1973. 'Samuel Beckett and his "Whoroscope"', *Moderna Språk* (Stockholm), 67, 4–6.

OTHER WORKS CONSULTED

Ackerley, C. J., and Gontarski, S. E. (eds.). 2004. *The Grove Companion to Samuel Beckett*, New York: Grove Press.

Ackerley, C. J. 2006b. 'Obscure Locks, Simple Keys: the annotated *Watt*', *Journal of Beckett Studies*, (n.s.) 14: 1 & 2.

– 1998. 'Demented Particulars: the annotated *Murphy*'. *Journal of Beckett Studies*, (n.s.) 7: 1 & 2.

Admussen, Richard L. 1979. *The Samuel Beckett Manuscripts: a study*. Boston, MA: G. K. Hall.

Aeschylus. 1956. *The Oresteian Trilogy* (trans. Philip Vellacott). Harmondsworth: Penguin.

Alighieri, Dante. 1971. *The Divine Comedy of Dante Alighieri* (Italian text with translation and commentary by John D. Sinclair). London, Oxford, New York: Oxford University Press.

Atik, Anne. 2001. *How It Was: a memoir of Samuel Beckett.* London: Faber and Faber.

Augustine. 1907. *The Confessions of St Augustine* (trans. E. B. Pusey). London: J. M. Dent & Co Ltd.

Barnett, Anthony. 2007. *Listening for Henry Crowder.* Lewes, East Sussex: Allardyce Books/AB Fable Recordings.

Beck, Jean. [?1910]. *La Musique des troubadours.* Paris: Henri Laurens Editeur.

Belmont, Georges. 2001. *Souvenirs d'outre-monde.* Paris: Calmann-Lévy.

Bérard, Victor. 1944. *Odyssée.* Paris: Armand Colin.

Bryden, Mary, Julian Garforth and Peter Mills (eds.). 1998. *Beckett at Reading: Catalogue of the Beckett Manuscript Collection at the University of Reading.* Reading: Whiteknights Press and the Beckett International Foundation.

Caselli, Daniela. 2000. 'The "Florentia Edition in the ignoble Salani collection": a textual comparison', *Journal of Beckett Studies*, (n.s.) 9:2, 1–20.

Cauvin, Jean-Pierre and Mary-Ann Caws (eds.). 1982. *Poems of André Breton: a bilingual anthology.* Austin, TX: University of Texas at Austin.

Cohn, Ruby. 2001. *A Beckett Canon.* Ann Arbor: University of Michigan Press.

– 1962. *Samuel Beckett: The Comic Gamut.* New Brunswick, NJ: Rutgers University Press.

Cronin, Anthony. 1996. *Samuel Beckett: The Last Modernist.* London: Harper Collins.

Cunard, Nancy. 1969. *These Were the Hours: Memories of my Hours Press, Réanville and Paris, 1928–1931* (ed. Hugh Ford). Carbondale and Edwardsville: Southern Illinois University Press.

Davis, Robin J. 1979 (with supplement checklist 1977–84). *Samuel Beckett / Checklist and Index of his Published Works. / 1967–1976.* University of Stirling: The Library.

Dolan, T. P. 1999. *A Dictionary of Hiberno-English.* Dublin: Gill and Macmillan.

Duthuit, Georges. 2006. *Les Fauves* (ed. Rémi Labrusse, reprinted from the first French edition published by Editions des Trois Collines, Geneva, 1949). Paris: Editions Michalon.

– 1950. *The Fauvist Painters* (translated by Ralph Manheim, from the first French edition published by Editions des Trois Collines, Geneva, 1949, with the uncredited assistance of Samuel Beckett). New York: Wittenborn, Schultz Inc.

Federman, Raymond, and John Fletcher (eds.). 1970. *Samuel Beckett: his works and his critics*, Berkeley and Los Angeles, CA: University of California Press.

Feldman, Matthew. 2006. *Beckett's Books: a cultural history of Samuel Beckett's 'Interwar Notes'*. London: Continuum.

Freud, Sigmund. 2001. *The Standard Edition of the Complete Psychological Works of Sigmund Freud* (ed. James Strachey), vol. XVII. London: Vintage, The Hogarth Press and the Institute of Psycho-Analysis.

Glenavy, Beatrice. 1964. *Today We Will Only Gossip*. London: Constable.

Gordon, Lois. 1996. *The World of Samuel Beckett 1906–1946*. New Haven and London: Yale University Press.

Harmon, Maurice (ed.). 1998. *No Author Better Served: The Correspondence of Samuel Beckett and Alan Schneider*. Cambridge, MA; London, England: Harvard University Press.

Harvey, Lawrence E. 1970. *Samuel Beckett: Poet and Critic*. Princeton, NJ: Princeton University Press.

Haynes, John, and James Knowlson. 2003. *Images of Beckett*. Cambridge: Cambridge University Press.

Hoy, Peter C. (ed.; with Robin J. Davis). 1972. *Calepins de Bibliographie: Samuel Beckett*. Paris: Lettres Modernes, Minard.

Joyce, James. 1992. *Poems* and *Exiles*. Harmondsworth: Penguin (ed. J. C. C. Mays).

– 1992. *A Portrait of the Artist as a Young Man*. Harmondsworth: Penguin (ed. Seamus Deane).

– 1992. *Dubliners*. Harmondsworth: Penguin (ed. Terence Brown).

– 1991. *Poems and Shorter Writings*. London: Faber and Faber (eds. Richard Ellmann, A. Walton Litz and John Whittier-Ferguson).

– 1964. *Finnegans Wake*. London: Faber and Faber.

– 1960. *Ulysses*. London: John Lane/The Bodley Head.

Knowlson, James, and John Pilling. 1979. *Frescoes of the Skull: The later prose and drama of Samuel Beckett*. London: John Calder.

Knowlson, James. 1996. *Damned to Fame: the Life of Samuel Beckett*. London: Bloomsbury.

– (ed.) 1992, 1993. *The Theatrical Notebooks of Samuel Beckett*, I–IV. London: Faber and Faber.

– 1971. *Samuel Beckett: an exhibition*. London: Turret Books.

Lake, Carlton (ed.). 1984. *No Symbols Where None Intended: Samuel Beckett at the Humanities Research Center*. Austin, TX: University of Texas at Austin, 1984.

Laloy, Louis. [?1910]. *La Musique chinoise*. Paris: Henri Laurens Editeur.

Lawlor, Seán. 2011. '"That's how it was and them were the days", in: Mark Nixon (ed.), *Publishing Samuel Beckett*, London: The British Library, 23–33.

Mahaffy, J. P. 1901. *Descartes*. Edinburgh and London: William Blackwood.

Mauthner, Fritz. 1923. *Beiträge zu einer Kritik der Sprache*. Leipzig and Munich: Felix Meiner (3 vols.; 3rd edition).

McMillan, Dougald. 1975. *Transition 1927–38: the history of a literary era*. London: Calder and Boyars.

Murphy, P. J. 1999. *Reconstructing Beckett: Language for Being in Samuel Beckett's Fiction*. Toronto: University of Toronto Press.

Nixon, Mark. 2011. 'George Reavey – Beckett's first literary agent', in Mark Nixon (ed.), *Publishing Samuel Beckett*, London: The British Library, 41–55.

Nordau, Max. 1895. *Degeneration* (translator unknown). London: William Heinemann.

O'Brien, Eoin. 1986. *The Beckett Country*. Dublin: Black Cat Press in association with Faber and Faber.

O'Connell, Sandra. 2010. 'Brian Coffey and George Reavey: a friendship of lasting importance', in: Benjamin Keatinge and Aengus Woods (eds.), *Other Edens: the life and work of Brian Coffey*, Dublin: Irish Academic Press.

Perloff, Marjorie. 2005. '"In Love with Hiding": Samuel Beckett's War', *Iowa Review*, 35, no. 2, 76–103.

Pilling, John, and Seán Lawlor. 2011. 'Beckett in Transition', in: Mark Nixon (ed.), *Publishing Samuel Beckett*, London: The British Library, 83–95.

Pilling, John. 2011. *Samuel Beckett's 'More Pricks than Kicks': in a strait of two wills*, London: Continuum.

– 2006. 'Beckett and Mauthner Revisited', in: S. E. Gontarski and Anthony Uhlmann (eds.), *Beckett after Beckett*, Gainesville, FL: University Press of Florida, 158–66.

– 2005. 'Dates and Difficulties in the *"Whoroscope" Notebook*', *Journal of Beckett Studies*, (n.s.) 13:2, 39–48.

Proust, Marcel. 1983. *Remembrance of Things Past* (trans. Terence Kilmartin, C. K. Scott Moncrieff and Andreas Mayor). 3 vols. Harmondsworth: Penguin.

Robertson, J. G. 1931. *A History of German Literature*. Edinburgh: Blackwood and Sons. (2nd revised edition).

Schopenhauer, Arthur. 1909. *The World as Will and Idea* (trans. R. B. Haldane). 3 vols. London and Manchester: Kegan Paul, Trench, Trubner and Co.

Schwob, Marcel. 1903. *La Lampe de Psyche*. Paris: Mercure de France.

Shovlin, Frank. 2003. *The Irish Literary Periodical 1923–1958*. Oxford: Oxford University Press.

Thackeray, William Makepeace. 1908. *Vanity Fair*. London: J. M. Dent and Son.

Vasari, Giorgio. 1927. *The Lives of the Painters, Sculptors and Architects* (trans. A. B. Hinds). London: Dent.

Windelband, Wilhelm. 1907. *A History of Philosophy* (trans. James H. Tufts). New York and London: The Macmillan Company. (2nd edition, revised and enlarged).

Index of Titles and First Lines

Asterisked page references for titles are to unrevised texts printed in the Appendix. Page references following semicolons are to main entries in the Commentary. For titles of translations, the author of the original is given in square brackets.

.